GEORGE RAFT

ALSO BY EVERETT AAKER

Encyclopedia of Early Television Crime Fighters:
All Regular Cast Members in American Crime and Mystery
Series, 1948–1959 (McFarland, 2006; paperback 2011)

Television Western Players of the Fifties: A Biographical Encyclopedia
of All Regular Cast Members in Western Series, 1949–1959
(McFarland, 1997; paperback 2007)

GEORGE RAFT
The Films

Everett Aaker

McFarland & Company, Inc., Publishers
Jefferson, North Carolina, and London

ISBN 978-0-7864-6646-7
softcover : acid free paper ∞

LIBRARY OF CONGRESS CATALOGUING DATA ARE AVAILABLE

BRITISH LIBRARY CATALOGUING DATA ARE AVAILABLE

On the cover: George Raft in *Scarface*, 1932 (United Artists/
Photofest); background images © 2013 Shutterstock

Manufactured in the United States of America

*McFarland & Company, Inc., Publishers
Box 611, Jefferson, North Carolina 28640
www.mcfarlandpub.com*

To the late George Raft

ACKNOWLEDGMENTS

Thanks are due to the following people who shared their personal
recollections of George Raft with me: the late Tony Curtis,
Sybil Danning, the late Anne Francis, Alan Frank, Coleen Gray,
the late Jane Greer, Will Hutchins, the late Sidney Pink,
the late Don Sharp and the late Marie Windsor.

Also to the following: Tom Weaver, David Ragan, the late Leslie Halliwell,
David Redfern, Peter Swan, Tony Hutchinson, Boyd Magers,
Dennis Howells, Michael Selby, Trevor Brown, the late John Buttery,
the late Robin Ray, Brian Beard, Jeremy Baker, Terry Beard,
Robin Clapton, Peter Ferguson, Derek Southall, Steve Coates
and all the other members of "the Black Bird Club."
Bob and Janet Ainsley, Graham Main, John and Katy Andrew,
David Haley, Andrew and Suzanne Hight, Ian Morrison,
Susan Poole, Dave Harris and my sister.

TABLE OF CONTENTS

PREFACE

George Raft was an actor who specialized in playing gangsters with style and charisma. Since gangsters had a financial interest in clubs where he danced in his pre–Hollywood days, he became an acquaintance of many of them which made his characterizations frighteningly realistic. As Raft said, "If you were an entertainer on Broadway in those days, you would have to be blind and lame not to associate with gangsters. They owned the clubs and that's where the work was." He became a star flipping a coin in one of his earliest movies, *Scarface* (1932). He was highly regarded within his own lifetime as a performer, but after he died his reputation went into a steep decline.

Actors can be assessed in different ways and according to different criteria. One yardstick these days tends to be in terms of classical acting; here Raft was a non-starter. He did not perform Shakespeare or Chekhov. He did, however, have the one element essential for a successful career in Hollywood motion pictures, namely charisma or star quality. He was a leading exponent of the art of personality acting. Assessed according to that standard, he came close to hitting the jackpot. He was a spontaneous actor who was at his best during the first two or three takes.

Raft starred in many movies. His track record in films was one of the better ones among Hollywood movie stars largely because he established himself during the early years of the talkies. His peak years coincided with the best years of the Hollywood movie factory so that even his weaker films had a surface gloss, decent production values, capable direction, plenty of extras and reliable actors in the supporting roles. The fact that many of his films had high action content helped them consid-

erably. Crime still exists in a myriad of forms so his work dates less than that of many actors of the period. There were very few total duds in his filmography.

The time now seems right for a reappraisal of his films. All of Raft's movies are covered in this book with details on the casts, the characters, technical credits, a story synopsis and relevant comments. All of these movies, except the lost ones, have been viewed by the author and, except where stated, the opinions are derived from personal viewing, not from secondary sources. There are three excellent biographies of George Raft by James Robert Parish, Lewis Yablonsky and Stone Wallace. The purposes of this book are to make it the definitive study of his films, to dispel a number of myths surrounding his career and to give the reader, whether dedicated film buff or casual viewer, an insight into the production of all his films.

Many of Raft's best films were directed by four "A" list directors: Henry Hathaway, Howard Hawks, Raoul Walsh and Billy Wilder. Two of these directors, Hawks and Wilder, directed him only once, but the resulting films, *Scarface* (1932) and *Some Like It Hot* (1959), started and finished the most productive period of his career. All of his starring films featured at least one strong female character. None of his starring films had all-male casts.

The fact that Raft's career declined is indisputable. The causes were rather more complex than some writers have indicated. The rise of Humphrey Bogart and his acceptance of roles that Raft rejected in the early forties is frequently cited as the only cause. The fact that three of Raft's films were among the top-grossing movies of 1944–1945 hardly suggests an actor who was completely over the hill. The reasons for his decline include rejection of roles in movies which were accepted by other actors and became big commercial successes; advancing age; his work for independent producers whose scripts and production values were sometimes not up to previous standards; his refusal, from the early forties onwards, to play gangsters or to die onscreen; the fact that when the mercurial Howard Hughes assumed control of RKO — a studio where Raft had made some good films — Hughes ran it into the ground; changes in the type of movies audiences most favored during the fifties; and Raft's lack of a theatrical background to sustain him when film roles became scarce. Nevertheless, many actors would have crawled over hot coals to have George Raft's career.

In a sense George Raft's life is an affirmation of one of the more positive aspects of the American way of life, namely that a person from such humble origins could triumph, become world-famous and an enduring legend of the silver screen. Raft is one star who has never been forgotten. The public in general and a subsequent generation of actors, the one portraying gangsters in particular, went on imitating his mannerisms long after people stopped going to see his movies. His legend continues principally via his loyal fanbase on the Internet and the DVD revolution, which has introduced him to a new generation of film buffs and enabled his films to continue to entertain decades after he died.

INTRODUCTION

The Eighteenth Amendment and Prohibition, i.e., the Volstead Act, was established in the United States without much opposition in a burst of idealism. Prohibition in 1920 coincided with the new decade which aimed for the joyous abandonment of every rule and code and a short, wild ride through life. Virtually from the start, the Volstead Act proved impossible to enforce, particularly when the president of the United States himself, Warren Harding, held drinking parties in the White House.

Fronted by gangsters, speakeasies thrived. Those whose job it was to enforce the act faced apathy from a war-weary public. Smuggling liquor, hijacking of alcoholic drink intended as medical supplies and manufacturing of illegal booze reached epic proportions. There were big financial rewards awaiting the Prohibition racketeer in the Roaring Twenties, a decade notorious for the number of hoodlums and gangsters who flourished. The era began around 1920 when Johnny Torrio hired Al Capone as his lieutenant and reached its apogee with the St. Valentine's Day Massacre in 1929. Items such as fast cars and sub-machine guns accompanied the rise of the gang-ster. Gangsters did not confine themselves to illegal booze. They were also involved in gambling, prostitution and sadistic protection rackets. In fact, Prohibition achieved the opposite effect of that intended and it has been said that its introduction gave organized crime the financial backing which enabled gangsterism to continue for decades in America. That way of life was curtailed by the stock market crash of 1929 and the subsequent repeal of Prohibition.

The American public and indeed the public all over the world became fascinated by the gangsters' lifestyle, flashy clothes, slang, weapons and the fashionable molls frequently seen hanging on their arms. Films featuring gangsters quickly caught on with audiences. During the early part of the thirties a number of films were not only enormous commercial successes, but became classics of the genre artistically. The actors in the leading roles were charismatic and became household names virtually overnight. Debate still rages among film buffs as to which of these players was the most convincing and authentic of all. A strong body of opinion would put forward the name of George Raft.

BIOGRAPHY

George Raft was born George Ranft in the notorious Hell's Kitchen district of New York. The exact date is a subject of controversy. For many years film encyclopedias gave it as September 27, 1903. Later the year was altered to 1900. On a radio broadcast in England during the sixties, Raft gave his year of birth as 1898. When he was indicted on income tax evasion charges in 1964, his birthday was given as September 26, 1895. This date was usually quoted and is the one which appears on both his death certificate and tombstone. More recent research derived from a census of 1910 and his local Draft Board in 1940 makes his date of birth September 26, 1901. This still seems a little odd since many thespians try to retain their youth as long as possible in Hollywood, and it would have to be one of the few instances where a star ever claimed to be older than he actually was.

Raft was the son of Conrad Ranft and Eva Glockner. His father (1876–1929) was German, while his mother (1878–1937) was of mixed German-Italian ancestry. His parents married in 1896. His father worked for 27 years as a department store delivery man and in the summers ran a merry-go-round at Coney Island. According to Hollywood press releases, George had four younger brothers and a younger sister. Three brothers were killed in World War I and the remaining one was killed working construction on a skyscraper. His sister died young of tuberculosis. But the census of 1910 reveals that he only had a sister and no brothers.

Growing up in an extremely tough environment, George joined the most fearsome of the street gangs, the Gophers. A childhood friend of his, Liverpool, England–born Owney

Madden (1892–1965), led the Gophers and bankrolled George early in his Hollywood career. Raft was a student at P.S. 169 and later at St. Catherine's elementary school, but he spent little time there. As a child he was entranced by Broadway, the nickelodeons and baseball, which remained a lifelong passion.

After a fight with his father, he became a school dropout, sleeping in all manner of strange places (mainly pool halls, lofts and derelict buildings) and working at various jobs until World War I. During the teens he joined a semi-professional baseball team, but soon realized that he was not going to make the grade as a full-time player. This was also when he first began to use the surname Raft, although he didn't legally change it until 1935. He also became a professional boxer and, according to *The Ring* magazine, had 14 bouts under a few different names. He was even less successful at this than baseball. After one particularly vicious beating in the ring, he quit.

He frequented dance halls where he began to learn the art of dancing. He had no formal training, but imitated others. He became a fast Charleston dancer and secured a few engagements as a specialty dancer. To earn extra money he entered and won dance contests. At one club he encountered Rudolph Valentino, who suggested that Raft join him at another where they were both paid to dance with women. This made him a taxi dancer. There are also unconfirmed reports that Raft was a gigolo, receiving money not only for his dancing but also for sexual favors. This was an allegation which Raft vehemently denied all his life. His resemblance to Valentino meant that after Valentino's success, George found himself in demand at various New York theaters as a substitute for the star. When Valentino died in 1926, there were those who wanted Raft to become a second Valentino, but Raft found the notion ghoulish and decided to continue with a career founded entirely upon his own individuality.

Raft made the acquaintance of agent Stanley Burns, who eventually partnered him with vaudevillian dancer Eve Shirley on a tour of New England states and later with Lily Field. Afterwards he joined a group of vaudevillians who toured small towns for two and a half years. This was where Raft honed his dancing skills. He was one-third of a vaudeville act called Pilcer, Douglas and Raft which toured the Paramount Publix circuit. During the 1920s he met a man named Max Greenburg. Greenburg later changed his own name to Mack Gray, and he was nicknamed "Killer" by Carole Lombard even though he had never killed anyone. (Gray's nickname was derived from a Yiddish word: When he was ill in a hospital, Lombard visited him and Gray told her he had a *killa* which was the Yiddish word for hernia.) During the thirties Gray joined Raft in Hollywood as his chauffeur, handyman and general gopher. He also played small parts in films which starred Raft. They parted company in 1952 and Gray went to work for Dean Martin.

In 1919 Raft obtained a job as a dancer at the College Arms, a Coney Island club. Although this did not last long, he was befriended by a piano player at another club, the College Inn, where he also secured employment for a while. The name of the piano player was Jimmy Durante. Durante was subsequently bankrolled (probably by the Mob) in a Manhattan club called Club Durant which gave him the chance to employ Raft full-time. Raft later went to work at the El Fey nightclub (fronted by the legendary hostess Texas Guinan) where he danced and did some minor bootlegging on the side. He met Feets Edson, a bootlegger, who taught him how to drive a car gangland-style.

In 1925 he won a role in the Broadway show *The City Chap* where he had a specialty number. At one time he worked simultaneously in two theaters and two nightclubs. He toured Europe as part of a dancing act in 1926. While in London he met the Prince of Wales, whom he taught to dance the Charleston. As Fred Astaire once said, "Raft was an extraordinary dancer who did the fastest, most exciting Charleston I ever saw." Upon his return to New York he was featured in another Broadway revue, *Padlocks of 1927*, which starred Texas Guinan. Bandleader Ben Bernie gave Raft a career boost by recommending him for a booking at the famed Palace Theatre in 1926. Raft also managed prizefighter Maxie Rosenbloom in his early days. During the twenties he had affairs with the singer-actress Helen Morgan and Winnie Lightner.

When Guinan received an offer from Warner Brothers to go to Hollywood to appear in a film called *Queen of the Nightclubs* (1929), loosely based on her life, it was decided that Raft should accompany her as a bodyguard and have a number in the film. This marked his screen debut. After the completion of two films, he returned to New York where the stock market had crashed and the night life for a while was quiet. Deciding in favor of a career in the movies, Raft relocated to Hollywood where he struggled for quite some time. Director-screenwriter Rowland Brown encountered him at the Brown Derby and told him that he would be suitable for a small role as a hood-bodyguard in *Quick Millions* (1931).

There were rumors floating around Hollywood that Raft was acting as an advance man for the Mob. The police brought him in on suspicion of robbing the home of actress and sometime girlfriend Molly O'Day, which Raft denied. He was on the point of being exiled from the state, but he had a contract at Fox for a movie called *Hush Money* (1931) as a gangster threatening Joan Bennett. Winfield Sheehan, then Fox's head of production, convinced D.A. Buron Fitts and the police that

Raft was intent on a career as an actor and managed to save him. Samuel Goldwyn chose him to play a gangster in an Eddie Cantor vehicle, *Palmy Days* (1931). James Cagney, who had known Raft from his New York days and liked him, recommended him to Warner Brothers for an unbilled bit as a dancer whom he slugs in *Taxi!* (1932).

Raft spent a night at the fights in the company of director Howard Hawks, who cast Raft in the career-making part of the loyal henchman Guido Rinaldo in *Scarface* (1932) with Paul Muni in the title role. Raft's lack of acting experience was concealed in the film by his habit of flipping a coin, a mannerism which he borrowed from one of his New York mob acquaintances. Hawks rather astutely said, "The camera likes some people and it liked George Raft." When the film was released it was a sensational success and propelled Raft far up the Hollywood ladder. While the film was showing in Chicago, Raft was summoned to see Al Capone, upon whose life the film was allegedly based. By all accounts, Capone liked the film and Raft.

There were a number of studios competing to put Raft under contract. He inked an exclusive lifetime deal with Paramount where his salary was increased to $1,500 a week in 1933 and $2,500 a week in 1934. Although Paramount signed Raft for tough guy roles, he was at his most animated during his early years there and appeared in his widest diversity of parts during the thirties. The deadpan style came later. His salary in 1935 was $90,000, in 1936 $51,041 and in 1937 $219,399. In 1938 Gary Cooper was interviewed by the FBI and he advised that Raft was an individual who was somewhat unable to keep pace with the salary he was receiving and that Raft had a distorted sense of loyalty to his old New York associates who were not always of the best type. Raft said, "Playing the parts I played, those of gangsters and hoodlums, I seemed to attract the real thing and believe me it was better to say, 'Hello' to those guys than ignore them."

During his later years at Paramount, Raft became increasingly difficult over scripts and his appearances became fewer. He was on suspension at Paramount a record 22 times. During the late thirties, Raft acquired a reputation for appearing in films with actors who were much more highly regarded than he, but somehow he more than held his own opposite them. Notable examples included Gary Cooper in *Souls at Sea* (1937), Henry Fonda in *Spawn of the North* (1938) and James Cagney in *Each Dawn I Die* (1939).

Disagreements over scripts and salary brought about an extremely acrimonious split from Paramount on January 22, 1939, and it was thought that he would not work for them again. Cagney and director William Keighley went after Raft to co-star with Cagney in Warners' exciting *Each Dawn I Die*, which reestablished his reputation and contained one of his best performances as "Hood" Stacy. On the strength of this success he signed with Warners on July 15, 1939, at a salary of $5,000 per week. Temperament intervened again and Raft began to turn down scripts by the yard. He only made four additional films under his Warner Brothers contract, but earned a total of $288,396.82 while he was there. The most familiar version of how Raft came to leave Warner Brothers in December 1942 is that recalled by Jack Warner. Allegedly Warner telephoned Raft, invited him to a meeting and offered to settle the matter for $10,000. Owing to a misunderstanding, Raft thought that he should pay Warner that amount of money instead of the other way around so he wrote out a check and gave it to Warner. Warner practically ran with it to the bank and cashed it. Other stars have indicated, however, that they bought themselves out of contracts with Warner Brothers so Warner's version of what happened may not be quite accurate. Raft made a terse comment on that studio when he said, "At the studio Jack Warner made the place seem like Alcatraz."

In view of the number of leading men who

were away in the armed forces during World War II, it seems surprising that Raft did not make more films during this period. He was classified by the Draft Board as 4F. His main contribution to the war effort was *Cavalcade of Sports*, wherein a number of fighters participated in boxing matches at different military bases. Raft himself frequently refereed the bouts. Bankrolling this from his own funds cost him $50,000. In December 1944 it was said that Raft was in need of funds and that he had not acted in movies for the past three years. During that period he had apparently been replaced by Humphrey Bogart in "bad man" roles.

In 1941 a press release announced that the Frolics Club in Miami was being remodelled and that Raft would run the club. There was an attempt by the FBI in July 1942 to look into the sources of Raft's income, but the investigation went nowhere. In November 1944 the FBI reported that sizable libraries of obscene films were possessed by Raft, Lou Costello *et al.* Raft was in the press in 1944 as a result of an allegedly loaded dice game in the apartment of Brooklyn baseball manager Leo Durocher; Martin Shurin claimed he lost $18,500 to Raft. Raft hit the headlines again in 1945 when he allegedly beat up Hollywood attorney Ed Raiden, who was representing Betty Doss, a nineteen-year-old girl who had been one of Raft's mistresses. Raiden asserted that Raft "by trick and device" took from the possession of Miss Doss personal property which belonged to her and five days later Miss Doss retained Raiden to recover the alleged love gifts. Raft was investigated briefly by the FBI in 1946 in connection with general criminal activities in the Los Angeles area. The investigation was based upon the possibility of a white slave violation arising out of the Raiden matter and the suspicion of Raft being a fingerman on a number of big jewel robberies. The investigation was dropped when no tangible evidence was forthcoming. In 1947 Raft succeeded underworld figure Tony Cornero as front man for a gambling ship, the SS *Lux*. In July and August 1947, attempts were made to extort money from Raft for the negative of an incriminating photo. The perpetrator was never caught. In 1949 the Los Angeles office of the FBI reported that a syndicate headed by Raft had purchased the Desert Retreat Hotel in Palm Springs for $250,000. It was noted that Billy Mann would be general manager and Raft would be a silent partner. In 1950 the Los Angeles office of the FBI reported that Raft continued to be closely associated with sneak gambling games operating in the Los Angeles area. He received no publicity in this regard at that time and it appeared that he acted as a steerer of motion picture celebrities to the gambling games. Raft was in the news when he vouched for John Capone, brother of Al, after John was arrested in Los Angeles in 1953. Interviewed by bureau agents in 1938 and 1953, Raft exhibited on both occasions an outwardly cooperative attitude. In 1954 Raft visited San Juan, Puerto Rico, for the purpose of opening a European-style casino with associates. Their efforts were unsuccessful.

In 1952 and 1953 Raft was interviewed by the FBI. Attempting to locate Raft at his residence in Beverly Hills, agents discovered that his house was occupied by a young woman who Raft later advised was his girlfriend. He stated that he allowed the girl to live in his house with her parents while he was absent from California and upon returning found that her parents were ill and he could not move them from the house so he took a Beverly Hills apartment where he was interviewed. Agents observed that Raft was small in stature, had a limp handshake and gave the personal impression quite contrary to that which he portrayed in motion pictures.

Raft was unfortunate enough to become involved with Benny "Bugsy" Siegel, a gangster and vicious contract killer, who went to Hollywood in 1937 with a view to increasing the influence of the Mob in California. That same year he contacted Raft, whom he had previously known in New York. Siegel's financial interests including gambling places on the Los Angeles waterfront, a dog racing track and a luxury gambling ship (named *Rex*) operating outside the twelve-mile limit. Some of his funding came from Hollywood producers. In 1945, using money from organized crime, Siegel decided to build a new hotel and casino, subsequently called the Flamingo, in Las Vegas. It would be a Mecca for gamblers from all over the country.

The casino opened on December 26, 1946. William Randolph Hearst had passed the word around the front offices of all the studios that any star attending risked his or her career. Raft himself did not want to attend, but Siegel threatened him if he was a no-show. The only stars whom Raft could persuade to attend were Charles Coburn, Sonny Tufts and George Jessel. By January 1947 the casino had sustained $500,000 in gambling losses. Siegel closed down the gambling facility until the hotel section could be opened up. Then Siegel antagonized the New York underworld when they did not receive the return on their investment which they expected. Siegel was marked for death when word reached the Mob that he had a bankroll of $600,000 and was planning to join his moll Virginia Hill, who was then in Europe. Siegel had allegedly married Hill in Mexico in 1946.

In early June 1947, Siegel borrowed $100,000 from Raft which was never repaid. On June 20, 1947, Raft and Siegel were together at Raft's home. Siegel told him that he wanted to go to a Hollywood restaurant for dinner around 9 P.M., but Raft had an evening business engagement with producer Sam Bischoff. Raft agreed to drop in afterwards at the house on Linden Drive being rented by Virginia Hill. It may also be speculated that Bischoff had been warned not to let Raft leave before 9 P.M. Their meeting finished later than intended, but instead of going to Linden Drive, Raft went to play bridge. He was interrupted when actor Dewey Robinson burst in on the game to tell Raft that Siegel had been shot to death at the house around 9 P.M. Shortly afterwards, gangsters entered the Flamingo and told the startled staff that there was a change in the management.

During this postwar period while Raft was not exactly deluged with film offers, his agent Charles K. Feldman negotiated successfully for a number of "one off" or pact deals which kept Raft's career going for the remainder of the forties. Raft found himself working for such mildly eccentric independent producers as Benedict Bogeaus, whose product lacked the polish and production values which Raft was used to. Most of these independent films were released through United Artists. Raft shot four films at RKO Radio, of which the first ranked among his best: He played the title role in *Johnny Angel* (1945), an eerie deep-sea mystery which the studio had little faith in, but which turned out to be a box office bonanza. Raft set up his own production company, Star Films, in partnership with Sam Bischoff to make three films, but only two were made. Raft's personal fortunes took a downturn in 1947 when he was declared bankrupt. His finances were rocky from then onwards.

With the climate of the film industry changing in 1950, Raft was forced to find work abroad. He was also paid a retainer by racketeer Frank Costello to coach him prior to giving testimony before the Kefauver Rackets Committee. Since there were no acceptable film offers forthcoming, Raft turned to television with a syndicated series called *I'm the Law*. He went to England where he fulfilled a six-week tour of the British Isles. While there, he was approached by producer Bernard Luber to star in three quickie features which were subsequently released by Lippert. On March 22, 1954, a Silver Anniversary Testimonial Dinner was given for Raft at the Friars Club in Beverly Hills. Jack Warner, Dore Schary of MGM and Darryl F. Zanuck of 20th Century–Fox attended. In the midst of the ribbing, Raft made an emotional appeal for a job. Warner remained flint-hearted, but Schary found Raft a role as gangster Dan Beaumonte in *Rogue Cop* (1954) which brought him his best notices in years. Zanuck cast him as a police detective investigating a theatrical murder in *Black Widow* (1954).

As a foretaste of what Raft was to suffer in future years, producer Mike Todd invited Raft to play a cameo in his all-star *Around the World in 80 Days* (1956). Raft did not face the cameras again for three years. Instead he became a talent scout for the Flamingo Hotel in Las Vegas. He was offered shares for $65,000, but had to file an application with the Nevada State Gaming Control Board. The Nevada State Tax Commission refused him a gambling casino stockholder's permit because of his past associations. They made a meticulous search of his background, but could find no reason for denying him a permit, so the decision was later reversed. Raft reportedly told the Tax Commission he raised the money for his two percent interest by borrowing $30,000 on his Coldwater Canyon home, $20,000 on his insurance annuities and $10,000 from his agent, Charles K. Feldman. He claimed that he had repaid all of the loans through earnings from *A Bullet for Joey* (1955).

This experience as a talent scout qualified him to become entertainment director of the Capri Hotel in Havana, Cuba, which he did for a stint in the spring of 1958 to booming business. In June he returned to Hollywood where he appeared in his last outstanding film role, that of Spats Columbo in Billy Wilder's classic *Some Like It Hot* (1959). Rather reluctantly he left for Havana to resume his duties at the Capri Hotel over Christmas and New Year's. This activity came to an abrupt end when Fidel Castro's forces overran the country and overthrew the corrupt Batista regime. Castro took control of the country's gambling casinos and closed them down. Raft was captured during the revolution, but after a tense period he was allowed to fly back to the United

States. He did not receive any financial compensation for his lost earnings. His memoirs had been serialized in *The Saturday Evening Post* in 1957 and he was paid $25,000. He subsequently sold the film rights to his life story for $5,000 to Allied Artists. The resulting film was released under the title *The George Raft Story* (1961) in America and as *Spin of a Coin* in Europe. Ray Danton played Raft, but Raft would have preferred Tony Curtis.

In 1960, a professed fan and businessman approached Raft with the idea of setting up a consumer discount store chain, Consumer Marts of America, with Raft to act in a public relations capacity. The first store opened in Chicago with a dozen others following over the next two years. Raft was paid expenses, modest fees for his name and given stock options. Subsequently he was made a vice-president of the company, which gave him financial liability without any authority or further remuneration. In 1964 he was told by the corporate accountant that the company had gone into liquidation with the most serious financial consequences for Raft. In the proceedings that followed, he lost most of his assets including his Beverly Hills home. In 1965 he was indicted on six counts of income tax evasion. After pleas of leniency from show business pals Bob Hope, Bing Crosby, Frank Sinatra, Red Skelton, Lucille Ball, George Murphy and Jimmy Durante, and a hearing, Raft pleaded guilty to one count and was given a suspended sentence and a $2,500 fine. Sinatra gave him a blank check up to the value of $1,000,000 to help his defense.

Afterwards he went to France at the behest of actor Jean Gabin to appear second-billed in the gangster film *Rififi in Panama* (1966), which was well-received. Next he flew to London to become chairman and host of George Raft's Colony Sporting Club, a swank gaming establishment in Berkeley Square, Mayfair. Former co-stars such as Alice Faye and William Holden came to see him there and he attended various public relations events. He did radio and television work and there was even talk of a new film, *Midnight Man*, using the club as a background. He was to spend nine months of each year there for an indeterminate period of time with a three-month vacation for the baseball season back in the States. He owned ten shares in the club, was paid a modest salary with the use of a chauffeur-driven Rolls-Royce and an apartment in Bilton Towers, Cumberland Place, which came with a full-time maid.

The rest of the shares were owned by a syndicate which reputedly had links to organized crime. The company's articles contained two unusual clauses. The first specified that directors need not retire at the age of 70. The second said that they need not hold shares in the company. The enterprise was financed by Dino Cellini, who set up a company called Travel Resorts Enterprises Limited operating out of Miami, Florida, to organize gambling junkets to the Colony Club. When a welshing gambler returned to the States, the New England Mob was there to collect. If he could not pay, he and his family were threatened with violence and even killed. Reports to the Board of Trade described Raft as a promotions consultant and Cellini as a technical adviser.

On February 25, 1967, while Raft was on his first vacation in the States, the British Home Secretary Roy Jenkins barred him from re-entering the country because of his alleged associations. (Jenkins later told Parliament that eight American citizens had been declared "prohibited immigrants" during the previous year because of their alleged connection with crime and gambling.) On March 14, 1967, Senator George Murphy rang the FBI and informed them that he had received a call from Raft. He stated that he did not consider Raft to be a personal friend and had never stuck his neck out for him. The Senator did however state that on one occasion he had interceded for Raft with the Internal Revenue Service when Raft was in serious trouble. Raft asked him to write a letter to the British government on his behalf and to contact the FBI so Raft

could look at his file; Murphy refused. He did tell Raft he would set up an appointment with the FBI so that Raft could make any statement to them that he desired. Walter Winchell also wrote a letter to J. Edgar Hoover at Raft's request, asking Hoover to clarify the matter. Hoover refused to meet Raft. On April 4, 1967, there was a letter written by the FBI to Raft confirming that the FBI had no jurisdiction in England and that it had no control over governmental action taken by a foreign country. On April 21, 1967, Raft sent a letter to the FBI stating that his solicitor had been informed by an unknown source that a dossier about Raft had been given by the FBI to the United States ambassador in London, who transferred it to the Home Secretary. This was vehemently denied by the U.S. ambassador, who said that he did not even know Raft was in England until the papers reported that he had been declined re-entry.

The legal hassle is probably what prevented Raft from appearing in cameos in such films as *Madigan's Millions* and *Don't Make Waves*. He was pursued by creditors and was forced to sell his Coldwater Canyon house for $63,000 and move into a one-bedroom Beverly Hills apartment. The Colony Club closed its doors for the last time in 1969. He was refused permission to re-enter Britain in 1971 and 1974. In 1970 Raft was the subject of an inquiry into crime and gambling and agreed to answer questions before a New York grand jury about alleged associations with the Mafia. Raft denied being a member of any gang.

He remained in debt to the IRS to the amount of $75,000 and survived on a small pension from the Screen Actors Guild and Social Security payments. He had a hand in organizing various nostalgia events and earned some money from commercials for Pontiac, Alka-Seltzer, Maxwell House and the Merchants National Bank in Indianapolis, Indiana. In the seventies he was appointed goodwill ambassador to the Riviera Hotel, Las Vegas, but operated out of the Los Angeles office. In

1973 he moved into a small apartment in the Century City complex.

Raft allegedly married for the first time in the teens to a much older woman who bore him a son who eventually made him a grandfather. This has never been verified. The second marriage took place on June 15, 1923, to Grayce Mulrooney, a welfare worker, in Pennsylvania. They were together for only a short period, but as she was a Catholic she refused to divorce him until she died in 1968. Since they were legally separated, however, she was given ten percent of his earnings for life.

His most important relationship was with Virginia Pine (1912–1984) who had a daughter, Joan, born in 1933. Born Virginia Peine in Chicago, the daughter of affluent businessman Augustus Peine, Virginia moved to Hollywood to pursue a career as an actress after divorcing Edward Lehman, Jr. She was introduced to Raft at a Hollywood racetrack in 1935 by Jock Whitney, a wealthy playboy. In 1937 Raft built a lavish house for her in Coldwater Canyon, part of the Bel Air section of Los Angeles. Their relationship ended in 1939, partly because Raft could not obtain a divorce and partly because they were one of the subjects of an infamous *Photoplay* magazine article, "Hollywood's Unmarried Husbands and Wives," which created a scandal. When Raft returned to the house after a social event, he found Virginia and Joan gone. Virginia later issued a press statement that she had gone to New York to find a proper school for Joan and to search for legitimate stage work for herself. In 1942 she married Quentin Reynolds. She was married five times in total.

Raft escorted Norma Shearer (1902–1983), MGM star and widow of studio executive Irving Thalberg, home from a party at Jack Warner's mansion. She already had two children, Irving Junior and Katherine. In July 1939 Raft attended a premiere of *Each Dawn I Die* in New York. While dining with Charles Boyer and his actress wife Pat Paterson, he accepted an invitation to attend the World's Fair.

They invited Shearer to go with them and the foursome went everywhere together. The others were sailing to Europe on the *Normandie* and Raft made a snap decision to go with them. There were several celebrities including Shearer and the Boyers at the dock, but a huge crowd turned up. So great was Raft's popularity that the others were virtually ignored. By the time Raft and Shearer returned to Hollywood, their relationship had become the talk of the town. She had considerable influence on his life and there was talk of them appearing together in films at MGM and Warner Brothers which did not materialize. Their relationship ended in 1941 because Raft could not obtain a divorce and pressure from the more conservative element in Hollywood convinced Shearer that Raft was not suitable husband material. In 1942 she married ski instructor Martin Arrouge.

Raft's last serious relationship was with Betty Grable (1916–1973), whom he met in 1941. Raft used a mutual friend, Mary Livingstone, as a sounding board to see whether Grable would go out with him. This was unnecessary because Grable was eager to date him. He would pick her up at 20th Century–Fox studios after she had finished work. Then they would go for dinner at the Brown Derby and he would take her home. They both liked to shop at drug stores. After they arrived at her home, they would play gin rummy until 8:30 P.M. Betty was in bed by 9 P.M. On Saturdays they would go dancing (they were both experts). They enjoyed football, the races and boxing matches. Raft, who was still making up for the family life he never had, enjoyed taking the Grable family out en masse. Their relationship lasted until 1943 when Grable went on a USO tour. While she was away, she did some thinking and decided her life was not the way she wanted. When she returned, Raft was waiting for her. After working hard at the studios all day, she played hostess at the Hollywood Canteen in the evenings so she had less time for Raft. The wedge that finally came between them was Raft's inability to obtain a divorce. She finished with him by telephone.

On July 11, 1943, she eloped to Las Vegas and married Harry James, whom she divorced in 1965. Raft later renewed acquaintance with both her and her husband and they sometimes used to go around as a threesome. She later said, "I would have married George Raft the week I met him. I was so desperately in love." Actor Will Hutchins recalls, "When I was a lad, my granddad would take me out to the ball park to see the L.A. Angels play. And who would we see? Why, none other than the most glamourous couple in town: George Raft and Betty Grable."

During the 1970s, Raft's health began to fail. In 1972 he underwent a hernia operation and in 1980 came down with pneumonia. He suffered very badly during his last years from emphysema and was in and out of hospital for six months before he died in the New Los Angeles Hospital on November 24, 1980, from cardio-respiratory arrest, acute bronchopneumonia, emphysema and leukemia.

Hospital spokesman Dr. Ruxford Kennamer said, "George had been in no pain. He simply went to sleep." Raft had been in the hospital about a week before he died. At the time of his death he left a $10,000 life insurance policy together with a few pieces of furniture. He reckoned that he had earned $10 million from his films, but most of it was spent on women and horse racing. As he expressed it, "I was a soft touch. If anybody asked me for money, I figured they needed it. I suppose I'd be a millionaire today if I hadn't spent so much on broads." He is buried in the Courts of Remembrance Sanctuary of Light at Forest Lawn Cemetery, Hollywood Hills, in a crypt engraved simply "George Raft 1895–1980." He has two stars on the Hollywood Walk of Fame. Pete Hamill in *The New York Post* wrote possibly the best epitaph for Raft when he penned, "I wish someone would give him a long coat and machine gun, a pair of spats and a blonde and let him flip a silver dollar in the air before shooting it out with the cops. George Raft, of all people, should be allowed to go out in style."

THE FILMS

Queen of the Night Clubs (1929)

Cast: Texas Guinan (Texas Malone), John Davidson (Don Holland), Lila Lee (Bea Walters), Arthur Housman (Andy Quinland), Eddie Foy, Jr. (Eddie Parr), Jack Norworth (Phil Parr), George Raft (Gigola), Jimmy Phillips (Nick), William Davidson (Assistant District Attorney), John Miljan (Lawyer Grant), Lee Shumway (Crandall), Joseph Depew (Roy), Agnes Franey (Flapper), Charlotte Merriam (Girl), James T. Mack (Judge).

Credits: Director and Producer: Bryan Foy; Assistant Director: Freddie Foy; Screenplay: Addison Burkhard and Murray Roth; Photography: Edwin B. DuPar. Released by Warner Bros. on February 24, 1929. Black and white. 60 minutes.

Synopsis: A popular night club entertainer falls victim to jealous rivals.

Comments: This is understood to be a lost film. Raft made an inauspicious screen debut in this film in which he does a specialty dance number. Texas Guinan was an early mentor for Raft. In *Queen of the Night Clubs* she urged "a big hand" for him although few took notice then. A short clip from this film, with Guinan and Raft conducting a band, can be seen in *Winner Take All* (1932).

Biography: Bryan Foy was born in Chicago, Illinois, on December 8, 1896. He entered show business in a hugely popular vaudeville act with his father Eddie Foy Sr. and "The Seven Little Foys." He left the act in 1918 to go to Hollywood, where he progressed to producing and directing two-reelers at Fox. In the mid-twenties he joined Warner Bros. where his experience on Vitaphone shorts led to him directing "the first 100 percent all-talk-ing picture" *Lights of New York* (1928). After directing other films, Foy became a producer, heading the B unit at Warner Bros. where he became known as "The Keeper of the B's." He died in Los Angeles on April 20, 1977, aged 70, of heart failure.

Biography: Texas Guinan was born Mary Louise Cecelie Guinan in Waco, Texas, on January 12, 1884. She made her screen debut in 1917. She rose to fame making a number of short Westerns in which she was billed as "The Female Bill Hart." In 1921 she set up her own film production company, but found the going tougher than she expected. Closing the company, she left Hollywood in 1922 to appear in a musical at New York's Winter Garden Theater. A chance meeting with entrepreneur Larry Fay led to the opening of a number of night clubs in the New York area, which paid off handsomely. During the Prohibition era her talents for entertaining and self-promotion fused and led to a successful career as a hostess in night clubs and speakeasies. Within a year she earned over a million dollars and came to epitomize both the Roaring Twenties and Prohibition. Her famous greeting for her patrons was "Hello, suckers," which they loved. Her final film was *Broadway Thru a Keyhole* (1933) in which she played herself. She died in Vancouver, Canada, while making a personal appearance on November 5, 1933, aged 49, of amoebic dysentery. Her film biography *Incendiary Blonde* (1945) starred Betty Hutton.

Side Street (aka The Three Brothers) (1929)

Cast: Tom Moore (Jimmy O'Farrell), Owen Moore (Dennis O'Farrell aka Barney Muller),

Matt Moore (John O'Farrell), Emma Dunn (Mrs. Nora O'Farrell), Kathryn Perry (Kathleen Doyle), Frank Sheridan (Tom O'Farrell), Charles Byer (Maxse Kimball), Arthur Housman (Henchman Silk Ruffo), Mildred Harris (Bunny), Walter McNamara (Patrick Doyle), Edwin August (Henchman Mac), Irving Bacon (Henchman Slim), June Clyde (Judy the Singer), Heinie Conklin (Drunk at Party), Al Hill (Henchman Blondie), George Raft (Georgie Ames the Dancer), Ray Turner (Muller's Butler), Dan Wolheim (Henchman Pinkie).

Credits: Screenplay and Director: Mal St. Clair; Producer: William LeBaron; Screenplay: George O'Hara and Jane Murfin; Adaptation: Eugene Walter and John Russell; Photography: William Marshall; Original Music: Oscar Levant. Released by RKO Radio on September 15, 1929. Black and white. 70 minutes.

Synopsis: The story of three brothers, one of whom is a cop, the second a surgeon, the third a gangster. The gangster's henchmen lay a trap for the cop without informing the gangster. When he discovers their plot, the gangster rushes to the scene where his men shoot him, leaving him to die in the arms of his brothers.

Comments: This was one of the earliest films released by RKO Radio. It is the only film in which the three Moore brothers appear together. This early sound effort is extremely primitive, marred by many sound recording defects and static camera angles. Much of the acting, including that of the leads, is truly awful. Raft has a small part as a gangster.

Biography: Mal St. Clair was born in Los Angeles on May 17, 1897, of Irish parents. A former newspaper cartoonist, he joined Mack Sennett in 1915 as a bit player and gag writer. He began directing shorts for Sennett in 1919. Freelancing from 1921 onwards, he directed his first feature in 1923. His career reached its apogee directing sophisticated comedies in the mid-twenties. In the early thirties his career nosedived and, although he remained busy until 1948, none of his later films were partic-

ularly well-received. He died in Pasadena, California, on June 1, 1952, aged 55.

Quick Millions (1931)

Cast: Spencer Tracy (Daniel J. "Bugs" Raymond), Marguerite Churchill (Dorothy Stone), John Wray (Kenneth Stone), Warner Richmond ("Nails" Markey), Sally Eilers (Daisy De Lisle), George Raft (Jimmy Kirk), John Swor (Contractor), Leon Waycoff [Leon Ames] (Hood), Bob Burns ("Arkansas" Bob Smith), Oscar Apfel (Police Captain), Ward Bond (Cop in Montage), Eddie Hart (Henchman), Edgar Kennedy (Cop in Brawl), Henry Kolker (District Attorney McIntyre), Dixie Lee (Stone's Secretary), Tom London (Atlas Newsreel Man), Louis Mercier (Chauffeur), Paul Panzer (Robbery Victim), Bob Perry (Racetrack Tout in Speakeasy), Oscar Smith (Oscar).

Credits: Director: Rowland Brown; Producer: William Fox; Screenplay: Rowland Brown and Courtney Terrett; Additional Dialogue: John Wray; Photography: Joseph H. August; Sound Recorder: W.W. Lindsay, Jr.; Costumes: Sophie Wachner. Released by Fox on May 3, 1931. Black and white. 72 minutes.

Synopsis: After a fight with a cop, truck driver "Bugs" Raymond finds himself broke. His loyal but common girlfriend Daisy De Lisle threatens to leave him. Raymond joins forces with "Nails" Markey, who owns a fleet of trucks and controls the produce market. Together they offer protection to garage owners in exchange for a weekly fee. At a testimonial dinner for "Nails" Markey, gangsters from Chicago under Raymond's control rob some dignitaries of incriminating letters which can be used as blackmail if the civic leaders try to arrest them. Raymond meets socialite Dorothy Stone, sister of construction industry financier John Stone. During a strike, Stone has no trucks to move building materials. Raymond and his henchman Jimmy Kirk go to see Stone and provide him with trucks.

Raymond becomes a director of the John

Stone Building Corporation. He takes Dorothy to the races and the opera. When Daisy protests, he beats her. He tells Markey not to bring his men to the office any longer. Markey accuses him of going high hat and ignoring his men and their core business. Markey asserts himself and tells the gangsters that he is now their boss. He arranges for Jimmy to carry out a hit on a prominent anti-racketeering journalist outside of the organization. This causes a massive roundup of underworld figures. The police captain tells Raymond that Jimmy was seen leaving the hotel where the murder took place. When Kirk rings Raymond and confesses to the murder, Raymond tells him to go to Lefty's garage at ten that night where there will be a car and money for him. When Kirk goes to the garage, he is shot to death.

When Raymond proposes to Dorothy, she rejects him and tells him that she is already engaged. Raymond has become so infatuated with her that he decides to kidnap her on her wedding day at the church with the aid of his henchmen. On the way to the church, Raymond tells Markey that he is still looking for the guy who hired Kirk. Markey draws a gun and shoots and kills him. As the car passes the church, Raymond's derby hat is flung from the car window, signifying symbolically that his reign of terror is over.

Comments: *Quick Millions* was the only time that Raft was directed by Rowland Brown. Spencer Tracy in this, his second film, as "Bugs" Raymond, the guy with a one-ton brain who's too nervous to steal and too lazy to work. This movie did much to establish Tracy as a strong screen presence and won praise for Brown's imaginative direction. The theme of the film was that successful racketeering involves infiltration of big business and that violence is a method of achieving this rather than an end in itself. Although there were violent scenes, they were usually shown in an offbeat way. Warner Richmond is fine as Tracy's partner and eventual killer. Raft is equally good as Tracy's henchman. This movie was instrumen-

tal in Raft landing a career-making role in *Scarface*.

Despite a strained beginning Tracy and Raft became good friends while shooting this film. There was a battle of screen chemistry here. In scenes where they were together, it was easy to forget Tracy who was delivering important dialogue to other characters and instead concentrate on Raft in the background, seemingly doing very little. One highlight of this film was Raft's softshoe dance at a party. The camera focused on his legs, the intention of which seemed to be to demonstrate his slick steps, but in fact was a preamble to the next time the viewer saw his legs in an expertly shot murder scene. Raft was particularly good when he nonchalantly departed the scene of the killing.

Biography: Rowland Brown was born in Akron, Ohio, on November 6, 1897. He was educated at the University of Detroit and Detroit School of Fine Arts. Originally a fashion illustrator and sports cartoonist, he arrived in Hollywood in 1928 and started as a laborer on the Fox lot, working his way up to being a property boy and gag writer. By 1930 he was on the payroll as a screenwriter. He directed his first film *Quick Millions* (1931) and two other acclaimed films before being blacklisted. He became known as "the director who slugged a producer" after punching David O. Selznick. He continued to contribute scripts and stories as the basis for films (including a couple starring Raft) until 1952. He died at his home in Costa Mesa, California, on May 6, 1963, aged 65.

Biography: Spencer Bonaventure Tracy was born in Milwaukee, Wisconsin, on April 5, 1900, the son of John Edward Tracy, a truck dealer, and Caroline Brown. In 1930 he scored a major triumph on Broadway in *The Last Mile* which led to his film debut in *Up the River* (1931). He was initially with Fox and in 1935 he signed with MGM where he became one of their most popular and enduring stars. He was Oscar-nominated nine times and won back-to-back Best Actor Oscars for *Captains*

Courageous (1937) and *Boys Town* (1938). In 1923 he married stage actress Louise Treadwell. They had two children, a son John (1924–2007) and daughter Louise (1932). He was never divorced from his wife, but was estranged from her for years. He had a long personal and professional relationship with Katharine Hepburn. He died in Beverly Hills on June 10, 1967, aged 67, of heart failure. Raft appeared in two films with Tracy, *Quick Millions* and *Goldie*.

Goldie (1931)

Cast: Spencer Tracy (Bill), Warren Hymer (Spike Moore), Jean Harlow (Goldie), Jess De Vorska (Gonzales), Leila Karnelly (Wife), Ivan Linow (Husband), Lina Basquette (Constantina), Eleanor Hunt (Russian Girl), Maria Alba (Dolores), Eddie Kane (Barker), Billy Barty (Child), Dorothy Granger (Nanette, Girl in Café), Alberto Morin (Carnival Customer), Edmund Mortimer (Fashion Show Extra), George Raft (Pickpocket at Carnival), Julian Rivero (Bartender), Harry Tenbrook (Nanette's Man in Café).

Credits: Director: Benjamin Stoloff; Producer: William Fox; Screenplay: Gene Towne and Paul Perez; Photography: Ernest Palmer; Editor: Alex Troffey; Original Music: R.H. Bassett and Hugo Friedhofer. Released by Fox on June 28, 1931. Black and white. 68 minutes.

Synopsis: Spike, a sailor, finds a book containing the addresses of prostitutes. When he dates each of these girls, he finds that they are all similarly tattooed. Spike sets out to find the pervert who left his mark on each of the girls and thrash him in a fight. But he finds Bill, who is the culprit and also a sailor, they become good buddies. In Calais, Bill becomes enamored of a carnival high diver named Goldie. Bill warns Spike that Goldie will live up to her name and is only interested in stealing his money. Goldie tries to work her way into Spike's heart, but he is not so easily deceived. When

Spike discovers that Goldie is marked with Bill's tattoo, he abandons her in disgust.

Comments: This is a remake of *A Girl in Every Port* (1928). Appearing in his second Spencer Tracy film, Raft has a very minor role as a pickpocket.

Biography: Benjamin Stoloff was born in Philadelphia, Pennsylvania, on October 6, 1895. Educated at the University of Southern California, he began as a director of shorts. Later he joined Fox where he directed several series of shorts and his first full-length feature in 1926. He was more noted for the quantity of his films rather than quality. He died in Hollywood on September 8, 1960, aged 64.

Hush Money (1931)

Cast: Joan Bennett (Janet Gordon), Hardie Albright (Stuart Elliott), Owen Moore (Steve Pelton), Myrna Loy (Flo Curtis), C. Henry Gordon (Jack Curtis), Douglas Cosgrove (Captain Dan Emmett), George Raft (Maxie), Henry Armetta (Bootlegger), George Byron (Flannegan), Joan Castle (Miss Stockton), Andre Cheron (Silvio), Ronnie Cosby (Baby), George Irving (Mr. Stockton), Louise Mackintosh (Housekeeper), Nella Walker (Mrs. Stockton), Huey White (Puggie).

Credits: Director: Sidney Lanfield; Story and Screenplay: Philip Klein and Courtney Terrett; Dialogue: Dudley Nichols; Photography: John F. Seitz; Music: Glen Knight. Released by Fox on July 12, 1931. Black and white. 68 minutes.

Synopsis: Janet Gordon becomes part of a criminal gang led by Steve Pelton. The gang is captured and sentenced. Janet, the first to be paroled, vows to go straight and becomes an interior decorator. She meets and marries Stuart Elliott without telling him about her past. When Pelton is released, he tries blackmailing Janet. Policeman Dan Emmett circulates the information to the underworld that Pelton received a reduced sentence by informing on the rest of the gang. The criminal fraternity exact vengeance by eliminating Pelton, leaving Janet to enjoy her life.

Comments: This was the first of four films in which Joan Bennett appeared with Raft. In the other three they were co-stars, but here Raft has a bit part as a gangster. Bennett met Raft for the first time on the set of this film.

Biography: Director Sidney Lanfield was born in Chicago, Illinois, on April 20, 1898. Originally from vaudeville and a jazz musician, he went to Hollywood in 1926 as a gagman for Fox and from 1928 as a screenwriter. He directed his first feature in 1930 and shot a number of movies until 1952, mainly at 20th Century–Fox and Paramount. In 1952 he switched to television where he directed over 200 episodes. He was married to actress Shirley Mason from 1927 until his death in Marina Del Rey, California, on June 30, 1972, aged 74, from a heart attack. In spite of being married to an actress, he had a reputation for being extremely cruel to the players on his sets.

Palmy Days (1931)

Cast: Eddie Cantor (Eddie Simpson), Charlotte Greenwood (Miss Helen Martin), Barbara Weeks (Joan Clark), Spencer Charters (Mr. A.B. Clark), Paul Page (Steve Clayton), Charles Middleton (Yolando), George Raft (Joe, Yolando's Henchman), Harry Woods (Plug Moynihan, Yolando's Henchman), Busby Berkeley (Fortune Teller), Arthur Hoyt (Man at Séance and at Party), Sam Lufkin (Hypnotizing Detective), Edmund Mortimer, Herbert Rawlinson, Bill Elliott (Party Guests), Loretta Andrews, Edna Callaghan, Nadine Dore, Mildred Dixon, Ruth Eddings, Betty Grable, Virginia Grey, Amo Ingraham, Jean Lenivich, Betty Lorraine, Neva Lynn, Nancy Nash, Faye Pierre, Nita Pike, Dorothy Poynton, Betty Slocum, Hyca Slocum, Betty Stockton, Dorothy White, Toby Wing, Hazel Witter (Goldwyn Girls).

Credits: Director: A. Edward Sutherland; Producer: Sam Goldwyn; Story & Dialogue: Eddie Cantor, Morrie Ryskind, David Freedman; Continuity: Keene Thompson; Photography: Gregg Toland; Editor: Sherman Todd; Music: Con Conrad, Harry Akst; Musical Director: Alfred Newman; Dances and Ensembles: Busby Berkeley; Art Direction: Richard Day, Willy Pogany; Sound Recorder: Vinton Vernon; Costumes: Alice O'Neill; Released by United Artists on October 3, 1931. Black and white. 77 minutes.

Musical Numbers:

"Bend Down Sister" by Ballard MacDonald and Con Conrad, sung by Charlotte Greenwood and the Goldwyn Girls.

"There's Nothing Too Good for My Baby" by Benny Davis, Harry Akst and Eddie Cantor, sung by Eddie Cantor in blackface.

"My Honey Said Yes, Yes" by Cliff Friend, sung by Eddie Cantor, performed by the Goldwyn Girls, later reprised by Cantor and Charlotte Greenwood.

Synopsis: Mr. Clark's bakery comes complete with a gym full of showgirls which is run with military precision by Miss Helen Martin. Yolando, a fake medium, and Eddie Simpson, his idiot assistant, run a service for business people. Miss Martin wants a husband and Yolando promises her one. Simpson turns up at the bakery where he is put through a vigorous physical training program by Miss Martin. Clark tells Yolando that he needs an efficiency expert in his business. Yolando tells Joe to go to the bakery at noon and get the job. At the stroke of noon, Simpson is on the run from Miss Martin and is accidentally appointed to the job. Simpson, in search of an office, meets Clark's pretty daughter Joan and wants to engage her as his secretary. Owing to a misunderstanding, Simpson believes that Joan is in love with him whereas she really loves boyfriend, Steve Clayton.

Clark has allocated $25,000 bonus money in cash for his employees. At the bakery, Yolando watches Simpson put it in the safe. Simpson writes the combination of the safe on a piece of yellow paper. Yolando tells his henchmen to steal it from Simpson so they go to the office to obtain it. The gangsters pursue Simpson, who disguises himself as a woman and hides in a laundry basket. While searching the locker room, the gangsters find the safe combination. They open the safe, but the money is gone: Simpson has beaten them to it. He has put it in some dough which he then cooks in the oven.

At the engagement party for Joan and Steve, Clark is told that the money is no longer in the safe. Simpson is accused of theft and taken away by police from whom he escapes with Helen. They drive to the bakery where they find the loaf with the money in it, but are surprised by Yolando and his henchmen. A madcap chase ensues. Via telephone, Simpson alerts Clark to the crookedness of Yolando. Simpson hides the money in the coat of the mystic, which is nearly burned. In the nick of time, the police arrive to arrest the gangsters. Simpson gives Clark back the money and is acclaimed a hero. He realizes he is genuinely in love with Helen and marries her at the climax.

Comments: *Palmy Days* was the first of two films in which Raft was directed by Eddie Sutherland. It was Samuel Goldwyn's second annual Eddie Cantor production, a merry mixture of laughs, dance numbers and smiling chorus girls. The fact that it is set in a bakery with a gym allows free rein for some inventive Busby Berkeley dance routines. It contains some good musical numbers, some snappy dialogue and some funny chase scenes. Raft as Joe, one of Yolando's henchmen, has several scenes. He first appears about twenty minutes into the film, dressed in a mystic's costume, when he is told by Yolando to land the efficiency expert job. He reappears about ten minutes later explaining to Yolando why he has not been given the job. In the two main chase sequences he is seen pursuing Simpson. At the climax while he is searching Helen, she knocks him unconscious. He is last seen being led away by police. Raft was always very effective in this kind of role. *Palmy Days* was one of the year's top-grossing films with domestic rentals of $1,000,000.

Biography: A. Edward Sutherland was born in London on January 5, 1895, the son of professionals Al Sutherland and Julie Ring. He started out as a performer, appearing in vaudeville, stock and musical comedy. He began his motion picture career as a stuntman and bit part actor in a Helen Holmes serial in 1914. Later he joined Charlie Chaplin's directorial staff. He directed his first feature in 1925. His particular penchant was directing comedy films. He was married five times: to Marjorie Daw, Louise Brooks, Ethel Kenyon, Audrey Henderson and Edwina Sutherland. He died in Palm Springs on December 31, 1973, aged 78.

Biography: Eddie Cantor was born Edward Israel Iskowitz in New York on January 31, 1892. The son of Russian immigrants who died when he was a child, he became a professional entertainer at the age of fourteen. After working as a singing waiter at Coney Island, he became popular in burlesque, vaudeville and on Broadway. He made his screen debut in 1926 and became especially popular during the thirties. He was awarded a special Oscar in 1956. He was married to Ida Tobias from 1914 until she died in 1962; they had five daughters. He died in Beverly Hills on October 10, 1964, aged 72, of a heart attack.

Taxi! (1932)

Cast: James Cagney (Matt Nolan), Loretta Young (Sue Riley Nolan), George E. Stone (Skeets), Guy Kibbee (Pop Riley), Leila Bennett (Ruby), Dorothy Burgess (Marie Costa), David Landau (Buck Gerard), Ray Cooke (Danny Nolan), Berton Churchill (Judge West), Donald Cook (Movie Star in Movie Clip), Eddie Fetherston (Dance Contest M.C.), Ben Hendricks, Jr. (Moving Man), Aggie Herring (Cleaning Lady), Evalyn Knapp (Movie Star in Movie Clip), George MacFarlane (Father Nulty), Matt McHugh (Joe Silva), Robert Emmett O'Connor (Cop with Jewish Man), Nat Pendleton (Bull Martin, Truck Driver), Lee Phelps (Onlooker), Russ Powell (Dancing

Judge Presenting Cup), George Raft (William Kenny), Sam Rice (Man in Elevator), Hector Sarno (Mr. Lombardy, Monument Maker), Cliff Saum (Head Mechanic), Ben Taggart (Detective), Harry Tenbrook (Tom, Cab Driver), Polly Walters (Polly, Danny's Date).

Credits: Director: Roy Del Ruth; Producer: Robert Lord; Based on the play *The Blind Spot* by Kenyon Nicholson; Adaptation and Dialogue: Kubec Glasmon and John Bright; Photography: James Van Trees; Editor: James Gibbon; Art Director: Esdras Hartley; Vitaphone Orchestra Conductor: Leo F. Forbstein; Makeup: Perc Westmore. Working Titles: *Taxi Please!* and *The Blind Spot*. Released by Warner Bros. on January 23, 1932. Black and white. 70 minutes.

Synopsis: A war between taxi cab owner Consolidated and independent cab drivers has spilled over into violence. Consolidated enforcer Buck Gerard tells taxi cab owner Pop Riley to abandon the site where he has been stationed for years. Riley ignores this warning, but when a trucker on Gerard's instructions plows into his taxi, Riley shoots and kills him. For this he is sentenced to ten years in the penitentiary where he subsequently dies. Independent taxi driver Matt Nolan, who is fighting Consolidated, invites Riley's daughter Sue to a meeting where she urges restraint. This infuriates Nolan, but in spite of this he falls in love with Sue and marries her. At a restaurant he becomes involved in a fight with Gerard, who stabs and kills Nolan's brother. Nolan refuses to tell the cops who did it, but seeks vengeance. A tip leads him to an apartment where Gerard and his moll, Marie Costa, are hiding out. Nolan intends to shoot Gerard, but the cops arrive. In trying to escape, Gerard falls to his death.

Comments: This was the first of four films in which Raft was directed by Roy Del Ruth. It's a highly entertaining film done with pace in the best Warner Bros. tradition. Stars James Cagney and Loretta Young made an attractive, gutsy combination. Raft has a memorable bit as a hoofer who competes with Cagney and Young in a dance contest. The final was between Raft and his partner and Cagney and Young. When Raft was declared the winner, he said to Cagney, "How do you like that, wise guy?" Cagney reacted by slugging him.

Dancers in the Dark (1932)

Cast: Miriam Hopkins (Gloria Bishop), Jack Oakie (Duke Taylor), William Collier, Jr. (Floyd Stevens), Eugene Pallette (Gus), Lyda Roberti (Fanny Zabowolski), George Raft (Louie Brooks), Maurice Black (Max), De Witt Jennings (Sgt. McGroady), Paul Fix (Benny), George Bickel (Spiegel), James Bradbury, Jr. (Happy, Trombonist), Sam Coslow (Vocal Double for Jack Oakie), Adelaide Hall (Vocal Double for Miriam Hopkins), Claire Dodd (Girl at Bar), Eduardo Durant (Orchestra Leader), Paul Gibbons (Orchestra Member), Mary Gordon (Cleaning Lady), William Halligan (Terry, Trumpeter), Walter Hiers (Ollie), Al Hill (Smitty, Bouncer), Frances Moffett (Ruby), Kent Taylor (Saxophonist), Alberta Vaughn (Marie), Fred Warren (Al, Pianist).

Credits: Director: David Burton; Based on the play *Jazz King* by James Ashmore Creelman; Screenplay: Herman J. Mankiewicz; Adaptation: Brian Marlow and Howard Emmett Rogers; Photography: Karl Struss; Music: W. Franke Harling, John Leipold, Stephen Pasternacki and Dana Suesse. Song "St. Louis Blues" by W.C. Handy. Released by Paramount on March 20, 1932. Black and white. 74 minutes.

Synopsis: This drama is set in the world of nightclubs and taxi dancers. Men go to a nightclub called "The Dance Palace" to dance with girls, paying ten cents a dance. Duke Taylor, a bandleader, thinks his young friend, saxophonist Floyd Stevens, will be corrupted by his engagement to taxi dancer Gloria Bishop. To protect him, Duke arranges with nightclub owner Max to fire Floyd so that he will have to sign with Barton, a rival bandleader, and leave town for four weeks. In his absence, Duke finds himself falling for Gloria, with whom he had an earlier relationship. She rejects him. When Floyd returns, he finds Duke in a clinch with Gloria. Duke reassures Floyd that Gloria has been faithful to him, but nevertheless Floyd slugs him.

A jealous gangster, Louie Brooks, regards Gloria as his moll. When Louie and his accomplice Benny rob a jewelry store, Louie shoots and kills the proprietor. Gloria asks Louie if she can leave town with him. Before they can do so, the police arrive at the nightclub searching for Louie. Benny has been arrested and told the police that Louie killed the jeweler. The police search the nightclub for Louie, who pulls a gun and holds Duke at gunpoint. Duke manages to alert the cops by arranging to have the band play "St. Louis Blues," Louie's favorite song. When he realizes what Duke has done, Louie shoots him. Pursued by cops, Louie climbs onto a ledge outside the club and falls to his death. The wounded Duke tells Floyd that Gloria has never been unfaithful to him. The two lovers are reunited while Duke is taken to a hospital in a squad car.

Comments: This was the only time George Raft was directed by David Burton. The dance hall set where nearly all the action takes place was atmospheric with shadows being cast in all directions, giving the film a German Expressionistic look. This was the first and better of the two films Raft made with Miriam Hopkins, whom he hated working with. Raft played one of his most sinister characters in this film and since the world of nightclubs and taxi dancers was one he understood, he was totally convincing. This was the first film he made under his contract with Paramount and was a major stepping stone on his route to stardom. It was actually shot after *Scarface,* but released earlier. Although Raft was sixth-billed, he had a much larger role than William Collier, Jr., who had relatively little footage despite his prominent billing. One of the most memorable features of

Raft's character was his single-minded liking for the song "St. Louis Blues," particularly when Gloria sang it. Her aura of vulnerability together with the dangerous appeal of Raft gave their scenes together an erotic and sadistic edge. On the strength of this film, critics dubbed Raft "a fascinating, new kind of villain."

Biography: David Burton was born in Odessa, Ukraine, Russia, on May 22, 1886. Upon coming to America, he changed his name. Educated in Philadelphia, he worked for many years as stage manager for Charles Frohman productions. He traveled all over the world in the course of his theatrical work. He directed a number of 1930s films which were not particularly distinguished. He died in New York City on December 30, 1963, aged 77.

Scarface (1932)

Cast: Paul Muni (Antonio [Tony] "Scarface" Camonte), Ann Dvorak (Francesca [Cesca] Camonte), Karen Morley (Poppy), Osgood Perkins (Johnny Lovo), C. Henry Gordon (Insp. Ben Guarino), George Raft (Guido Rinaldo), Vince Barnett (Angelo), Boris Karloff (Gaffney), Purnell Pratt (Mr. Garston, Publisher), Tully Marshall (Managing Editor), Inez Palange (Mrs. Camonte), Edwin Maxwell (Detective Chief), Henry Armetta (Pietro, Barber), Gus Arnheim (Orchestra Leader), Maurice Black (Jim, Headwaiter), Gino Corrado (Waiter at Columbia Cafe), Virginia Dabney (Mabel), Eddie Fetherston (Reporter), Paul Fix (Hood with Gaffney), Howard Hawks (Man in Bed), Hank Mann (Stag Party Janitor), Warner Richmond (Cesca's Dance Partner), Bert Starkey (Epstein, Lawyer), George E. Stone (Reporter at Police Station), Helen C. Thompson (Sadie Thompson), Harry J. Vejar (Big Louis Costillo), John Kelly, Jack Perry, Charles Sullivan, Harry Tenbrook (Costillo's Hoods), Eugenie Besserer, William B. Davidson, Brandon Hurst (Citizens Committee Members), Francis Ford (Prison Guard in alternate ending), William Burress (Judge in alternate ending).

Foreground left to right: Osgood Perkins, Vince Barnett, Paul Muni, Karen Morley and George Raft in *Scarface*.

Credits: Director: Howard Hawks; Producers: Howard Hughes and Howard Hawks; Assistant Director: Richard Rosson; Based on the Book by Armitage Trail; Story: Ben Hecht; Continuity and Dialogue: Seton I. Miller, John Lee Mahin and W.R. Burnett; Photography: Lee Garmes and L.W. O'Connell; Editors: Edward Curtiss and Lewis Milestone; Musical Directors: Adolph Tandler and Gus Arnheim; Art Direction: Harry Oliver; Sound Recorder: William Snyder; Released by United Artists on April 17, 1932. Black and white. 93 minutes.

Synopsis: A prologue states, "This picture is an indictment of gang rule in America and of the callous indifference of the government to this constantly increasing menace to our safety and our liberty. Every incident in this picture is the reproduction of an actual occur-

rence and the purpose of this picture is to demand of the government: 'What are you going to do about it?' The government is your government. What are you going to do about it?" Big Louis Costillo, who runs Chicago's South Side, is shot and killed in his own restaurant by his bodyguard Tony "Scarface" Camonte on the instructions of gangster Johnny Lovo. Inspector Guarino picks up both Camonte and his henchman, Rinaldo, but they are soon released on a writ of Habeas Corpus. Camonte is appointed Lovo's chief lieutenant and meets Lovo's arrogant mistress, Poppy. Camonte tells him that he wants to take over O'Hara's business on the North Side, but Lovo tells him to stay out of it because O'Hara is still too powerful a figure to cross.

Lovo, Camonte and Rinaldo go to the First Ward social club where Costillo's mob is gathered. Lovo tells them that he is taking over the South Side and will be supplying all the beer there. Camonte starts a campaign of violence which strongarms club proprietors into buying their beer. Camonte tries delivering an order of beer on the North Side which angers Lovo. As they are leaving the club, a speeding car dumps the body of one of their gangsters together with a stark warning, "Keep out of the North Side." Camonte sends Rinaldo over to O'Hara's flower shop, where he kills O'Hara. Sexually aroused by the violence, Poppy switches allegiance from Lovo to Camonte.

Gaffney, a rival gangster, inherits O'Hara's empire. He opens a shipment of machine guns that O'Hara had imported into the state. Gaffney and his mob take the guns, pile into cars and speed to a restaurant where Camonte is eating and blaze away. Their attempt to kill him is unsuccessful. Gaffney's mob also attack the athletic club where Lovo is wounded. Camonte and his gang retaliate by creating mayhem on the North Side. He orchestrates the notorious St. Valentine's Day Massacre, carried out by his gangsters (dressed as cops) wiping out most of Gaffney's cohorts. Camonte is told that Gaffney has taken refuge at a bowling alley. After attending a theatrical performance of *Miss Sadie Thompson,* Camonte and his mob go to the bowling alley where they murder Gaffney.

As Camonte leaves the family home, an attempt is made by mysterious gunmen to murder him. A chase ensues, but Camonte miraculously survives. Believing that Lovo is behind the attempt on his life, Camonte and Rinaldo go to the social club where Lovo panics and, on instructions, Rinaldo shoots him to death. Camonte assumes complete control of Lovo's criminal empire and takes up with Poppy.

Camonte has what appears to be an incestuous relationship with his sister Cesca. After seeing Cesca throw a coin to an organ grinder, Rinaldo becomes enamored of her. While Camonte is out of town Cesca goes to see Rinaldo and they form a dangerous romantic liaison.

Cesca buys a place of her own and leaves the family house. When Camonte returns from the trip, he extracts Cesca's new address from his mother. He goes to the apartment and is shocked when Rinaldo opens the door. Before Rinaldo can speak, Camonte guns him down. After Rinaldo's death, Cesca tells Camonte that she and Rinaldo were married the previous day.

Inspector Guarino and a squad of men arrive at Camonte's property to arrest him for the murder of Rinaldo. As Camonte enters, the police converge and open fire. When Poppy phones, Camonte is so stunned that he cannot think straight nor talk to her properly. He is joined by the still grieving Cesca. She has a gun which she intended to use on Camonte, but is unable to do so. A volley of police bullets kills Cesca first. Tear gas is fired into the room which overcomes Camonte. He comes rushing down the stairs begging the police not to shoot. Ignoring Guarino, he hurtles outside where he is machine gunned to death while a neon sign outside flashes, "The World Is Yours." In an alternative ending which can be found among the DVD extras, Guarino arrests Camonte and takes him in alive. A jury finds him guilty and a stern judge delivers a lecture before sentencing him to hang on December 10, 1931. The execution is shown taking place.

Comments: This was the only occasion in which Raft was directed by Howard Hawks. *Scarface* cemented Raft's career: The sinister gunman he played had a habit of flipping a coin in the air. This was a piece of business which was invented by Hawks for Raft to camouflage his lack of acting experience. It was so effective that it appeared Raft had been acting for years. Raft thought so highly of Hawks that he desperately wanted to make another film with him, but the opportunity never arose. Hawks said, "George was just a bodyguard, but having him flip the coin made him a character. The coin represented a hidden attitude, a defiance, a held-back authority, a coolness which hadn't been found in pictures up to that time."

One of Raft's most spellbinding pieces of acting was where Camonte and Rinaldo go to see Lovo. Lovo begs Rinaldo to have a drink. Rinaldo refuses by shaking his head, spinning the coin and then killing Lovo. He says nothing. Raft's acting was so chilling in this scene that it was easily possible to read his mind before the killing. The only scene where his acting came across as awkward was the one where he professed his love for Cesca. Rinaldo appeared early in the film at a barber shop where he disposed of his gun before being taken in by police. This character lasted until he was gunned down in the 77th minute of the movie. His death scene, where he slid down the door, was another impressive piece of acting. Reference books list Raft's character as Guido, but on the tickertape after his murder his character was called Guino. Camonte called him "Little Boy."

Scarface ran into trouble with the censors largely because of the violence and some of its themes such as the incestuous relationship between Tony and his sister Cesca. Despite the fact that the film was named one of the ten best of the year by both the National Board of Review and *Film Daily,* it did not recoup its costs when first released. The film was reworked to less effect in *Scarface* (1983) with Al Pacino. *The Picturegoer's Who's Who* (1933) stated, "Raft, at this showing, looks as if he is going to be one of the big names in the future — but please refrain from calling him a second Valentino which is the label that at the moment is being most indiscreetly applied to him. Apart from the acting, there is a wonderful scope of cinema activity and no picture has more vividly portrayed gun fights with all their attendant evils." Raft was listed in the Honors List compiled by the same publication: "For making the small role of the lover of a gang leader's sister one of the high lights in *Scarface* and for his death scene.... [He is] an artiste of unusual ability and of distinctive type."

Biography: Howard Winchester Hawks was born in Goshen, Indiana, on May 30, 1896. Educated at Phillips Exeter Academy, New Hampshire, the family moved to California when Howard was ten. Later he studied mechanical engineering at Cornell University. During summer vacations he worked in the property department of Famous Players–Lasky. During World War I he served as a pilot in the Army Air Corps and after his discharge designed planes in an aircraft factory. He decided that he preferred the film industry so he went to Hollywood where he worked his way up from cutter to scriptwriter. He made his directorial debut with *The Road to Glory* (1925). He went on to become one of the most proficient directors in the history of the cinema, tackling most genres with outstanding results. Surprisingly he was only nominated once for a Best Director Oscar, for *Sergeant York* (1941). He did however receive an Honorary Oscar in 1975. He was married and divorced three times, to Athole Shearer, Nancy "Slim" Gross and Dee Hartford. He had one adopted son, one natural son and two daughters. He died in Palm Springs on December 26, 1977, aged 81, from complications as a result of a concussion sustained in a fall.

Biography: Paul Muni was born Muni Weisenfreund in Lemburg, Austria, on September 22, 1895. The son of professional actors Phillip Weisenfreund and Sally Weisberg, he arrived in America in 1902 and became a stalwart of the Yiddish theater. In 1926 he made his English-language stage debut in the Broadway production *We Americans.* He made his screen debut in *The Valiant* (1929). He signed a contract with Warner Bros. for whom he did much of his best work. He was nominated for a Best Actor Oscar five times and won for *The Story of Louis Pasteur* (1936). Disagreement over roles led to the termination of his Warner Bros. contract. His movie career declined thereafter, but he scored a notable triumph on Broadway in *Inherit the Wind* (1955). In later years he suffered from poor health and advancing blindness. He married

Bella Finkle in 1921. He died in Montecito, California, on August 25, 1967, aged 71, of a heart ailment.

Biography: Ann Dvorak was born Ann McKim in New York City on August 2, 1911. She was the daughter and only child of Edwin McKim, a director, and Anna Lehr, an actress. She was educated at St. Catherine's Convent in New York City and the Page School for Girls in Los Angeles. In 1920 her parents divorced and she lived with her mother. When she entered films, she chose the stage name Dvorak, derived from her mother's ancestors in Bohemia. She was an assistant dance director at MGM and a chorine in *The Hollywood Revue of 1929*. Her big break came when Howard Hughes cast her in *Scarface*. She signed a contract with Warner Bros., but her time with them was marred by constant conflict. In 1940 she and her first husband, Leslie Fenton, returned to his native England, where she drove an ambulance for the duration of the war and appeared in three British films. In 1945 she resumed her film career, which continued until 1951. She later divided her time between homes in Malibu Beach and Honolulu. She was married and divorced from Fenton (1932–1946) and dancer Igor Dega (1947–1951). She wed architect Nicholas Wade in 1951, but was widowed in 1975. She died in Honolulu on December 10, 1979, aged 68, of stomach cancer.

Night World (1932)

Cast: Lew Ayres (Michael Rand), Mae Clarke (Ruth Taylor), Boris Karloff ("Happy" MacDonald), Dorothy Revier (Jill [Mrs. "Happy"] MacDonald), Russell Hopton (Klauss), Hedda Hopper (Mrs. Rand), Clarence Muse (Tim Washington, the Doorman), Dorothy Peterson (Edith Blair), Bert Roach (Tommy), George Raft (Ed Powell), Gene Morgan (Joe), Huntley Gordon (Jim), Robert Emmett O'Connor (Policeman Ryan), Arletta Duncan (The Cigarette Girl), Florence Lake (Miss Smith), Paisley Noon (Clarence), Greta Granstedt (Blonde), Louise Beavers (Maid), Sammy Blum (Salesman), Harry Woods (Gang Leader), Eddie Phillips (Vaudevillian), Tom Tamarez (Gigolo), Geneva Mitchell (Florabelle), André Cheron (Frenchman from Schenectady), Frankie Farr (Trick Waiter), Jack La Rue (Henchman "Limpy"), Ray Turner (Wash Room Attendant), Alice Adair, Hariette Hagman, Amo Ingraham (Chorines); Helene Chadwick, Byron Foulger, Pat Somerset, Robert Livingston, Larry Steers (Night Club Customers).

Credits: Director: Hobart Henley; Producer: Carl Laemmle, Jr.; Associate Producer: E.M. Asher; Story: P.J. Wolfson, Allen Rivkin; Screenplay: Richard Schayer; Photography: Merritt Gerstad; Editor: Ted Kent; Supervising Film Editor: Maurice Pivar; Musical Score: Alfred Newman; Musical Director: Hal Grayson; Dances Staged by Busby Berkeley; Art Direction: John J. Hughes; Sound Recorder: C. Roy Hunter. Released by Universal on May 5, 1932. Black and white. 57 minutes.

Synopsis: Happy's Club in New York City, "Happy's" wife is having an affair with Klauss, the choreographer. "Happy" is also experiencing problems with bootleggers demanding to know why he is still doing business with their rival, Casey. Michael Rand is well on his way to being an alcoholic after his mother shot and killed his adulterous father, (she was acquitted). Rand becomes involved in an argument and "Happy" is forced to knock him out. When Michael recovers, Ruth takes him into "Happy's" office. They are discovered there by Ed Powell, a gangster who regards himself as Ruth's boyfriend and who has previously arranged a date with Ruth. Powell invites her to his apartment, but Ruth is reluctant to go. Rand orders Powell to leave and says that he will see Ruth home. A fight ensues in which Rand knocks out Powell.

When "Happy" finds Jill in a tryst in his office with Klauss, he fires him. When Jill tries to walk out on him, "Happy" refuses her a divorce and insists that she is going to stay with him. The others leave the club, but Michael and Ruth remain behind. Michael tells Ruth that he is going away and invites her to go with him to Bali as husband and wife. Two gangster bootleggers burst into the club. "Happy" tries to shoot it out with them, but realizes that his wife has removed his gun's bullets. The gangsters shoot them in cold blood. Then they catch sight of Michael and Ruth. They are about to kill them when a uniformed police officer shows up and shoots both the hitmen. Michael and Ruth are told that the police will not detain them long at headquarters and Ruth agrees to go with Michael to Bali.

Comments: This was the only time Raft was directed by Hobart Henley. Henley handled the material well and moved it along at a brisk pace. The action took place in one location in the course of a single night and involved a number of different characters and plots. In that sense it emerged like another *Grand Hotel*, but done on a minor scale. The name of the club, "Happy's," was a misnomer because none of the characters was particularly happy. There were also a few dances arranged by Busby Berkeley in his trademark style.

Raft had only three main scenes. One was where he was greeted by Boris Karloff and they exchanged some tough talk. Secondly, when Raft fixed up the date with Mae Clarke. Thirdly, when he came upon Lew Ayres and Clarke in "Happy's" office and was later knocked cold by Ayres. This was the right kind of environment for Raft and he handled his scenes effectively.

Biography: Hobart Henley was born in Louisville, Kentucky, on November 24, 1887, and educated at the University of Cincinnati. In 1923 he went to New York where he set up his own company as a producer and director. He later worked for MGM, Warner Bros. and Paramount. He retired from films in 1936. He died in Beverly Hills on May 22, 1964, aged 76.

Winner Take All! (1932)

Cast: James Cagney (Jim Kane), Marian Nixon (Mrs. Peggy Harmon), Guy Kibbee (Pop Slavin), Dickie Moore (Dickie Harmon), Virginia Bruce (Joan Gibson), Alan Mowbray (Forbes), Esther Howard (Ann), Clarence Muse (Rosebud), Clarence Wilson (Ben Isaacs), Ralf Harolde (Legs Davis), John Roche (Roger Elliott), Ernie Alexander (Elevator Operator), Sheila Bromley (Joan's Friend), Charles Coleman (Joan's Butler), Jay Eaton (Mr. Wingate), George "Gabby" Hayes (Intern), Selmer Jackson (Ring Announcer), John Kelly (Fight Spectator), Allan Lane (Monty), Chris-Pin Martin (Pice's Manager), Larry McGrath (First Referee), John T. Murray (Pettigrew), Harvey Parry (Al West), Bob Perry (Tijuana Referee), Lee Phelps (Ring Announcer), Julian Rivero (Joe Pice), Rolfe Sedan (Stork Club Waiter), Phil Tead (Reporter), Billy West (Joe's Second in Tijuana), Renee Whitney (Lois), Texas Guinan (Herself), Arthur Housman (Nightclub Patron), Charlotte Merriam (Blonde in Nightclub), George Raft (Nightclub Bandleader).

Credits: Producer and Director: Roy Del Ruth; Original Story: Gerald Beaumont; Screenplay: Robert Lord and Wilson Mizner; Photography: Robert Kurrie; Editor: Thomas Pratt; Musical Score: W. Franke Harling; Music Conductor: Leo F. Forbstein; Art Direction: Robert Haas; Costumes: Orry-Kelly; Makeup: Perc Westmore; Stunts: Harvey Parry. Released by Warner Bros. on July 16, 1932. 66 minutes.

Synopsis: Burnt-out boxer Jim Kane, who is temporarily a resident of a health spa ranch in New Mexico, meets widow Peggy Harmon again. She needs $600 more to continue her sickly son's treatment there. To assist her, Kane risks a beating in a "winner take all" match in Tijuana. Subsequently he returns to the ring while Peggy stays in New Mexico. In New York he falls for Park Avenue gold-digger Joan Gibson and finds himself split between two women. He undergoes plastic surgery to please Joan, but becomes a "powder puff" boxer to avoid spoiling his new looks. At a championship fight where Joan is absent, he beats the champ and then dashes to a ship at the docks on which the faithless Joan is about to elope. He gives her a kick in the backside and reconciles with Peggy.

Comments: Marian Nixon played Peggy, whose background was as a singer at Texas Guinan's club. Early on in the film, when Kane and Peggy first met, there was a flashback to the nightclub where for a few moments the camera flashed on a conductor vigorously conducting the band. This character was played by George Raft. This nightclub scene is stock footage lifted from *Queen of the Nightclubs* (1929).

Madame Racketeer
(aka *The Sporting Widow*) (1932)

Cast: Alison Skipworth (Martha Hicks aka Countess von Claudwig), Richard Bennett (Elmer Hicks), George Raft (Jack Houston), John Breeden (David Butterworth), Evalyn Knapp (Alice Hicks), Gertrude Messinger (Patsy Hicks), Robert McWade (James Butterworth), J. Farrell MacDonald (John Adams), Rita Carlyle (Inquisitive Convict), Oscar Apfel (J. Harrington Hagney), Jessie Arnold (Frankie), Irving Bacon (Gus, the Desk Clerk), George Barbier (Warden George Waddell), Ed Brady (Taxi Driver), Anna Chandler (Stella), Arthur Raymond Hill (Shanks), Robert Homans (Chief of Police), Arthur Hoyt (Shiffern), Frank Beal, William Humphrey, Alfred P. James, Edgar Lewis, Scott Seaton (Bank Directors), Kate Morgan (Maxine), Cora Shumway (Matron), Walter Walker (Arthur Gregory), Eleanor Wesselhoeft (Mrs. Dunkenspiel).

Credits: Directors: Alexander Hall and Harry Wagstaff Gribble; Producer: Harry Wagstaff Gribble; Screenplay: Malcolm Stuart Boylan and Harvey Gates; Photography: Henry Sharp; Music: John Leipold. Released by Paramount

on July 23, 1932. Black and white. 72 minutes.

Synopsis: International confidence trickster Martha Hicks is paroled after yet another stay in prison and decides to treat her rheumatism with a stay at her estranged husband Elmer's hotel at a Wisconsin spa. There, incognito, she checks on the two daughters she abandoned as infants. Alice, the older daughter, wishes to marry David Butterworth, an upstanding young man and a banker. He is the son of priggish bank president James Butterworth. The latter wants his son to marry money. The younger, more impressionable daughter Patsy has taken up with a hoodlum confidence trickster, Jack Houston. Martha uses her skills to try to put her family back on track. She recognizes Houston as a crook and they form an uneasy alliance.

Martha, masquerading as the Countess von Cloudwig, pretends to deposit non-existent securities in a satchel with banker Butterworth. He does not check the securities, but she forges his signature on a receipt. When she makes an application for a $10,000 loan, she makes it appear that Butterworth has stolen the securities. She demands restitution of the money or she will expose him to the press. To keep her quiet, he agrees to pay with $10,000 to be delivered to her shortly before his son's wedding to Alice takes place in the hotel.

At the hotel, Martha tells Houston a fictitious tale and persuades him to try to arrest John Adams, a genuine detective who has known her for years, but Adams arrests Houston instead. Houston tells Adams that the countess is planning a theft and Adams temporarily releases him. At the hotel, Butterworth gives the money to Martha. Alice and John Butterworth are married. With Elmer's help, Martha eludes Adams and escapes, boarding the train to Chicago with the money. On the train she is horrified to discover Houston and Patsy, who have eloped. Martha tries to warn Patsy that Houston is a crook. When Patsy refuses to listen, Martha and Houston fight and he pushes her out of the railway carriage into the corridor. Adams and Elmer are pursuing the train in a car. When Martha pulls the communication cord, Adams comes on board and arrests her for a parole violation. Martha admits the theft of the money, but tells Adams that Houston was her accomplice. Adams finds some of the money on Houston (she slipped it into his pocket during the fight). Disillusioned with Houston, the naive Patsy accompanies her father Elmer back to the hotel. The final scene shows Martha back in jail regaling the other inmates with stories of the spa hotel. While she is doing so, a gift from Elmer of a music box is delivered to her.

Comments: This was the first of five films in which Alexander Hall directed George Raft. In this one, Hall shared a directing credit with Harry Wagstaff Gribble. Although Raft had prominent billing, Skipworth, who was a bargain basement Marie Dressler, was the undisputed star. Raft first appeared in about the fortieth minute and had a few good scenes. He was seen setting up a scam with Skipworth and later arguing with her on the train. He tried to arrest J. Farrell MacDonald, but was arrested himself. He was also seen swimming, dancing and romancing Gertrude Messinger. In his last scene he was sitting with MacDonald and Skipworth most unhappily after his schemes have gone awry.

The title of the film *Madame Racketeer* was a misnomer because it suggested a hard-edged gangster movie with a tough female lead and plenty of violence. Although crime was a theme throughout the film, it was played as more of a comedy. There was at least one slapstick scene where Skipworth fell into a mudbath. The film had a rapidly paced and well-photographed chase climax. The film was however grounded in truth since there have been people who in reality have fallen for the kind of scams depicted in this movie.

Biography: Alexander Hall was born in Boston, Massachusetts, on January 11, 1894. He was educated at Columbia University and served in the U.S. Navy in World War I. After the war he stayed in France gaining experience both in front of and behind the camera. In 1921 he returned to America. During the twenties he worked his way up from editor to assistant director. In 1932 he signed with Paramount and made his directorial debut. He stayed at Paramount until 1938 when he moved over to Columbia where he did his best work, notably *Here Comes Mr. Jordan* (1941) for which he was nominated for a Best Director Oscar. He retired in 1956. He was married to Lola Lane and Marjorie Hunter. He died in a San Francisco hospital after a stroke on July 30, 1968, aged 74, survived by a son.

Biography: Harry Wagstaff Gribble was born in Sevenoaks, Kent, England, on March 27, 1896. Between 1910 and 1912 he was educated at Emmanuel College, Cambridge. From 1914 to 1918 he served as a private in the London Regiment and in the 27th Division of the New York National Guard. He started as a stage actor in 1915. His career as a playwright and producer lasted until 1947. He only produced and co-directed this one motion picture, however. Throughout the greater part of his life he resided in New York. He died in New York City on January 28, 1981, aged 84.

Night After Night (1932)

Cast: George Raft (Joe Anton), Constance Cummings (Miss Jerry Healy), Wynne Gibson (Iris Dawn), Mae West (Maudie Triplett), Alison Skipworth (Miss Mabel Jellyman), Roscoe Karns (Leo), Louis Calhern (Dick Bolton), Bradley Page (Frankie Guard), Al Hill (Blainey), Harry Wallace (Jerky), George "Dink" Templeton (Patsy), Marty Martyn (Malloy), Tom Kennedy (Tom, the Bartender), Bill Elliott (Escort), Patricia Farley (Hatcheck Girl), Theresa Harris (Ladies Room Attendant), Dennis O'Keefe (Drunk on Table), Leo White (Kitchen Staff Member), Paul Porcasi (Chef).

Credits: Director: Archie Mayo; Producer: William Le Baron; Based on the Story "Single

Mae West and Raft in *Night After Night*.

Night" by Louis Bromfield; Screenplay: Vincent Lawrence; Continuity: Kathryn Scola; Photography: Ernest Haller; Original Music: Ralph Rainger and Bernhard Kaun; Costumes: Walter Plunkett. Released by Paramount on October 30, 1932. Black and white. 73 minutes.

Synopsis: Ex-boxer and prohibition tough guy Joe Anton runs a New York City speakeasy and gambling casino called Number 55. Joe is considering selling the speakeasy and discusses it with his minder, Leo. He is also tired of his girlfriend Iris Dawn, whom he considers common. His ambition is to become a society gentleman. To reduce the competition with his own nightclub, gangster Frankie Guard goes to see Joe and offers him $50,000, but Joe refuses to sell for less than $250,000.

Because Joe has become interested in a mysterious but glamourous woman who patronizes his place unescorted night after night, he hires Mrs. Mabel Jellyman, a middle-aged schoolteacher, to teach him the proper method of speaking and etiquette. Eventually Joe becomes acquainted with the woman, Jerry Healy of Park Avenue, who patronizes the club mainly because the speakeasy happens to be the man-

sion she had lived in years ago until the Depression ruined her family and they lost their home.

When Joe starts paying attention to Jerry, Iris becomes jealous and vows not to lose Joe. An ex-girlfriend of Joe's, Maudie Triplett, arrives at the club and interrupts a private dinner which Joe is having with Jerry and Mrs. Jellyman. Maudie and Mrs. Jellyman start boozing together while Joe and Jerry go on a tour of inspection around the club. Frankie Guard returns and Joe, who is desperate to become a legitimate businessman and falling in love with Jerry, accepts his revised offer of $200,000. When Iris threatens Jerry, Joe orders Leo to throw her out of the club. She begs Leo to let her remain and promises to make no further trouble. In a weak moment Leo relents. Instead she confronts Joe and Jerry during their club inspection and pulls a gun. Joe manages to distract and disarm her. This incident seems to be an aphrodisiac to Jerry, who calls Joe "Pirate" and kisses him passionately. Joe spends a sleepless night rationalizing that Jerry must be in love with him.

When Joe goes to Jerry's apartment, he tells her that he wants her to marry him. She demurs, telling him that her kiss only meant that she was carried away with the thrill of the previous evening. She tells him she is intending to go abroad with fiancé Dick Bolton whom she admits she is marrying for his money. Joe returns to the club where he tells Frankie Guard that he is no longer going to sell his club, much to Leo's approval even though Frankie threatens violence. Joe also cancels his lessons with Mrs. Jellyman. Jerry angrily goes to the club where initially she repels Joe and destroys his murals and his paintings. Frankie and his mob arrive at the club and begin wrecking the place. Joe and Leo initially grab their guns for battle, but when Jerry begs him not to fight Frankie and declares her undying love for him, Joe says about Frankie, "Tell 'em to stop. They're only wrecking their own joint."

Comments: This is the first of two films in which Raft was directed by Archie Mayo. The film began with the credits superimposed in front of a mansion with the underscoring of "There's No Place Like Home." With the credits still rolling, a brief history of the mansion was told: It was first seen with a "For Sale" board, followed by a board reading "Home for Rent" and finally a sign reading "Sold at Public Auction" before the list of credits. It faded out with the street number of the house, 55. The working title of the film was *Number 55*. A final shot behind the closing credits showed "Frankie Guard's Playground."

This was the first time that Raft was the top-billed star of a film. It was an entertaining amalgam of genres, namely gangster thriller, comedy and musical. A number of popular tunes of the day, many introduced in recent Paramount pictures, were heard as instrumentals and background music, especially during the night club sequences when the orchestra plays.

It was also risqué and sizzling with sex. Raft took a bath in an early scene and it is quite obvious he was naked which was designed to please his army of female fans. Much of the best dialogue was spoken by Mae West. She was on the telephone and mentioned a couple of times, but only appeared after forty minutes. When a hatcheck girl exclaimed about West's diamonds, "Goodness, what beautiful diamonds!" West's reply was, "Goodness had nothing to do with it, dearie!" Raft had casting approval so he agreed to West, but she took over the movie when she sashayed in. As Raft ruefully recalled, "In that picture she stole everything but the cameras." Raft appeared with West again in the dire *Sextette* (1978), his penultimate movie, and died three days after

she did. One major demerit of *Night After Night* was that it ended abruptly as if the budget had been exceeded before the final projected shootout and it was decided to omit it.

Biography: Archie Mayo was born in New York City on January 29, 1891, the son of a tailor. He was educated at New York public schools and Columbia University. He spent his early career in musical shows touring Australia, Europe and America. Film experience began in 1916 when he secured work as an extra. Then he became a gag man in 1917 and directed comedy shorts. His first feature film was *Money Talks* (1926). He directed numerous films, mainly at Warner Bros. and Fox. The loss of his wife Lucille Wolf in 1945, together with his surly attitude towards actors and other studio personnel, cost him his career as a director. He briefly surfaced a decade later as a producer. He died in Guadaljaka, Mexico, on December 4, 1968, aged 77, of cancer.

Biography: Constance Cummings was born Constance Halverstadt in Seattle, Washington, on May 15, 1910. Her parents were Dallas Vernon Halverstadt and Kate Logan Cummings. Her parents separated when she was seven and her mother took her to California. Her ambition was to be a dancer and when she finished high school at 16, her mother took her to New York where she studied dancing. She was understudying a part in a play when she was seen by a reporter who wrote a flattering piece about her in a newspaper which was read by a Hollywood talent scout. She was sent to Hollywood for a screen test and was cast in a film starring Ronald Colman. Two days into shooting, she was fired. Colman arranged for her to be cast in another film, *The Criminal Code* (1931), which marked her screen debut. On the strength of this she was signed to a seven-year contract with Columbia. She was busy both at her home studio and on loan-outs such as *Night After Night*. She married the English writer and subsequent M.P. Benn Levy in 1933. She went on to enjoy a 70-year career primarily in the West End, Broadway and films. She was awarded C.B.E. in 1974 and won a Tony award on Broadway as Best Actress in 1979. She was widowed in 1973. She died in Oxfordshire, England, on November 23, 2005, aged 95. She was survived by two children and six grandchildren.

Biography: Wynne Gibson was born Winifred Gibson in New York City on July 3, 1898, the daughter of Frank W. Gibson and Elaine Coffin. She was educated at Wadleigh School for Girls in New York. She was a chorus girl and appeared in vaudeville as part of *The Melody Charmers*. Her major Broadway appearance was in *Jarnegan* (1928) where she was seen by an agent who thought she should be in films. She made her screen debut in *Nothing but the Truth* (1929) and continued in films until 1943, frequently in hard-bitten roles. She also appeared in the portmanteau film *If I Had a Million* in which Raft featured in a different episode. Later she appeared in recurring roles in radio and television soap operas and did summer stock on the East Coast. During 1955 and 1956 she was chairperson of the Equity Library Theater which gave free shows to the public. She shared a large house for many years with another retired actress, Beverly Roberts. She briefly married and divorced twice. She died in Laguna Niguel, California, on May 15, 1987, aged 88, after a stroke.

Biography: Mae West was born Mary Jane West in Brooklyn, New York, on August 17, 1893, the daughter of "Battlin'" Jack West, an Irish former boxer turned livery stable owner and his German-Jewish wife Hilda Doelger. Mae began her career in 1897 with Hal Clarendon's stock company in New York and on the road, playing child parts in many plays. Mae made her Broadway debut in *A La Broadway* (1911) and until 1926 appeared in revues and vaudeville. Then her mother encouraged her to write her own material so she wrote plays with racy themes and titles and a legend was born. George Raft suggested her for the role in *Night After Night* which marked her screen debut. She signed a contract with Paramount

and between 1932 and 1938 starred in eleven films for them. She was one of the Top Ten Box Office stars in 1933 and 1934. She quit the screen in 1943 but much later starred in *Myra Breckinridge* (1970) and *Sextette*. Her autobiography *Goodness Had Nothing to Do with It* was published in 1959. She died in Los Angeles on November 22, 1980, aged 87, of a cerebral thrombosis. Her only marriage was to singer Frank Wallace, whom she wed in 1911. They were estranged for many years before their divorce in 1942.

Biography: Alison Skipworth was born in London on July 25, 1863, the daughter of Dr. Richard Ebenezer Groom and Elizabeth Rodgers. She was educated privately and was originally a model. *A Gaiety Girl* (1894) marked her first stage appearance in England. She went to America and made her first Broadway appearance in *An Artists Model* (1895). Between 1925 and 1930 she claimed to have appeared in twenty-one consecutive stage failures so she was glad to accept an offer of a Paramount film contract. Her final film was *Wide Open Faces* (1938). Her last Broadway appearance was *Lady of the Valley* (1942). She was married and divorced from artist Frank Markham Skipworth. She died in New York on July 5, 1952, aged 86. She appeared with Raft in *Madame Racketeer, Night After Night* and *Midnight Club*. Both Raft and Skipworth appeared in different episodes of *If I Had a Million*.

If I Had a Million (1932)

Cast: Gary Cooper (Steve Gallagher), Charles Laughton (Phineas V. Lambert), George Raft (Eddie Jackson), Jack Oakie (Private Mulligan), Richard Bennett (John Glidden), Charlie Ruggles (Henry Peabody), Alison Skipworth (Emily La Rue), W.C. Fields (Rollo La Rue), Mary Boland (Mrs. Peabody), Roscoe Karns (Private O'Brien), May Robson (Mrs. Mary Walker), Wynne Gibson (Violet Smith), Gene Raymond (John Wallace), Frances Dee (Mary Wallace), Hooper Atchley (Hotel Desk

Clerk), Irving Bacon (China Shop Salesman), Eddie Baker (Second Desk Clerk), Reginald Barlow (Otto K. Bullwinkle), Vangie Beilby, Clara T. Bracy, Effie Ellsier, Louise Emmons, Lydia Knott, Ruby Lafayette, Ida Lewis, Margaret Mann, Gertrude Norman, Emma Tansey, Joy Winthrop (Idylwood Residents), Harry C. Bradley (Uniformed Bank Guard), Bob Burns (Marine Sergeant), James P. Burtis (Marine Jailer), James Bush (Bowen — Teller at Second Bank), Arthur S. Byron (Murphy's Beds Proprietor), Berton Churchill (Warden); Wallis Clark (Mr. Monroe — Bank Executive), Joyce Compton (Marie — Waitress), Cecil Cunningham (Agnes — Emily's Friend), Lester Dorr (Pedestrian at Accident), Bess Flowers (China Store Customer), Blanche Friderici (Mrs. Garvey), Frank Hagney (Carnival Bouncer), Lilian Harmer (Idylwood Receptionist), Samuel S. Hinds (Lawyer), Fred Holmes (China Shop Clerk), Robert Homans (Detective), Lew Kelly (Prison Barber), Fred Kelsey (Prison Jailer), Tom Kennedy (Joe — Carnival Bouncer), Marc Lawrence (Henchman of Mike, the Gangster), Edward LeSaint (Mr. Brown), Lucien Littlefield (Zeb — Hamburger Stand Driver), Charles McMurphy (Mike — Bank Plainclothesman), Grant Mitchell (Prison Priest), William V. Mong (Harry — Jackson's Fence), Clarence Muse (Singing Prisoner), Gail Patrick (Secretary at Idylwood), Jack Pennick (Sailor with Violet), Walter Percival (Carnival Concessionaire), Russ Powell (Bartender at Violet's Hangout), Tom Ricketts (Dancing Partner at Idylwood), Dewey Robinson (Papadopoulos — Idylwood Cook), Fred Santley (Marvin — Glidden Assistant), Syd Saylor (Driver), Margaret Seddon (Mrs. Small), Edwin Stanley (Mr. Galloway — Bank Manager), Herbert Moulten, Willard Robertson, Larry Steers, John St. Polis (Glidden Associates), Kent Taylor (Bank Teller), Jerry Tucker (Crying Boy with Balloon), Morgan Wallace (Mike — Jackson's Gangster Associate), Edith Yorke (Idylwood Resident with Parkinson's Disease).

Credits: Directors: James Cruze ("Death Cell"), H. Bruce Humberstone ("The Forger"), Ernst Lubitsch ("The Clerk"), Norman Z. McLeod ("China Shop" and "Road Hogs"), Stephen Roberts ("Violet" and "Grandma"), William A. Seiter ("The Three Marines"), Norman Taurog ("Prologue" and "Epilogue"), Lother Mendes; Executive Producer: Emanuel Cohen; Associate Producers: Benjamin Glazer and Louis D. Lighton; Production Supervisor: Ernst Lubitsch; Photography: Harry Fischbeck ("The Clerk"), Charles Edgar Schoenbaum ("Death Cell" and "The Three Marines"), Gilbert Warrenton ("China Shop"), Alvin Wyckoff ("Road Hogs"); Assistant Directors: Arthur Jacobson ("Death Cell"), Paul Jones ("Violet," "Grandma" and "The Three Marines"), William J. Scully ("China Shop"); Writers: Robert D. Andrews ("Windfall" story), Claude Binyon ("The Three Marines" adaptation), Whitney Bolton ("Grandma" story), Malcolm Stuart Boylan ("The Three Marines" adaptation), John Bright, Sidney Buchman, Lester Cole, Isabel Dawn, Boyce De Gaw, Oliver H.P. Garrett ("The Forger" story), Harvey Gates ("The Three Marines" story), Grover Jones ("Grandma" and "Prologue" adaptation), Ernst Lubitsch ("The Clerk" story and adaptation), Lawton MacKall, Joseph L. Mankiewicz ("Violet," "China Shop" and "The Three Marines" adaptation), William Slavens McNutt ("Grandma" and "Prologue"), Robert Sparks ("China Shop" and "Prologue"); Original Music: John Leipold, Stock Music: Bernhard Kaun; Sound Recorders: Frank Grenzback, Philip Wisdom; Released by Paramount on December 2, 1932. Black and white. 88 minutes.

Synopsis: Tycoon John Glidden, dying though still vigorous, is so dissatisfied with his relatives and associates that rather than will his money to any of them, he decides to give it away in $1,000,000 amounts to strangers picked at random from the telephone book. He ends up with a meek china salesman, a prostitute, a forger, two ex-vaudevillians who hate road hogs, a condemned man, a mild-mannered clerk, a boisterous Marine and an oppressed inmate of an old ladies home. Raft played the forger, whose identity becomes so well known to the police and banks that he cannot cash the check which he has been given. Eventually cold and hungry, he goes to a flophouse where he exchanges the check for a night's lodging. Once he is there, the owner rings the police and calmly lights his cigar with the check.

Comments: While the segments involving Charles Laughton and W.C. Fields have been established as milestones of mirth in Hollywood history, unfortunately the Raft segment was not in the same class as drama and was a bridge between some of the more lively sketches. This film served as the basis of the fifties television series *The Millionaire*.

Biography: H. Bruce Humberstone was born in Buffalo, New York, on November 18, 1901, and educated at Miami, Florida, Military Academy. His nickname was "Lucky." He entered films in his teens as a script clerk and then became an assistant director. He was a director from 1932 onwards, mainly at 20th Century–Fox. He was later a prolific television director. He died in Woodland Hills, California, on October 11, 1984, aged 82, from pneumonia.

Under-Cover Man (1932)

Cast: George Raft (Nick Darrow), Nancy Carroll (Lora Madigan), Roscoe Karns (Dannie), Lew Cody (Kenneth Mason), Gregory Ratoff (H.L. "Marty" Martoff), Noel Francis (Connie), David Landau (Inspector Conklin), Paul Porcasi (Sam Dorse), William Janney (Jimmy Madigan), Leyland Hodgson (Gillespie), George Davis (Bernie, the Chauffeur), Robert Homans (Fake Officer Flannigan), Jack Kennedy (Paddy Kilbane), Frances Moffett (Secretary at Shooting Scene), Kent Taylor (Russ), Wilhelm Von Brincken (Maitre d' at Padlock Club).

Credits: Director: James Flood; Story: John Wilstach; Screenplay: Garrett Fort and Francis Edwards Faragoh; Adaptation: Thomson Burtis; Photography: Victor Milner; Original Music: Herman Hand and John Leipold; Stock Music: Karl Hajos. Released by Paramount on December 3, 1932. Black and white. 74 minutes.

Synopsis: A series of bond robberies have been taking place in New York. The gang responsible is headed by outwardly respectable Kenneth Mason and Marty Martoff. The latter runs an estate management investment firm. When Sam Dorse refuses to accept bonds from a recent robbery, he is shot dead by Martoff. Dorse's son Nick Darrow turns up at Inspector Conklin's office and says that he wants to join the department as an undercover operator. When her brother, Jimmy, a runner, is stabbed to death by Mason to obtain the bonds he is carrying, Lora Madigan goes to see Conklin. She is glimpsed by Darrow. When Ollie Snell, a racketeer with an introduction to Martoff, is arrested, Darrow assumes his identity to infiltrate the gang. Darrow goes to see Martoff and pretends to be in the business of handling stolen bonds.

Martoff agrees to do business with him and suggests that Darrow go to the Padlock Club. Darrow and Lora join forces to track down the killers of her brother and his father. Darrow tells her to change her address and her name so she becomes Lora Clark. Together they go to the Padlock Club where they quickly become acquainted with Mason and his moll, Connie. With some revellers, Nick and Lora accompany Mason and Connie back to his apartment. While Mason makes a lunch date for the following day with Lora, he instructs Connie to cozy up to Darrow and find all she can about him. Lora finds the murder weapon, a knife in a fountain pen, hidden in Mason's desk. Mason goes to Connie's apartment where he overhears Connie warning Darrow to beware of Mason. After Darrow leaves, Mason roughs her up and finds Darrow's handkerchief with his real initials on it.

At lunch, Mason pumps Lora for information about Ollie Snell. He invites her to accompany him to California. Darrow goes to see Martoff in his apartment where Martoff pulls a gun and tells him about the discovery of the handkerchief. Mason and Dannie, a hitman, enter. They test Darrow with an ingenious ploy, but he outsmarts them. When a former associate of Snell's, Paddy Kilbane, turns up at the apartment, he is shot dead before he can reveal that Snell is an imposter.

Mason tells Darrow to stay with Martoff. The next robbery is $500,000 worth of bearer bonds from an investment company. Once the bonds are stolen, Mason tells them that he will be with Lora at the Sundown apartments. Fake guards murder the real guards and steal the bearer bonds. In the getaway car, Martoff admits to Darrow that he killed Sam Dorse. Darrow kills him. Darrow switches the bonds to a car driven by Dannie. Lora makes a slip and reveals both her own and Darrow's real identities to Mason. When Mason tells Dannie to kill Darrow, Nick attacks them both. When Mason tries to kill Darrow with the knife, Lora screams a warning. Dannie holds them all at gunpoint until Inspector Conklin and his squad arrive. Dannie is revealed to be an undercover operative and the one who killed Paddy Kilbane. Mason is taken to jail and Nick and Lora are free to pursue their romance.

Comments: This was the first and by far the better of the two films in which Raft was directed by James Flood, one of the least esteemed of the directors Raft worked for. The ingredients (a solid cast, intriguing plot and good dialogue) were well mixed. There was a considerable feeling of tension throughout the film and the final fight sequence was excitingly done, but Darrow's dis-

posing of Martoff took place off screen which was disappointing for the viewer. Nevertheless this was still one of Raft's better early movies because he was always at his most convincing in the crime genre. He was in cracking form as Nick Darrow, alias Ollie Snell, who outsmarted the criminals while showing his more vulnerable side to Carroll, who also did well in this crime film. Noel Francis was appropriately hard-bitten as a drunken moll in league with the criminals while trying to entice Nick. The other disappointing aspect of this film was that after some intriguing scenes, her character disappeared without explanation. Lew Cody and Gregory Ratoff made a pair of particularly nefarious villains.

Biography: James Flood was born in New York City on July 31, 1895. He entered films in 1912 as an assistant director at Biograph and in the early twenties began directing at Fox and Warner Bros. His wife Lucial was the sister of director William Beaudine. Flood died in Hollywood on February 4, 1953, aged 57, of complications after surgery.

Biography: Nancy Carroll was born Ann Veronica Lahiff in New York on November 19, 1903. Her parents were Thomas and Ann

Nancy Carroll and Raft in *Under-Cover Man.*

Lahiff, who were Irish. She was educated at Holy Trinity School in New York. She left school at the age of sixteen, worked in an office and took part in amateur entertainment nights at a local theater. Her stage surname Carroll was derived from the surname of the M.C. there. She made her Broadway debut in the chorus of *The Passing Show of 1923*. While dancing in *The Passing Show of 1924* she met and married her first husband, Jack Kirkland, with whom she had a daughter Patricia, born in 1925. They divorced in 1931. His career as a playwright took them to Hollywood. She made her screen debut in *Ladies Must Dress* (1927) and became a star in *Abie's Irish Rose* (1928). She was nominated for a Best Actress Oscar in *The Devil's Holiday* (1930), but temperament destroyed her career and she made her last film in 1938. She married twice more. She was appearing in the play *Never Too Late* in Nyack when she was found dead in her New York apartment on August 6, 1965, aged 61.

Biography: Noel Francis was born Noel Frances Sweeney in Temple, Texas, on August 31, 1906. She grew up in Dallas and attended Southern Methodist University and Columbia University in New York. She started her career as a dancer in the Ziegfeld Follies. Her biggest stage hit was with Wheeler and Woolsey in *Rio Rita*. After making her screen debut in *Fox Movietone Follies* (1930), she was under contract to Warner Bros., which produced some of her most characteristic roles as prostitutes and molls. In 1937 her screen career ended in B Westerns starring Buck Jones. In the forties she moved to San Francisco where she worked as a radio producer. She started a talent agency with a business partner using her Hollywood connections to find work for their clients. Within a couple of years, the business went bust. Little more was heard of her until she died prematurely in Los Angeles on October 30, 1959, aged 53.

Biography: Lew Cody was born Louis Joseph Coté in Berlin, New Hampshire, on February 22, 1884. The son of French parents,

he was educated at McGill University in Canada and intended to pursue a medical career. Becoming bored, he opted instead to become an actor. He played in vaudeville and stock and at one time owned five stock companies. He made his screen debut in *The Mating* (1915). He went on to become a highly successful screen actor, sophisticated comedy being his real forté. Off-screen he was one of the legendary wits of Hollywood and one of the most in-demand and highly paid after-dinner speakers. He made a smooth transition to talkies. The second and third of his three wives were actresses Dorothy Dalton and Mabel Normand. He died in Beverly Hills on May 3, 1934, aged 50, of a heart attack in his sleep. He is buried at St. Peters Catholic Cemetery in Lewiston, Maine.

Pick-Up (1933)

Cast: Sylvia Sidney (Mary Richards), George Raft (Harry Glynn), Lilian Bond (Muriel Stevens), William Harrigan (Jim Richards), Clarence Wilson (Sam Foster), Brooks Benedict (Tony), Robert McWade (Jerome Turner), Purnell Pratt (Prosecuting Attorney), Charles Middleton (Mr. Brewster), Oscar Apfel (The Warden), George Meeker (Artie Logan), Louise Beavers (Magnolia), Florence Dudley (Freda), Patricia Farley (Sadie), Eddie Clayton (Don), Dorothy Layton (Peggy), Alice Adair (Sally), Eleanor Lawson (Matron), Al Hill (Johnson, the Reporter), Lona Andre, Gail Patrick (Party Girls).

Credits: Director: Marion Gering; Producer: B.P. Schulberg; Story: Vina Delmar; Screenplay: S.K. Lauren and Agnes Brand Leahy; Adaptation: Sidney Lazarus; Photography: David Abel; Original Music: Ralph Rainger, Rudolph G. Kopp and John Leipold; Stock Music: W. Franke Harling and George Steiner. Released by Paramount on March 24, 1933. Black and white. 76 minutes.

Synopsis: Mary Richards has just been released from prison where she has served a two-year stretch for playing a confidence trick with her husband that resulted in a victim killing himself. Her husband Jim, who still has three years to serve, demands to see her. When she visits him, he tells her to search out his friend Tony, but Mary tells him that she is finished with a life of crime and never wants to see him or his associates again. Back in the city and virtually destitute, during a rainstorm she climbs into a Diamond Taxicab driven by Harry Glynn. Initially annoyed by her, Glynn relents and takes her back to his own apartment. He gets Mary a job working on the switchboard at Diamond Taxis. There she works under the false name Molly Fuller. Foster, the boss, lusts after her, but she rebuffs him. She lives with Harry and they gradually fall in love. She blames him for his lack of ambition, in particular for not buying an interest in a garage. When Foster fires both of them, Harry buys an interest in the garage.

Harry proposes to Mary, but she is forced to decline because she is still wed to Jim. Jim's gangster pal Tony traces Mary to Norwood Park where Harry has his garage. When rich bitch Muriel Stevens and her acquaintances are stranded in the river in a car, Harry rescues her and takes her to her home. She invites both Harry and Mary to a party where all the guests are dressed as young children. Muriel tries to seduce Harry which infuriates Mary. Mary leaves the party early followed by Harry. At home they quarrel.

Mary goes to visit Muriel and tells her that she and Harry are not married. Muriel says she fancies Harry and will do anything to win him. Dejected, Mary goes to see a judge who tells her that since her husband has been in prison for three years, she can obtain a divorce within two weeks. Muriel turns up at the garage and invites Harry to a weekend of passion at her vacation cabin in the woods. She deliberately leaves a map behind so that Harry can follow her. When Mary returns home, she is elated because a decree has annulled her marriage. When Harry goes back to the apartment, he informs Mary that he is yearning for Muriel. Harry goes to the cabin where he asks Muriel to marry him, but Muriel ridicules him.

Raft and Lilian Bond in *Pick-Up*.

Jim arrives at Harry's apartment and tells Mary that he has been paroled. He informs Mary that he intends to kill Harry when he returns. Mary agrees to go away with him to an apartment Tony has found for them. When they arrive at the apartment, Jim rummages through her bag for car keys. He finds the decree annulling their marriage. He accuses her of double crossing him and tells her that he was not paroled but broke out of prison, killing a guard in the process. Mary manages to lock Jim in the apartment and then calls the police. When they arrive, they arrest both Jim and Mary.

The story makes front page news and is seen by Harry. Harry goes to see leading criminal attorney Jerome Turner and begs him to take Mary's case. In the courtroom the prosecuting attorney tries to establish that Jim had no intention of killing Harry and that Mary aided and abetted Jim escaping jail because she loves him. In a finale worthy of Perry Mason, Turner gives Jim his gun to identify. Instead Jim goes berserk and tries to shoot Harry in the courtroom, but the gun is loaded with blanks and Jim is overpowered. Mary is released. Outside she is picked up by Harry and taken to his apartment. He suggests that they should stop off en route to pick up a marriage licence.

Comments: This was the first and better of the two films which Raft made for director Marion Gering. His direction, particularly the adult party where all the guests were dressed as children, was quite imaginative. This well-plotted film was the first and best of three that Raft made with co-star Sylvia Sidney. Raft played a character who was less cynical and streetwise, but more gullible than usual. Raft's character was also depicted as lacking in ambition. The way Sidney made him keener to progress was well depicted.

It was no secret in the film that Harry and Mary were living together and there was no condemnation of this from a moral standpoint which made it quite contemporary in attitude. The film was also unusual in that the burden of the climax was entirely carried by character actors, mainly William Harrigan, Purnell Pratt and Robert McWade, who made the most of the opportunity. Neither Sidney nor Raft featured prominently in the courtroom climax. Lilian Bond was also excellent playing an upper bracket femme fatale. This film was a box office hit.

Biography: Marion Gering was born in Rostov-on-Don, Russia, on June 9, 1901. Educated at the Gates Theatrical College in Moscow, he came to America in 1924 as part of a trade commission for Siberian furs. Finding that New York producers regarded his slight knowledge of English a handicap, he bought the rights to a play, founded the Chicago Play Producing Company and produced it himself. Between 1927 and 1930 he produced and directed plays in New York. Between 1930 and 1936 he was a film director at Paramount and between 1937 and 1939 he was a film director at Columbia. Later attempts to revive his moribund career in countries such as Cuba between 1947 and 1949 met with little success. There are unconfirmed reports that he later worked as a technical assistant and caretaker in further education colleges. He married actress Dorothy Libaire in 1930. He died in New York City on April 19, 1977, aged 76.

Biography: Sylvia Sidney was born Sophia Kosow on August 8, 1910, in the Bronx, New York, the only child of Russian-Jewish immigrants Victor Kosow and Rebecca Saperstein. She was adopted by her mother's second husband, dentist Dr. Sigmund Sidney. She was educated at Washington Irving High School. In 1925 she joined the Theatre Guild School and made her Broadway debut in *The Squall* (1927). She made her screen debut in *Thru Different Eyes* (1929). She secured a Paramount contract on the strength of her Broadway success in *Bad Girl* (1930). She was discovered by female agent Ad Schulberg who recommended Sidney to her husband, head honcho B.P. Schulberg, who became her lover. She became a star in *City Streets* (1931) and went on to become one of Paramount's most popular stars of the thirties, most notably in highly dramatic roles in which she suffered greatly. She returned to the theater in 1937. Her stature as an actress gradually declined and her physical appearance changed, although she continued to appear sporadically in films into the 1990s. She wrote a book on needlepoint and lived for many years in Connecticut where she bred prize dogs. In 1974 she received an Academy Award nomination as Best Supporting Actress for *Summer Wishes, Winter Dreams.* She was married (and divorced) three times: to publisher Bennett Cerf from 1935 to 1936, to actor Luther Adler from 1938 to 1946 and to agent Carlton Alsop from 1947 to 1951. With Adler she had a son named Jacob (1939–1987). She died in New York on July 1, 1999, aged 88, of throat cancer. She appeared with George Raft in three films: *Pick-Up, You and Me* and *Mr. Ace.*

Biography: Lilian Bond was born in London, England, on January 18, 1908, the daughter of a tea shop owner. A graduate of Brompton Oratory School, she made her first appearance on the stage in pantomime in *Dick Whittington* (1924). While rehearsing another show, *Sunny* (1926), she married for the first time to Harry Schulman, dropped out of show business for a year and then divorced. She emigrated to the United States where she made her screen debut in 1927. Her best remembered film roles were in *The Old Dark House* (1932) and as Lily Langtry, the object of Judge Roy Bean's (Walter Brennan) lust, in *The Westerner* (1940). Her second marriage (1935 to 1944) was to Sydney Smith, a wealthy New York broker and big game hunter. After their 1944 divorce, she had a minor role in another Raft film, *Nocturne,* but her scenes were deleted prior to the film's release. She married for the third time to writer Michael Fessier in 1950 and was widowed in 1988. She died in Reseda, California, on January 25, 1991, aged 83, of cardiac arrest after a bout with cancer. She was survived by a stepson and stepdaughter. She is buried with Fessier at Hollywood Forever Cemetery.

Midnight Club (1933)

Cast: Clive Brook (Sir Colin Grant), George Raft (Nick Mason), Helen Vinson (Iris Whitney), Alison Skipworth (Lady Edna Barrett-Smythe), Sir Guy Standing (Assistant Commissioner Arthur Hope), Alan Mowbray (Arthur Bradley), Ferdinand Gottschalk (George Rubens), Forrester Harvey (Thomas Roberts), Ethel Griffies (The Duchess), Billy Bevan (First Detective), Charles McNaughton (Second Detective), Rita Carlyle (Mason's Landlady), Charles Coleman (Carstairs), Jean De Briac (Headwaiter), Teru Shimada (Nishi), Leo White (Waiter).

Credits: Directors: Alexander Hall and George Somnes; Producer: Bayard Veiller; Assistant Director: Eric Locke; Original Story: E. Phillips Oppenheim; Screenplay: Seton I. Miller and Leslie Charteris; Photography: Theodor Sparkuhl; Editor: Eda Warren; Music: W. Franke Harling and Howard Jackson; Sound Recorders: Gene Merritt and Philip Wisdom; Special Effects: Gordon Jennings. Released by Paramount on July 29, 1933. Black and white. 64 minutes.

Synopsis: Assistant Commissioner Hope sends detectives to London's Midnight Club to keep a gang headed by Sir Colin Grant under surveillance. Hope believes the gang is behind a series of audacious, high-class jewel robberies. After a robbery committed by the gang at Roberts' jewellers, the proprietor Mr. Roberts accompanies Hope to the club where he identifies the gang, but they have been under surveillance all night by Hope's detectives. Unbeknownst to Hope, whenever they commit their crimes, they leave a group of lookalikes behind in the club to pretend they were there while the robberies are being committed.

Gang member Iris Whitney drives the getaway car. Grant professes his love for her and suggests that she temporarily flee to Paris, but she refuses. By a trick, Nick Mason, an alleged jewel thief, obtains the stolen Roberts jewels from her. Grant invites Mason to join the four thieves at their table at the club. Grant tells Mason to return the stolen Roberts jewels to him, but Mason brushes him off and tells him to call the police. Much to the amusement of the gang, Mason is arrested and taken to see Hope. There it is revealed that Mason is an undercover detective temporarily on assignment to Scotland Yard. Mason shows Hope the jewels he obtained from Iris. At the club, Grant meets Lady Barrett-Smythe who invites him to a soirée at her house the following evening. At the party, Mason steals the diamonds of Lady Barrett-Smythe, puts them in a box inside the house and addresses it to himself. Grant spots it as he is leaving and purloins the diamonds, leaving the box behind.

When Grant returns to the club, he agrees to let Mason join the gang with the intention of doublecrossing him. The gang members go to Mason's apartment. While they are there, the box arrives, and Mason finds it is full of rocks, much to his annoyance. Grant tells him that a duchess is holding a ball and that he wants Mason to steal her famous emerald. Mason escorts Iris to the ball where he charms her while dancing with her and she takes the opportunity to tell him about the lookalikes. Mason's ingenuity in stealing the emeralds impresses Grant, who shows him the laboratory where jewels are separated from their fittings and inserted into vases for shipment to America. At the club, while Mason is dancing with Iris, Grant spots Mason's badge and handcuffs and deduces that Mason is a detective. The gang members inveigle Mason into a quiet room where they overpower him, handcuff him and make a getaway.

The police raid the club. Iris returns, handcuffs herself to Nick and is arrested. Hope promises Iris her freedom if she reveals the location of Grant's hideout, but she refuses. Grant rings Hope and then goes to Mason's apartment. Mason tells Grant that Iris is in jail because of him and that he is turning him in. Before he can do so, Hope arrives with Iris and

tells Mason that Grant has surrendered himself in return for Iris's freedom. While Hope accompanies Grant to Scotland Yard, Mason is left to romance Iris.

Comments: This was the second of the five films in which Raft was directed by Alexander Hall. Here again Hall shared the directorial reins, this time with George Somnes. This was a minor film in the Raft filmography. It was an ensemble piece rather than a star vehicle for any one member of the cast. Once upon a time the idea of a lookalike seemed very farfetched, but since there is a flourishing industry in them nowadays together with the fact that several heads of state in different countries have used them for security reasons, perhaps the idea is no longer so implausible.

The film dealt with the upper classes and was totally devoid of any sordid or gritty elements. The plot was developed in a fairly light vein and was intended primarily as entertainment. The special effects in the scenes involving the lookalikes were well done. From a contemporary perspective it is easy to take this for granted, but in 1933 it was fascinating to watch actors handing objects to each other in the split screen.

Although the acting styles of Raft and Clive Brook could not be more dissimilar, Raft was effective in his role. As Sir Guy Standing expressed it, "No one would expect a man with a face like that to be a detective." The romance which developed between Raft and Vinson was rather unconvincing. It was hard to believe that she would abandon Brook and fall in love with Raft. The main weakness of the film is that the lookalikes who were not hardened criminals would have been well aware of the purpose for which they had been hired and the police would have been able to discover the ruse fairly easily.

Biography: Georges Somnes was born Georges Carleton Flye in Newcastle, Maine, on July 7, 1887. He provided no more than a footnote to the history of motion pictures in that he co-directed four motion pictures during the early thirties. He reportedly died in Denver, Colorado, on February 8, 1956, aged 68.

Biography: Clive Brook was born Clifford Hardman Brook in London on June 1, 1887, the son of George Alfred and Charlotte Mary Brook. Because his father wanted him to be a lawyer, Clive was sent to Dulwich College. At the age of fifteen he had to leave after the family's finances declined. He switched to a polytechnic to study elocution and held a number of jobs after that. At the outbreak of World War I in September 1914 he enlisted as a private and rose to the rank of major in the Machine Gun Corps. He sustained shell shock at the Battle of Messines in June 1918 and was invalided out. After recovering his health he went on the stage. He made his screen debut in *Trent's Last Case* (1920).

When *The Royal Oak* (1923) was seen in Hollywood, he received offers from three studios. He was under contract at different times to Thomas Ince, Warner Bros., RKO Radio and Paramount. His career reached its apogee when he starred as Robert Maryott in *Cavalcade* (1933), which won an Oscar as Best Picture. In 1935 he returned to England permanently because of threats to kidnap his children. He continued to be active in British films until 1944 and he made several stage and television appearances in England during the fifties. His final film appearance was *The List of Adrian Messenger* (1963). He resided in a lavish apartment in Eaton Square, London, with winters spent in the Bahamas. He married Charlotte Elisabeth Mildred Evelyn in 1920 and they had two children, Faith (1922–2012) and Lyndon (1926–2004), both of whom became thespians. He died of age-related causes in London on November 17, 1974, aged 87.

Biography: Helen Vinson was born Helen Rulfs in Beaumont, Texas, on September 17, 1907. Her father, Edward A. Rulfs, was a Texas Oil Company executive. She was educated at the University of Texas for two years before leaving to make her professional stage debut in 1927. Her screen debut was in *It's a Deal* (1930). She spent a year under contract to Warner Bros., but obtained her release and freelanced successfully after that. Vinson was tall and experienced difficulties dancing with George Raft in *Midnight Club* because he was on the short side. She married and divorced Harry Neilson Vickerman and British tennis champion Fred Perry. She married Donald Hardenbrook, a wealthy New York stockbroker, in 1946, and at his request gave up her acting career, which she found traumatic. Her final acting credit was *The Thin Man Goes Home* (1944). She was widowed in 1976. After her acting days were over, she obtained a degree at the New York School of Interior Design. During the last years of her life she divided her time between Chapel Hill, North Carolina, and Nantucket. She died at Chapel Hill on October 7, 1999, aged 92.

The Bowery (1933)

Cast: Wallace Beery (Chuck Connors), George Raft (Steve Brodie), Jackie Cooper (Swipes McGurk), Fay Wray (Lucy Calhoun), Pert Kelton (Trixie Odbray), Oscar Apfel (Ivan Rommel), Herman Bing (Max Herman), Ferdinand Munier (Honest Mike), George Walsh (John L. Sullivan), Lillian Harmer (Carrie Nation), Irving Bacon (Hick in Clothes Store), John Bleifer (Mumbo the Mute), Phil Bloom, Kid Broad, Pueblo Jim Flynn, Joe Glick, Mack Gray, Jack Herrick, Al McCoy, Sailor Vincent (Pugs), James Burke (Recruiting Sergeant), Heinie Conklin (Drunk/Fight Spectator), Jimmy Conlin (Enlistee), Lester Dorr (Cynic), Bobby Dunn (Cockeyed Violinist), Kit Guard (Arsonist Henchman), Pat Harmon (Fireman), Harold Huber (Slick), John Ince (Crony), John Kelly (Lumpy Hogan), Fred Kelsey (Detective Kelsey), Charles Lane (Doctor), Charles McAvoy (Waiter), Charles Middleton (Detective), Frank Mills, Tammany Young (Firemen), Frank Moran (Bettor), Fletcher Norton (Googy Cochran), Hal Price (Editor), Harry Semels

Left to right: Raft, Jackie Cooper and Wallace Beery in *The Bowery*.

(Artist), Phil Tead, Harry Tenbrook (Touts), Andrew Tombes (Collar Salesman).

Credits: Director: Raoul Walsh; Producer: Darryl F. Zanuck; Associate Producers: William Goetz, Raymond Griffith; Based on a novel by Michael L. Simmons and Bessie Roth Soloman; Screenplay: Howard Estabrook and James Gleason; Photography: Barney McGill; Editor: Allen McNeil; Music: Alfred Newman; Art Director: Richard Day; Double for George Raft: Harvey Parry. Released by 20th Century Pictures/United Artists on October 7, 1933. Black and white. 92 minutes.

In the Gay Nineties New York had grown up into bustles and balloon sleeves ... but the Bowery had grown younger, louder and more rowdy, until it was known as the "Livest mile on the face of the globe" ... the cradle of men who were later to be world famous.

Synopsis: In New York's Bowery, Swipes McGurk is a homeless boy whom Chuck Connors has adopted. Connors and Steve Brodie are bitter rivals who are perpetually playing practical jokes on one another and run rival fire brigades. After Swipes smashes a window, a fire breaks out and both fire brigades respond. A brawl ensues in which Brodie's men are trounced, effectively ending his tenure as fire chief. Next they become rival prizefight managers. A fight is promoted between Connors' boxer Bloody Butch and Brodie's fighter "The Masked Marvel" who is in actuality John L. Sullivan. Sullivan fells Bloody Butch with one punch.

Demure Lucy Calhoun arrives from Albany at Connors' saloon looking for work. Since she is homeless, he takes her to live with him at his apartment where she becomes cook and housekeeper. This upsets Swipes, who leaves in a huff and goes to live with Brodie. Brodie goes to see Connors, but instead finds Lucy. He falls for her, but mistakenly believes she is a prostitute. Nevertheless they go out together and fall in love.

Two characters named Slick and Googy offer to murder Connors if Brodie will pay them $500, but Brodie will have none of it which makes him their enemy. Brodie is approached by two businessmen brewers named Herman and Rummell whose beer is sold all over the world, but not in the Bowery. They want to set up a saloon with Brodie acting as frontman. To make Brodie and the saloon famous from the Bowery to Brooklyn, they need a stunt. Brodie devises the idea of leaping from the Brooklyn Bridge. Connors bets Brodie that he does not have the nerve to do it, but if he succeeds Brodie will become sole owner of Connors' saloon.

Brodie's plan is to throw a wax dummy of himself off the bridge, but only Brodie himself, Swipes and Mumbo the Mute know this. When the dummy is stolen by Slick and Googy, Brodie is forced to make the jump himself. Despite a police blockade, Brodie manages to get onto the bridge and makes the jump successfully. Connors is prevented from witnessing this when his saloon is raided by temperance reformer Carrie Nation. Since Brodie now owns the place, Connors turns it over to Carrie Nation and her cohorts to wreck it. In spite of this, the saloon opens again with Brodie as proprietor and becomes a great success with Brodie hailed as "King of the Bowery." Brodie is given a newspaper bearing the headline that an American battleship has been blown up by the Spaniards, starting the Spanish-American war.

Connors becomes a penniless derelict and has to let Lucy go. Connors enlists in the army to go to Cuba. Afterwards he goes back to his hotel where he has a tearful reunion with Swipes. Outside his room, Slick and Googy are waiting for him. They tell him that Brodie did not jump off the Brooklyn Bridge and show him the dummy which they have stolen.

This infuriates Connors and he goes looking for Brodie with murder in his heart. He finds him in his saloon and accuses him of deception. They agree to settle the matter with their fists aboard Grogan's barge at 12:30 that night.

A crowd gathers on the shore. The two men row out to the barge where they brawl. A rowboat comes back with a victorious but bloody Connors on board. His victory sparks a celebration in which he is joined by Swipes. During the celebration, the police turn up to arrest Connors for assault and battery on Brodie. Lucy goes to the hospital to comfort the badly beaten but still forceful Brodie. The police bring Connors to the hospital for identification by Brodie, but he refuses to identify Connors and instead tells the police that he slipped and fell. After the police leave, Swipes persuades them to shake hands and they start laughing about the fight. Connors and Swipes help Brodie out of his hospital bed. Brodie also enlists and the two men (aided by the stowaway Swipes) bid a touching farewell to Lucy and set off to war together.

Comments: This was the first of five films in which Raft was directed by Raoul Walsh. It was the first movie of the newly formed 20th Century Pictures, which released its product through United Artists until it merged with Fox in 1935, creating 20th Century–Fox. *The Bowery* was a rowdy film full of larger-than-life personalities, rich in atmosphere and packed with incident. Raft was at his most animated and personable. He and Beery reportedly did not like each other off-screen and there was friction on the set. A recurring gag throughout the film was exploding cigars which Raft kept giving to Beery. The characters they played were based on real people, Steve Brodie (1863–1901) and Chuck Connors (1852–1913). The names Chuck Connors and Steve Brodie were later used by real-life actors.

The film depicted a way of life which has long gone including singing waiters, rough bartenders, prostitutes from Suicide Hall being pushed into a Black Maria and tailors grabbing helpless victims off the street and forcing them to buy suits they don't want. The film played havoc with history because it indicated that Brodie's jump from the Brooklyn Bridge in 1886 was almost contemporaneous with the Spanish-American War which in reality began in 1898. It was also the least politically correct film Raft appeared in, largely because of a notorious scene involving Chinese tenement dwellers trapped by fire.

Fay Wray registered strongly as the object of Raft's affection. Pert Kelton made a major contribution in the early stages of the film as a saloon entertainer with her energetic songs and dances, but she was largely absent in the latter stages of the movie. George Walsh, the former silent screen leading man who played John L. Sullivan, was the brother of Raoul Walsh. The film was a huge commercial success and, with rentals of $2,000,000 in the U.S. and Canada alone, was widely regarded as being one of the best movies that Raft ever appeared in.

Biography: Raoul Walsh was born Albert Edward Walsh in New York City on March 11, 1887, the son of an Irish clothing designer father and Spanish mother. He was educated at Seton Hall University in New York City. Following a two-year tour of Europe after graduating from college, he began studying play writing. He was seen on the stage for a brief period in 1910 and became a film actor in 1912. D.W. Griffith gave him his first chance to direct. Walsh's acting career ended when he was playing the lead of the Cisco Kid *In Old Arizona* (1929): On the way to a location, he was involved in a car accident which robbed him of the sight of one eye. He still directed the film, however. He became one of Hollywood's top directors with many of his best films being released through Warner Bros. Walsh was married three times: to Miriam Cooper, Lorraine Miller and Mary Simpson. He died in Simi Valley, California, on December 31, 1980, aged 93, of a heart attack.

Biography: Wallace Beery was born in Kansas City, Missouri, on April 1, 1885, the son of Noah and Margaret Beery. His father was a police officer. He ran away from home at the age of sixteen to join the Ringling Brothers Circus as an elephant trainer. After two years experience he went to New York and became a chorus boy in musical comedies. His screen debut was with Essanay in Chicago in 1914 as a Swedish maid in the *Sweedy* series. He lost a fortune in the stock market crash of 1929 and thereafter acquired a reputation as one of the legendary tightwads of Hollywood. He was under contract to MGM where he remained one of their most durable stars. He was twice nominated for a Best Actor Oscar and won for *The Champ* (1931). He died in Beverly Hills on April 15, 1949, aged 64. He married and divorced twice (to Gloria Swanson and Rita Gilman). He adopted a daughter, Carol Ann Beery, in 1933.

Biography: Jackie Cooper was born John Cooperman in Los Angeles on September 15, 1922. His father was a studio production manager, his mother a stage pianist. Director Norman Taurog was his mother's brother. In 1930 a crying scene in an *Our Gang* short produced by Hal Roach prompted Paramount to borrow him to star in *Skippy*, directed by Taurog. Because of the excellence of his performance, he became the youngest player to be nominated for a Best Actor Oscar. In 1931 Taurog arranged for MGM to buy Cooper's contract from Hal Roach. Cooper starred opposite numerous MGM stars until his appeal began to wane and he was dropped by MGM. A skilled drummer, he served in the U.S. Navy during World War II touring South Pacific bases in a band. Upon his discharge he went to New York where he studied acting. He subsequently gained a reputation as a reliable television actor and starred in two series, *The People's Choice* (1955–1958) and *Hennessey* (1959–1962). In 1964 he became an executive with Screen Gems and for over five years headed the company. He was married and divorced from June Horne and Hildy

Parks. He was married to Barbara Krause from 1954 until she died in 2009. He died in Beverly Hills on May 3, 2011, aged 88. He was survived by two sons, but both of his daughters predeceased him.

Biography: Fay Wray was born in Alberta, Canada, on September 15, 1907, the daughter of rancher Joseph H. Wray. When she was a child, her family moved from Canada to California, then to Arizona and to Salt Lake City. She was educated at public schools there and later at Hollywood High School. While on a school vacation in 1923, she began to work in films as an extra. Her big break came when Erich von Stroheim chose her to play Mitzi in *The Wedding March* (1926). She made a smooth transition to talkies and hit another peak in the early thirties, especially when she played Ann Darrow in *King Kong* (1933). She made some films in England in the mid-thirties and continued to play leads in B pictures until the early forties. In the early fifties, after a decade's absence, she emerged as a character actress both in films and on television. Her memoirs *On the Other Hand* were published in 1989. She married three times and had three children. She died in Manhattan on August 8, 2004, aged 96.

All of Me (1934)

Cast: Fredric March (Don Ellis), Miriam Hopkins (Lyda Darrow), George Raft (Honey Rogers), Helen Mack (Eve Haron), Nella Walker (Mrs. Darrow), William Collier Sr. (Jerry Helman), Gilbert Emery (The Dean), Blanche Friderici (Miss Haskell), Kitty Kelly (Lorraine), Guy Usher (District Attorney), John Marston (Nat Davis), Edgar Kennedy (Guard), Jill Dennett (Molly), Laura La Marr (Lil), Astrid Allwyn (Ray), Patricia Farley (Bee), Al Hill (Mickey), Leslie Palmer (Paul), Lillian West (Jennie), Jason Robards Sr. (Man in Speakeasy), Barton MacLane (First Cop), Bruce Mitchell (Second Cop), Harry Stubbs (Second Man in Speakeasy), Eleanor Bullen

(Woman in Speakeasy), James Burke (Welfare Island Guard), Helena Phillips Evans (Mrs. Haron), Mack Gray (Tough Guy).

Credits: Director: James Flood; Producer: Louis D. Lighton; Based on the play *Chrysallis* by Rose Albert Porter; Screenplay: Sidney Buchman and Thomas Mitchell; Dialogue Director: Thomas Mitchell; Photography: Victor Milner; Editor: Otto Lovering; Music: Ralph Rainger, Leo Robin and Karl Hajos. Released by Paramount on February 3, 1934. Black and white. 70 minutes.

Tagline: "There are two kinds of woman, but only one kind of love!"

Synopsis: At Clay College, Massachusetts, Don Ellis is an engineering lecturer who is in love with one of his students, unconventional Lyda Darrow. Lyda loves him but does not want to marry him. Don is offered a new job out west at Boulder Dam and wants Lyda to come with him, but she hesitates.

Don and Lyda go to a speakeasy where they encounter Honey Rogers, a prisoner on parole, and his girl Eve Haron. When Eve becomes ill, Lyda calls her a cab. Lyda accidentally leaves her purse, which Honey sees and keeps. Lyda spots Honey with the purse in his pocket, but does nothing about it. When Eve finds out, she is furious with Honey. At the boarding house where Eve lives, loan shark Davis turns up claiming that Rogers owes him $50. An argument turns to violence when Rogers hits him. Lyda later tells Don that she is pregnant. Then Don says that he is not joining the Boulder Dam project after all. Lyda confesses that she invented the baby so that he would not go. Lyda and Don break off their engagement.

In a letter, Eve tells Lyda that she is now living at the Rose Manor reformatory and insists on seeing her. Eve tells Lyda that she is pregnant and that after the fracas Honey was sent back to the island to complete his sentence and Eve cannot communicate with him. She begs Lyda to contact Honey. Lyda goes to see Honey in prison and reassure him. Rogers tells her he is going to break out and help Eve.

Rogers does escape, but in the process kills a guard. Rogers and Lyda go to the home where Rogers takes Eve away. They hide out in the woods overnight and the following day drive into town where they check into a hotel. The police surround the hotel, but before they can burst in, Honey and Eve jump to their deaths from a hotel window. Don tries to persuade Lyda to sign a statement to the effect that Honey and Eve forced her to help them, but she demurs because she does not regard Honey and Eve as criminals but as victims of society. Don and Lyda face the future together.

Comments: This was the second film in which Raft was directed by James Flood. This was the second, and by far the worse, of the two films which Raft made with Miriam Hopkins. It is hard to envisage any gangster named Honey, let alone George Raft. Fredric March and Raft had totally different acting styles, and with a better screenplay much could have been made of the conflict between the two, but alas they only shared one short scene together. The film had two plots which ran concurrently, but did not mesh into a satisfying whole.

Raft had a relatively small role. His character appeared within the first twenty minutes, but then disappeared until the last third. He did however figure prominently in the best scene in which he carried the sanctimonious matron of the lodge over to the closet where the residents locked her in. The scenes in the reform home had a credibility and spontaneity which the other scenes lacked. This film was similar to the Warner Bros. "social conscience" films of the thirties, but somehow the stilted dialogue and ridiculous situations undermined its impact. The reviews were universally bad and it was a box office flop.

Biography: Fredric March was born Ernest Frederick Mcintyre Bickel in Racine, Wisconsin, on August 31, 1897. The son of John F. Bickel and Cora Marcher, he studied economics at the University of Wisconsin and, after fighting in World War I, worked in a bank. When given a year's leave in 1920 he went on the stage. For three years he was with a stock company in Denver, Colorado. He refused to go into films until talkies came. He was appearing on stage in *The Royal Family* (in which he parodied John Barrymore) when he was invited to enter films and signed a contract with Paramount. His "Mr. Average America" appearance and personality made him one of the most distinguished actors of his generation. He was nominated five times for a Best Actor Oscar and won for *Dr. Jekyll and Mr. Hyde* (1931) and *The Best Years of Our Lives* (1946). He married Ellis Baker in 1923, but divorced her in 1927. That same year, in Mexico he wed Florence Eldridge, with whom he adopted a daughter in 1932 and a son in 1935. He died in Los Angeles, on April 14, 1975, aged 77, of cancer.

Biography: Miriam Hopkins was born Ellen Miriam Hopkins in Savannah, Georgia, on October 18, 1902, the daughter of insurance salesman Homer A. Hopkins and Ellen Cutler. She was raised by her maternal grandmother in Bainbridge, Georgia, and educated at Goddard Seminary, Vermont, and Syracuse University. While appearing as Kalonika in *Lysistrata* on Broadway in 1930, she commuted to Paramount's Astoria Studios to make her screen debut in *Fast and Loose*. She became one of Paramount's busiest actresses until 1935 when she moved over to Sam Goldwyn and then to Warner Bros. in 1939. She received a Best Actress Oscar nomination for playing the title role in *Becky Sharp* (1935). She returned to the stage in 1943 and continued to be a regular stage player for the next twenty years, only making occasional feature films. She was married and divorced four times: to Brandon Peters, Austin Parker, Anatole Litvak and Ray Brock. She adopted a son, Michael, in 1932. She died in New York on October 9, 1972, of a heart attack, aged 69.

Biography: Helen Mack was born Helen MacDougall in Rock Island, Illinois, on November 13, 1913, the daughter of William and Regina MacDougall. Her parents took her to

New York when she was a child and in 1921 enrolled her in Professional Children's School where she acquired her stage name. She appeared in silent films which were shot in and around New York. Her career as a mature film star commenced in 1931 and continued until 1945. Among the films in which she appeared was *The Son of Kong* (1933), but unlike Fay Wray, it brought her nothing like the same degree of recognition. She later became a successful radio producer and director, scriptwriter and playwright. She was married twice and had two sons. She died in Beverly Hills on August 13, 1986, aged 72, of pancreatic cancer at the home of writer friend Aleen Leslie, where she was living at the time.

Bolero (1934)

Cast: George Raft (Raoul De Baere), Carole Lombard (Helen Hathaway), Sally Rand (Annette), Frances Drake (Leona), William Frawley (Mike De Baere), Gertrude Michael (Lady Claire D'Argon), Ray Milland (Lord Robert Coray), Gloria Shea (Lucy), Martha Barnattre (Belgian Landlady), Frank Dunn (Hotel Manager), Gregory Golubeff (Orchestra Leader), Mack Gray (Club Patron), Dell Henderson (Theater Manager), John Irwin (Porter), Adolph Milar (Beer Garden Manager), Paul Panzer (Bailiff), Ann Shaw (Young Matron), Phillips Smalley (Leona's Angel).

Credits: Director: Wesley Ruggles; Original Story: Carey Wilson and Kubec Glasmon; Screenplay: Horace Jackson; Idea: Ruth Ridenour; Photography: Leo Tover; Editor: Hugh Bennett; Based on the composition *Bolero* by Maurice Ravel; Original Music: Bernhard Kaun, John Leipold and Ralph Rainger; Musical Direction: Nathaniel Finston; Stock Music: Karl Hajos, W. Franke Harling and Rudolph G. Kopp; Choreography: LeRoy Prinz; Dance Double for George Raft: Veloz; Dance Double for Carole Lombard: Yolanda. Released by Paramount on February 23, 1934. Black and white. 83 minutes.

Taglines: "He rose to fame on a ladder of dancing ladies!" and "His dancing partners were but stepping stones to fame!"

Synopsis: In 1910 Raoul De Baere works as a miner by day and an unsuccessful solo dancer by night. He is an unscrupulous individual who intends to use dancing as a route to fame. Told that he would win contests with a female partner, he borrows money from his half-brother Michael to set up a dancing act for himself and a partner at a Hoboken beer garden. With Leona, he rises to being a featured attraction at the Café Hag in Paris. He joins forces professionally with cool, ambitious Helen Hathaway, with whom he becomes most successful. They go to England where he meets fan dancer Annette.

Opening his own nightclub Chez Raoul in Paris, he decides to dance the Bolero on opening night with Helen, surrounded by natives pounding on drums. During their debut performance, patrons appear to be more interested in discussing the outbreak of World War I than watching them dance. Raoul aborts his performance and makes an eloquent announcement about enlisting in the service of his native country, Belgium. When Helen discovers Raoul has enlisted in the Belgian army only as a publicity stunt, she abandons him in disgust. Raoul endures a horrific time during the war. When the war ends in 1918, Raoul, a victim of poison gas, returns to civilian life diagnosed with a bad heart and weak lungs.

After the armistice, ignoring the advice of his doctors, Raoul decides to reopen his nightclub, hoping to renew his quest for fame by performing *Bolero*. He finds Annette again down on her luck, dancing for rent money in a low saloon. Helen has since married Lord Robert Coray. Both are in the audience to watch the reopening of Chez Raoul. When Annette arrives at the club too drunk to perform, Raoul fires her and decides to substitute a solo dance. Michael, seriously worried about Raoul, goes to Helen's table and asks if she will agree to appear as Annette's substitute.

Raoul and Helen dance the *Bolero*, which is a tremendous success. The strain proves too much for Raoul, who suffers a heart attack and dies, leaving Helen distraught. Michael declares, "He was too good for this joint!"

Comments: This was the only time that Raft was directed by Wesley Ruggles. In *Bolero* he gave one of his best performances and it was his favorite of his own films. The theme of this film was ambition and Raft so understood Raoul that he had the character nailed down. Although this was a musical, there were virtually no songs or vocalizing. Instead there were instrumental dance numbers and background

Raft and Carole Lombard in *Bolero*.

music from popular songs of the period which helped to create and sustain the mood. (Maurice Ravel's *Bolero* was written in 1928 so it would have been impossible for Raft and Lombard to perform a dance routine in 1918.) Raft said that Lombard was his best dancing partner. The audition scene where she stripped down to her underwear to dance was very sexy.

A major asset of this film was Leo Tover's cinematography. He dramatically captured the dances as well as emphasizing the performances of the actors with light and shadow. The gruesome carnage of World War I was shown as a montage, but it was a major turning point in the plot. The long-term effects of poison gas really did ruin the lives of soldiers who survived the war itself. Raft made a number of films during the thirties and early forties with a musical background, but this was the only one which really looked like an expensive, classy feature. Most of the rest were cheaper-looking, and lacked the production values, excellent script and superior direction of *Bolero*. Raft and Lombard were teamed together the following year in a vastly inferior film, *Rumba*. This was Raft's best musical and a big box office hit.

Biography: Wesley Ruggles was born in Los Angeles on June 11, 1889. He appeared as an actor in musical comedy, minstrel shows and stock. He entered films in 1914 as a Keystone Cop. By 1918 he was directing for Morosco. He directed *Cimarron* (1931) which won a Best Picture Oscar. In 1944 he was invited by MGM to go to England to direct for them. He did not shoot any films for them, but instead independently directed and produced *London Town* (1946) which was such a debacle that it ended his career. His brother was the famous actor Charlie Ruggles. Wesley was married to Arline Judge, from whom he was divorced, and later to Marcelle Rogez. He died in Santa Monica on January 8, 1972, aged 82, after a stroke. He was survived by Rogez and a son.

Biography: Carole Lombard was born Jane Alice Peters in Fort Wayne, Indiana, on October 6, 1908, the daughter of Frederick C. Peters and Elizabeth Knight. Her parents divorced when she was eight and her mother took her to live in California. She was spotted in the street by director Allan Dwan who cast her in *A Perfect Crime* (1921). She left school at fifteen to join a theatrical company. In 1924 she signed a contract with Fox, but a car accident the following year left her with a scarred face which despite makeup and careful lighting was visible in her films. Fox fired her so she became a Mack Sennett Bathing Beauty in 1927 and changed her name to Carol Lombard. In 1930 she was signed by Paramount who added an "e" to her Christian name. She went on to become one of their most popular stars. She was nominated for a Best Actress Oscar in *My Man Godfrey* (1936). After America entered World War II she flew to Indiana for a war bond rally which was hugely successful, raising $2 million. On January 16, 1942, she was on board TWA Flight 3 en route back to Hollywood when the plane crashed into Table Rock Mountain about thirty miles south west of Las Vegas, killing all 22 people on board including Carole, aged 34, and her mother. She was married to William Powell from 1931 until their divorce in 1933 and to Clark Gable in 1939; he survived her.

The Trumpet Blows (U.K. title: *The Trumpet Calls*) (1934)

Cast: George Raft (Manuel Montes), Adolphe Menjou (Pancho Montes/Pancho Gomez), Frances Drake (Chulita Valdes), Sidney Toler (Pepe Sancho), Edward Ellis (Chato), Nydia Westman (Carmela Ramirez), Katherine De Mille (Lupe), Lillian Elliott (Senora Ramirez), Douglas Wood (Senor Ramirez), Francis McDonald (Vega), Morgan Wallace (Police Inspector), Gertrude Norman (Grandma Albrentez), Joyce Compton (Blonde on Train), Hooper Atchley (Detective), Mischa Auer (Chato's Assistant), Al Bridge (Policeman), Howard Brooks (Priest), E. Alyn Warren (Stationmaster), Charles Stevens (Mojias).

Credits: Director: Stephen Roberts; Story: Peter Emerson Browne and J. Parker Reade, Jr.; Screenplay: Bartlett Cormack and Wallace Smith; Photography: Harry Fischbeck; Editor: Ellsworth Hoagland; Music: Ralph Rainger and Leo Robin; Art Direction: Wiard Ihnen. Released by Paramount on April 14, 1934. Black and white. 72 minutes.

All Saints Day in Mexico — when on November 1 the memory of the dead is celebrated not sadly — but with songs recalling their virtues.

Synopsis: Rancher Pancho Montes and his right hand man Pepe arrive at a cemetery to lay a wreath at the grave of the notorious Robin Hood–type bandit, Pancho Gomez. Gomez was allegedly shot and killed by police. In reality Montes is Gomez; he dressed up a dead body to make it appear that Gomez had been killed. Later they meet the train carrying Pancho's younger brother Manuel, who has been attending college in America. Manuel aspires to be a matador under the guidance of stern trainer Chato, but Pancho tries to discourage him.

Pancho organizes a lavish party and hires a troupe of lovely dancers to perform in honor of his brother's graduation. Both Manuel and Pancho fall in love with the prettiest dancer, Chulita, who prefers Manuel. Manuel leaves the ranch with Chato to become a bullfighter, rather than hurt his brother. Chato becomes a successful bullfighter and both brothers turn up in Corrales where Chulita is dancing.

Manuel goes to see Chulita and they kiss and make up. Pancho sees them kissing, lambasts them both and leaves. Manuel is so upset that in the arena he is gored by a bull. Chato, who did not witness this, returns from Mexico City where he tells Manuel that he has arranged a contract for him to fight in the capital. Manuel loses his courage and turns to drink. Chulita, who thought it would be romantic to be a bullfighter's sweetheart, admits she has made a mistake. Forced to decide between bullfighting and Chulita, Manuel chooses to pursue his career, which causes Chulita to walk out.

Chulita goes to Pancho's unoccupied ranchhouse. As she waits in the darkness, Pancho and Pepe arrive on horseback from one of their robberies. Chulita tells Pancho that Manuel is in no condition to fight bulls in Mexico City and begs Pancho to go to him, but he refuses. When the police arrive and tell Pancho about the robbery and that a peon has recognized one of the outlaws as the allegedly deceased Pancho Gomez, Chulita realizes that Pancho is the bandit leader. After the police have gone, Chulita tells Pancho she understands why he cannot go to Mexico City as he will be recognized and arrested. Pancho ridicules her, so Pancho, Chulita and Pepe go to Mexico City.

In the Mexico City bullring, Pancho and Chulita are seated in the audience when two detectives spot Pancho and take a seat nearby. Manuel makes a brave attempt with the cape, but when he sees his brother being led away by police, he loses his cool and is injured by the bull. After Pancho jumps into the ring to save his brother, Manuel is able to recover sufficiently for both brothers to escape from the bull. Manuel later returns to the bullring where he manages to kill the bull to the delight of the crowd. At the entrance the two detectives tell Pancho that they have found a witness who can identify the real Pancho Gomez. The witness turns out to be the faithful Pepe, who tells the detectives that the real Pancho Gomez has the tattoo of a skull and crossbones on his arm. When the detectives examine his arm and find nothing, they believe they are mistaken and release Pancho. The two brothers are reconciled and Manuel tells Chulita he was wrong and that he really loves her more than bullfighting.

Comments: This was the only time Raft was directed by Stephen Roberts. This was the most deliberate attempt Paramount made to force Raft into the Rudolph Valentino mold by casting him as a bullfighter similar to Valentino's triumph in *Blood and Sand*. The fact that *The Trumpet Blows* was one of the weakest films Raft made for Paramount (and a box office failure) virtually ended the comparison. The plot made little sense and the casting was absurd. There was not one member of the cast who was convincing as a Mexican and not one of them spoke with a genuine Mexican accent. There were however some good atmospheric shots and footage of real bullfighting.

Frances Drake was better served by this film than in her other film with Raft, *Bolero,*

Raft and Frances Drake in *The Trumpet Blows.*

where she appeared as one of his early temperamental partners. She had a couple of excellent dance scenes in *The Trumpet Blows*. The first was where she did a wild dance in a skimpy costume at a party under Raft's appreciative eye. The second was at Corrales where she did a dance pretending to be a matador, while a half-naked dancer clad in white pretended to be the bull. This was a rather surreal scene with lesbian overtones.

Raft and Menjou were so physically different that casting them as brothers was ludicrous. This was the only film Raft and Menjou did together, but they had met back in the twenties when Menjou was a Broadway actor and Raft a dancer. Menjou came into a club one night after hours where Raft was performing and insisted that Raft be awoken from sleep and perform a dance number for him. Afterwards he expressed his appreciation to Raft, but left without giving him a tip for the special performance. When they met up in Hollywood on the set of this film, Raft reminded Menjou that he owed him some money.

Biography: Stephen Roberts was born in Summersville, West Virginia, on November 23, 1895. After graduating from college he entered the United States military and became an expert aviator and flying instructor during World War I. After the Armistice he took up trick and exhibition flying, but an accident at El Paso, Texas, obliged him to abandon his flying career. He became an assistant director under Thomas H. Ince and William S. Hart. In 1922 he directed his first short for Educational, where he remained until 1931. He signed with Paramount in 1932 and remained with them until his untimely death in Beverly Hills on July 17, 1936, aged 41, after a heart attack.

Biography: Adolphe Menjou was born Adolph Jean Menjou in Pittsburgh, Pennsylvania, on February 18, 1890. His parents were Jean Adoph Menjou, a French-born restaurateur, and Nora Joyce. He was raised and educated mainly in Cleveland, Ohio. He went to

Cornell University to study mechanical engineering, later switching to liberal arts, but did not graduate. In 1912 he decided he wanted to be an actor so he went to New York. He made his screen debut in *The Man Behind the Door* (1915). After service in World War I, he decided to relocate to Hollywood to reactivate his screen career. He became a household name when he starred in *A Woman of Paris* (1923) directed by Charles Chaplin. When talkies arrived, despite an excellent speaking voice, he was regarded as finished. He scored a big hit and was nominated for a Best Actor Oscar in *The Front Page* (1931) as Walter Burns. He enjoyed a successful career for another fifteen years before his aggressive support of the House UnAmerican Activities Committee made him extremely unpopular within the industry. He frequently won the accolade of being voted the Best Dressed Actor in Hollywood. He died in Beverly Hills on October 29, 1963, aged 73, of chronic hepatitis. He was survived by his third wife, Verree Teasdale.

Biography: Frances Drake was born Frances Morgan Dean in New York City on October 22, 1908, the daughter of Edwin Morgan Dean, a mining businessman who lost a fortune in the Wall Street Crash. She was educated at Havergal College, Toronto, and at a finishing school in Arundel, England. Under her real name she danced in night clubs in London and made her screen debut in *The Jewel* (1932). This secured her passage to Hollywood and a Paramount contract. The studio changed her name to Frances Drake and she made her first appearance for them in *Bolero*. She was another actress who liked Raft personally. She married Hon. Cecil John Arthur Howard, son of the nineteenth Earl of Suffolk, in 1939 and retired after *The Affairs of Martha* (1942). She was widowed in 1985. In 1992 she married David Brown, who survived her. She died in a Beverly Hills hospital on January 17, 2000, aged 91.

Limehouse Blues (Reissue title: *East End Chant*) (1934)

Cast: George Raft (Harry Young), Jean Parker (Toni Talbot), Robert Loraine (Inspector Sheridan), Kent Taylor (Eric Benton), Anna May Wong (Tu Tuan), Montagu Love (Pug Talbot), Billy Bevan (Herb), E. Alyn Warren (Ching Lee), Wyndham Standing (Assistant Commissioner Kenyon), Louis Vincenot (Rhama), John Rogers (Smokey), Robert Adair (Alfred), Eric Blore (Slummer), Rita Carlyle (Wife), Forrester Harvey (McDonald), Keith Hitchcock (Policeman), Colin Kenny (Davis), Eily Malyon (Woman Who Finds Pug), Dora Mayfield (Annie, the Flower Seller), James May (Taxi Driver), Tempe Pigott (Maggie), Elsie Prescott (Woman Employment Agent), Desmond Roberts (Constable), Colin Tapley (Man Fighting with Wife), Otto Yamaoka (Chinese Waiter on Boat).

Credits: Director: Alexander Hall; Producer: Arthur Hornblow, Jr.; Original Story: Arthur Phillips; Screenplay: Arthur Phillips, Cyril Hume and Grover Jones; Photography: Harry Fischbeck; Editor: William Shea; Music: Sam Coslow and John Leipold; Art Direction: Hans Dreier and Robert Usher; Makeup: Wally Westmore. Released by Paramount on December 11, 1934. Black and white. 65 minutes.

Synopsis: In London's Limehouse, Eurasian Harry Young owns The Lily Gardens, a front for a big-time smuggling operation. He lives in an ornate apartment above the club. Police Inspector Sheridan drops in to see him after a crime and warns him to stay away from the River Thames as it will not be healthy from then onwards. Pickpocket Toni Talbot runs into The Lily Gardens with a man's watch she has stolen and Young protects her from the police. She is the stepdaughter of rival smuggler

Jean Parker and Raft in *Limehouse Blues*.

Pug Talbot. The violent Talbot, who is informed that Toni is involved with Young, feels that Young has been cutting in on his business and declares that he intends to be top smuggler on the river again. The following night when Young goes down to the river to collect smuggled goods from a ship, Talbot informs the police, but Young eludes them. Pug is invited by Young to his club to settle matters. The following evening while Young and his Chinese mistress Tu Tuan are performing "Limehouse Blues" on stage, Pug is stabbed to death by Young's henchman Rhama.

Young invites Toni to be his "eyes and ears" and to live in a former store room above The Lily Gardens. Tu Tuan tells Young that Toni must go, but he refuses because he is falling in love with Toni even though it is not reciprocated. On a shopping spree in the West End, Toni meets Eric Benton and falls in love with him. Toni gives Young back the money he has given her and tells him that she wants to find herself a proper job, but Young spreads the word that no one in Limehouse is to employ her. Tu Tuan warns him that Toni is making a fool of him and will not marry him because he is not wholly white. When Young refuses to listen, Tu Tuan tells him that she is finished at The Lily Gardens. Benton proposes to Toni, but she tells him that she is a pickpocket and has been kept by Young and tries to break off the relationship.

Benton turns up at the club, confronts Young and tells him that he loves Toni. Young invites him to his apartment that night with the intention of having Benton killed. A horrified Tu Tuan spots Benton leaving the club, surmises what Young is intending and alerts Inspector Sheridan, who guarantees her safety. A distraught Tu Tuan stabs herself to death. It is Chinese New Year and Young and Toni are invited to dinner on a freighter which is being used as a front for smuggling activity.

When Young tells Toni that Benton will never trouble her again, Toni realizes that Young intends to murder Benton and begs him to call off the killing. Now aware that Toni genuinely loves Benton and will never love him, Young starts back to the dock in his boat with Toni to try to prevent Benton's murder. They are pursued on the Thames and fired on by Inspector Sheridan and his men. The wounded Young and Toni dash through the Limehouse streets only to find that Benton has already arrived at Young's apartment. Young manages to prevent Rhama from murdering Benton. Toni and Benton are reunited and Young enables them to escape. A triumphant Inspector Sheridan arrives and exclaims, "You won't escape from me this time!" "Yes I will. You shoot too straight," replies Young as he falls dying. With his dying breath, he exonerates Toni from all involvement in his crimes.

Comments: This was the third and best of the five Raft films which Alexander Hall directed. It was a richly atmospheric evocation of the East End of London. Hall's direction was very inspired in places and there were several exciting scenes. Although not a commercial success when first released, this was one of Raft's most unusual films and was his only opportunity to work with Anna May Wong. He also had a memorable dance sequence with Wong. Raft was well-suited to playing the role of Harry Young because his face was inscrutable and he brought an enigmatic personality to the character. The weakest link in the acting chain was Robert Loraine, who was competent but not outstanding, as the dogged police officer. The film showed some signs of haste in the production. In one scene Jean Parker (talking to Kent Taylor) twice called him "Harry"—the name of Raft's character, not Taylor's, in the film.

Biography: Robert Bilcliffe Loraine was born in New Brighton, Wirral, England, on January 14, 1876. His stage debut was made in the English provinces in 1889 and his first appearance on the London stage in 1894. He appeared in Shaw's *Man and Superman* on Broadway in 1905 to great acclaim. He was also a famous aviator who was the first to fly across the Irish Channel and land on the Isle of Wight and the first to send a Marconi wireless message from a plane. He joined the Royal Flying Corps at the outbreak of World War I, shot down several German planes, was twice badly wounded, rose to the rank of Lt.-Colonel and was subsequently awarded the M.C. and D.S.O. After the war he continued his career on the London and New York stages. He made his screen debut in *Bentley's Conscience* (1922). At the tail end of his career he played a few character roles in American films. He died in London on December 23, 1935, aged 59. In 1897 he married Julie Opp whom he soon divorced and then in 1921 Winifred Lydia Strangman with whom he had three daughters who survived him. His estate amounted to £2,689.

Biography: Jean Parker was born Lois Stephanie Zelinska of Polish-French parents in Butte, Montana, on August 11, 1912. She was raised in California and graduated from Pasadena High School. She made her screen debut in 1932 and appeared regularly in films until 1944, notably as the spunky heroine of several films shot by Paramount's Pine-Thomas unit. Between 1944 and 1950 she devoted herself to stage work. From 1950 onwards she again appeared occasionally in films. She taught drama in later years and did television commercials. She was married and divorced four times: to George MacDonald, Douglas Dawson, Curtis Grotter and actor Robert Lowery, with whom she had a son, Robert Jr., who was born in 1952. She died at the Motion Picture Country Home and Hospital in Woodland Hills, California, on November 30, 2005, aged 93, of complications from a stroke.

Biography: Anna May Wong was born Wong Liu Tsong (Frosted Yellow Willow) in Los Angeles on January 3, 1905, the daughter of laundry owner Sam Wong and Lee Gon Toy. She was educated at a mission school in Chinatown and Los Angeles High School. She began doing extra work in films in 1919. Her

big break came when she was cast as the Mongol Slave in *The Thief of Bagdad* (1924). She became an international celebrity in the late twenties shooting films in England, France and Germany. She signed a contract with Paramount in 1931. Of her films for this studio the most acclaimed was *Shanghai Express* (1932). During World War II she worked tirelessly for USO and China War Relief. In 1951 she starred in a short-lived television series, *The Gallery of Madame Liu-Tsong*, and she later made TV guest appearances. She died in Santa Monica on February 3, 1961, aged 56, of a massive heart attack in her sleep. She never married.

Rumba (1935)

Cast: George Raft (Joe Martin), Carole Lombard (Diana Harrison), Lynne Overman (Flash), Margo (Carmelita), Gail Patrick (Patsy Fletcher), Iris Adrian (Goldie Allen), Monroe Owsley (Hobart Fletcher), Jameson Thomas (Jack Solanger), Soledad Jiminez (Aunt Maria), Paul Porcasi (Uncle Carlos), Samuel S. Hinds (Henry Harrison), Virginia Hammond (Mrs. Harrison), Richard Alexander (Cop), Hooper Atchley (Doctor), Luis Barrancos, Olga Barrancos, Laura Puente (Rumba Dancers), Brooks Benedict (Man in Audience), James Burke, James Burtis (Reporters), E.H. Calvert (Police Captain), Rafael Corio (Alfredo), Helen Curtis, Dorothy Dalton, Janette Dickson, Nora Gale, Patsy King, De Don Blunier, Lora Lane, Alma Ross, Jean Ross (Chorus Girls), Donald Gray (Watkins), Mack Gray (Assistant Dance Director), Raymond McKee (Dance Director), Frank Mills (Bouncer), Dennis O'Keefe (Man in Diana's Party at Theater), Jack Raymond (Gangster), Craig Reynolds (Bromley), Dick Rush (Policeman), Robert "Buddy" Shaw (Ticket Taker), Don Brodie, Charles Sullivan (Gangsters), Akim Tamiroff (Tony, Café Proprietor), Elinor Vanderveer (Audience Member), Bruce Warren (Dean), Zora (Specialty Dancer).

Credits: Director: Marion Gering; Producer: William LeBaron; Original Idea: Guy Endore and Seena Owen; Screenplay: Howard J. Green; Screenplay Contributor: Paul Girard Smith; Additional Dialogue: Harry Ruskin and Frank Partos; Photography: Ted Tetzlaff; Music and Lyrics: Ralph Rainger; Original Music: Jose Padilla; Orchestrators: Herman Hand, John Leipold and Tom Satterfield; Dances and Ensembles: LeRoy Prinz; Specialty Dance Creators: Veloz and Yolanda; Spanish Lyrics: Francois B. De Valdes; Art Direction: Hans Dreier and Robert Usher; Sound Recorder: Jack A. Goodrich; Costumes: Travis Banton; Special Photographic Effects: Dewey Wrigley. Songs include: "I'm Yours for Tonight," "The Magic of You," "The Rhythm of the Rumba," "Your Eyes Have Said" and "If I Knew." Released by Paramount on February 23, 1935. Black and white. 71 minutes.

Synopsis: In Havana, hoofer Joe Martin wins $5,000 in a lottery. When he goes to collect his winnings with dancing partner Goldie Allen and journalist turned manager "Flash," he discovers that his lottery ticket is a fake. The person with the winning ticket is heiress Diana Harrison who coincidentally turns up at The Rolling Tar, the club where Martin and Allen dance. She goes to his dressing room where she offers him her winnings, but he refuses. Diana's boyfriend, Hobart Fletcher, takes offense and slugs Martin. A fight breaks; Martin is blamed and fired. Martin decides to stay in Cuba while Goldie returns to Broadway.

When Carmelita goes to his aunt's store, Martin serves her. They become acquainted and go to the fiesta where Martin persuades her to become his dance partner in a new act. Hearing the rumba — the dance of love — at the fiesta gives him the idea for his act. He opens the club "El Elefante" where they dance the rumba under the stage name of "Jose Marinez and Carmelita." On opening night when Diana turns up at the club, Martin teaches her the rumba while simultaneously romancing her. Her disturbed parents, afraid of a scandal, insist that she return home to the States.

Martin and Diana have a rendezvous in which initially he rejects her, but when she tells him about the wire from her parents and professes her love, he has a change of heart and they embrace. Carmelita, whom Martin also invited, witnesses this. Both girls are deeply upset and leave separately. Diana returns to New York where her parents inform her that private detectives have compiled a report on Martin and have uncovered his unsavory past (he fled to Cuba to escape gangsters whom he was once involved with). Diana tells her parents that she is not going to see Martin again, but she has also broken off her engagement to Hobart.

Producer Jack Solanger begs Martin to return to New York to topline his new revue. When Martin reads in the newspaper about Diana's broken engagement, he instructs "Flash" to inform Solanger that he will accept the offer. In his New York dressing room, Martin receives a note apparently from gangsters threatening to murder him during his act if he performs in New York. Reporters overhear Martin telling "Flash" about the note, which creates a furor in the press. At the appointed hour, cops are planted all over the theater. When the highly strung Carmelita faints and is unable to appear, Martin says he is going to do the routine as a single. Instead Diana rushes to him and insists on going on in Carmelita's place. They dance the rumba together. Not only are they a smash hit, but no attempt is made to murder Martin. When the dance is over, Martin tells Solanger that Diana is his new dance partner. "Flash" confesses that the death threats note was written by him as a publicity stunt which succeeded beyond his wildest expectations.

Comments: This was the second of two Raft films directed by Marion Gering. *Rumba* reunited the team of Raft and Carole Lombard from *Bolero*, but this was a vastly inferior film and a box office flop. Whereas *Bolero* was a fine drama about the rise and fall of an ambitious dancer, *Rumba* emerged as an unmemorable musical with a soap opera plot. When they made the first movie together, Raft and Lombard reportedly got along splendidly. This time however there was some antagonism largely because Lombard's jokes were frequently aimed at Raft's lack of formal education, a subject about which Raft was extremely sensitive.

The cast and production values were up to standard. The chief culprit here was the script, which was laden with clichés. A lot of scribes made a contribution to it which suggests that there were script problems from early on. Conflict between women works better when one is a bitch. This was not the case here since Margo was a decent human being who was badly treated by the insensitive Raft. The equivalent character in *Bolero* was played by Frances Drake as a virago and was therefore much better defined. The ending which revealed the death threats to be a hoax was also extremely disappointing. One other story weakness occurred when Raft went to see Lombard at her house and found her immediately. There was no indication of how he gained access to the interior of the place. *Rumba* did not compare favorably with the Technicolor Latin musicals of 20th Century–Fox during the forties.

Biography: Margo was born Maria Margarita Guadalupe Teresa Estella Castilla Bolado y O'Donnell in Mexico City on May 10, 1917, the daughter of Dr. Amedio Bolado, a Spanish surgeon. She was raised in the United States where she was taught dancing by Eduardo Cansino and began performing at the age of ten. She made her debut at the Mexican Theatre in Los Angeles. She first appeared as a dancer in cabaret at the Wardorf-Astoria in New York with the band of her uncle, Xavier Cugat. For a time she was also the dance partner of George Raft at the Paramount Theatre. She made her screen debut in *Crime Without*

Passion (1934). She made her Broadway debut as Miriamne in *Winterset* (1935) to great acclaim and appeared in the film version in 1936. Possibly her best remembered film role was as Maria, the rapidly aging Shangri-La refugee in *Lost Horizon* (1937). She married actor Francis Lederer in 1937, but divorced in 1940. She then married Eddie Albert in 1945. With him she had a son, Edward Albert, Jr. (1951–2006), and adopted a daughter in 1954. She and her second husband performed a nightclub song-and-dance act during the fifties. In 1974 she was appointed Commissioner of Social Services in Los Angeles. At the time of her death she was a steering committee member on the President's Committee on the Arts and Humanities and a member of the Board of the National Council of the National Endowment of the Arts. She died at her home in Pacific Palisades on July 17, 1985, aged 68, of brain cancer.

Biography: Lynne Overman was born in Maryville, Missouri, on September 19, 1887. His parents were William James Overman and Dora Alice Johnson. He was educated at Blees Military Academy and Missouri University. His first profession was as a racetrack jockey, but he thought that acting seemed easier so he joined a troupe of vaudeville minstrels in 1907. During World War I he served in the Navy. Afterwards he worked in stock and vaudeville both as a single act and in sketches. He made his Broadway debut in *Fair and Warmer* (1916) and his London West End debut in *Just Married* (1924). He went to Hollywood in 1934 where he made his first film, *Midnight*. Paramount signed him to a contract and he made nearly all his films there. His trademark was his inimitable singsong voice. He appeared in two other films with Raft, *Yours for the Asking* and *Spawn of the North*. He died in Santa Monica on February 19, 1943, after two heart attacks. He was married to Emily Helen Drange. His estate amounted to approximately £36,000.

Stolen Harmony (1935)

Cast: George Raft (Ray Angelo alias Ray Ferraro), Ben Bernie (Jack Conrad), Grace Bradley (Jean Loring), Iris Adrian (Sunny Verne), Lloyd Nolan (Chesty Burrage), Goodee Montgomery (Lil Davis), Charles Arnt (Clem Walters), William Cagney ("Schoolboy"), Leslie Fenton (Joe Harris), Paul Gerrits (Ted Webb), Ralf Harolde (Dude Williams), Jack Norton (Dick Philips), Robert Emmett O'Connor (Warden Clark), William Pawley (Turk Connors), Cully Richards (Pete, the Cabbie), Christian Rub (Mathew Huxley), Fred "Snowflake" Toones (Henry, the Bartender), Stanley Andrews (Patrol Chief), Earl Askam (State Trooper), Harry Bernard (Peanut Vendor), Jack Burnette (Pianist), Ruth Clifford (Nurse), Edgar Dearing (Motorcycle Cop), Eddie Dunn (Hotel Clerk), Kit Guard (Convict in Orchestra), Jack Herrick, Jack Perry, Eddie Magill (Prisoners), Carol Holloway (Mother of Six Kids), Ada Ince, Lois January, Adele Cutler Jerome, Margaret Nearing (Girls in Sextette), Jack Judge (Photographer), John Kelly (Bates, Prison Bandleader), James T. Mack (Pop, the Doorman), Arthur Millett (Deputy Sheriff), Jack Hill, Ted Oliver (Cops), Constantine Romanoff (Piccolo Player), Ernest Shields (Elevator Operator), Oscar Smith (Chimes Player in Prison), Eddie Sturgis (Musician), Ben Taggart (Sergeant, Cop at Motel), Billy Wilson (Sheriff), Duke York (Duke, Bus Driver). Cast of *Fagin Youse Is a Viper*: John "Dusty" King (Fagin), Frank Prince (Hero), Purv Pullen (Little Nell), Billy Wilson (Sheriff), Mickey Garlock (The Working Girl), Al Goering (Lady), Dick Stabile (Minister), Manny Prager (Nell's Father).

Credits: Director: Alfred L. Werker; Producer: Albert Lewis; Original Story: Leon Gordon and Harry Ruskin; Screenplay: Leon Gordon; Dialogue: Claude Binyon and Lewis R. Foster; Photography: Harry Fischbeck; Editor: Otto Lovering; Lyrics and Music: Mack Gordon and Harry Revel; Composer of Incidental Music: John Leipold; Dance Specialties: LeRoy Prinz; Art Direction: Hans Dreier and Bernard Herzbrun; Songs include "Would There Be Love," "Let's Spill the Beans," "I Never Had a Man to Cry Over" and "Fagin Youse a Viper." Released by Paramount on April 20, 1935. Black and white. 74 minutes.

Synopsis: Jack Conrad, leader of his own big band, is present at a jail where he sees an orchestra playing. He hires ex-con Ray Ferraro, who does the orchestrations, to play sax on a tour of the West. Knowing the problem his background could cause, Conrad changes his name to Ray Angelo. Conrad introduces him to Jean Loring, a hoofer and vocalist with the band. When her regular partner Ted Webb is unable to perform through drunkenness and is fired, Ferraro substitutes and promptly falls in love with Jean.

Ex-con Joe Harris, Ferraro's cellmate, catches up with Ferraro and tries to persuade him to rob the safe of the bus, but Ferraro wants nothing to do with it. Shortly afterwards the safe is robbed. Ferraro goes to a fleabag hotel where Harris has a room. A fight ensues in which Ferraro knocks Harris out and recovers the money. When a cop arrives, he finds Ferraro and the money, but Harris has fled. The cop takes Ferraro back to Conrad, who shows loyalty to Ferraro by accepting the recovered money and vouching for him to the police. Jean stands by him, but the rest of the band members ostracize him. Conrad tells Ferraro that it might be better for him to leave the bus at Kansas City. When Jean wants to accompany him since they are a team, Ferraro tells her to stay put.

When the bus gets a flat tire, an armed gang spots them and holds them up at gunpoint. Ferraro recognizes them as the Burrage gang, the most wanted gang in America. The gang hijacks the bus and takes the band to their hideout where they force Conrad and the rest of the band to perform for them. A police search is launched to find the missing bus and band. Ferraro pretends to join the Burrage gang and suggests to Burrage that to evade capture the gang all board the bus and, when stopped by police, pretend to be part of the band. When the bus is spotted, the police seek an explanation for their disappearance and give them an escort across the county line. The gang later commandeers a big car and, at Ferraro's suggestion, returns to Omaha with Ferraro at the wheel. En route Ferraro deliberately crashes the car and runs to a nearby police station, alerting them to the Burrage gang. A terrific gunfight ensues in which the gang are wiped out. In a radio broadcast, Conrad pays tribute to Ferraro's bravery while Ferraro is shown in hospital recovering from his wounds with the adoring Jean at his side.

Comments: This was the first and only time that Raft was directed by Alfred L. Werker. The movie contained some witty dialogue and elaborate musical numbers. It was the first of three Raft films in which Lloyd Nolan played a villain. The musical and crime elements in this film fused quite successfully. Raft and Grace Bradley were at their most charming and attractive. The show performed by the band was very typical of the period and was highlighted by a number with all the band members in costume for an operetta. Ben Bernie was the composer of "Sweet Georgia Brown" which ironically was Raft's signature tune although it was not performed in this film. Raft only did a few dance steps here for close-ups while the medium and long shots of the dance numbers were filmed using a double whose build did not match Raft's so the subterfuge was obvious. What does remain most vividly in the memory about this film was Conrad's incredible bus which the band used to travel to different locations! A recurring gag in the film was Clem Walters' pursuit of performer Lil Davis via taxi because he wants to marry her and settle down.

Biography: Alfred Lewis Werker was born in Deadwood, South Dakota, on December 2, 1896. He went to Hollywood in 1917 and entered the industry as a continuity clerk, became a prop man for the Mary Pickford unit and was then promoted to director. He signed a contract with Fox in 1928 and went on to direct a number of entertaining films. He retired from films after a clutch of minor Westerns in 1957. He died in Orange County, California, on July 28, 1975, aged 78.

Biography: Grace Bradley was born in Brooklyn, New York, on September 21, 1913. Her background was as a concert pianist. She was dancing in a New York night club when she attracted the attention of a Paramount talent scout who signed her to a contract in 1933. Although she continued to appear in comedies for Hal Roach until 1943, she largely gave up her career in 1937 when she married William Boyd of *Hopalong Cassidy* fame. After his death in 1972, she devoted much time

Raft and Grace Bradley in *Stolen Harmony*.

and effort to perpetuating his memory. As a member of the South Coast's Medical Center Foundation Board based in Laguna Beach she studied and taught Tai Chi. She died at Dana Point, California, on September 21, 2010, on her 97th birthday. She was interred with her husband at Forest Lawn Memorial Park in Glendale.

Biography: Ben Bernie was born Benjamin Anselvitz in Bayonne, New Jersey, on May 30, 1891. This bandleader's nickname was "The Old Maestro" and his sentimental signature tunes "It's a Lonesome Old Town" and "Au Revoir Pleasant Dreams" were catnip to audiences in the Depression. He was educated at New York College of Music, City College of New York and Columbia School of Mines. He gave up the study of engineering to become a violin salesman. In 1910 he made his vaudeville debut as an accordion player and in 1922 scored a hit in New York as an orchestra leader. His dance band had long runs in major hotels and on radio during the years between 1931 and 1941. He also had a mock feud for years with Walter Winchell. He divorced his wife Rose in 1935; they had one child. He died in Beverly Hills on October 20, 1943, aged 52, after a lingering illness.

Biography: Lloyd Nolan was born in San Francisco, California, on August 11, 1902, the son of James Charles Nolan, a shoe manufacturer from Ireland, and Margaret Elizabeth Shea. He graduated from Santa Clara Preparatory School and studied English at Stanford University, but was forced to drop out after flunking his first year exams. He entered show business in 1924 and scored a notable Broadway hit in *One Sunday Afternoon* in 1933. Paramount signed him to a contract and he made his screen debut in *Stolen Harmony*. He went on to amass a huge number of film credits notably at 20th Century–Fox. In the fifties he returned to the stage, scoring a success in *The Caine Mutiny Court-Martial.* He also starred in three television series: *Martin Kane, Private Investigator, Special Agent 7* and *Julia.*

He died in Los Angeles on September 27, 1985, aged 83, of respiratory arrest and lung cancer. He married Mary Mell Efird in 1933 and they remained wed until she died in 1981. With her he had a daughter (born in 1941) and a son (1943–1969). He subsequently married Virginia Dabney who survived him. He appeared in two other films starring Raft, *She Couldn't Take It* and *The House Across the Bay.*

The Glass Key (1935)

Cast: George Raft (Ed Beaumont), Edward Arnold (Paul Madwig), Claire Dodd (Janet Henry), Rosalind Keith [Culli] (Opal "Snip" Madwig), Charles Richman (Senator Henry), Robert Gleckler (Shad O'Rory), Guinn Williams (Jeff), Ray Milland (Taylor Henry), Tammany Young (Clarkie), Harry Tyler (Henry Sloss), Charles Wilson (D.A. Farr), Emma Dunn (Mom), Matt McHugh (Puggy), Pat Moriarity (Mulrooney), Mack Gray (Duke), Ann Sheridan (Nurse), Irving Bacon (Waiter), Vera Buckland (Landlady), Alfred Delcambre (Reporter), George Ernest (Boy), Herbert Evans (Senator Henry's Butler), George Lloyd (Hood), Michael Mark (Swartz), Frank Marlowe (Walter Ivans), Percy Morris (Bartender), Frank O'Connor (McLaughlin), George Reed (Black Servant), Henry Roquemore (Rinkle), Phillips Smalley (Man in Barber Chair), Kathrin Clare Ward (Gossip).

Credits: Director: Frank Tuttle; Producer: E. Lloyd Sheldon; Executive Producer: Henry Herzbrun; Assistant Director: Russell Mathews; Based on the novel by Dashiell Hammett; Screenplay: Kathryn Scola and Kubec Glasmon; Additional Dialogue: Harry Ruskin; Photography: Henry Sharp; Editor: Hugh Bennett; Original Music: Heinz Roemheld, John Leipold and Tom Satterfield; Art Direction: Hans Dreier and A. Earl Hedrick; Sound Recorder: Jack Goodrich. Released by Paramount on June 15, 1935. Black and white. 80 minutes.

Tagline: "He carries his love in his iron fists."

Synopsis: Widower Paul Madwig is a political fixer backing the re-election of Senator Henry and intends to marry Henry's daughter Janet. When Paul's daughter Opal Madwig borrows $300 from Ed Beaumont, Madwig's number one lieutenant, Beaumont becomes suspicious and follows her. She goes to a hotel and gives the money to Taylor Henry, son of Senator Henry, whom she believes is in love with her. Taylor Henry needs the money to repay a gambling debt to Shad O'Rory, saloon owner, racketeer and inveterate enemy of Paul Madwig. Beaumont turns up and insists on taking Opal home over Taylor's objections. Paul Madwig has forbidden her to see Taylor and is furious about her disobedience. Madwig goes to the Senator's home to break up the relationship.

Later, walking at night, Beaumont comes upon the body of Taylor Henry. Beaumont returns to Madwig's house and tells him that Taylor is dead. Shad O'Rory arranges for Henry Sloss, another enemy of Paul Madwig, to go to the police and claim that he saw Madwig having a violent argument with Taylor Henry at the scene of the crime. D.A. Farr tells Beaumont that he intends to indict Madwig for murder. Beaumont and Madwig go to one of the saloons owned by O'Rory where they row in public, leading Beaumont to slug Madwig. In disgust Beaumont leaves Madwig's employ. The information is conveyed to O'Rory who invites Beaumont to see him. O'Rory tells him that he will stake him to a fine gambling house if Beaumont will join his team. When O'Rory informs him that Henry Sloss is the witness who went to the police, Beaumont tells him that Sloss is unreliable. After O'Rory produces Sloss's affidavit, Beaumont reveals that he is still loyal to Madwig by throwing the affidavit in the fire. When Beaumont tries to leave, he is attacked by O'Rory's dog.

Beaumont is taken to a secret address where he is knocked unconscious and held prisoner by O'Rory's thuggish henchman, Jeff. Even though he is badly hurt, Beaumont manages to make good his escape by starting a fire. In the hospital, Beaumont tells Madwig that Sloss is the witness and that Madwig needs to reach him and silence him. Madwig finds Sloss and by a mixture of threats and bribery persuades him to leave town.

When this is reported in the newspapers, public opinion turns against Madwig. Janet Henry, believing Madwig to be guilty, pretends to befriend Opal and takes her to the Senator's house where they intend to trick her into making an accusation against Paul. Beaumont is able to prevent this by slugging Opal. When Sloss is murdered, Beaumont goes back to the location he previously escaped from, where Jeff invites him to have a private drink prior to beating him up again. Beaumont's idea is to ply Jeff with liquor to

Raft and Edward Arnold in *The Glass Key*.

make him drunk enough to tell the truth. Before he can put this plan into action, O'Rory turns up. When Jeff blurts out that he killed Sloss, he and O'Rory brawl and Jeff kills O'Rory.

When D.A. Farr arranges to call all the witnesses together, Beaumont manages to obtain a cane from Senator Henry's house. The cap of the cane was recently changed because the original was bloodstained and found at the scene of the crime. This reveals that the murderer of Taylor Henry was Senator Henry, who killed his son with the cane after a violent argument. This satisfies D.A. Farr regarding both murders. Once Paul Madwig is cleared, Beaumont and Opal Madwig go out on a date.

Comments: This was the first of two films in which Raft was directed by Frank Tuttle. It was the first version of a fine, hardboiled novel by Dashiell Hammett and represented the only time Raft played a Hammett hero. A splendidly sinister figure whether planning strategy or networking, Raft was in exactly the right milieu. Raft met Hammett when the author visited the set while the film was in production. The "glass key" of the title was a figure of speech referring to the close relationship between Madwig and Senator Henry which might shatter at any time. The film was remade in 1942. Contemporary thinking is that the original was a straightforward thriller, while the remake was a film noir. This is because the Raft version lacked a femme fatale and the perverted edge which were present in the latter version.

The original film was greatly enhanced by brisk direction and snappy dialogue. The car crash which opened the film is still genuinely shocking. The film was made highly watchable by such touches as odd camera angles, stark shadows and a swinging lamp while a murder was being committed. There were also a couple of well-shot montages where members of the general public questioned Paul Madwig. The main theme of the film was loyalty in that Raft was totally loyal to Arnold even when the audience was led to believe that he had changed

sides. Raft was prepared to take a savage beating at the hands of the sadistic Guinn Williams to find out the truth. The leading male players were uniformly fine. The leading actresses were competent rather than outstanding, but Ann Sheridan had a memorable bit as a hospital nurse. This film was one of Raft's biggest box office hits of the thirties.

Biography: Frank Tuttle was born in New York City on August 6, 1892. He was educated at Yale University where he was at one time president of the Yale Dramatic Society and thus gained his first experience of theatricals. Originally he was assistant editor of *Vanity Fair* magazine and a publicist. His screen career began as a continuity writer for Paramount in the twenties. After a while he organized the Film Guild and directed five films. Returning to Paramount, this time as a full-fledged director, he handled a number of films efficiently. During the McCarthy era he was called before the House UnAmerican Activities Committee where he admitted to past membership in the Communist Party and denounced many of his colleagues as fellow travelers. This combined with his propensity for alcohol caused his fall from grace and, although he was never officially blacklisted, his career declined precipitously. He was married three times. He died at Mount Sinai Hospital in Hollywood on January 6, 1963, aged 70, after a heart attack.

Biography: Edward Arnold was born Guenther Schneider in New York City on February 18, 1890. At ten he was an orphan living in a New York tenement. He had jobs in a meat market and jewelry store until sent to school at the East Side Settlement House where he had his first experience of acting in *The Merchant of Venice* as Lorenzo. In 1907 he appeared on stage with Ethel Barrymore in *Dream of a Summer Night*. In 1915 he signed a contract with Essanay in Chicago and appeared in many Western two-reelers. He played supporting roles in a number of features before returning to the stage between 1919 and 1931. In 1932 he returned to Hollywood and went on to appear in over a hundred films, initially as a star. His film *Sutter's Gold* (1936) was one of the most costly flops in Hollywood history so he morphed into a star character actor. He was particularly good in two films directed by Frank Capra, *You Can't Take It with You* (1938) and *Mr. Smith Goes to Washington* (1939). Many of his best films date from his longterm contract with MGM during the forties. The fact that he was never Oscar-nominated was a dreadful oversight. He died in Encino, California, on April 26, 1956, aged 66, after a cerebral hemorrhage. He married three times and had three children.

Biography: Claire Dodd was born Dorothy Ann Dodd in Des Moines, Iowa, on December 29, 1908, the daughter of Walter Dodd and Ethel Cool. She was raised in Little Rock, Arkansas. Her father abandoned the family when Claire was ten. She left school in her teens, had a number of jobs and struggled in the Depression. She was working as a model when she was spotted by a talent scout, brought to Hollywood and given a screen test. Sam Goldwyn liked the test and cast her as a showgirl in *Whoopee* (1930). She joined Florenz Ziegfeld's *Smiles* on Broadway and then signed with Paramount. In films she frequently played "the other woman." She married and divorced Jack Milton Strauss, with whom she had a son. In 1940 she married H. Brand Cooper, with whom she had three more sons and a daughter. She retired in 1942. She died in Beverly Hills on November 23, 1973, aged 64, of cancer.

Biography: Rosalind Keith was born Rosalind Culli in Belleville, Illinois, on December 6, 1916. She began her career when only five years of age playing in local companies and then joined a professional company, the Kendall Players. Paramount spotted her when she appeared in a Hollywood presentation and gave her a contract. She retired from films in 1944 and went with her husband to live at Oak Hill Farm in Glenwood, Arkansas. She died in Glenwood on February 24, 2000, aged 83.

Every Night at Eight (1935)

Cast: George Raft ("Tops" Cardona), Alice Faye (Dixie Foley aka Dixie Dean), Frances Langford (Susan Moore), Patsy Kelly (Daphne O'Connor), Walter Catlett (Colonel Day, Master of Ceremonies), Harry Barris (Harry), Herman Bing (Joe Schmidt), Boothe Howard (Martin), John Dilson (Huxley), Louise Carver (Mrs. Snyder), Ted Fio Rito (Leader of Ted Fio Rito Orchestra), Henry Taylor, Jimmie Hollywood, Eddie Bartel (Three Radio Rogues), Florence Roberts (Mrs. Murgatroyd), Claude Allister (Rich Bore), Herbert Ashley (Piano Remover), Lynton Brent (Mail Sorter), Stephen Chase (Barrymore), Eddie Conrad (The Bewildered Baritone), Phyllis Crane (Telephone Operator), Eddie Fetherston (Gold Strike Cigarettes Ad Man), Charles Forsythe (Sound Effects Man), Nina Gilbert (Chief Operator), Florence Gill (Henrietta, Chicken Lady Singer), Gertie Green (Telephone Operator), Harry Holman (Colonel from Jacksonville), Louise Larabee (New Employee), James Miller (Singer), Dillon Ober (Drummer in Band), Richard Powell (Sailor).

Credits: Director: Raoul Walsh; Producer: Walter Wanger; Assistant Director: Eric Stacey; Based on the Story "Three on a Mike" by Stanley Garvey; Screenplay: Gene Towne and C. Graham Baker; Additional Dialogue: Bert Hanlon; Photography: James Van Trees; Editor: W. Donn Hayes; Original Music: Frederick Hollander, Paul Mertz and Clifford Vaughan; Musical Arranger: Paul Mertz; Musical Setting: S.K. Wineland; Art Direction: Alexander Toluboff; Sound: Hugo Grenzbach; Costumes: Helen Taylor. Songs: "I Feel a Song Comin' On" by Dorothy Fields and George Oppenheimer, sung by Alice Faye; "I'm in the Mood for Love" by Dorothy Fields and Jimmy McHugh, sung by Frances Langford; "Take It Easy," "Speaking Confidentially" and "Every Night at Eight" by Dorothy Fields and Jimmy McHugh; "Then You've Never Been Blue" by Ted Fio Rito, Joe Young and Frances Langford.

Left to right: Raft, Alice Faye, Patsy Kelly and Frances Langford in *Every Night at Eight*.

Released by Paramount on August 2, 1935. Black and white. 80 minutes.

Synopsis: Three talented amateur singers, Dixie, Susan and Daphne, work as a secretary and switchboard operators for Huxley's Mint Julep Company, but are fired for insubordination by Colonel Huxley himself. Desperate, they enter an amateur radio contest. Although they lose because Susan collapses from hunger, they team up with eventual winner "Tops" Cardona, leader of an orchestra made up of tradesmen. He reinvents them as the "The Three Swanee Sisters" from way down south. Initially they sing for Joe Schmidt in his cafe but graduate to radio, creating a sensation and ironically being sponsored by Colonel Huxley's Mint Julep Company. They sing in the studio every night at eight.

Susan falls in love with the arrogant Cardona, who has become a control freak. When an ignorant society matron invites them to meet bluebloods aboard a boat and take them for a three-day cruise, the girls stage a rebellion against Cardona and accept. Once a radio broadcast of their show begins without them, the girls realize their place is with "Tops" and the common people rather than with society snobs so they abandon the party and head for the studio where they arrive just in time for the end of the show. Susan professes her love for "Tops" on radio via the song, "I'm in the Mood for Love." In turn he realizes that he is no good without them and they save him from becoming "Flops" Cardona.

Comments: This was the second of five Raft features directed by Raoul Walsh. It was an atypical film from this director, who was usually associated with vigorous action. This was a modest but highly entertaining musical which benefited from good songs and plenty of repartee. During the singing on the wireless of the number "I Feel a Song Comin' On," Raft did some very fancy footwork while conducting the orchestra, a feat which could only be appreciated by a movie audience, not by a radio one. One rather intriguing aspect of this movie was that Frances Langford (billed fourth in the opening credits, but third in the closing credits) provided the romantic interest with Raft rather than the expected Alice Faye–George Raft combination. Faye agreed to wear a black wig in order to look like Frances Langford and Patsy Kelly, but her home studio 20th Century–Fox did not want her screen image as a blonde changing. Consequently, this idea was relegated to a joke in the middle of one scene with the final words of Raft, "I changed my mind, turn her back and make her a blonde!" This film was a box office success.

Biography: Alice Faye was born Alice Jeanne Leppert in Hell's Kitchen, New York City, on May 5, 1912. She was educated at P.S. 84 and after training under Chester Hale she became a chorine in clubs. She acquired her stage name from comedian Frank Fay. While appearing in *George White's Scandals*, she was spotted by its star Rudy Vallee who signed her as lead singer on his radio show and band tours. In 1934 she and Vallee appeared together in a screen version of *Scandals of 1934*. This led to a contract at Fox.

Twentieth Century–Fox hit on a winning formula for musicals. With Faye as star, movies such as *Alexander's Ragtime Band* (1938) and *Hello Frisco Hello* (1943) were smash hits for the studio. When she tried to turn dramatic with the film noir *Fallen Angel* (1945), she so loathed the result that she walked out on the studio and her contract. She was married to Tony Martin from 1937 until their divorce in 1940. She then married Phil Harris in 1941. With him she had a stepson, Phil Jr., and two daughters: Alice, born in 1942, and Phyllis, born in 1944. She was widowed in 1995. With her second husband she did a network radio show from 1948 to 1954 which sustained her

popularity. She lived for years in Rancho Mirage, California, on the grounds of the Thunderbird Country Club. She died in Rancho Mirage on May 9, 1998, aged 86, of stomach cancer.

Biography: Frances Langford was born in Lakeland, Florida, on April 4, 1913, the daughter of Vasco Langford and Ann Newbern. She was educated at Southern College, Florida, where she majored in music. She sang on a local Tampa radio show where she was heard by Rudy Vallee, who introduced her on his national radio show. In 1933 she made her Broadway debut in *Here Goes the Bride* and was signed to a film contract by Walter Wanger. *Every Night at Eight* was her debut film and she went on to appear in nearly 30 others. She became a major radio star, notably on the shows of Bob Hope, and in 1938 she was voted America's No. 1 female singer. During World War II she accompanied Hope on his tours of the war zones where she became known as "Sweetheart of the Fighting Forces."

She and Don Ameche co-hosted two early television series and she starred in a couple of prime time specials in 1959 and 1960. By the end of the decade she had virtually retired to Florida and ownership of a coastal resort restaurant and nightclub called The Outrigger where she occasionally sang. She died at Jenson Beach, Florida, on July 11, 2005, aged 92. She was married first to Jon Hall from 1938 until their divorce in 1955, secondly to Ralph Evinrude, outboard motor magnate, from 1955 until she was widowed in 1986, and third to Harold Stuart in 1994, who survived her. She had no children.

Biography: Patsy Kelly was born Bridget Veronica Kelly in Brooklyn, New York, on January 12, 1910. She was a dance teacher for three years before she went on the stage. She began as a chorus girl at the Palace Theatre, then became the stooge of comedian Frank Fay in his act; afterwards she was a featured comedienne in Broadway shows. She was brought by Hal Roach to Hollywood where she made her screen debut in *Going Hollywood* (1933) and spent a decade as a wisecracking supporting actress whose name was sometimes worth more than the nominal star of a feature. She also made a series of hilarious two-reelers partnered with Thelma Todd and later Lyda Roberti. During the early forties she was in a sanitarium for several weeks according to different sources to cure a drink problem or for obesity. When she returned, she found the film industry closed to her and survived by making radio and later television appearances and a role in stock productions of *Dear Charles* provided by a close friend, Tallulah Bankhead. She made a film comeback in *Please Don't Eat the Daisies* (1960) and a spectacular return to Broadway in *No, No, Nanette* (1971) for which she won a Tony award as the tap-dancing maid. She resided for many years in a Hollywood apartment. She died at the Motion Picture Country Home and Hospital in Woodland Hills, California, on September 24, 1981, aged 71, of cancer following a stroke. She never married.

She Couldn't Take It
(U.K.: *Woman Tamer*) (1935)

Cast: George Raft (Joe "Spot" Ricardi/Joe Rickett), Joan Bennett (Carol Van Dyke), Walter Connolly (Dan Van Dyke), Billie Burke (Mrs. Van Dyke), Lloyd Nolan (Tex), Wallace Ford ("Fingers" Boston), James Blakeley (Tony Van Dyke), Alan Mowbray (Alan "Ham" Barlett), William Tannen (Cesar), Donald Meek (Uncle), Stanley Andrews (Wyndersham), Frank Austin (Railroad Attendant), Irving Bacon (Man at Toll Gate), Wyrley Birch (Dr. Schaeffer), Frank Conroy (Frank Raleigh), Kernan Cripps (Guard), Peppino Dallalic (Don), Jack Duffy, James B. Kenton, Victor Potel (Farmers), Frank Fanning (Warden), Mack Gray (Ike), Eddie Gribbon (Detective), Jack Holmes (Prison Doctor), Maynard Holmes (Edgar), Olaf Hytten (Butler), John Ince (Prison Official), Thomas E. Jackson, Harrison Greene (Spielers), Tom Kennedy (Slugs), Donald Kerr (Sailor), Mike Lally, W.E. Lawrence (Photographers), Ivan Lebedeff (Count), Maxine Lewis (Crooner), George Lloyd (Turnkey), George McKay (Red), Robert Middlemass (Desk Sergeant), Joseph North (Butler), Franklin Pangborn (Secretary), Lee Phelps (Bailiff), Lon Poff (Judge), John Quillan (Bellboy), Frank Rice (Milkman), Loren Riebe (Human Fly), Ted Oliver, Ky Robinson (Motorcycle Cops), Philip Ronalde (Waiter), Oscar Rudolph (Newsboy), Henry Sylvester (Stage Manager), Ray Turner (Janitor), Walter Walker (Judge), George Webb (Editor), Huey White (Eddie Gore), C.A. Beckman, James P. Burtis (Traffic Cops), Jack Daley, Edgar Dearing, Gene Morgan (District Attorney's Men), Charles Sherlock, Antrim Short, Emmett Vogan, Billy West (Reporters), Stark Bishop, Joe Clive, Tom Costello, James Harrison, Stanley Mack, Al Ferguson, Frank LaRue, Frank Marlowe, Walter Perry, Robert Wilber (Prisoners).

Credits: Director: Tay Garnett; Producer: B.P. Schulberg; Original Story: Gene Towne and C. Graham Baker; Screenplay: Oliver H.P. Garrett; Photography: Leon Shamroy; Editor: Gene Havlick; Original Music: Howard Jackson and Louis Silvers; Art Direction: Stephen Goosson; Sound Recorder: Edward Bernds. Released by Columbia on October 8, 1935. Black and white. 77 minutes.

Synopsis: The wealthy Van Dyke family is constantly in the news for their outrageous behavior and extravagance much to the annoyance of family head Dan Van Dyke. His self-centered airhead wife has a fondness for foreign imports and his spoiled children, Tony and Carol, have constant run-ins with the law. When Dan himself ends up with a five-year prison term for income tax evasion, he becomes cellmates with ex-bootlegger Joe "Spot" Ricardi. Ricardi lectures Dan on his lack of control over such a family so a dying Dan makes him sole trustee of his estate. Shortly afterwards, Dan takes his last breath.

After his release from prison, Ricardi meets

his old pal "Fingers" Boston and other former members of his mob, now headed by Tex. They want him to become involved in a kidnapping racket, but Ricardi refuses. Carol Van Dyke, under the guise of a reporter, goes to see Ricardi to find out what his plans are for the family. Carol makes a slip and Ricardi realizes her true identity. He calls a press conference where he announces that Carol has split from her worthless longtime fiancé, actor Alan "Ham" Barlett. At a dinner party, Carol repudiates this. They all go to Coney Island where Carol proudly shows reporters the car, formerly owned by Ricardi, which she is going to drive when she marries Alan. To prevent this, Ricardi drives away in the car with Carol. In the middle of nowhere, Ricardi lets the car roll off a cliff so he and Carol are forced to walk.

Ricardi and his friends intimidate Barlett until he flees the altar. Carol files suit against Ricardi wanting to have him removed as trustee.

Carol sends for Tex and his gang, intending that they should pretend to kidnap her so that Ricardi will have to pay a ransom which they will share. A ransom note is delivered to Mrs. Van Dyke with instructions. Believing that he is involved with the kidnappers, the police pursue Ricardi. "Fingers" tells Carol that Tex and the gang are going to keep the ransom money and murder her instead. For this, Tex shoots "Fingers" in cold blood and, after picking up the ransom, the gang leaves his body at the collection point as a warning to Ricardi.

Ricardi finds that "Fingers" has left a message alerting him to the whereabouts of Carol, but warning him not to pay the ransom because Carol will be killed. Before Ricardi can act, he is picked up by the police. He manages to gain control of the car and leaves them behind. Other police pick up his trail, but are delayed by a train. Ricardi reaches the hideout where he pretends to have the police with him. The gang, except for Tex, all flee and are soon

Lloyd Nolan and Raft in *She Couldn't Take It*.

arrested by the police. Tex surprises Ricardi at gunpoint, but Ricardi sees his reflection in a mirror and shoots him. Ricardi and the Van Dyke family are reunited with Carol.

Comments: This was the first and only time that Raft was directed by Tay Garnett. Raft and Joan Bennett developed such a rapport with Garnett that he later said his most abiding recollection of this film was that it gave him a lifelong friendship with both of them. Raft made this Columbia film on loanout from his home studio. It was the second of the four times that he appeared with Joan Bennett, but the previous time she was the star and he was playing a bit, whereas now they had equal billing. It was the second of three Raft films in which Lloyd Nolan played a villain.

This film was intended by Columbia to be similar to their runaway success *It Happened One Night* (1934), and it was meant to fall into the subgenre known as screwball comedy highlighted by the madcap police car chases which occurred at both the start and end. This film was nowhere near as good as its classic predecessor. The comedy and criminal elements did not jell into a satisfactory whole. For the first hour the comedy elements prevailed. After that, the film took a most unpleasant turn. Most of the plot complications were not in the least bit funny. In particular, the killing of "Fingers" was vicious. The kidnapping of the Lindbergh baby had only happened a few years earlier and kidnapping, whether of an infant or an adult, was certainly not a subject for levity.

One of the fundamentals of good scriptwriting is that one or more of the characters in a film has to have an experience which shifts the relationships and leads to some kind of change within the character as a direct result of the drama. At the end of this movie, there was no indication that the largely worthless Van Dykes, and in particular Carol, have learned anything. Although he had a sense of humor in real life and appeared in one landmark comedy film, *Some Like It Hot*, comedy was a genre to which Raft was most ill-suited. He seemed much more at home in the serious parts of the film.

Biography: Tay Garnett was born in Los Angeles on June 13, 1894. He served as a flight instructor with the Naval Air Service in San Diego during World War I. During a training flight he suffered an injury which left him with a permanent limp. His service lasted until 1922 during which he was assigned to write and stage shows for servicemen. Upon his discharge he gravitated to Hollywood where he found temporary employment as a gagman and later scriptwriter for Hal Roach and other comedy producers. He became a director in 1928 and helmed some excellent films for Paramount, Warner Bros. and MGM. He later became a prolific television director. He was married three times: to Patsy Ruth Miller, Helga Moray and Mari Aldon. He died in Sawtelle, California, on October 3, 1977, aged 83, from leukemia.

Biography: Joan Geraldine Bennett was born in Palisades, New Jersey, on February 27, 1910, the daughter of Richard Bennett and Adrienne Morrison. Her two sisters Constance and Barbara both became well-known actresses. She was educated privately and at boarding schools in Connecticut and France. She made her Broadway debut opposite her father in *Jarnegan*. While appearing in this play she was seen by Samuel Goldwyn and brought to Hollywood where she made her screen debut in *Bulldog Drummond* (1929). In 1931 she signed a two-year contract with Fox. She went on to star in numerous films over the next twenty years, many of them produced by her third husband Walter Wanger. She featured in one major scandal on December 13, 1951, when a jealous Wanger, believing that she was having an affair with her agent Jennings Lang, shot him in the groin. In 1952 Wanger was imprisoned for four months. In 1953 she returned to the stage in two national touring companies. Between 1966 and 1970 she was the star of the daytime television serial *Dark Shadows*. She died at her Scarsdale, New York, home on December 7, 1990, aged 80, of a heart attack. She married four times and had four children. She appeared with Raft in three other films: *Hush Money, The House Across the Bay* and *Nob Hill.*

It Had to Happen (1936)

Cast: George Raft (Enrico Scaffa), Rosalind Russell (Beatrice Newnes), Leo Carrillo (Guiseppe Badjagaloupe), Arline Judge (Miss Sullivan), Alan Dinehart (Rodman Drake), Andrew Tombes (Dooley), Arthur Hohl (Honest John Pelkey), Paul Stanton (Mayor John Trotter), Pierre Watkin (District Attorney), Stanley Fields (Mug), George Irving (Foreman of Grand Jury), Thomas E. Jackson (Joe, Mayor's Secretary), Harry C. Bradley (Beatrice's Secretary), Clay Clement (Joe McCloskey, Scaffa's Attorney), Paul Hurst (Aggressive Workman), Lynn Bari (Voice of Secretary), George Bookasta (Italian Boy), Tommy Bupp (Shoe Shine Boy), James Burke (Ditch Foreman), Wallis Clark (Immigration Officer), John Dilson (Juror), Pauline Garon (French Maid), Herbert Heywood (Trainer), John Hyams (Man in Café), Edward Keane (Politician), Charles Lane (State Examiner Hillburn), Lou Loy (Chinese Man), Matt McHugh (Elevator Man on Ship), Frank Meredith (Motorcycle Cop), Torben Meyer (Sign Painter), John Kelly, Frank Moran (Moving Men), James C. Morton (Bartender), Robert Emmett O'Connor (Policeman), Inez Palange (Italian Mother), John Sheehan (Mark Cooper, Pelkey's Secretary), Harry Stubbs (Bailiff), Ben Taggart (New York Cop), Ray Turner (Zeke), Lloyd Whitlock (Man in Café), Jack Curtis, G. Pat Collins, Jimmie Dundee, Ben Hendricks, Jr., Harry Woods (Workmen), Franklyn Ardell, Sam Ash, Jack Hatfield, J. Anthony Hughes, Cully Richards, Emmett Vogan (Reporters).

Credits: Director: Roy Del Ruth; Producer: Darryl F. Zanuck; Associate Producer: Raymond Griffith; Assistant Director: Ben Silvey; Based on the Story "Canavan, The Man Who Had His Way" by Rupert Hughes; Screenplay: Kathryn Scola and Howard Ellis Smith; Photography: J. Peverell Marley; Editor: Allen McNeil; Original Music: Arthur Lange; Art Direction: Hans Peters; Costumes: Gwen Wakeling; Sound Recorders: Eugene Grossman and Roger Heman; Released by 20th Century–Fox on February 15, 1936. Black and white. 79 minutes.

Synopsis: Beatrice Newnes, "the richest girl in the world," is returning to the United States aboard an Italian ship. To avoid reporters, she descends to steerage and makes her exit. While there, she is seen by two Italian immigrants, Enrico Scaffa and Guiseppe Badjagaloupe. Flat broke in New York, they are reduced to standing in line waiting to be hired to dig ditches. When they show the superintendent a letter addressed to "Honest John" Pelkey, he hires them immediately.

While Scaffa is at work, he is given a red flag with which he can control traffic, giving him an illustration of what power means. Among the vehicles he stops are ones carrying Beatrice Newnes and the mayor of New York. When the foreman comes to the scene and threatens Scaffa for holding up the mayor, an enraged Scaffa slugs him, much to the amusement of the mayor. The foreman fires both Scaffa and Badjagaloupe. The mayor sends for Scaffa and expresses admiration for his courage in not being pushed around. He appoints him at $35 a week as one of his assistants.

Over the next four years Scaffa rises to become an ombudsman and powerbroker helping many needy people. When the Eastside Branch of the Hudson Investment Trust runs into financial trouble, the books are confiscated for an audit by the state examiner. The trust is headed by Rodman Drake, husband of Beatrice Newnes. Scaffa summons the district attorney and asks him to convene the grand jury so that if there is a political scandal, he wants indictments against all of those involved. Scaffa tells Rodman and Beatrice Drake that Rodman is going to be indicted unless he refunds $4 million to the investors who lost money. Scaffa summons "Honest John" Pelkey to his office. Pelkey has been collecting donations for a new hospital amounting to $15,000, but kept $4,000 of it for his own use. Scaffa gives him two weeks to return the money which earns him Pelkey's enmity. Beatrice goes to see Scaffa and gives him $4 million to make good the deficit. Rodman Drake flees to Cuba in case Scaffa cannot prevent an indictment. In his absence, Scaffa goes to Saratoga where he romances Beatrice Drake, who is there for the races.

Ignorant of this, Rodman comes back from Cuba to the hotel in Saratoga where Beatrice is staying. Beatrice confronts Rodman, tells him that she is in love with Scaffa and wants a divorce. In light of the potential scandal, he begs her to remain with him. Beatrice sees Scaffa and tells him that Rodman has returned and that she has agreed not to divorce him for a few months. In the meantime she tells Scaffa they had better not see one another. "Honest John" Pelkey goes to see Rodman Drake and browbeats him into admitting that he has given Scaffa $4 million to make good the investment company loss. As proof, Drake gives

Pelkey the cablegram from Scaffa telling him he can now return from Cuba. Pelkey lies to Rodman that Scaffa has kept the money for himself. Beatrice goes to Scaffa and asks what happened to the money. Scaffa assures her that he found a way to place the $4 million in the Hudson Trust account. Beatrice tells Scaffa that she now wants to divorce Rodman and marry him.

Scaffa receives a call from Miss Sullivan, his secretary, telling him that the D.A.'s men are in his office going through his files. Scaffa tells her he is returning to New York. Once there he learns the D.A. has turned the cablegram over to the grand jury. Scaffa is urged by his attorney to flee to Canada because he has committed a felony. Beatrice urges him to confront the grand jury because he has done nothing wrong. Appearing before the grand jury, he is able to prove that the $4 million was deposited in the account of Hudson Trust and there was no deficit or bribery. On the strength of this, the grand jury investigation is discontinued and no charges are brought against Scaffa. On the way out, he knocks Pelkey cold. A determined Scaffa then tells Beatrice that he loves her and that he has chartered a plane so they can fly to Reno where she can obtain a divorce and marry him.

Comments: This was the third time Raft was directed by Roy Del Ruth. The previous times he only had bit parts, but now he was the star. This film marked another of Raft's loanouts, this time to the newly formed 20th Century–Fox studio. This was a highly entertaining film similar in theme to those which were being directed by Frank Capra around the same time in that it dealt with one in-

Rosalind Russell and Raft in *It Had to Happen*.

corruptible individual versus big business interests. In light of all the recent scandals involving financial institutions, it is also quite relevant to modern times. The plot development was enthralling throughout, leading up to a satisfying dénouement before the grand jury.

Raft was accused of taking a massive bribe, but although not guilty of this, he was taking a considerable risk in becoming involved with Russell. What made her attractive to Raft was that she came from the opposite end of the social scale. This kind of relationship does happen in real life and their relationship and love for each other was credible. Although Russell was one of the classiest actresses Raft ever worked with, it was his scenes with sexy, sassy Arline Judge as his secretary which had spontaneity and sparkle. One example of her spunk was where Judge proved to be as tough as the guys who came to confiscate Raft's files by punching one of them out. One of her most amusing scenes was where, despite Raft's orders, she delayed Russell from entering his office and Raft gives Judge a light tap on the head for her cheek! Actually it might have been more realistic if Raft had ended up marrying Judge in this film. *It Had to Happen* was a box office hit and deserves to be better remembered.

Biography: Roy Del Ruth was born Roy Morgan in Delaware, Michigan, on October 18, 1887. He was educated at schools in Philadelphia, Williamsport and Brooklyn. He lived in London for a time, then returned to America and went into journalism. His film career began in 1915 as a scenarist with Mack Sennett. In 1917 he began directing two-reelers. Graduating to features in 1925, he became an efficient studio director mainly at Warner Bros. and MGM. He is frequently cited as a solid craftsman whose career flourished under the studio system, then went steadily downhill as a freelance. He died at his home in Sherman Oaks, California, on April 27, 1961, aged 73, after a heart attack. He was survived by his widow, actress Winnie Lightner, whom he wed in 1934, and by two sons, one of whom, Thomas Del Ruth, became a distinguished cinematographer.

Biography: Rosalind Russell was born in Waterbury, Connecticut, on June 4, 1907, the daughter of trial lawyer James Edward Russell and Clara McKnight. She was educated at Marymount College in Tarrytown, New York, and the American Academy of Dramatic Arts. She commenced her career with two stock companies, one at Saranac Lake, New York, and the other E.E. Clive's stock company in Boston. In 1930 she made her Broadway debut in *The Garrick Gaieties*. She originally went to Hollywood to be screen-tested by Universal, but when they hesitated she signed a contract with MGM in 1934 as a possible threat to Myrna Loy. She made her screen debut in *Evelyn Prentice* (1934). She went on to receive Best Actress Oscar nominations for *My Sister Eileen* (1942), *Mourning Becomes Electra* (1947) and *Auntie Mame* (1958), but did not win on any occasion. Her health began to fail from 1960 onwards. She eventually died in Los Angeles on November 28, 1976, aged 69, of cancer. In 1941 she married Frederick Brisson, who survived her along with a son named Lance, who was born in 1943.

Yours for the Asking (1936)

Cast: George Raft (Johnny Lamb), Dolores Costello Barrymore (Lucille Sutton), Ida Lupino (Gert Malloy/Nancy Carstairs), Reginald Owen (Dictionary McKinney/Colonel Evelyn Carstairs), James Gleason (Saratoga), Edgar Kennedy (Bicarbonate), Lynne Overman (Honeysuckle), Richard "Skeets" Gallagher (Perry Barnes), Walter Walker (Mr. Crenshaw), Robert Gleckler (Slick Doran), Richard Powell (Benedict), Betty Blythe (May), Harry C. Bradley (Art Dealer), John Byron (Chauffeur), Keith Daniels (Henchman), Huntley Gordon (Clark Bering), Arthur Stuart Hull (Deaf Mute), Louis Natheaux (Dealer), Albert Pollet

(Headwaiter), Ralph Remley (O'Rorke), Charles Requa (Mr. Ames), Henry Roquemore (Pot-bellied Man), Max Barwyn, Edward Peil, Jr., Francis Sayles (Waiters).

Credits: Director: Alexander Hall; Producer: Lewis E. Gensler; Assistant Director: James Dugan; Original Story: William R. Lipman and William H. Wright; Screenplay: Eve Greene, Harlan Ware and Philip MacDonald; Photography: Theodor Sparkuhl; Editor: James Smith; Musical Direction: Boris Morros; Stock Music Composers: Phil Boutelje, Ralph Rainger and Tom Satterfield; Art Direction: Hans Dreier, Roland Anderson; Sound Recorders: Harry Lindgren and John Cope; Costumes: Travis Banton. Released by Paramount on August 20, 1936. Black and white. 72 minutes.

Synopsis: After her father dies, socialite Lucille Sutton is down on her luck. When she gambles and loses at the Miami club run by Johnny Lamb, he refuses to advance money on her jewels. Since she has no money for cab fare, Lamb takes her home to the family mansion. She tells him that bailiffs are arriving the following day. He suggests that they turn her house into a high-class casino and become partners. A tentative romance develops much to the disgust of Lamb's cronies and employees.

One visitor to the new casino is Gert Malloy, an attractive confidence trickster whose favorite scam is to pretend to be an heiress to steal from men. Lamb's cronies track down Gert and her friend Dictionary McKinney. They hire them to masquerade as Nancy Carstairs and her uncle, Colonel Evelyn Carstairs. The plan is for Nancy to trick Lamb into falling in love with her and then abandon him so that he will be cynical about society women forever. At a party which Lamb organizes for Nancy to meet Lucille, Lucille realizes that Nancy is a fraud. When Nancy fakes a heart attack, Colonel Carstairs sends for Lamb, who believes Nancy is dying. Carstairs says that Nancy must go to Spain for her health and they try to fleece Lamb of $15,000 as a loan on their property which he is unaware is rented.

When Lucille tells Lamb that she is going away, Lamb says he will give her money for her end of the business. When Lamb's cronies arrive with $15,000, they think it is for Lucille. When his friends subsequently accuse Lucille of fleecing Lamb of

Raft and Dolores Costello in *Yours for the Asking.*

$15,000, she tells him she is genuine and to investigate Nancy and Colonel Carstairs instead. Lamb discovers that some heirlooms the Carstairses have sold him are worthless fakes.

Lamb goes to the Carstairs villa where a confrontation takes place and the Carstairses are unmasked. Lamb is joined by his cronies, but ignores them when he finds out that they originally hired the Carstairses even though they were not in on the scam. Later Lamb pays off Lucille as promised. When Lamb discovers that his men have retrieved the $15,000, he forgives them. He tells them he is going into a legitimate business and that they will all be joining him in this new enterprise. When Lucille departs, Lamb goes after her and brings her back, realizing he is in love with her.

Comments: This was the fourth of five Raft films directed by Alexander Hall. It's also one of Raft's most obscure films and deserves to be. One indication that the script ran into trouble was the number of credited scribes involved in it. This film proved once again that situation comedy was not Raft's forte, especially when the situation was not particularly funny. It is also a little hard to believe that a man as streetwise as Raft in this film would fall victim to a confidence trick like buying fake heirlooms. Raft's two best scenes were at the start where he battles gangsters trying to steal money from his gambling den and at the end when he knocks out the Carstairses' pugnacious butler. The three actors (James Gleason, Edgar Kennedy and Lynne Overman) playing Raft's minders were all noted scene-stealers and just about kept the film afloat. The final scene (which did not feature Raft at all) involved these three actors; perhaps this was Alexander Hall's way of allowing them to take a bow.

The weakest link in the cast was Dolores Costello, one of Raft's most colorless leading ladies. It was perhaps significant that she did not play any part in the climax at all. Ida Lupino, in the first of three appearances opposite Raft, was in fine form. He had one good scene with her where they danced the rumba with music lifted from his previous film of the same title. Probably the best scene was at the climax in which Raft's minders have a fight with the Carstairses and, in particular, where James Gleason slapped Ida Lupino's bottom. Generally the best scenes were the ones Raft was not involved in. When Hall went to the exclusive Coronado Island beach to film location scenes, Groucho Marx, Charlie Ruggles and Tookie Spreckles were there already and they became extras in the background (they are not visible in the film). In spite of the shortcomings of this film, it showed a marginal profit.

Biography: Dolores Costello was born in Pittsburgh, Pennsylvania, on September 17, 1905, the daughter of professional actors Maurice Costello and Ruth Reeves. Her sister Helene was also a well-known actress. As a child she acted in her father's films and went around the world with him. Later she became a New York model and was signed for movies when she was a chorus girl while in Chicago on tour in *George White's Scandals.* Her first major adult role was in *The Little Irish Girl* (1926). Her career gained stature when she was cast opposite John Barrymore in *The Sea Beast* (1926). She made a smooth transition to talkies. Her best-remembered later role was as Isabel Amberson in *The Magnificent Ambersons* (1942). She retired in 1943. She died at Fallbrook, California, on March 1, 1979, aged 73, of emphysema. In 1928 she married John Barrymore with whom she had a daughter and a son, actor John Jr., before divorcing him in 1934. She married physician John Vruwink in 1939, but divorced him in 1951.

Souls at Sea (1937)

Cast: Gary Cooper (Michael "Nuggin" Taylor), George Raft ("Powdah"), Frances Dee (Margaret Tarryton), Henry Wilcoxon (Lt. Stanley Tarryton), Harry Carey (Captain of the *William Brown*), Olympe Bradna (Babsie),

Robert Cummings (George Martin), Porter Hall (Court Prosecutor), George Zucco (Barton Woodley), Virginia Weidler (Tina), Joseph Schildkraut (Gaston de Bastonet), Gilbert Emery (Captain Martisel), Lucien Littlefield (Tina's Father, the Toymaker), Paul Fix (Violinist), Tully Marshall (Mr. Pecora), Monte Blue (Mate on the *William Brown*), Stanley Fields (Captain Paul M. Granley), Norman Ainsley (Ticket Taker), Stanley Andrews (First Mate), Robert Barrat (The Reverend), Lina Basquette (Brunette in Saloon), Wilson Benge (Doctor), Frank Benson (Gardener), George Beranger (Henri), Matthew Betz (Slaver), Arthur Blake (Prime Minister), Eugene Borden, Rolfe Sedan (Friends of de Bastonet), Allan Cavan (Dignitary), Davison Clark (Bailiff), Harvey Clark (Court Clerk), Ethel Clayton (Passenger), Herbert Clifton (Ticket Clerk), David Clyde (Butler), G. Pat Collins, Francis Ford (Slavers), Clyde Cook (Hendy — Coachman), Cecil Cunningham (Lady Torrington), Lowell Drew (Jury Foreman), John M. Sullivan, John Elliott, Phillips Smalley (Dignitaries), Franklyn Farnum (Court Bailiff), Leslie Francis (Woodley's Secretary), Phyllis Godfrey (Housemaid), Mary Gordon (Cook), Pauline Haddon (Blonde), Grayce Hampton (Old Knitting Woman), Forrester Harvey (Pub Proprietor), Fay Holden (Mrs. Martin), Olaf Hytten (Proprietor), Colin Kenny (Military Guard), Crauford Kent (Navy Clerk), George Lloyd (Sailor), Rollo Lloyd (Parchy, Mate on Slaver); George MacQuarrie (Doctor), Charles Middleton (Jury Foreman), Belle Mitchell (Fortune Teller), Henry Mowbray (Bus Man), Forbes Murray (Associate Justice), Carlyle O'Rourke (Puppeteer), Lee Shumway (Mate), William Stack (Judge), Paul Stanton (Taylor's Defense Attorney), Ben Taggart (Ship's Officer), Colin Tapley (Donaldson), Viva Tattersall (Queen Victoria), Jameson Thomas (Pelton), Luana Walters (Eloise), Paul Walton (Puppeteer), Robert Warwick (Vice

Olympe Bradna, Raft, Frances Dee and Gary Cooper in *Souls at Sea*.

Admiral), Blue Washington (Ship Slave), Jane Weir (Barmaid), Gloria Williams (Passenger).

Credits: Director and Producer: Henry Hathaway; Assistant Director: Hal Walker (Oscar winner); Original Story: Ted Lesser; Screenplay: Grover Jones and Dale Van Every; Photography: Charles Lang, Jr., and Merritt Gerstad; Editor: Ellsworth Hoagland; Musical Director: Boris Morros (Oscar nominee); Original Music: W. Franke Harling and Milan Roder (Oscar nominees); Songs: Ralph Rainger and Leo Robin; Orchestrations: John Leipold; Art Direction: Hans Dreier and Roland Anderson (Oscar nominees); Sound Recorders: Harry Mills and John Cope; Costumes: Edith Head; Special Photographic Effects: Gordon Jennings. Released by Paramount on September 3, 1937. Black and white. 90 minutes.

Synopsis: This film is told in flashback. Michael "Nuggin" Taylor is on trial, accused of killing several people when the *William Brown* sank on April 19, 1841. Previously Taylor and his friend "Powdah" were officers aboard the slave ship *Blackbird*. Sadistic Captain Paul Granley is killed while whipping slaves, but before he dies he turns over command of the ship to "Nuggin" and "Powdah" and tells them to deliver some papers to Updyke and Morgan when the ship reaches Savannah. A change of course by "Nuggin" leads to their capture by a British patrol ship. The cargo of slaves has disappeared, presumably thrown overboard, but there is no tangible evidence of this. Lt. Tarryton, a British officer, is in favor of drowning them. Instead "Nuggin" and "Powdah" are hung by their thumbs from the mast until they agree to talk.

"Powdah" tells the British captain that they rescued "Nuggin" when his own ship floundered and that he did not know until after he was signed up by the rescuing captain that it was a slave ship. "Nuggin" tells the British that no slaves were killed. (Actually, when nightfall came, he hugged the coast and allowed the slaves to swim the short distance to shore.)

Tarryton makes a mistake in referring to Granley as a well-known slave trader which makes "Nuggin" realize that he is secretly in league with the slave traders.

In Liverpool "Nuggin" and "Powdah" are released, but "Nuggin" tells "Powdah" that he thinks it is a trick by the British. In a pub, "Nuggin" meets Barton Woodley. Woodley works for British Intelligence and tells him he believes "Nuggin" is secretly waging a one-man war against the slave trade. He wants him to go to work for the British. Woodley shows "Nuggin" the log and papers of the *Blackbird* including a letter from Granley to his associates detailing the routes of every one of his slave ships for the next few months. Woodley wants "Nuggin" to go to Savannah by the fastest possible route and deliver the doctored letter so that the slave trade will be defeated. "Nuggin" is booked on the *William Brown*.

Tarryton tells Pecura, his partner in the slave trade, that he needs to reach America fast to capitalize on Granley's death by taking over his operation. Pecura books his passage on the *William Brown*. Margaret, Tarryton's sister, rushes to the docks to beg her brother not to go. When Pecura realizes that Margaret is aware of some their plans, he warns Tarryton that Margaret must not leave the ship, but accompany him to America. On board ship, when "Nuggin" goes to his cabin, he finds "Powdah" there. Margaret is put in the same cabin as Babsie, a maid seeking a new life in America, and they become fast friends. Another passenger, a little girl named Tina, provides much of the entertainment. In the course of the voyage "Nuggin" falls in love with Margaret, while "Powdah" romances Babsie.

While giving a recitation, Tina forgets her lines, but "Nuggin" finishes the poem for her. In gratitude Tina insists on giving him her Indian musical box. She goes to her berth to fetch it and accidentally breaks an oil lamp which causes a massive fire. When the fire reaches the powder room, there is an explosion which kills Tina and the ship capsizes. When

"Nuggin" returns to his cabin, he finds Tarryton has ransacked it and discovered Granley's letter. Tarryton holds him at gunpoint and tells him he is going to kill him. In the melee, "Nuggin" knocks him unconscious and retrieves the letter.

There is only one lifeboat left. Tarryton comes to and tries to kill "Nuggin." There is a fistfight which ends when "Nuggin" knocks him out and he drowns, which repels Margaret. Nevertheless he pushes her into the boat. "Powdah" finds "Nuggin," tells him that Babsie has been killed in her cabin and that he is going back to join her. He knocks "Nuggin" into the lifeboat and then returns to the dead Babsie. The lifeboat is overloaded and a piece of the mast falls into it, nearly wrecking it, but "Nuggin's" seamanship keeps it afloat. In the process, several people are killed. "Nuggin" manages to steer the boat into port and then goes on to Savannah to deliver the letter.

"Nuggin" is tried for murder and found guilty in Philadelphia. Then Barton Woodley arrives to tell the court the truth. "Nuggin" is granted a new trial where he will no doubt be exonerated. Margaret realizes that she was wrong and that "Nuggin" will soon be free to continue their romance.

Comments: This was the first of three Raft films directed by Henry Hathaway, who recalled Raft years later as a timid man masquerading as a tough guy. *Souls at Sea* was one of Raft's finest films and he gave one of the best performances of his career under Hathaway's assured direction. This was one of the very few historical films for Raft. He initially turned down the role of "Powdah" and was suspended by the studio. Lloyd Nolan and Anthony Quinn stood by to replace him. Once the part was more sympathetically written, Raft readily accepted it. As the character, he wore crimped hair and an earring. Scenes in which Raft romanced Bradna were very touching and extremely well written.

It had been intended as a roadshow special, but was switched to normal release instead and trimmed to 90 minutes which made for a tauter, more exciting narrative. It was a huge commercial success worldwide. There were two heartbreaking scenes, one when "Powdah" returned to the dead Babsie and tenderly put his mother's wedding ring on her finger. The other was when Tina came running along the ship's passageway crying for her father, but was killed in the explosion. The very fine musical score deservedly received an Oscar nomination. The special effects, especially the sinking of the *William Brown*, were spectacular indeed. This was also the first of a few films dating from this period in which Raft appeared with an actor, Gary Cooper in this case, who was deemed to be superior, but somehow matching the quality of performance given by the other male lead. In its review *Variety* wrote, "Cooper and Raft are outstanding — the former up to his usual standard; Raft a bit of a surprise as a sympathetic player who meets his dramatic opportunities more than half way."

Biography: Henry Hathaway was born Marquis Henry Leonard de Fiennes in Sacramento, California, on March 13, 1898. He was the son of an actress and a stage manager and the grandson of a Belgian marquis. In 1914 he joined Universal as a prop boy and then played in juvenile roles. After U.S. Army service he spent a year in business, but disliked this so much that he resumed his film career with the Goldwyn Company. He commenced his directing career shooting Westerns for Paramount in 1932. He became one of Hollywood's best directors, mainly at Paramount and 20th Century–Fox. Surprisingly he was only nominated once for a Best Director Oscar, for *The Lives of a Bengal Lancer* (1935). He died in Hollywood on February 11, 1985, aged 86, after a heart attack.

Biography: Gary Cooper was born Frank James Cooper in Helena, Montana, on May 7, 1901. The son of Charles H. Cooper (1866–1946), a judge, and Alice Brazier (1873–1946), he was educated at Dunstable, an English public school, and later Grinnell College, Iowa.

He had some talent as an artist, but when he failed to make the grade, he began working as an extra in films. He changed his name to Gary at the suggestion of his agent, Nan Collins, whose home town was Gary, Indiana. He made his screen debut in 1925 and his first substantial role was in *The Winning of Barbara Worth* (1926). He made an easy transition to talkies and went on to become one of the industry's most popular male film stars. He was under contract to Paramount and later Warner Bros. He won Best Actor Oscars for *Sergeant York* (1941) and *High Noon* (1952). He died in Los Angeles on May 14, 1961, aged 60, of lung cancer. He married Veronica "Rocky" Balfe in 1933 and had one daughter, Maria, who was born in 1937.

Biography: Olympe Bradna was born in Paris, France, on August 12, 1920, the daughter of Joseph and Jeanne Bradna, professional entertainers. She was named after the Olympia Theater in Paris where her parents were performing at the time. She became an acrobatic dancer at the Follies-Bergere and originally came to America in 1934 as part of the Follies troupe that toured there. She later performed at the French Casino in New York. She was signed to a contract by Paramount in 1936. She retired in 1941 after marrying millionaire socialite Douglas Wood Wilhoit. She died in Stockton, California, on November 5, 2012, at age 92.

You and Me (1938)

Cast: Sylvia Sidney (Helen Roberts [Dennis]), George Raft (Joe Dennis), Barton MacLane (Mickey Bain), Harry Carey Sr. (Jerome Morris), Roscoe Karns (Cuffy), George E. Stone (Patsy), Warren Hymer (Gil Carter, aka Gimpy), Robert Cummings (Jim), Adrian Morris (Knucks), Edward Pawley (Dutch), Roger Gray (Bath House Man), Cecil Cunningham (Mrs. Mary Morris), Vera Gordon (Mrs. Abie Levine), Egon Brecher (Abie Levine), Willard Robertson (Dayton, Parole Officer), Guinn "Big Boy" Williams (Taxi), Bernadene Hayes (Nellie), Joyce Compton (Curly Blonde Shopper), Carol Paige (Torch Singer), Ernie Adams (Nick), Max Barwyn (German Waiter), Harlan Briggs (Thomas McTavish), Sheila Darcy (Perfume Clerk), William B. Davidson (Borton, Attorney-at-Law), Hal K. Dawson (Information Clerk), Jane Dewey (Clerk), Ellen Drew (Cashier), Jimmie Dundee (Greyhound Bus Driver), Fern Emmett (Mother), Julia Faye (Secretary), Joe Gray (Red), Paula De Cardo, Harriette Haddon (Cigarette Girls), Oscar "Dutch" Hendrian (Lucky), Robert Homans (Security Guard in Store), Arthur Hoyt (Mr. Klein), Herta Lynd (Swedish Waitress), Joyce Mathews (Clerk), John McCafferty (Policeman), Matt McHugh (Newcomer), James McNamara (Big Shot), Sam Ash, Jack Mulhall (Floorwalkers), Paul Newlan (Bouncer at Danceland), Jack Pennick (Gangster), Margaret Randall (Shoplifter), Ruth Rogers (Salesgirl), Marion Weldon, Barbara Salisbury, Barbara Jackson (Demonstrators), Gwen Kenyon, Louise Seidel (Hat Check Girls), Harry Tenbrook (Bartender), Blanca Vischer (Flower Girl), Phil Warren (Secretary).

Credits: Director and Producer: Fritz Lang; Original Story: Norman Krasna; Screenplay: Virginia Van Upp; Photography: Charles Lang, Jr.; Editor: Paul Weatherwax; Musical Direction: Boris Morros; Musical Adviser: Phil Boutelje; Music: Kurt Weill; Lyrics: Sam Coslow; Art Direction: Hans Dreier and Ernst Fegté; Sound Recorders: Harry Lindgren and Walter Oberst. Released by Paramount on June 3, 1938. Black and white. 93 minutes.

Tagline: "Every time she says 'I Love You' she breaks the law!"

Synopsis: Benign Jerome Morris runs a New York department store where the majority of employees are ex-cons on parole. Joe Dennis, one of the salesmen, falls into this category. He intends to leave for California, but changes his mind when his girlfriend Helen Roberts proposes to him. Unbeknownst to him, she is also an ex-convict, so their marriage is forbid-

Raft and Sylvia Sidney in *You and Me*.

ing for them. Morris lectures the ex-convicts about honesty and then tells them he wants them all back on the job the following day. He then leaves them to Helen, who mathematically proves that each robber's cut for stealing the stolen goods would only have amounted to $113 plus a jail sentence. The sheepish robbers depart. In the meantime, gangsters working for a powerful rival crime boss murder Mickey Bane.

The parole board members refuse to give Helen's new address to Joe and tell him that no parolee has any civil rights so the marriage is not valid. Joe enlists the aid of his former gang to find Helen. Gimpy eventually finds Helen in the general hospital where she has just given birth to a son. Joe and Helen are joyfully reunited and rewed.

den. They marry and move into her apartment. Mary becomes pregnant, but does not tell Joe.

Gangster Mickey Bain tries to persuade Joe to return to a life of crime, but Joe resists. Another ex-convict, Gimpy, is contacted by Bain and told to bring Joe to a meeting with the gang on Christmas Eve. At the meeting, Bain tells Joe the gang will be robbing Morris's store on Christmas Day. When Joe refuses to join them, Bain informs him that Helen is also an ex-convict out on parole. When Joe returns home, he tricks Helen into confirming that she is an ex-convict. Joe walks out and agrees to join the gang for the robbery.

Gimpy tries to forewarn Helen that the store is going to be robbed and to keep Joe with her that evening, but it is too late. In turn, Helen warns Jerome Morris. When the gang breaks into the store, the police are wait-

Comments: One of Raft's oddest films, *You and Me* was the second of the three films in which Raft was paired with Sylvia Sidney. It was the only time he was directed by Fritz Lang, an "A"-list director who helmed some fine films. *You and Me* unfortunately was not one of them. It was a curious brew of genres incorporating crime, comedy, drama, soap opera and musical elements. Raft was so foolish in rejoining his old criminal gang that it was hard to feel any sympathy for him. He alienated the audience who probably thought he deserved another jail sentence.

Kurt Weill composed 23 music cues for *You and Me*, but Paramount did not like his work much and used only nine of them. Weill was possibly trying to replicate on film the kind of experimental theater which was his forté. In one memorable scene, the ex-convicts remembered their time in jail in which the montages were accompanied by a rhythmic voiceover narration. In another, Sylvia Sidney gave the convicts a lesson in economics in the department store to prove that crime did not pay. It was however difficult to believe that hardened criminals would not have had sufficient brains to realize themselves that no one was likely to become rich from this heist. Sidney succeeded in having Richard Wallace, the original director assigned to this film, replaced by Lang, who had directed her two previous films. *You and Me* was a box office flop.

Biography: Fritz Lang was born Friedrich Christian Anton Lang in Vienna, Austria, on December 5, 1890. He intended to be an architect, but became an artist instead. He studied in Munich and went to Paris in 1913 as a fashion designer. During World War I he served in the Austrian army. When his war service ended in 1916 he wrote scenarios and obtained a contract with the German film company DECLA. From 1919 onwards he was a film director of his own scenarios, frequently in collaboration with his wife Thea Von Harbou. He directed several classic films in Germany during the twenties and early thirties. When he was invited by Dr. Joseph Goebbels, Hitler's minister of propaganda, to make films for the Nazis, he fled to Paris that evening by train because he was afraid that his Jewish origins would be discovered. In 1935 he arrived in Hollywood where he directed a multitude of films until studio politics drove him out in 1956. He went to Germany where he directed a couple more films and then returned to America where he lived in retirement until he died in Beverly Hills on August 2, 1976, aged 85. He was married three times, to Lisa Rosenthal, Thea Von Harbou and Lily Latte.

Spawn of the North (1938)

Cast: George Raft (Tyler Dawson), Henry Fonda (Jim Kimmerlee), Dorothy Lamour (Nicky Duval), Akim Tamiroff (Red Skain), John Barrymore (Windy Turlon), Louise Platt (Dian "Di" Turlon), Lynne Overman ("Jack" Jackson), Fuzzy Knight (Lefty Jones), Vladimir Sokoloff (Dimitri), Duncan Renaldo (Ivan), John Wray (Dr. Sparks), Michio Ito (Indian Dancer), Stanley Andrews (Partridge), Richard Ung (Tom), Slicker (Himself), Irving Bacon, Monte Blue (Cannery Officials), Henry Brandon (Davis), Egon Brecher (Erickson), Harvey Clark, Edmund Elton (Pursers), Bob Kortman (Fisherman at Party), Adia Kuznetzoff (Vashia), Robert Middlemass (Davis), Eddie Marr, Frank Puglia, Leonid Snegoff (Members of Red's Gang), Arthur Aylesworth, Wade Boteler, Galan Galt, Rollo Lloyd, Lee Shumway, Archie Twitchell (Fishermen), Guy Usher (Grant), Alex Woloshin (Gregory).

Credits: Director: Henry Hathaway; Producer: Albert Lewin; Associate Director: Richard Talmadge; Original Story: Barrett Willoughby; Screenplay: Jules Furthman and Talbot Jennings; Photography: Charles Lang, Jr.; Process Photography: Farciot Edouart; Editor: Ellsworth Hoagland; Musical Direction: Boris Morros; Music: Dimitri Tiomkin; New Songs: Frank Loesser and Burton Lane; Art Direction: Hans Dreier and Roland Anderson; Sound Recorders: Harry Mills and Walter Oberst; Special Photographic Effects: Gordon Jennings. Honorary Academy Award for Outstanding Achievements in Creating Special Photographic and Sound Effects. Released by Paramount on September 9, 1938. Black and white. 110 minutes.

Years ago the Vigilantes forced a respect for law upon the desperadoes of the old west. The same struggle took place against fish-pirates of the Alaskan frontier. This is the story of that struggle. In the early summer myriads of salmon return to their native rivers to spawn.

Synopsis: Tyler Dawson and Jim Kimmerlee are friends working in the Alaskan fishing industry. Dawson has made a down payment on a new fishing schooner and asks Kimmerlee, who runs a fishing cannery, to join his enterprise, but Kimmerlee declines. Hotelier Nicky Duval is in love with Dawson, but is jealous because of the stories she has heard about him being involved with other women. Windy Turlon, owner and editor of the local newspaper, goes to the docks where a ship has arrived. He welcomes his daughter Dian, whom he has not seen in eight years while she has been educated in the United States. Dian stays in Nicky's hotel where longtime friend Kimmerlee meets her. At a dance, Dian and Kimmerlee begin a romance. Red Skain, a salmon fishing pirate, makes an unwelcome appearance at the dance, where he suggests that Dawson join forces with him.

Fishermen have little time for anything else when the salmon are running. With the canneries working at full capacity, the fishermen preserve the catch by chipping ice from the huge icebergs near the fishing grounds. Kimmerlee sails to the icebergs where he encounters Dawson and Skain's boats. Attempts to loosen the ice result in an avalanche from which Dawson rescues Kimmerlee. On board Dawson's boat, Kimmerlee notices that the fish have no net marks so obviously they have been stolen from other fishermen's traps. Kimmerlee is worried and shows Dawson a notice which states that anyone found on fishing traps having no business there will be killed. Kimmerlee warns Dawson that the legitimate fishermen mean business and will not stand for the thefts.

Out on patrol with the other fishermen, Kimmerlee comes upon a boat stealing fish from traps. Skain makes good his escape, but two of his men are left behind. The honest fishermen later arrive at Skain's headquarters where they find him and his men nonchalantly playing cards. They bring in the dead bodies of Skain's henchmen and give him a stern warning. The other fishermen depart, but as Kimmerlee is leaving he notices "Skipper," Dawson's pet seal. A moment later, Dawson enters the room unaware of what has happened until he sees the dead bodies.

Dawson agrees to join Skain's plan to steal fish from the maximum number of traps. Kimmerlee and the fishermen discover Dawson and a couple of Skain's men stealing from the traps. In the ensuing battle Skain's men are overpowered, but Kimmerlee shoots Dawson. Later Kimmerlee finds Dawson and takes him back to Nicky's hotel where a doctor and Nicky tend his wounds. Kimmerlee tells Dian that Dawson is not to blame, but Skain is. He loads his gun ready to hunt for Skain, but Dian professes her love for him and begs him not to go.

Dawson sends Nicky for Skain. Once he arrives, Dawson tells him they need to make sure their stories tally. When Kimmerlee shows up, Dawson pretends to be hostile towards him and tells him to leave. Skain is convinced of Dawson's enmity towards Kimmerlee. Dawson tells Nicky that he is not angry with Kimmerlee and intends to prove it. Kimmerlee confronts Dian and tells her that he has to bring Skain to justice. Kimmerlee goes out alone in his boat. In a panic, Nicky finds Dian and tells her that Dawson has disappeared and she believes that Skain has taken him on board his boat.

Skain spots Kimmerlee's boat and heads towards him. By a trick, Dawson locks Skain in the cabin. Kimmerlee has Dawson in his sights, but Dawson turns the boat towards an iceberg. Sounding the horn causes an avalanche to fall on Skain's boat, killing both Dawson and Skain. While Nicky is devastated by the tragedy, Kimmerlee and Dian are now free to marry, leaving Windy and his assistant Jackson to eulogize Tyler Dawson, who is set to become a legend.

Comments: This was the second of the three Raft films directed by Henry Hathaway, and one of Raft's most exciting. Raft was paired with another actor, Henry Fonda, who was regarded as superior to Raft and once again Raft's acting was of the same high quality as Fonda's. The theme of the film was loyalty of the two men to each other and the dialogue and situations were totally credible. Raft had an especially memorable scene in which he was lying injured in bed and smoked a cigarette. When exhaling, the smoke came out through his chest! If Raft and Fonda had shot this film decades later, they would both have spent considerable time in Alaska on location. At this stage in the history of the cinema, they went no further than the back lot of Paramount in Hollywood because the studio built a wharf, jetty and miscellaneous buildings to replicate the look of an Alaskan fishing village.

The script, direction, cast and special effects were all top-notch. In terms of the sheer expertise with which this film was assembled, it was hard to beat. It was originally intended to star Cary Grant and Randolph Scott, but they were dropped and Raft and Fonda substituted. For this film they were a better combination. Fonda later said that he made some films for artistic reasons and others just for the money. This film was one for the money, but when he saw how it turned out, he was very pleased he starred in it.

Of the supporting cast, Akim Tamiroff as a menacing pirate with no redeeming features, John Barrymore as a garrulous newspaper editor and Lynne Overman as his cynical assistant were all outstanding. Lamour was the big surprise because, deglamorized in frumpy clothing, she revealed the fine actress beneath the attractive facade. She played most of her scenes with Raft. They had good chemistry together, the depiction of their love-hate relationship was most convincing and they brought a fine emotional intensity to their scenes. This film was a big box office hit. A *Variety* critic wrote, "Impressive scenes of the Alaskan waters backgrounded by towering glaciers which drop mighty icebergs into the sea, imperilling doughty fishermen and their frail craft, lift *Spawn of the North* into the class of robust out-of-door films where the spectacular overshadows the melodrama." The film was remade as *Alaska Seas* (1954).

Biography: Henry Jaynes Fonda was born in Grand Island, Nebraska, on May 16, 1905, son of William Brace and Herberta Jaynes Fonda. When he was six months old, the family moved to Omaha where his father ran a printing shop. In 1925 he was persuaded by a family friend to join the Omaha Community Playhouse where he stayed for three years. He then joined a group of aspiring thespians at the University Players where he acquired substantial experience. On Broadway in 1934 he received excellent notices for playing in *The Farmer Takes a Wife*. He went to Hollywood to reprise the role. Very rapidly he became a star and by the end of the thirties an international name. He reached the peak of his early career playing Tom Joad in *The Grapes of Wrath* (1940) which earned him a Best Actor Oscar nomination.

In 1942 he enlisted in the Navy in which he served for three years. His first role upon his return was as Wyatt Earp in the classic Western *My Darling Clementine* (1946). During the seven years (1948–1955) that he

Raft and Dorothy Lamour in *Spawn of the North.*

was absent from films, he scored his greatest Broadway triumph in the title role in the play *Mister Roberts*. From the mid-fifties onwards he was active in all media including starring in two television series, *The Deputy* (1959–1962) and *The Smith Family* (1971–1973). He finally won a Best Actor Oscar for his last released film, *On Golden Pond* (1981), and a Special Oscar in 1981. He died at Cedars-Sinai Hospital Medical Center, Los Angeles, on August 12, 1982, aged 77, of cancer and cardiorespiratory arrest. Fonda was married five times. His fifth and final wife (from 1965 onwards) was Shirlee Mae Adams. He was survived by his widow and two natural children, actors Jane and Peter.

Biography: Dorothy Lamour was born Mary Leta Dorothy Slaton in New Orleans, Louisiana, on December 10, 1914, the daughter of John Slaton and Carmen La Porte. She adopted her stage name from her stepfather's surname, Lambour. While working as a secretary, she won the beauty title of Miss New Orleans in 1931. She became a lift operator in Chicago and joined a theatrical company. She then worked as a singer and radio performer before signing a contract with Paramount in 1936. Her second film *The Jungle Princess* (1936) was a big success. In this she wore a sarong which became her trademark and made her a popular pinup during World War II. Her greatest fame probably came during the forties and early fifties with the *Road* series with Bing Crosby and Bob Hope. She was married to bandleader Herbie Kaye from 1935 until divorced in 1939. In 1943 she married William Ross Howard III with whom she had two sons. She was widowed in 1978. She died in North Hollywood on September 21, 1996, aged 81, from cardiac arrest and arteriosclerosis.

The Lady's from Kentucky (1939)

Cast: George Raft (Marty Black), Ellen Drew (Penelope "Penny" Hollis), Hugh Herbert (Mousey Johnson), ZaSu Pitts (Dulcy Lee), Louise Beavers (Aunt Tiny), Lew Payton (Sixty), Harry Tyler (Carter), Forrester Harvey (Nonny Watkins), Edward Pawley (Spike Cronin), Gilbert Emery (Pinkney Rodell), Eugene Jackson (Winfield), Jimmy Bristow (Brewster), Stanley Andrews (Doctor), George Anderson (Joe Lane), Robert Milasch (Big Longshoreman), Hooper Atchley (Surgeon), Irving Bacon (Information Clerk), Bill Cartledge (Jones), Gus Glassmire (Pole Judge), Roger Gray (Waiter), Bob Perry (Dealer), Frank Moran, Jack Raymond (Customers), Virginia Sale (Cashier), John Merton, Paul Newlan, Bob Stevenson (Gamblers), George Melford, Carl Stockdale (Veterinarians), Charles Trowbridge (Charles Butler), Harry Tenbrook, George Turner (Longshoreman), Archie Twitchell (Radio Announcer in Gambling Den), Frankie Van (Taxi Driver), Fern Emmett, Nell Craig, Carol Holloway, Gloria Williams (Nurses), Hal K. Dawson, Tom Hanlon (Announcers).

Credits: Director: Alexander Hall; Producer: Jeff Lazarus; Original Story: Rowland Brown; Screenplay: Malcolm Stuart Boylan; Photography: Theodor Sparkuhl; Editor: Harvey Johnston; Original Music: John Leipold and Leo Shuken; Stock Music: Stephen Foster; Art Direction: Hans Dreier and John Goodman; Sound Recorders: Hugo Grenzbach and Walter Oberst. Released by Paramount on May 1, 1939. Black and white. 76 minutes.

Synopsis: Marty Black and Mousey Johnson, compulsive gamblers, pay $100 for a gambling den to Carter, a bookie who is absconding. One race virtually bankrupts them. In checking I.O.U.s left by gamblers, they find a half ownership in Roman Son, a thoroughbred racehorse. The other half of the horse is owned by Penny Hollis, daughter of the late Major Hollis. Both owners are delighted when the horse wins a "baby race." Penny tries to pay off Marty and Mousey, but they refuse. She takes the horse back to the Hollis farm in Kentucky where Marty and Mousey find her. Conflict develops because Marty wants to enter the horse in the Bidwell Stakes, but Penny claims Roman Son is not ready. Marty and Penny develop a romance, but fall out when Marty secretly enters the horse in the Bidwell Stakes. The horse wins, but suffers from exhaustion. After it recovers, Penny enters it in the Kentucky Derby and Marty bets heavily on it. Once a stewards' objection is overcome by Marty assigning his half to Penny, the horse is allowed to race. Despite injury, Roman Son wins and Marty and Penny are reconciled.

Comments: This was the fifth and final time Raft was directed by Alexander Hall. The theme of this film was compulsive gambling and the degree to which a viewer will enjoy it depended upon an individual's attitude towards that addiction. Since in real life Raft was a compulsive gambler, he had the character nailed down. The first fifteen minutes of this comedy, far from being funny, are a harrowing nightmare of the depths compulsive gamblers sink to, including giving blood and being penniless. It was a big comedown from the better "A" movies in which Raft had most recently appeared and was much more similar to the kind of films he was making during the earlier part of the thirties. This film was very similar to the superior quality movies which 20th Century–Fox was making around the same time in color. This film cried out for color. One of the better aspects of this film was the use of an instrumental version of "Camptown Races" both over the opening credits and in the background. This was an economy measure since the tune was probably in the public domain. This was Raft's final film under his Paramount contract. Since he was about to leave Paramount, the studio slotted him into an inferior movie to gain some additional revenue before Raft left the lot.

Biography: Ellen Drew was born Ester Loretta Ray in Kansas City, Missouri, on November 23, 1915, daughter of a barber. She was raised in Kansas City, Chicago and Englewood, Illinois. She was educated at Chicago's Parker High School, which she was forced to leave at

sixteen to help her mother. After winning a local beauty contest, she went to Hollywood. She worked as a waitress and soda jerk before being discovered by actor and agent William Demarest, who was instrumental in having her signed to a contract by Paramount. She had small parts in films in which she was often billed as Terry Ray. Her career gained stature when she appeared in *Sing You Sinners* (1938) opposite Bing Crosby. She went on to enjoy a dozen years of stardom until 1951. She was married four times and had a son. She died in Palm Desert, California, on December 3, 2003, aged 88, of a liver ailment.

Each Dawn I Die
(aka *Killer Meets Killer*) (1939)

Cast: James Cagney (Frank Ross), George Raft (Judson "Hood" Stacey), Jane Bryan (Joyce Conover), George Bancroft (Head Warden John Armstrong), Maxie Rosenbloom (Fargo Red), Stanley Ridges (Mueller), Alan Baxter ("Polecat" Carlisle), Victor Jory (Assistant D.A. Grayce), John Wray (Pete Kassock), Edward Pawley (Dale), Willard Robertson (Lang), Emma Dunn (Mrs. Ross), Paul Hurst (Garsky), Louis Jean Heydt (Joe Lassiter), Joe Downing (Limpy Julien), Thurston Hall (D.A. Jesse Hanley), William B. Davidson (Bill Mason), Clay Clement (Lockhart, Stacey's Attorney), Charles Trowbridge (Judge), Harry Cording (Warden Temple), Abner Biberman (Shake Edwards), John Dilson (Parole Board Member), Earl Dwire (Judge Crowder), James Flavin (Policeman), Arthur Gardner (Man in Car), Jack A. Goodrich (Accident Witness), Fred Graham (Guard in Cell), Mack Gray (Joe, Gangster), Chuck Hamilton (Court Officer), John Harron (Lew Keller, Reporter), Al Hill (Johnny, Gangster), Max Hoffman, Jr. (Gate Guard), Stuart Holmes (Accident Witness), Robert Homans (Mac, a Guard), Selmer Jackson (Patterson, Editor), Wilfred Lucas (Bailiff), Walter Miller (Turnkey), Bert Moorhouse (Lawyer), Wedgewood Nowell (Parole Board

Member), Frank O'Connor (Guard in Movie Room), Henry Otto (Guard in Warden's Office), Bob Perry (Bud, Gangster), Jack Perry (Hoodlum), Lee Phelps, Dick Rich (Guards), John Ridgely (Jerry Poague, Reporter), Cliff Saum (Accident Witness), Napoleon Simpson (Mose, Convict), Garland Smith (Man in Car), Emmett Vogan (Prosecutor), Leo White (Taxi Driver), Maris Wrixon (Girl in Car), Joe Sully (Man), Jack C. Smith (Guard), Mike Lally, Paul Panzer, Hector Sarno, Charles Sullivan, Elliott Sullivan, Harry Tenbrook, Jack Wise (Convicts),

Credits: Director: William Keighley; Executive Producer: Hal B. Wallis; Associate Producer: David Lewis; Assistant Director: Frank Heath; Original Story: Jerome Odlum; Screenplay: Norman Reilly Raine, Warren Duff and Charles Perry; Photography: Arthur Edeson; Editor: Thomas Richards; Music: Max Steiner; Musical Directors: Leo F. Forbstein and Hugo Friedhofer; Art Direction: Max Parker; Sound Recorder: Everett A. Brown; Costumes: Howard Shoup; Makeup: Perc Westmore; Stunts: Mike Lally and Harvey Parry; Technical Advisor: William Buckley. Released by Warner Bros. on August 19, 1939. Black and white. 92 minutes.

Synopsis: Crusading newspaper reporter Frank Ross is out to expose corrupt District Attorney Jesse Hanley, who is running for governor. In the dead of night Ross witnesses ledgers being burned by Assistant District Attorney Grayce. When a description of this incident appears in the *Banton Record* under his own byline, the crooked politicians have Ross framed in a car accident in which three people are killed. "Polecat" Carlisle and Shake Edwards make it appear that Ross was drunk at the wheel of his car. Ross is found guilty of manslaughter and sentenced to twenty years hard labor at Rocky Point.

En route to the pen, he is handcuffed to hardened gangster "Hood" Stacey, who is in for a life sentence. Stacey discovers that Limpy Julien, an old enemy whom he believes in-

formed on him, is also back in prison. Limpy makes an attempt to murder Stacey, but is foiled by Ross. While watching a movie in the prison cinema, Limpy is stabbed to death with Stacey's knife. Stacey tells Ross that he did not kill Limpy, but if Ross will go to the head warden and inform him that Stacey is the guilty party, Stacey will be tried for murder in the courthouse from which he can escape. On the outside he can use his connections to find out who framed Ross and why. Initially Ross refuses, but when his mother and girlfriend, Joyce Conover, visit and tell him that they have been unable to find Shake Edwards, Ross changes his mind. He does however slip a note to Joyce informing her that there is going to be action in the courthouse at Stacey's trial and to have a reporter and cameraman standing by.

Ross informs on Stacey to honest head warden Armstrong. After Armstrong sends for Stacey, Stacey attacks Ross, which is as good as a confession. When Stacey is brought to trial, reporters from the *Banton Record* are there in force when he makes good his escape. Once the corrupt assistant district attorney W.J. Grayce is appointed chairman of the parole board, Ross realizes he will have no parole. Months later Joyce is taken to Stacey's hideout where she begs him to keep his promise to find Shake Edwards. Stacey informs her that Ross double-crossed him because he told Ross to keep his mouth shut about Stacey's escape, but instead Ross informed his newspaper and the courtroom was full of reporters and cameramen. Joyce tells Stacey that Ross has been in solitary confinement for the past five months for refusing to betray him.

After she has gone, Stacey instructs his gang to hunt down Shake Edwards so that he can be forced to tell the truth and Ross can have a new trial. Joyce goes to see Armstrong, who tells her that Ross is the most insubordinate prisoner he has known in 35 years. While Joyce is there, he sends for Ross and tells him that if he behaves himself he will come out of

Foreground left to right: William B. Davidson, Raft and James Cagney in *Each Dawn I Die*.

solitary confinement with a good conduct record and that he will recommend him to the parole board. Ross becomes a model prisoner. But when he comes before the parole board, he finds Grayce in charge. His parole is refused for the next five years.

Stacey's gang tracks down Shake Edwards, who tells them that while he identified Ross, it was actually "Polecat" Carlisle who framed Ross on instructions from Hanley and Grayce. When reporters came close to finding out the truth, the villains had "Polecat" picked up, convicted on an old charge and sent to Rocky Point to watch Ross. Feeling an obligation to Ross, Stacey surrenders to prison authorities to obtain revenge against "Polecat." Once there, Stacey is placed in solitary confinement. When Lassiter, a prisoner, dies at the hands of Kassock, the most sadistic of the wardens, the prisoners kill Kassock and make a break.

They are confronted by Armstrong, who tries to reason with them but is overpowered. The mob intends to kill him, but Ross prevents this by reminding them that Armstrong is needed to open up solitary confinement and release Stacey and other prisoners. Stacey and Ross are reunited. When the prisoners try to escape, they are confronted by the National Guard with machine guns and gas bombs. Many are killed and Stacey is wounded. Nevertheless they take "Polecat" to where Armstrong can overhear the conversation. Stacey forces "Polecat" to confess that Ross is innocent and was framed for manslaughter. Ross begs Stacey to surrender, but Stacey tells him it is too late. Stacey takes "Polecat" to the door at gunpoint and both are killed. When guards storm the prisoners' stronghold, they find Ross and Armstrong alive.

A *Banton Record* headline shows "Governor Hanley charged with murder. Grayce named as accessory. Warden of Rocky Point, corroborated by dying deputy, accuses pair of Ross Frame-Up." As he is being released from prison, with the loyal and loving Joyce waiting, Ross is handed a photo by Armstrong of Stacey inscribed to Ross, "I finally found a square guy!"

Comments: This was the only time that George Raft was directed by William Keighley. Keighley directed with tremendous zest and drew excellent performances from the entire cast, which was predominantly male. In his first film as a freelance actor, Raft gave one of his best performances; it was instrumental in landing him a long-term contract with Warner Bros. Even though some aspects of the film strained belief (such as Raft voluntarily returning to prison), it was compulsive viewing from first to last because of Keighley's direction, the acting and the exciting script.

James Cagney and Raft enjoyed working with each other and this translated into the finished product. Their chemistry was one of the film's greatest assets. This was another film where Raft was teamed with a powerhouse actor, Cagney, but raised the level of his own performance to that of his co-star. Raft had known Cagney back in his New York days and had previously played bits in two Cagney films. The pity was that the duo never again appeared on screen together. Raft wanted to work with Cagney again, but none of the possible ideas worked out. According to the review in *Variety*, "Raft is a plausible, gripping, underworld bigtimer. He rates the co-starring classification." This film was a big box office hit with domestic rentals of $1,111,000. It was reportedly Joseph Stalin's favorite film.

Biography: William Keighley was born in Philadelphia, Pennsylvania, on August 4, 1889. He dropped out of vocational school at 17 and worked as a messenger boy and railroad clerk while attending the Ludlum School of Dramatic Art. In 1912 he joined a touring company specializing in Shakespearean roles. He first acted on Broadway in 1915 and directed a New York play in 1928. He entered films and, after working as an assistant director and dialogue

director, began directing films in 1932. He was a Warner Bros. contract director throughout the greater part of his career, being particularly adept at gangster movies and comedies. Upon his retirement in 1953 he moved to Paris to devote himself to still photography before returning to reside in New York in 1972. He was married to actress Genevieve Tobin from 1938 until he died in New York City on June 24, 1984, aged 94, of a stroke and pulmonary embolism.

Biography: James Cagney was born James Francis Cagney, Jr., in New York City, on July 17, 1899. He was the son of an Irish barman and a half–Irish, half–Norwegian mother. In 1920 he joined the cast of a Broadway show and toured for five years. He made his screen debut in *Sinner's Holiday* (1930). Warner Bros. signed him to a seven-year contract and he became a star with *The Public Enemy* (1931), a seminal gangster film, as Tom Powers. He became one of the most popular stars of the thirties and won a Best Actor Oscar for playing George M. Cohan in *Yankee Doodle Dandy* (1942). He then left Warners to freelance via his own production company with disappointing results. In 1949 he made a sensational comeback in Warners' *White Heat* and enjoyed another successful decade of screen acting until he retired in 1961. His last film appearance, as Police Commissioner Rheinlander Waldo in *Ragtime* (1981), was an extremely unfortunate coda to his screen career. He died at his home, Verney Farms, in Stanfordville, New York, on March 30, 1986, aged 86. In 1922 he married Frances Willard Vernon (nicknamed "Bill") and they adopted two children.

Biography: Jane Bryan was born Jane O'Brien in Los Angeles on June 11, 1918. She did not come from a show business background and obtained a screen test via Jean Muir's Theatre Workshop. She signed a contract with Warner Bros., made her screen debut in *The Case of the Black Cat* (1936) and went on to appear in over a dozen films including two with Raft, *Each Dawn I Die* and

Invisible Stripes (1940). She married Justin Dart in 1939 and with him had two sons and a daughter. She largely abandoned her career for marriage. Her husband purchased the Rexall Drug Chain in 1945 and founded the conglomerate Dart-Kraft Incorporated. The Darts were close friends of Ronald Reagan and were extremely influential backing Reagan's bid for the presidency in 1980. She was widowed in 1984. She died at Pebble Beach, California, on April 8, 2009, aged 90, after a long illness.

I Stole a Million (1939)

Cast: George Raft (Joe Lourik/Joe Harris), Claire Trevor (Laura Benson), Dick Foran (Paul Carver), Henry Armetta (Nick Respina), Victor Jory (Patian), Joseph Sawyer (Detective Billings), Stanley Ridges (George Downs), Robert Elliott (Peterson), Tom Fadden (Verne), John Hamilton (District Attorney Wilson), Ernie Adams ("The Mooch"), Irving Bacon (Simpson), Raymond Bailey (Cabbie), John Berkes (Tramp), Virginia Brissac (Nurse), Arthur Q. Bryan (Manager), John Butler (Logan, Cab Manager), Hobart Cavanaugh, Billy Engle (Bookkeepers), Eddy Chandler (Baggage Car Guard), George Chandler (Clerk in Clothing Store), Wallis Clark (Jenkins), Hal K. Dawson (Member of Patian's Gang), Drew Demorest (Reporter), Eddie Dunn (Superintendent), Ralph Dunn (Bartender), Dick Elliott (Small Town Doctor), Fern Emmett (Visitor in Hospital), Dot Farley (Woman), Sammy Finn (Cabbie), Mary Forbes (Customer in Flower Shop), Lee Ford (Usher), Mary Foy (Matron), Jack Gardner (Reporter), Mack Gray (Bank Robber), Al Hill (Guard), Harold Hoff (Garage Attendant), Edward Fliegle, J. Anthony Hughes, Harry Stafford (Members of Patian's Gang), Lloyd Ingraham (Sympathetic Man), Charles Irwin (Theater Manager), Mike Lally (Croupier), Edmund MacDonald (Cop), Mary MacLaren (Nurse), Jerry Marlowe (Photographer), Larry McGrath (Gas Station Attendant), Mira McKinney (Mrs. Loomis), Malcolm "Bud" McTaggart (Reporter), Margaret McWade (Woman), Harold Minjir (Jewelry Salesman), Frances Morris (Prisoner), Lee Murray (Jockey), Jimmy O'Gatty (Mug), Sarah Padden (Lady in Post Office), Tom Steele, Dick Wessel, Emory Parnell (Cops), Edward Peil Sr., Jim Farley (Doormen), Russ Powell (Watchman), Joey Ray (Clerk), Betty Roadman (Matron), Jason Robards Sr. (Bank Teller), Frances Robinson (Elsie, Movie Cashier), Constantine Romanoff (Wrestler), Henry Roquemore (Manager), William Ruhl (Detective), Dave Sharpe (Cabbie), Landers Stevens (Businessman), Charles Sullivan (Gas Station Helper), Ben Taggart (Police Captain), Phil Tead (Charlie), Harry Tyler (Kibitzer at Dice Game), Emmett Vogan (Theater Manager), Billy Wayne (Mild Cabbie), Claire Whitney (Matron), Arthur Yeoman (Telegrapher).

Credits: Director: Frank Tuttle; Associate Producer: Burt Kelly; Assistant Director: Vernon Keays; Original Story: Lester Cole; Screenplay: Nathanael West; Photography: Milton R. Krasner; Editor: Ed Curtiss; Music: Frank Skinner and Ralph Freed; Musical Director: Charles Previn; Art Direction: Jack Otterson; Sound Supervisor: Bernard B. Brown; Sound Recorder: William R. Fox; Costumes: Vera West. Released by Universal on August 22, 1939. Black and white. 80 minutes.

Synopsis: Joe Lourik is a San Francisco taxi driver who is desperate to own his vehicle. His methods alienate the other drivers. They retaliate by taking the brake off his cab when his back is turned, causing the vehicle to roll into the bay. Wrongly accused of a crime, he refuses to accompany the police to the station and escapes. He hops a freight to another town. One of the hobos tells him when the train arrives in San Diego to disembark and go to see Patian.

Patian turns out to be the mastermind behind a series of bank robberies. Lourik reluctantly agrees to drive the getaway car. At the scene of the robbery, Lourik is framed for theft by Patian, but he escapes with the police in hot pursuit. He eludes them and confronts Patian, accusing him of a double cross. Patian gives him $100 together with the address of a Sacramento rooming house run by an ex-con named Simpson. Patian promises to send Lourik $1,500. When his money runs out and Simpson demands more rent, Simpson tells him that Patian has no intention of sending him the money.

Lourik goes to a flower shop intending to commit robbery. Instead he meets and falls in love with Laura Benson. With money obtained from robbing an illegal gambling business, he buys a legitimate garage business in Amesville. Over the next twelve months the business prospers, he marries Laura and she becomes pregnant. After police trace him to the garage, he persuades Simpson to send him a phony telegram offering to buy the garage for $2,000. This gives Lourik the excuse to go to San Diego to see Patian. When Patian tries to pull a gun on him, Lourik disarms him and takes $2,000 from Patian's wallet. He arranges for Laura to enter a private hospital and sends her a telegram. Shortly afterwards he is attacked by Patian's men, robbed of his money and thrown from a moving cab.

He discovers that Laura has been taken to a charity ward. Desperate for money, he robs a post office. In the process he drops the telegram so the police are able to identify him. He finds a newspaper in the street which tells him that Laura has given birth to a baby daughter and has been discharged, but is still under police surveillance. At one point Laura is sent to prison for aiding and abetting a criminal. Later Laura goes to the district attorney to beg him for clemency if Lourik surrenders. Despite extenuating circumstances from the early crime, the D.A. can promise nothing. He allows Laura to arrange a meeting, but warns her that detectives will be watching. At Lourik's hideout there is an emotional reunion between Joe and Laura. Lourik tells her that he is going to escape with her and the baby.

Laura tells him that it will not work and that his only recourse is to surrender. Lourik spots the police and at Laura's urging goes outside to be arrested and to serve a long jail sentence.

Comments: This was the second of two films in which Raft was directed by Frank Tuttle and the first of two films in which he co-starred with Claire Trevor. It was the second film which Raft made as a freelance and was one of his lesser films. Its theme was to show the way in which small crimes grow into major ones. If the film had been true to this theme throughout its running time, it would have been a punchy, hard-hitting crime drama. Unfortunately when Trevor entered the scene about twenty minutes into the film, it rapidly went downhill and became schmaltz. It never really recovered its lost momentum. Trevor was an actress who was so much more effective when she played characters with starch in their veins rather than saccharin as here. The best scene however was one that belonged to Raft and Trevor, namely where she fell in love with him while dancing. Their romantic dance was exquisitely done.

It was hard to believe that any character played by Raft would have behaved in such a way as to jeopardize his life in the manner depicted. Each of his actions seemed to be more foolish than the last and designed to cause even greater harm. Apparently when Raft was given the script of this film and discovered that he had to rob a post office, he allegedly said, "No gangster would do that! That's a federal rap!" In spite of this objection, the scene remained in the picture and provided the point of the title, *I Stole a Million*. This film was a box office flop.

Biography: Claire Trevor was born Claire Wemlinger in New York City on March 8, 1910, the daughter of Noel B. Wemlinger and Edith Morrison. Her father was a prosperous French merchant tailor who lost his business in the Depression. She was educated at Columbia University and the American Academy of Dramatic Arts. She commenced her stage career with the Repertory Players in Ann Arbor, Michigan, in 1929. She made her Broadway debut in *Whistling in the Dark* (1932). In 1933 she signed a five-year contract with Fox. The peak of her career was probably reached when she won a Best Supporting Actress Oscar for *Key Largo* (1948). She also received Best Supporting Actress Oscar nominations for *Dead End* (1937) and *The High and the Mighty* (1954). She officially retired in 1987. She wed Clark Andrews in 1938, but divorced in 1943. She then wed Navy Lt. Cyclos Dunsmoore in 1943, but divorced in 1947. With him she had a son, Charles (born in 1944), who was killed in a plane crash in 1978. In 1948 she married producer Milton Bren with whom she had two sons, Donald (born in 1949) and Peter (born in 1950). She was widowed in 1979. She died at Hoag Memorial Hospital, Newport Beach, California, on April 8, 2000, aged 90, of pneumonia and acute respiratory failure.

Invisible Stripes (1939)

Cast: George Raft (Cliff Taylor), Jane Bryan (Peggy), William Holden (Tim Taylor), Humphrey Bogart (Chuck Martin), Flora Robson (Mrs. Taylor), Paul Kelly (Ed Kruger), Lee Patrick (Molly Daniels), Henry O'Neill (Parole Officer Masters), Frankie Thomas (Tommy McNeil), Moroni Olsen (The Warden), Margot Stevenson (Sue), Marc Lawrence (Lefty Sloan), Joseph Downing (Johnny Hudson), Leo Gorcey (Jimmy), William Haade (Shrank), Tully Marshall (Old Peter), Joseph Crehan (Mr. Chasen), Chester Clute (Mr. Butler), John Hamilton (Police Captain Johnson), Maude Allen (Seated Lady at Dance), Irving Bacon (Human Resources Director), Raymond Bailey (Bookie), Bruce Bennett (Rich Man), Wade Boteler (Policeman Outside Garage), Sidney Bracey (Bank Guard), Frank Bruno (Pauly), Eddy Chandler (Police Driver), Lane Chandler (Detective), Cliff Clark (Police Sergeant), Richard Clayton (Hired Stockboy), G. Pat Collins (Alec), Ray Cooke (Pinky), William B. Davidson (McGovern), Joe Devlin (Henchman), Ralph Dunn (Doorman), Robert Elliott (Arresting Officer), Frank Faylen (Steve), Sammy Finn (Spotter), Jane Gilbert (Young Lady), Mack Gray (Hudson), Bert Hanlon (Shorty), Lew Harvey (Betting Room Door Guard), Al Hill (Getaway Driver at Bank Job), Al Hill, Jr. (Hired Stock Boy), Max Hoffman, Jr. (Chauffeur Showing Off Car), William Hopper (Society Gent), J. Anthony Hughes (Chauffeur), John Irwin (Prisoner), Selmer Jackson (Police Lieutenant), Harry Wilson, Walter James, Pat Flaherty (Workers), Victor Kilian (Loading Dock Foreman), Ethan Laidlaw (Cop Outside Police Station), Mike Lally (Henchman Driver), Marion Martin (Blonde), Frank Mayo (Prison Gate Guard), Stan Meyers (Dance Band Leader), Jack Mower (Detective Escorting Convicts), Pat O'Malley (Jailhouse Lieutenant), Emory Parnell (Policeman Outside Bank), John Ridgely (Employment Clerk), Harry Strang (Party Bartender), George Taylor (Smitty), Charles C. Wilson (Arresting Officer), Claude Wisberg (Older Boy), Dorothea Wolbert (Flower Seller).

Credits: Director: Lloyd Bacon; Executive Producer: Hal B. Wallis; Associate Producer: Louis F. Edelman; Assistant Directors: Elmer Decker and Don Alvarado; Dialogue Director: Irving Rapper; Original Book: Warden Lewis E. Lawes; Screenplay: Warren Duff; Story: Jonathan Finn; Photography: Ernest Haller; Editor: James Gibbon; Music: Heinz Roemheld; Orchestrations: Ray Heindorf; Musical Director: Leo F. Forbstein; Art Director: Max Parker; Sound Recorder: Dolph Thomas; Costumes: Milo Anderson; Makeup: Perc Westmore; Special Effects: Byron Haskin. Released by Warner Bros. on December 30, 1939. Black and white. 82 minutes.

Tagline: "Three Men and a Girl, Bound by Invisible Ties, Branded by Invisible Stripes."

Synopsis: Cliff Taylor and Chuck Martin are released on parole from Sing Sing Prison, New York. As they leave, the warden says that he has faith in Taylor, but none in Martin.

Taylor goes back to live with his understanding mother. He loses his girl, Sue, who tells him that she cannot marry an ex-convict. Gang boss Ed Kruger lets Martin back into the gang providing that he drops his vendetta against fellow gang member Lefty Sloan. As an ex-convict on parole, Taylor finds satisfactory employment hard to obtain because he is wearing invisible stripes. He accidentally encounters Martin and his girl Molly coming out of a movie theater. He declines Martin's offer to join the gang, which is making plenty of money illegally.

Taylor is eventually hired as a stock boy and is promoted to clerk. Although he is doing well, his life falls apart when he is picked up on suspicion after the store is robbed of $40,000 worth of furs. Although he is innocent, he is dismissed. Taylor's brother Tim, struggling to make enough money to marry his sweetheart Peggy, becomes unhappy to the point where he is prepared to embark on a life of crime. Cliff and Tim physically fight over this. Placing his own life in jeopardy, Cliff rejoins Martin and his former gang in a series of audacious bank robberies in order to buy a garage for Tim so that he can wed Peggy. Cliff covers up by telling his mother and brother that he is selling tractors. When the money is sufficient, Cliff quits the gang, alienating all the gangsters with the exception of Martin.

A later robbery goes seriously wrong. While escaping from the police, the gang implicates Tim by using his garage for their getaway. Martin tells Tim where the money for the garage really came from. Tim helps the wounded Martin reach Molly's apartment. When Tim returns to the garage, the police are waiting and he is arrested. Molly telephones Cliff to help Martin. Martin tells him that if Tim keeps his mouth shut, he will only receive a minimum sentence. Cliff does not want his brother to become a convict like himself, so he cuts a deal with the police captain that if Tim identifies the members of the gang and becomes a witness, the case against him will be dropped.

Cliff goes to Martin to try to help him escape. Leaving the police station, he is followed by men in league with the gang. Once the gang discovers the whereabouts of Taylor and Martin, they decide to exact revenge. In the ensuing shootout, Taylor and Martin are killed. Most of the gang are wiped out by the police. Tim shows Peggy his improved garage which is named "Taylor Brothers Garage." He informs the cop on the beat that Cliff is a silent partner.

Comments: This was the only time that Raft was directed by Lloyd Bacon. This was the first film Raft made under his new Warner Bros. contract. Its budget was $500,000. It was the first of two films in which Raft appeared with Humphrey Bogart. The theme of *Invisible Stripes* was that gangsters make plenty of money through crime, while honest people struggle to make a living. All of the elements of a classic gangster movie were present, yet the overall impression was one of disappointment. The last part of the film went awry and both Raft and Bogart were curiously ineffectual at the climax when they were killed, which was not characteristic of either actor. According to William Holden, during the fight scene between the brothers, Holden accidentally hit Raft in the eye with his head and opened a gash. Raft was good-natured about the incident. Flora Robson played Raft's mother but in real life she was younger than he was. One highlight of this film was Raft and Robson dancing the jitterbug together. One irony was that the film showing at the theater where Raft encountered Bogart was Bogart's *You Can't Get Away with Murder* (1939). *Invisible Stripes* made little impression at the box office.

Biography: Lloyd Francis Bacon was born in San José, California, on December 4, 1889. He was educated at Santa Clara College. After naval service in World War I, he commenced his film career as an actor with Lloyd Hamilton and he first began directing shorts in 1921, again with Hamilton. He directed his first feature in 1926. Much of his best work was done under contract to Warner Bros. and later to 20th Century–Fox. He died in Burbank, California, on November 15, 1955, aged 65, of a cerebral hemorrhage. He was married three times and had two sons.

Biography: Humphrey DeForest Bogart was born in New York City on December 25, 1899. He was the son of Belmont DeForest Bogart, a general practitioner, and Maud Humphrey, an artist. He attended Trinity School and Phillips Academy at Andover, Massachusetts. He joined the Navy in 1918 and served for two years in the North Atlantic. Afterwards he drifted through a number of posts before landing a job as an actor with a touring company. He went into films in the early thirties, but failed. He returned to the stage where he scored a resounding hit on Broadway as Duke Mantee in *The Petrified Forest*. He signed a seven-year contract with Warner Bros. in November 1935 and repeated the Mantee role in the screen version in 1936. He was nominated for a Best Actor Oscar in *Casablanca* (1942), but finally won one for *The African Queen* (1951) as Charlie Allnut. His first three marriages to actresses Helen Menken, Mary Philips and Mayo Methot all ended in divorce. In 1945 he wed Lauren Bacall with whom he had a son Stephen (born in 1949) and a daughter Leslie (born in 1952). He died in Los Angeles on January 14, 1957, aged 57, of cancer.

Biography: William Holden was born William Franklin Beedle, Jr., in O'Fallon, Illinois, on April 17, 1918. Holden was spotted in an amateur production and signed by Paramount for whom he made his screen debut in *Prison Farm* (1938). His second film *Golden Boy* (1939) won him both fan popularity and critical acclaim. During World War II he served as an Army lieutenant. After the war his career received an enormous boost when Billy Wilder cast him as Joe Gillis in *Sunset Blvd.* (1950), for which he received a Best Actor Oscar nomination, and as Sefton in *Stalag 17* (1953), which won him a Best Actor Oscar. He became one of the most popular film stars

of the fifties and was at one time the highest paid. His career declined as his consumption of alcohol grew. He was found dead in his luxury apartment in Santa Monica on November 16, 1981, aged 63, having bled to death following a fall. In 1941 he married actress Brenda Marshall, with whom he had two sons, but divorced in 1973. Holden and Raft both had cameo appearances in *Casino Royale*.

The House Across the Bay (1940)

Cast: George Raft (Steve Larwitt), Joan Bennett ("Lucky" Brenda Bentley), Lloyd Nolan (Slant Kolma), Walter Pidgeon (Tim Nolan), Gladys George (Mary Bogel), Peggy Shannon (Alice), June Knight (Babe), Joe Sawyer (Charley, Proprietor of Sorrento Cafe), Billy Wayne (Barney, Bartender), Edward Fielding (Judge), Virginia Brissac (Landlady), Cy Kendall (Crawley), Max Wagner (Jim), Frank Bruno (Jerry, Slant's Henchman), Herbert Ashley (Man in Park), Sam Ash (Broker), Peter Camlin (French Pilot), Marcelle Corday (French Maid), James Craig, Jack Lubell (Brenda's Boy Friends), George Renavent, Jean Del Val (French Officials), Sam Finn (Headwaiter), Mack Gray (Doorman Lookout), Harrison Greene (Irate Customer), Joseph Crehan, Charles Griffin (Federal Men), Kit Guard (Taresca's Driver), Harry Harvey (Man in Club), Max Hoffman, Jr., Donald Kerr (Drivers), Etta McDaniel (Lydia, the Maid), Miki Morita (Japanese Houseboy), Frances Morris (Slant's Secretary), Martin Cichy, Jim Farley, Franklyn Farnum, Al Ferguson, Pat O'Malley (Prison Guards), Elsa Peterson (Mrs. Hanson), John Bohn, Paul Phillips (Reporters), Dick Rush (Bailiff), Harry Tyler (Fur Peddler), Carol Adams, Kay Gordon, Edith Haskins, Pearlie Norton, Jean O'Donnell, Metzie Uehlien, Victoria Vinton (Chorus Girls), Maxine Leslie, Kitty McHugh, Helen Shipman, Dorothy Vaughan, Ruth Warren (Prisoners' Wives), Emmett Vogan (U.S. Official), Eddie Marr, Norman Willis (Taresca's Henchmen),

Isabel Withers (Woman in Club), Allen Wood (Newsboy), Freeman Wood (Mr. Hanson), Sam Wren (Draughtsman), Armand Wright (Barber).

Credits: Director: Archie Mayo; Producer: Walter Wanger; Assistant Director: Charles Kerr; Original Story: Myles Connolly; Screenplay: Kathryn Scola; Photography: Merritt B. Gerstad; Editors: Otho Lovering and Dorothy Spencer; Score and Musical Director: Werner Janssen; Choreographer: Sammy Lee; Art Direction: Alexander Golitzen and Richard Irvine; Sound Recorders: Frank Maher and Fred Lau; Costumes: Irene; Special Photographic Effects: Ray Binger; Stunts: Paul Mantz. Songs: "Chula Chi Hua Hua" by Sidney Clare, Nick Castle and Jule Style; "I'll Be a Fool Again" by Al Siegel; and "A Hundred Kisses from Now" by George R. Brown and Irving Actman. Released by United Artists on March 1, 1940. Black and white. 88 minutes.

Synopsis: Steve Larwitt runs a San Francisco nightclub with a gambling room which he rents out. He is initially antagonistic towards Brenda Bentley, a new chorus girl in his club, but when she wins him $15,000 on a bet, he revises his opinion of her. As a result he gives her a starring spot in his club show. They go out together for a week before he proposes marriage. She accepts. Over the next three years he becomes a business tycoon, but he has been cheating on his income tax.

Larwitt's lawyer, Slant Kolma, secretly lusts after Brenda. Kolma falsely tells Brenda that if Larwitt was convicted of income tax evasion, he would only receive a one-year jail sentence. To prevent business rivals from killing Steve, Brenda sends a letter with incriminating evidence to the I.R.S. As a result Larwitt is arrested by the FBI and tried. Kolma deliberately undermines Larwitt's business empire and conducts a worthless defense. Larwitt is found guilty and sentenced to ten years in Alcatraz. Brenda rents an apartment on Telegraph Hill where she can be close to Steve. Another wife visiting a prisoner on Alcatraz, Mary Bogel

becomes her good friend. They are offered a lift by Tim Nolan, a plane designer and pilot. Nolan becomes a friend of Brenda and their relationship develops.

Kolma has been keeping track of Brenda and encounters her at a restaurant where he is introduced to Nolan. Brenda goes to Kolma's hotel where he informs her that she is broke, but he will give her money and love. She is repelled and indignantly refuses. Kolma threatens to tell Larwitt that she gave information to the FBI. Brenda tells Mary that she must disappear. Brenda flees to Alameda where she reverts to her former profession as a chanteuse at the Sorrento Cafe. Mary tells a distraught Nolan where Brenda is and he tracks her to the cafe. Kolma goes to see Larwitt in Alcatraz and tells him that Brenda is having an affair with Nolan.

Larwitt escapes from Alcatraz by swimming ashore. Larwitt steals a car and some civilian clothes, goes to the club and waits for Brenda in her dressing room with vengeance in his heart. When Brenda appears, he advances menacingly towards her, intending to strangle her. Brenda blurts out the truth and says that it was Kolma who doublecrossed him. Nolan turns up with a gun, tells Larwitt that Brenda has never been unfaithful to him and that it was Kolma who stole all Larwitt's money. Brenda promises to try to help Steve escape. Convinced, Steve pretends to accept her offer, but tells her that he has a business matter to take care of and will meet her in an hour. He drives to Kolma's hotel where he finds Kolma and kills him. Attempting to return to Alcatraz, he is shot to death by police. While waiting for him at the club, Brenda learns of his death.

Comments: This was the second of two films in which Raft was directed by Archie Mayo. Alfred Hitchcock is believed to have shot a couple of scenes as a favor to Walter Wanger, for whose production company he had just helmed *Foreign Correspondent*. The title of this film referred to the famous penitentiary near San Francisco. This was the third of four films in which Raft appeared with Joan Bennett. In the course of this film, she sang three songs. Lloyd Nolan, in the third of his three Raft films, came across well as a shyster lawyer with a liking for Bennett. Raft dominated the first half-hour, but then largely disappeared until the climax. He did however remain the focal point of the plot and all the other characters talked about him. Raft's method of escaping from Alcatraz by swimming was factually inaccurate and ludicrous. No one ever escaped from the real Alcatraz that way. It may be that this was deliberate in that Alcatraz at the time was a working prison so depicting a possible real method of escape was deemed inadvisable. This film became a bone of contention between Raft and Warner Bros. because Raft was playing a gangster and died at the end. It was exactly the kind of part Raft was not prepared to play for his home studio, but would do for an independent producer like Wanger. Although it was in the gangster genre, it was one of Raft's lesser films and was not a box office hit.

They Drive by Night (UK: *The Road to Frisco*) (1940)

Cast: George Raft (Joe Fabrini), Ann Sheridan (Cassie Hartley), Ida Lupino (Lana Carlsen), Humphrey Bogart (Paul Fabrini), Gale Page (Pearl Fabrini), Alan Hale (Ed Carlsen), Roscoe Karns (Irish McGurn), John Litel (Harry McNamara), George Tobias (George Rondolos), Frank Faylen, Eddie Acuff, Eddie Fetherston, Pat Flaherty, Al Hill, Ralph Sanford, Charles Sherlock, Charles Sullivan, Dick Wessel (Drivers in Cafe), Marie Blake (Waitress), Eddy Chandler (Driver), Richard Clayton (Young Man), Joyce Compton (Sue Carter), Alan Davis (Driver), Joe Devlin (Fatso), Demetris Emanuel (Waiter), Claire James, Bess Flowers (Party Guests), Brenda Fowler (Prison Matron), Jesse Graves (Charles Culpepper), Mack Gray (Mike, Driver),

William Haade (Tough Driver), Charles Halton (Farnsworth), John Hamilton (Defense Attorney), Phyllis Hamilton (Stenographer), Carl Harbaugh (Mechanic), George Haywood (Policeman at Accident), Don Turner, Oscar "Dutch" Hendrian (Drivers), Howard C. Hickman (Judge), J. Anthony Hughes (Reporter), Paul Hurst (Pete Haig), Dorothea Kent (Sue), Mike Lally (Man Griping at Farnsworth), Vera Lewis (Landlady), George Lloyd (Barney), Wilfred Lucas (Bailiff), Frank Mayo (Motorist at Accident Base), Matt McHugh (Repairman), Edmund Mortimer (Man in Courtroom), Jack Mower (Deputy with Farnsworth), Henry O'Neill (District Attorney), Pedro Regas (Harry's Partner), John Ridgely (Hank Dawson), Cliff Saum (Man Outside Barney's), Harry Semels (Leo, Cashier), Dorothy Vaughan (Courtroom Matron), Max Wagner (Sweeney, Driver), Billy Wayne (Repairman), Frank Wilcox (Reporter), Norman Willis (Neves, Mike's Assistant), Jack Wise (Jake), Lillian Yarbo (Chloe, Lana's Maid).

Credits: Director: Raoul Walsh; Executive Producer: Hal B. Wallis; Associate Producer: Mark Hellinger; Assistant Director: Elmer Decker; Dialogue Director: Hugh MacMullen; Based on the Novel *The Long Haul* by A.I. Bezzerides; Screenplay: Jerry Wald and Richard Macaulay; Photography: Arthur Edeson; Editor: Thomas Richards; Music: Adolph Deutsch; Musical Direction: Leo F. Forbstein; Orchestrations: Arthur Lange; Art Direction: John Hughes; Costumes: Milo Anderson; Makeup: Perc Westmore; Special Effects: Byron Haskin and H.F. Koenekamp; Sound Recorder: Oliver S. Garretson; Montages: Don Siegel and Robert Burks; Stunts: Harvey Parry. Released by Warner Bros. on August 3, 1940. Black and white. 93 minutes.

Synopsis: The Fabrini brothers are trying to establish themselves in the trucking business. They have only one truck, however. Hauling a consignment of apples to Los Angeles, they are run off the road. Joe Fabrini hitches a ride to Barney's cafe to call for help.

There he encounters Cassie Hartley, a wise-cracking waitress. Mike Williams, for whom he was hauling the apples, owes Joe $300. Williams refuses to wire him the money so that Joe can buy a new tire. Instead he sends another trucker to haul the load into L.A. He also notifies Farnsworth, a financial company representative, of Joe's whereabouts because Joe is behind in his truck payments. Paul Fabrini, who dreams of a more secure existence with his wife Pearl, later turns up at the cafe with a replacement tire. The brothers then go to San Francisco where they barge into Williams' office and take the money they are owed by him.

En route to Los Angeles, they stop to pick up a woman who turns out to be Cassie. She has quit her job because her boss tried to become too familiar with her. They stop off at Mandel's cafe where they encounter a weary trucker named McNamara, who later falls asleep at the wheel and is killed in the resulting crash. The Fabrinis and Cassie, who are following behind, witness this accident. In Los Angeles, Joe finds Cassie a room where he falls asleep. In the morning while parking his truck close to the office of Ed Carlsen, he is involved in a vicious fight with another trucker which is witnessed by Ed and his shrewish wife, Lana. Lana, who knew Joe in the past, fancies him, but it is not reciprocated. Carlson arranges for Joe to pick up a consignment of lemons. They haul the lemons to San Francisco where they sell them at a big profit. Their rig is almost repossessed by Farnsworth. Joe pays the balance outstanding on the truck out of the proceeds from the lemon cargo. They buy another cargo, but on the road back Paul falls asleep at the wheel and the truck crashes. Joe is thrown clear, but Paul loses his right arm.

The truck is not insured. Joe loses his business and becomes desperate. At the insistence of his wife Lana, Ed appoints Joe traffic manager of his company. Joe does extremely well,

Left to right: Humphrey Bogart, Ann Sheridan and Raft in *They Drive by Night*.

but when he and Cassie go to Paul's for dinner, they find him extremely bitter about the loss of his arm and his unemployment. At the Carlsons' housewarming party, Lana tries to start a relationship with Joe, but he makes it clear that he is not going to play around with the boss's wife. After the party, Ed and Lana go to a nightclub where Ed becomes progressively drunker. When Lana drives Ed home, she deliberately leaves the motor of the car running in the garage. She uses the magic eye to close the garage door so that the by now unconscious Ed dies of carbon monoxide poisoning.

His death is ruled accidental. Lana gives Joe a 50 percent share in the company which he reluctantly accepts, but he is able to find Paul a job. Joe runs the company extremely efficiently for six months. When Lana goes to see Joe, she meets Cassie and promptly faints. Joe drives Lana home. When she arrives, she runs straight into the house. A day later Lana turns up at the office where she tries to proposition Joe, but Joe tells her that he is getting married to Cassie. Lana, berserk, shouts at Joe, "You made me kill Ed!"

In revenge she goes to the district attorney and accuses Joe of coercing her into killing Ed for the insurance money. The D.A. indicts Joe for murder. At the prison, Cassie begs Lana to tell the truth, but to no avail. The prison door has a magic eye similar to the one which closed the doors of Ed's garage. Seeing this makes Lana deranged. Nevertheless the situation looks bleak for Joe. On the witness stand Lana goes insane, screaming, "The doors made me do it!" The case against Joe is dismissed. After all that has happened Joe intends to divide up his share of the business among the employees for them to run as a cooperative and to go back on the road. Paul's wife is now pregnant. The men refuse to accept Joe's resignation and insist that he stay in charge. Joe and Cassie are happily reunited, intending to marry and looking forward to the future together.

Comments: This was the third of five films Raft made for director Raoul Walsh. Walsh's movies were noted for their vigor and *They Drive by Night* was no exception. This was the second time that Ida Lupino co-starred with Raft. Ann Sheridan had played bits in Paramount films starring Raft but this was the only time she had co-starring status with him. It was the second and final film Raft made with Bogart. Aside from *Some Like It Hot,* this is probably the best-remembered of Raft's films. The first and better part of the film dealt with the Fabrini brothers and how they earned their living in the road haulage business as independent truckers. As the brothers, Raft and Bogart were well cast.

The second and less successful half of the film told of Raft's involvement with Lupino, wife of powerful trucking baron Alan Hale. Studio boss Jack Warner was enraged by Lupino, who was heavily into astrology and caused costly delays by refusing to act on certain days when her astrologer warned her against it. Warner was inclined to forgive her when he saw the quality of her acting and when the film went on to gross over $4,000,000. If the film can be criticized, it's because the two halves of the film did not entirely mesh into one satisfying whole. This was probably not entirely surprising since the second half was a reworking of an older Warner Bros. movie called *Bordertown* (1935) with Bette Davis. The reason for the reworking was on account of a copyright dispute which arose between Warners and A.I. Bezzerides, the writer of the 1938 novel *The Long Haul* on which this movie was based. The film was remade in a disguised western format as *Blowing Wild* (1953). *They Drive by Night* is not to be confused with a Warner Bros. British film of the same name, released in 1938. This necessitated a U.K. change of title to *The Road to Frisco*. It is best remembered for its pace, some snappy dialogue, and for the star power of its leading players, all of them close to the top of their game. When Raft as Joe Fabrini says, "We're tougher than any truck that ever came off the assembly line," you can believe him!

Raft had one abiding memory of this film: "I could drive a car blindfolded. I learned how when I was helping to move booze, and the associate producer of the movie and my old pal, Mark Hellinger, must have known this when he assigned me to *They Drive by Night*. Some people say I got nothing from Owney Madden but a bad reputation — but the driving skill I acquired when I worked for him in New York years before undoubtedly saved my life and those of the people in the picture with me.

"In the scene, Humphrey Bogart, Ann Sheridan and I are highballing down a long hill in an old beat-up truck. Halfway down, the brakes really went out — a situation that wasn't in the script. Bogart saw me press the pedal and when nothing happened, he began to curse. 'We're going to get killed!' he yelled. Ann screamed and turned her eyes away from the road as I fought the wheel. I couldn't have been more scared myself. The speedometer hit 80 when I saw a break on the right where a bulldozer had started a new road. I pulled hard on the wheel and the truck went bouncing up the embankment where it finally stopped.

"Ann was too upset to talk, but Bogart said, 'Thanks, pal.'

"'Don't thank me,' I thought to myself because I didn't have the breath to answer. 'Write a letter to Owney Madden or Feets Edson.'"

Biography: Ann Sheridan was born Clara Lou Sheridan in Denton, Texas, on February 21, 1915, the daughter of George W. Sheridan and Lula Warren. She was educated at North Texas State Teachers College. In 1933 she won a beauty contest in which the first prize was an appearance in a Paramount film entitled *Search for Beauty.* She signed a contract with Paramount who featured her in small roles for eighteen months. In 1935 she moved over to Warner Bros., who dubbed her "The Oomph Girl" which made her a star. Once her film career was over in the fifties, she enjoyed some television success on the daytime soap opera *Another World* (1965–1966) and at the time of her death she was appearing in *Pistols 'n' Petticoats.* She died at the Motion Picture Country Home and Hospital in Woodland Hills, California, on January 21, 1967, aged 51, of cancer of the esophagus and liver. She married and divorced actors Edward Norris (1936–37) and secondly George Brent (1942–43). In 1966 she married Scott McKay, who survived her.

Biography: Ida Lupino was born in London on February 4, 1918, the daughter of Stanley Lupino and Constance Emerald, well-known professional entertainers. She studied at the Royal Academy of Dramatic Arts. She became a film star accidentally when she accompanied her mother to an audition for the leading role in a British comedy, *Her First Affaire* (1933). American director Allan Dwan preferred Ida to her mother and cast her in the leading role. Paramount brought her to Hollywood where she made her screen debut in *Search for Beauty* (1933). She became a star playing a Cockney spitfire in *The Light That Failed* (1939). During the 1940s her acting career peaked when Warner Bros. provided her with a number of strong dramatic roles. During the 1950s she became the only major female director in Hollywood, directing feature films with controversial themes and numerous television episodes. She married Louis Hayward in 1938, but divorced in 1945. She married secondly producer-writer Collier Young in 1948, but divorced in 1951. She married Howard Duff in 1951, but divorced in 1984. With him she had a daughter, Bridget, born in 1952. Ida Lupino died in Burbank, California, on August 3, 1995, aged 77, of bronchopneumonia and metastatic colon cancer. It is a travesty that she was never Oscar-nominated.

Manpower (1941)

Cast: Edward G. Robinson (Hank McHenry), Marlene Dietrich (Fay Duval), George Raft (Johnny Marshall), Alan Hale (Jumbo Wells), Frank McHugh (Omaha), Eve Arden (Dolly), Barton MacLane (Smiley Quinn),

Ward Bond (Eddie Adams), Walter Catlett (Sidney Whipple), Joyce Compton (Scarlett), Lucia Carroll (Flo), Egon Brecher (Antoine "Pop" Duval), Cliff Clark (Cully), Joseph Crehan (Sweeney), Ben Welden (Al Hurst), Barbara Pepper (Polly), Dorothy Appleby (Wilma), Murray Alper (Linesman), Jean Ames (Thelma, Café Cashier), Lynne Baggett (Hostess at Midnight Club), Leah Baird (Mrs. Taylor, Prison Matron), Diana Barrymore (Hostess at Midnight Club), Arthur Q. Bryan, Dick Elliott (Drunk Texans), Joyce Bryant (Mrs. Brewster), Georgia Caine (Head Nurse), Peter Caldwell (Boy Playing Baseball), Nat Carr (28 Club Waiter), Glen Cavender (Drunk Bounced from Midnight Club), Eddy Chandler (Detective in Raid), Chester Clute (Drug Store Clerk), Joe Devlin (Bartender), John Dilson (Jail Clerk), Roland Drew (Citizen Reporting Power Outage), Ralph Dunn (Man Calling Sweeney), Faye Emerson (Nurse), Eddie Fetherston (Power Company Telephone Operator), James Flavin (Orderly), Brenda Fowler (Mrs. Calkin, Saleslady), William Gould (Freeman, Police Desk Sergeant), Fred Graham, William Newell, Charles Sullivan, Elliott Sullivan, Dick Wessel (Linemen at Café Counter), Carl Harbaugh (Noisy Nash), John Harmon (Benny, the Counterman), Bobby Robb, Drew Roddy, Harry Harvey, Jr. (Boys Playing Baseball), Jeffrey Sayre, Al Herman, William Hopper (Power Company Telephone Operators), Herbert Heywood (Charlie, a Watchman), Frederick Hollander (Accompanist), Harry Holman (Justice of the Peace), Stuart Holmes (28 Club Bartender), John Kelly (28 Club Bouncer), Barbara Land (Marilyn), Vera Lewis (Wife of Justice of the Peace), Audra Lindley (Nurse), Jack "Tiny" Lipson (Midnight Club Bartender), Frank Mayo (Midnight Club Doorman), Pat McKee (Midnight Club Bouncer), Muriel Barr, Gayle Mellott (Models), Paul Panzer (28 Club Bartender), Lee Phelps (Detective in Raid), Jane Randolph (Hat Check Girl), Jack Richardson (Midnight Club Waiter), William Royle (Policeman in Raid), Robert Strange (Bailsman), Harry Strang (Fireman Sent to Line 191), Harry Tenbrook (Midnight Club Waiter), Dorothy Vaughan (Mrs. Boyle), Sailor Vincent (Sailor, a Linesman), Nella Walker (Floor Lady), Billy Wayne (Taxi Driver), Joan Winfield (Nurse Holding Baby), Isabel Withers (Head Nurse), Beal Wong (Wing Ling, Chinese Singer).

Credits: Director: Raoul Walsh; Executive Producer: Hal B. Wallis; Associate Producer: Mark Hellinger; Assistant Director: Russell Saunders; Dialogue Director: Hugh Cummings; Original Story: Fred Niblo, Jr.; Screenplay: Richard Macaulay and Jerry Wald; Photography: Ernest Haller; Editor: Ralph

Raft and Edward G. Robinson in *Manpower*.

Dawson; Music Score: Adolph Deutsch and Heinz Roemheld; Musical Director: Leo F. Forbstein; Art Direction: Max Parker; Sound Recorder: Dolph Thomas; Costumes: Milo Anderson; Makeup: Perc Westmore; Special Effects: Byron Haskin and H.F. Koenekamp; Technical Advisor: Verne Elliott. Songs: "I'm in No Mood for Music Tonight" and "He Lied and I Listened": Music by Frederick Hollander and Lyrics by Frank Loesser. Released by Warner Bros. on August 9, 1941. Black and white. 105 minutes.

Synopsis: The power linesmen of the Pacific Power and Light Company are relaxing in the 28 Club in the Los Angeles area. Outside a storm rages and the men are summoned by telephone to repair broken overhead lines. Hank McHenry saves the life of his friend Johnny Marshall, but receives an electric shock through one leg. Hank is unconscious, but Johnny manages to revive him. Hank is taken to a hospital where he recovers and is promoted to foreman.

One of the veteran linesmen, "Pop" Duval, is killed and Hank and Johnny break the news to this daughter Fay, a singer and hostess at the seedy Midnight Club. Ever since he accompanied her father to meet Fay when she was released from jail after serving a one-year sentence for alleged theft, Johnny has disliked Fay. Hank however rapidly becomes infatuated with her. Hank goes to the Midnight Club and wins her attention. She initially tries to persuade him not to go there because the place is too low-class for a decent fellow like him. Hank ignores her warnings and continues to frequent the club, talking to Fay until eventually he proposes marriage. Although she is not in love with him, but secretly fancies Johnny, she accepts because she wants to escape from her poverty-stricken lifestyle.

Not long after their marriage, Johnny suffers an industrial injury. Hank insists that Johnny recover at his new house. One night, suffering from insomnia, Fay declares her love for Johnny, but out of loyalty to Hank nothing happens

between them. After two months while Hank is away on a job, Fay leaves him to go to Chicago. On her way out of town, she drops in at the Midnight Club to say farewell to the other girls. While she is there, there is a police raid and Fay is taken to the police station along with the other girls. The police phone Hank, but Johnny answers the call. Johnny rushes to the jail and bails her out. When Fay again declares her love for him, he tells her that she is married to Hank and slaps her as a reminder.

Johnny returns to the crew, repairing overhead lines. Fay goes to the location where Hank is working in foul weather to tell him the whole story. While having a break, Hank enters the shed and finds Fay, who informs him of her love for Johnny. Hank jumps to the conclusion that Fay and Johnny have been conducting a clandestine affair. Rushing out into the rainswept night, he climbs a pole where Johnny is working on live wires. The two engage in a violent fight which ends when Hank accidentally falls from the pole. Before Hank dies, Johnny and Fay explain the truth to him. Afterwards Johnny goes to the bus stop where he dissuades Fay from leaving for Chicago.

Comments: This was the third film Raft made under his Warner Bros. contract. It was the fourth time he was directed by Raoul Walsh, who did his usual fine job. It was the first of two films in which Raft co-starred with Edward G. Robinson. It was the first of three films in which Raft appeared with Marlene Dietrich, but she only did a cameo in *Follow the Boys* and they both did cameos (although in the same sequence) of *Around the World in 80 Days*. There was some good, tough dialogue and plenty of rough, tough humor in *Manpower*, but overall it was disappointing. It was a reworking of an earlier film, *Slim* (1937), and a semi-remake of another, *Tiger Shark* (1932). One throwback to another earlier film was that the name of the club where Fay sang was the Midnight Club, which borrowed its name from the film of that title starring Raft. Recurrent rain scenes throughout the film made it necessary for special water tanks to be constructed on the sound stages. Four tanks holding 200 gallons each were installed. Estimates of water used during filming totalled over 75,000 gallons.

The plot was routine, consisting of little more than two men fighting over one woman, ground which had been covered in numerous "B" pictures. There were few if any surprises or unexpected plot twists. One of the main themes was electricity which, except for electrical engineers, was not an interesting subject for a film. Therefore to try to make it interesting, it had to be surrounded by a soap opera triangle. Despite its shortcomings, *Manpower* was a solid box office hit. Bosley Crowther in *The New York Times* stated in his review, "The principal participants in this drama are Edward G. Robinson and George Raft. And the inevitable lady in the case over whom the solid buddies dispute, is none other than Marlene Dietrich sporting every danger sign save a 'high voltage' sign. She does what she has to do well, but she's in to make trouble and that's all."

The fight in the film took second place to the conflict on the set of *Manpower*. It has been said that the real off-screen battle between Raft and Robinson was over the affections of Marlene Dietrich, who preferred Raft. Dietrich recalled, "George Raft was simply wonderful throughout the shooting." On April 18, 1941, Raft took exception to one of Edward G. Robinson's lines of dialogue. When Robinson stated that he had to speak the line and not Raft and found it quite acceptable, Raft directed towards Robinson a volley of obscene language with the intent of embarrassing and humiliating Robinson and lowering his standing in the eyes of his colleagues. Robinson left the set and went to his dressing room. In the opinion of Warner Bros. staff members, Raft's tirade was wholly uncalled for. The entire production was stopped for several hours resulting in a great financial loss to Warner Bros. A week

passed and, except as called for by the script and by the director, Raft and Robinson did not speak to one another.

Just before noon on Saturday, April 26, 1941, while shooting on Stage 11, Robinson was rehearsing a scene wherein the script called for him to be provoked into an attack on one of the other characters. During this scene Raft was supposed to make his entrance and to seek to quiet the disturbance. Instead of conducting himself as called for in the script, Raft immediately pushed Robinson around the set with a great deal of feeling and temper on Raft's part. In the presence of the cast and crew, Raft told Robinson to shut up, used profanity and threatened Robinson with bodily harm.

Robinson went to his dressing room, but a moment later returned and said, "George, what a fool you are for carrying on in such an unprofessional manner. What's the use of my going on? I have come here to do my work and not to indulge in anything of this nature. It seems impossible for me to continue." Raft again became verbally abusive, whereupon Raoul Walsh and assistant director Russell Saunders, fearing further violence on the set, jumped in and separated them. Robinson left the set and went to his dressing room. Production stopped between noon Saturday, April 26, and Monday, April 28, 1941. On the 28th, Walsh sent a note to Hal B. Wallis stating, "Robinson and Raft shook hands this morning and we are off to a good start. I will try to make up the time we lost." Raft said much later that he did not think Robinson was right for the role, which was written for a big guy such as Victor McLaglen. Robinson apparently told Raft how to say his lines on a few occasions and tried to explain film acting technique to him, which Raft deeply resented.

On June 13 there was another incident in which Raft objected to the climax having been changed from the script in one key respect. It was Raft's understanding that when he was holding Robinson by his belt, the belt would break so that the body fell to the ground by accident and not because the belt slipped out of the hand of Raft. "This will make me a heavy!" grumbled Raft. He refused to do the shot and after considerable argument said, "The hell with it!" and away he went. In the film the death is definitely depicted as the result of an accident.

Biography: Edward G. Robinson was born Emanuel Goldenberg in Bucharest, Rumania, on December 12, 1893, the son of Shia Moshe Goldenberg and Sara Gittel. His family moved to America in 1903 and he grew up on the Lower East Side of New York. He studied at the American Academy of Dramatic Art and made his Broadway debut in *Under Fire* (1915). Over the next fifteen years he became a frequent Broadway performer. He became famous when he played Rico Bandello in the gangster film *Little Caesar* (1930). Robinson was one of the most popular stars in Hollywood in the thirties and early forties. His career suffered a reversal when he was summoned before the House Un-American Activities Committee on three occasions for alleged Communist sympathies before he was able to clear his name. This enabled him to return to work where he continued as a star character actor until he died in Hollywood on January 26, 1973, aged 79, of bladder cancer. He was married to Gladys Lloyd from 1927 until their divorce in 1956. With her he had a son, Edward Jr. (1933–1974). In 1958 he married Jane Adler who survived him. On March 27, 1973, he was awarded a posthumous Special Oscar.

Biography: Marlene Dietrich was born Marie Magdalene Dietrich in Berlin, Germany, on December 27, 1901, the daughter of Louis Erich Otto Dietrich and Josefine Wilhelmina Elisabeth Felsing. She attended schools in Berlin and Dessau. She studied singing and the violin. From 1922 onwards she played roles in Berlin theaters. The film *The Blue Angel* (1930) made her a star. She arrived in Hollywood under contract to Paramount where her first film was *Morocco* (1930), for which she received a Best Actress Oscar nomination. She made many films for Paramount directed by Josef von Sternberg who did much to establish her legend. Her Paramount contract ended in 1937. She reinvented herself in the Western *Destry Rides Again* (1939) as the sexy, feisty saloon singer. During World War II she embarked on USO tours entertaining troops in North Africa and Europe. Her film career continued into the seventies, her last film being *Just a Gigolo* (1978). She became an even greater success on the international cabaret circuit from 1950 onwards and did television specials which were ratings hits. Her memoirs *Marlene Dietrich: My Life* were published in 1979. She married Rudolf Sieber in 1923 and with him had a daughter, Maria, born in 1924. She was widowed in 1976. She died in her sleep in Paris on May 6, 1992, aged 90.

Broadway (1942)

Cast: George Raft (Himself), Pat O'Brien (Dan McCorn), Janet Blair (Billie Moore), Broderick Crawford (Steve Crandall), Marjorie Rambeau (Lil), Anne Gwynne (Pearl), S.Z. Sakall (Nick), Edward S. Brophy (Porky), Marie Wilson (Grace), Iris Adrian (Maizie), Gus Schilling (Joe), Ralf Harolde (Dolph), Arthur Shields (Pete Dailey), Dorothy Moore (Ann), Elaine Morey (Ruby), Mack Gray (Himself), Nestor Paiva (Rinati), Abner Biberman (Trado), Damian O'Flynn (Jim "Scar" Edwards), Linda Brent (Hat Check Girl), Eddie Bruce (Photographer), Jimmy Conlin (Newsman), Kernan Cripps (Morgue Attendant), Arthur Loft, Joe Cunningham, Lee Phelps (Detectives), John Daheim (Andy), Fern Emmett (Will's Wife), Pat Gleason, Frank Ferguson (Reporters), James Flavin (Doorman), Joe Gray (Bootlegger), John Harmon (Harry), Jennifer Holt (TWA Stewardess), Tom Kennedy (Kerry the Cop), Charles Lane (Hungry Harry), Eve March (Mary), John Maxwell (Ed), Billy Nelson (Tommy), Jay Novello (Eddie), Larry McGrath, Jimmy O'Gatty, Charles Jordan, Tony Paton, Benny Rubin, Sammy Stein,

Charles Sullivan, Anthony Warde (Gangsters), Henry Roquemore (Will), Harry Seymour (Piano Tuner), John Sheehan (Oscar), Byron Shores (Manager), Kenny Stevens (Himself), Walter Tetley (Western Union Messenger), Harry Taylor (Wingy).

Credits: Director: William A. Seiter; Producer: Bruce Manning; Associate Producer: Frank Shaw; Assistant Director: Seward Webb; Based on a Play by Philip Dunning and George Abbott; Adaptation: Bruce Manning; Screenplay: Felix Jackson and John Bright; Photography: George Barnes; Editor: Ted Kent; Musical Director: Charles Previn; Musical Score: Frank Skinner; Dance Director: John Mattison; Art Direction: Jack Otterson; Sound Recorders: Bernard B. Brown and William Fox; Costumes: Vera West. Songs: "Dinah" by Joe Young, Sam Lewis and Harry Akst, sung by Marjorie Rambeau; "Sweet Georgia Brown" by Ben Bernie, Kenneth Casey and Maceo Pinkard; "Alabamy Bound" by Buddy De Sylva, Bud Green and Ray Henderson; "The Darktown Strutters Ball"; "Some of These Days" by Shelton Brooks; "Yes Sir, That's My Baby" by Gus Kahn and Walter Donaldson; "I'm Just Wild About Harry" by Eubie Blake and Noble Sissle, sung by Janet Blair. Released by Universal on May 12, 1942. Black and white. 91 minutes.

Synopsis: George Raft returns to his roots in New York City and recalls a story from the 1920s to Pete Dailey, a nightwatchman. At the time he was working at the Paradise Club as a dancer with six showgirls. Gangster Steve Crandall fancies Raft's partner, Billie Moore. Crandall tells nightclub owner Nick to organize a party at the club for friends of his. Bootleg whiskey comes into the club which Crandall has hijacked from "Scar" Edwards. Edwards

Left to right: **Iris Adrian, Elaine Morey, Pat O'Brien (in background at table), Marie Wilson, Raft, Dorothy Moore, Anne Gwynne and Janet Blair in** *Broadway.*

turns up at the club, demanding payment for the booze. Crandall pretends to make a deal, but then shoots him. The body is loaded in a truck, taken around the block and dumped.

From a fence jeweller Crandall buys a hot bracelet which he gives to Billie and insists she attend the party. Cop Dan McCorn arrives at the club. When Edwards' body is found, suspicion points at Crandall, but he has an alibi. McCorn is introduced to hoofer Pearl, whom he recalls from another club, The Golden Bowl, but she tells him he is mistaken. He recalls that she was Edwards' girl. McCorn suggests that Edwards has placed her in the club to act as his spy. When she learns that Edwards is dead, Pearl faints.

Raft and Crandall clash over Billie. Crandall frames Raft for Edwards' murder by planting on him the gun which was used. McCorn takes Raft to the morgue to view Edwards' body. Later cops interrogate Raft, but he denies all knowledge of the murder. Raft escapes, returning to the club where he and Billie do their specialty number which turns out to be a sensational success.

When Crandall arrives at the club, he intends to kill Raft. Raft confronts him in Nick's office where Crandall admits to murdering Edwards. This is overheard by Pearl, who has a gun. A violent fistfight between Raft and Crandall ends when Pearl shoots and kills Crandall. McCorn arrives and finds Crandall's body. He concludes that it was suicide. The following day Pearl confesses at the police station and subsequently receives a 15-year jail sentence.

Comments: *Broadway* was the only film in which Raft was directed by William A. Seiter. It was based on an original Broadway production staged by Jed Harris. It was a reworking of a 1929 film and it was tailored to the talents of Raft. It was the first of three films Raft made with Pat O'Brien. Marjorie Rambeau plays a Texas Guinan–type character, here disguised as Lil. Raft had wanted to star in a remake of *Broadway* for Universal, but Jack L. Warner refused to loan him so Raft spent eight months

on suspension. Eventually Warner relented and Raft shot the film. There was one amusing reference to this in the film. When Raft landed by plane in New York, he was met by an avalanche of reporters. One of them quipped, "Are you on vacation or on suspension?"

Despite suffering from a much too long preamble, it presented a vivid and atmospheric depiction of the "Roaring Twenties" complete with bootleggers, speakeasies, wild parties and chorus girls. Fourteen popular twenties tunes were utilized largely as background music although some were presented as song-and-dance numbers. A highlight was the dance sequences which clearly showed why Raft was regarded as one of the best dancers of the era. Janet Blair, who was strikingly attractive in this film, was an ardent admirer of Raft's and always credited this film with establishing her in Hollywood. It was a film which was very close to the heart of both Raft and Blair and this came across in their dancing.

The crime-solving parts involving O'Brien were less arresting, perhaps partly because the censorship code had become more rigid by the early forties. In the original version Pearl the murderess went unpunished by the law. The detective covered up the crime because he considered it justifiable. In this version O'Brien reached the same conclusion. Raft however revealed that Pearl confessed to the crime the following day and was given a lengthy jail sentence. A good lawyer could probably have proven justifiable homicide. Even if she had been found guilty, she would probably have been given a light sentence. This ending seemed to be very clumsy and could have been better scripted. One other aspect of this film which is irritating was the number of times O'Brien called the middle-aged looking Raft "kid." Despite its shortcomings, it still ranks among Raft's best films. The dancing, music and the ambience made it a hit with war-weary audiences.

Biography: Born in New York City on June 10, 1890, William Seiter was educated at Hudson River Military Academy. His first job was as a salesman of china and glassware in business with his father in New York. His first career was as an artist and writer. He joined the motion picture industry in its early days, first with the Selig Company and later with Reliance as an assistant director and screenwriter. He first became a director in 1918, initially helming shorts. He was a capable director of entertaining but usually lightweight features and worked at most of the studios. He directed several television episodes before he retired in 1959. Among his other attributes he was an excellent tennis player and horse rider and was reputed to be among Hollywood's best golfers. He was married to two actresses, Laura La Plante from 1926 until divorced in 1934 and Marian Nixon from 1934 until he died at his home in Beverly Hills on July 26, 1964, aged 74, after a heart attack.

Biography: Janet Blair was born Martha Janet Lafferty in Altoona, Blair County, Pennsylvania, on April 23, 1921, the daughter of Fred and Florence Lafferty. She derived her stage name from the county of her birth. She began singing with Hal Kemp's band at sixteen and was offered a contract with Columbia shortly after Kemp's death in a traffic accident. She made her screen debut in *Three Girls About Town* (1941). She staunchly maintained that the film which made her a star was *Broadway* which was done on loanout to Universal. Most of her other films were made under the Columbia pact which ended in 1948. In 1950 she started a new career in stage musicals playing Nellie Forbush in 1,673 consecutive performances of *South Pacific*. In the early seventies she co-starred with Henry Fonda in the television series *The Smith Family*. She was twice married and divorced and had two children. She died in St. Johns Health Center, Santa Monica, on February 19, 2007, aged 85, of pneumonia.

Biography: Pat O'Brien was born William Joseph Patrick O'Brien in Milwaukee, Wisconsin, on November 11, 1899. He was the son of William O'Brien, Sr., and Margaret McGovern. He grew up with Spencer Tracy and was a lifelong friend of James Cagney, with whom he appeared in several films. He served in the Navy during World War I. He was a law major at Marquette University before he and Tracy elected to study acting at the American Academy of Dramatic Arts. He commenced his career in vaudeville as a dancer and then moved to the legitimate theater with appearances on Broadway. His screen debut came in *Compliments of the Season* (1930). He established himself as a major screen actor with *The Front Page* (1931) as Hildy Johnson. In 1933 he joined Warner Bros. where he spent seven years, frequently playing priests. When he left Warners he had difficulty landing good parts, but he continued as a freelance mainly at Columbia and RKO playing tough heroes until 1949 after which his career declined precipitously. He did however remain active in show business for decades. He married actress Eloise Taylor in 1931. They adopted two sons and two daughters as well as having a natural daughter. His memoirs *The Wind at My Back* were published in 1963. He died in Santa Monica on October 15, 1983, aged 83, after a heart attack.

Biography: Broderick Crawford was born William Broderick Crawford in Philadelphia, Pennsylvania, on December 9, 1911, the son of Lester Crawford and Helen Broderick, professional show business people. He attended Dean Academy from 1924 until he graduated in 1928. He had a variety of jobs before breaking into show business via radio. He enjoyed excellent personal notices when he co-starred in *Point Valaine* (1935) on Broadway and as Lennie in the West Coast production *Of Mice and Men* (1938). He made an inauspicious screen debut in *Woman Chases Man* (1937). During 1942 he joined the United States Air Force where he served as a sergeant until his discharge in 1945 whereupon he resumed his acting career. His film career reached its apogee when he won a Best Actor Oscar as Willie

Stark in *All the King's Men* (1949). From 1954 to 1959 he became enormously popular on television when he played Patrol Chief Dan Mathews in the syndicated television crime series *Highway Patrol*. His later career declined to made-for-television movies, low-budget Westerns and minor European films. He was married three times. He died at Eisenhower Medical Center, Palm Desert, California, on April 26, 1986, aged 74, from respiratory arrest following a series of strokes.

Background to Danger (1943)

Cast: George Raft (Joe Barton), Brenda Marshall (Tamara Zaleshoff), Sydney Greenstreet (Colonel Robinson), Peter Lorre (Nikolai Zaleshoff), Osa Massen (Ana Remzi aka Ana Baronovitch), Turhan Bey (Hassan), Willard Robertson ("Mac" McNamara), Kurt Katch (Mailler), Georges Metaxa (L.V. Bastaki), Daniel Ocko (Igor Rashenko), Nino Bellini (Turkish Secretary), John Bleifer (Secretary), Walter Bonn (German Officer), Dick Botiller (Voice of Plane Announcer), Jack Chefe (Elevator Operator), Pedro de Cordoba (Baba, Old Turk), Fernanda Eliscu (Turkish Wife on Train), Rafael Corio (Turkish Husband on Train), Jean De Briac (Levantine Porter), Jean Del Val (Clerk), Charles De Ravenne (Bellboy), William Edmunds (Waiter with Information), Demetris Emanuel (Turkish Official), Hassan Ezzat (Turkish Conductor), Curt Furburg (Franz Von Papen), Steven Geray (Ludwig Rader), Frederick Giermann, Alfred Zeisler (Attaches), Lisa Golm (German Daughter), Carl Harbord, Dave Kashner (Men), Yeghishe Harout (Turkish Policeman), Ernst Hausman (Clerk), Charles Irwin (Hutchins — English Traveller), James Khan (Train Caller), Manart Kippen (Ivan), Kurt Kreuger (Chauffeur), Charles LaTorre (Typesetter), Liparit (Wagon Driver), Jerry Mandy (Italian on Train), Lou Marcelle (Voice of Commentator), Michael Mark (Hotel Night Clerk), Ray Miller (Chauffeur), Sylvia Opert

(Nautch Dancer), Nestor Paiva (Koylan), John Piffle (Fat Turk on Train), Paul Porcasi (Customs Official with Joe), Frank Puglia (Syrian Vendor), Frank Reicher (Rudick, the Assassin), Otto Reichow (Mailler's Henchman), Georges Renavent (Customs Official with Ana), Antonio Samaniego (Policeman), Irene Seidner (German Mother), Tom Steele (Thug at Newspaper Office), Bob Stevenson (German), Carl Harbaugh, Nick Thompson (Butlers), William Vaughn, John Van Eyck (Officials), Juan Varro (Policeman), William von Brincken (German Official), Hans Heinrich von Twardowski (German Officer), Leo White (Whispering Agent), Fred Wolff (Reiger), William Yetter, Sr. (Schneider — Mailler's Henchman).

Credits: Director: Raoul Walsh; Producer: Jerry Wald; Assistant Director: Russell Saunders; Dialogue Director: Hugh Cummings; Based on the Novel *Uncommon Danger* by Eric Ambler; Screenplay: W.R. Burnett, William Faulkner and Daniel Fuchs; Photography: Tony Gaudio; Editor: Jack Killifer; Original Music: Frederick Hollander; Musical Director: Leo F. Forbstein; Art Direction: Hugh Reticker; Sound Recorder: Dolph Thomas; Costumes: Milo Anderson; Makeup: Perc Westmore; Special Effects: Warren Lynch and Willard Van Enger; Technical Adviser: Nazim Kalkavan; Montages: Don Siegel and James Leicester. Released by Warner Bros. on June 9, 1943. Black and white. 80 minutes.

Synopsis: In 1942 Turkey, Colonel Robinson, a high-ranking Nazi, is instructed to create an international incident which will convince Turkey that the Russians are about to invade. This will give the Nazis the excuse they need to overrun the country. An attempt to achieve this by hurling a bomb at Fritz Van Papen, German ambassador in Ankara, narrowly fails. While on a train from Syria to Turkey, Joe Barton, an American agent masquerading as an oil refinery machine parts salesman, meets Ana Remzi (aka Ana Baronovitch), a Nazi spy. She tells him she is being

Left to right: Raft, Sydney Greenstreet, Brenda Marshall, Peter Lorre, Kurt Katch and William Yetter in *Background to Danger.*

followed by Russian agents. She begs Barton to take an envelope across the border which she will retrieve later. Once the train arrives at Ankara, Ana goes to a cheap hotel and calls Barton.

Barton checks the contents of the envelope and discovers that it contains maps of a phony Russian invasion of Turkey. When he arrives at Ana's hotel, he finds her dying. Barton hides when he sees Nikolai Zaleshoff arrive and search her room. As Barton leaves by the back way, he is seen by Tamara Zaleshoff, allegedly Nikolai's sister. Moments later Nikolai emerges, pursues Barton and hears him give the name of his hotel to a taxi driver. Barton hides the plans in his room before being kidnapped by Nazis pretending to be policemen and taken to Colonel Robinson who demands to know why he killed Ana and what became of the plans. When Barton refuses to talk, he is tortured. In the nick of time he is rescued by

Nikolai and Tamara. After Barton escapes, Robinson calls the police, informs them of Ana's murder and says that Barton is the murderer.

Barton is taken to an apartment where Nikolai admits that they are Russian agents. When Barton threatens to leave, Nikolai pulls out a gun and demands the plans, but Barton knocks him down and tells them to meet him at the Russian embassy in two hours when he will have the plans. When Barton returns to his hotel, he finds that the plans have gone and that he is wanted for murder. At a tobacconist's shop (a front for American secret service agents), he reports to McNamara his boss, who helps him. The trail leads to Istanbul.

Robinson gives the false plans to Bastaki, owner and publisher of the *Istanbul Crescent* newspaper. Bastaki promises to publish the plans in his newspaper, providing the Nazis restore his oil well interests and give him a high position in the new order. Robinson forces him to put a confession in writing. In Istanbul, Barton holds the Russians at gunpoint, but they deny having the plans and tell him that the Nazis must have taken them from his hotel room. On the trail of Robinson, Barton finds out that he is hiding at Bastaki's house. Barton breaks in, but is held at gunpoint by Robinson. Nikolai and Tamara have also been captured. Robinson instructs his goons to kill Barton and the Russians once he has departed.

After Robinson leaves, Barton and the Russians make a desperate bid for freedom. Nikolai is shot and killed, but Barton and Tamara make good their escape, hotly pursued by the Nazis. A high-speed car chase ends when the Nazis crash their car. Barton and Tamara find the newspaper publishing plant. Barton destroys the typesetting which contains the details of the false Russian invasion, forces Robinson to burn the original plans and to surrender the Bastaki confession which he hands over to the Turkish government. At the airport, Barton, Tamara and McNamara watch as Robinson is sent back to Berlin to be hung for failure on the orders of Himmler. Then Barton and Tamara board a flight to Cairo to continue the fight against the Nazis and their budding romance.

Comments: This was the fifth and final time that Raft was directed by Raoul Walsh. It was Raft's last film under his Warner Bros. contract. Eric Ambler, who wrote the source novel, was a pantheon thriller writer whose early novels had pace, thrills and topicality. One of the strengths of Ambler's writing was that he took ordinary men and placed them in extraordinary situations. Seldom was this better demonstrated than in *Uncommon Danger*, one of his best thrillers. The script diminished the strength of Ambler's writing by making the hero an American secret agent so he became a superhero in extraordinary circumstances which is not what Ambler intended. W.R. Burnett blamed Raft for making that change in the script.

It was one of a few Warner Bros. films of the period which sought to emulate the success of *Casablanca*. While *Background to Danger* was nowhere near that standard, it was atmospheric and exciting in its own right and did well at the box office. In particular the car chase where Raft tries to elude the Nazis was splendidly done. It was the only film in which Raft directly confronted the Nazis. It is principally remembered by film buffs because it was the only film in which Peter Lorre and Sydney Greenstreet were on opposite sides. Raft and Brenda Marshall must also have had the shortest on-screen romance of any of his films because they spent very little time alone together but were nevertheless an item by the finale. Considering that he did not serve during World War II and that there was a dearth of suitable leading men because so many were in the armed forces, Raft's lack of film output during these years is rather disappointing. Raft recalled, "In *Background to Danger*, the director had me tied up. Peter Lorre was sitting on a table in front of me. He was a mean little guy. Lorre blew cigarette in my face. I didn't like it. Lorre grinned. We had retake after retake. Lorre kept blowing smoke in my face. He kept getting closer and closer to my eyes with that cigarette. 'Untie me,' I said, before the next retake. I grabbed Lorre. 'You keep that cigarette out of my face,' I said. Lorre ran away and locked himself in his dressing room. When they had me tied up again, he comes prancing out. He sits on the table. He blows smoke in my face. And he flicks the cigarette around real close to my eyes. When I got outside, I slugged him. I told him he was a German spy. That upset him, but he didn't blow smoke at me again."

Biography: Brenda Marshall was born Ardis Anderson in Negros, the Philippines, on September 29, 1915. In 1930 her father, who owned a sugar plantation, sent her to live in San Antonio, Texas, where she attended high school and Texas State College for Women. In New York she studied at Maria Ouspenskaya's dramatic school. This led to her Broadway debut as Ardis Gaines in *Wives of Tomorrow* (1937). In 1939 a Paramount screen test was seen by Warner Bros., who signed her to a contract, changed her name and began to star her in films from *Espionage Agent* (1939) onwards. Warner Bros. eventually dropped her from contract. In 1937 she married Richard Gaines with whom she had a daughter, Virginia, born in 1938, before divorcing in 1941. In 1941 she married William Holden with whom she had sons Peter, born in 1945, and Scott, born in 1946. She did star in a few postwar films, the last of which was *The Iroquois Trail* (1950), to subsidize the family income because Holden's wartime absence had left them deeply in debt. In 1966 she separated from Holden and left him in Switzerland to return to America for good. They divorced in 1973. She died in Palm Springs on July 30, 1992, aged 76, of throat cancer.

Biography: Sydney Greenstreet was born in Sandwich, Kent, England, on December 27, 1879. His nickname was "Tiny." He was educated at Dane Hill School, Margate. One of eight children born to tanner J.J. Greenstreet and his wife Anne Baker, he originally worked as a tea planter in Ceylon and as an agent for a brewery in England before embarking on a stage career in 1900. He began with the Ben Greet Players, made his English stage debut in *Sherlock Holmes* (1902) and toured England in Shakespeare plays. He made his American debut in 1905 and spent the years until 1941 as a stage actor. He refused to make films until his screen debut in *The Maltese Falcon* (1941) for which he received a Best Supporting Actor Oscar nomination. His screen career lasted until 1949, much of his best work being done at Warner Bros. including eight films with Peter Lorre. In 1918 he married Dorothy Marie Ogden with whom he had a son, John Ogden. He died in Los Angeles on January 18, 1954, aged 74, of diabetes and Bright's Disease.

Biography: Peter Lorre was born Ladislav Loewenstein in Rozsahegy, Hungary, on June 26, 1904, the son of Alois and Elvira Lowen-

stein. He was raised in Vienna. He ran away from home at the age of seventeen and established his own theater company. By 1922 he was working as a bank clerk to fund his theatrical activities. He worked as an actor in Zurich, Vienna and Berlin where Fritz Lang gave him his first screen role as a child murderer in *M* (1931), which caused a sensation. In the early thirties he was guest of honor at a Nazi rally where he lampooned the party and was forced to flee the country. He went to France and England where he appeared in a couple of Hitchcock thrillers and then moved to Hollywood in 1935. At 20th Century–Fox he played Mr. Moto in a popular series of mystery thrillers. Much of his best work was done for Warner Bros., frequently in tandem with Sydney Greenstreet; they were described as an "Unholy Laurel and Hardy." He married Celia Lovsky in 1934, but divorced her in 1945. In 1945 he married Kaaren Verne but divorced her in 1950. That same year he married Anne Marie Brenning, with whom he had a daughter, but they separated in 1962. He died in Los Angeles on March 23, 1964, aged 59, of a stroke. Lorre also appeared in *Around the World in 80 Days* and *The Patsy,* films in which Raft made cameo guest appearances.

Stage Door Canteen (1943)

Cast: Cheryl Walker (Eileen Burke), William Terry ("Dakota" Ed Smith), Marjorie Riordan (Jean Rule), Lon McCallister ("California" Jack Gilman), Margaret Early (Ella Sue), Michael Harrison aka Sunset Carson ("Tex"), Dorothea Kent (Mamie), Fred Brady (Jersey Wallace), Patrick O'Moore (Australian Soldier), Marion Shockley (Lilian), Pat Flaherty (Army Sergeant), Mack Gray (Waiter), Eddie Hall (Soldier on Train), Louis Jean Heydt (Captain Robinson), John James (Don Brandt, Marine with Virginia Grey), Jack Lambert (Soldier Cutting in with Ina Claire), George Mathews (Marine Sergeant), Caleb Peterson (Johnny Jones), Ruth Roman (Hostess), Arthur Walsh

(Jitterbugging Soldier), Matt Willis (Soldier on Train). Guest Stars as themselves: Judith Anderson, Kenny Baker, Tallulah Bankhead, Ralph Bellamy, Edgar Bergen (with Charlie McCarthy and Mortimer Snerd), Ray Bolger, Ina Claire, Katharine Cornell, Dorothy Fields, Gracie Fields, Lynn Fontanne, Arlene Francis, Helen Hayes, Katharine Hepburn, Hugh Herbert, Jean Hersholt, George Jessel, Gertrude Lawrence, Gypsy Rose Lee, Alfred Lunt, Harpo Marx, Elsa Maxwell, Yehudi Menuhin, Ethel Merman, Paul Muni, Merle Oberon, George Raft, Lanny Ross, Martha Scott, Ethel Waters, Johnny Weissmuller, Ed Wynn. Supporting Stars as themselves: Henry Armetta, Benny Baker, Helen Broderick, Lloyd Corrigan, Jane Cowl, Jane Darwell, William Demarest, Virginia Field, Vinton Freedley, Billy Gilbert, Ann Gillis, Lucile Gleason, Vera Gordon, Virginia Grey, Sam Jaffe, Allen Jenkins, Roscoe Karns, Virginia Kaye, Tom Kennedy, Otto Kruger, June Lang, Betty Lawford, Bert Lytell (Canteen M.C.), Aline MacMahon, Horace MacMahon, Helen Menken, Peggy Moran, Ralph Morgan, Alan Mowbray, Elliott Nugent, Franklin Pangborn, Helen Parrish, Brock Pemberton, Selena Royle, Cornelia Otis Skinner, Ned Sparks, Bill Stern, Arleen Whelan, Dame May Whitty. With the Orchestras of: Count Basie, Xavier Cugat with vocalist Lina Romay; Benny Goodman with vocalist Peggy Lee; Kay Kyser, Guy Lombardo, Freddy Martin.

Credits: Director: Frank Borzage; Producer: Sol Lesser; Associate Producer: Barney Briskin; Assistant Directors: Lew Borzage and Virgil Hart; Screenplay: Delmer Daves; Photography: Harry Wild; Editor: Hal Kern; Musical Score: Freddie Rich (Oscar nomination); Musical Director: C. Bakaleinikoff; Music Arranger: Fletcher Henderson; Art Direction: Hans Peters; Sound Recorder: Hugh McDowell; Costumes: Albert Deano; Makeup: Irving Berns; Original Song "We Mustn't Say Goodbye" by Al Dubin (Lyrics) and James V. Monarco (Oscar nomination). Released by United Artists on May 12, 1943. Black and white. 132 minutes.

Synopsis: During World War II, four lonely soldiers en route overseas are given 48 hours leave. They make their way to New York City's American Theatre Wing's Stage Door Canteen where they meet numerous stars, and three have romances with hostesses there. One of them, "Dakota," proposes marriage to Eileen and she accepts, but before they can be wed, the soldiers are summoned back to their unit and sent overseas.

Comments: This was a moving tribute to the work of the Stage Door Canteen where World War II servicemen could meet and dance with stars of the American Theatre Wing. The romances depicted in this film were fictitious, but they provided a framework for numerous New York and Hollywood thespians to make cameo guest appearances. One of them was George Raft who in the first quarter of the film made a cameo appearance lasting about a minute. He was shown cleaning plates, making some small talk about boxing and baseball and then said that one team which will win is the American armed forces. The camera panned to show the huge numbers of them in the canteen. This was one of the top-grossing films of the year with $4,339,500 in domestic rentals alone.

Biography: Director Frank Borzage was born in Salt Lake City, Utah, on April 23, 1894. Leaving school at thirteen, he worked in the famous Silver King mine to earn money to go on the stage. At 15 he joined a stock company as a prop boy and utility player. Before he was 19 he became a leading man. In 1912 he gravitated to Hollywood where he was given movie roles by Thomas H. Ince. Borzage ran his own company for a time, playing the lead in eight Westerns before becoming a director at Fox. After his first big hit *Humoresque* (1920) he was awarded a contract with Fox. He won two Academy Awards as Best Director for *Seventh Heaven* (1927) and *Bad Girl* (1931). He was blacklisted for a decade during the

McCarthy era, but resumed his career in the late fifties. He died in Hollywood on June 19, 1962, aged 68, of cancer.

Follow the Boys (aka *Three Cheers for the Boys*) (1944)

Cast: George Raft (Tony West), Vera Zorina (Gloria Vance/Bertha Lindquist), Charley Grapewin (Nick West), Grace McDonald (Kitty West), Charles Butterworth (Louie Fairweather), George Macready (Walter Bruce), Elizabeth Patterson (Annie), Theodore von Eltz (William Barrett), Regis Toomey (Dr. Jim Henderson), Ramsay Ames (Laura), Martha O'Driscoll, Maxie Rosenbloom (Themselves), Spooks, a Dog (Junior), Frank Jenks (Chick Doyle), Molly Lamont (Miss Hartford, the Secretary), Mack Gray (Lieutenant Reynolds), Addison Richards (McDermott, *Life* Editor), Emmett Vogan (Harkness, *Life* Reporter), Cyril Ring (Laughton, *Life* Reporter), Charles D. Brown (Colonel Starrett), Nelson Leigh (Bull Fiddler), Jan Wiley, Odessa Lauren, Janet Shaw, Nancy Brinkman (Telephone Operators), John Meredith (Blind Soldier in MacDonald Number), John Estes (Patient), Ralph Gardner (Patient in MacDonald Number), Doris Lloyd, Baby Marie Osborne (Nurses), Lane Chandler (Ship's Officer), Frank La Rue (Mailman), Tony Marsh (Officer), Stanley Andrews (Australian Officer), Leslie Denison (Reporter), Leyland Hodgson (Australian Reporter), Bill Healy (Ship's Officer), Ralph Dunn (Loomis), Billy Benedict (Joe, a Soldier), Grandon Rhodes (George Grayson, Guild Member), Edwin Stanley (Taylor, Film Director), Roy Darmour (Eddie, Assistant Director), Carl Vernell (Terry Dennis, Dance Director), Wallis Clark (HVC Committee Man), Tony Hughes (Man), Richard Crane (Marine Officer), Frank Wilcox (Captain Williams, Army Doctor), Carey Harrison (Colonel), William Forrest (Colonel Edward Dobbs), Steve Brodie (Australian Pilot), Clyde Cook (Stooge), Tom Hanlon (Announcer), Bob Ashley, Lennie Smith (Jitterbugs), Duke York (M.P.), Lee Bennett (Acrobat), George "Shorty" Chirello (Assistant to Orson Welles), Nicodemus Stewart (Lieutenant Reynolds, USAF), George Eldredge (Submarine Officer), Bernard B. Thomas, Jimmy Carpenter, John Whitney, Walter Tetley, Joel Allen, Carlyle Blackwell, Mel Shubert, Stephen Wayne, Charles King, Don Kramer, Alan Cooke, Luis Torres, Nicholai, John Duane, Ed Browne, Clair Freeman, Bill Meader, Eddie Kover (Soldiers), Linda Brent, Janice Gay, Jane Smith, Marjorie Fectean, Doris Brenn, Rosemary Battle, Lolita Leighter, Mary Rowland, Eleanor Counts (Magic Maids), Jeanette MacDonald, Orson Welles' Mercury Wonder Show, Marlene Dietrich, Dinah Shore, Donald O'Connor, Peggy Ryan, W.C. Fields, The Andrews Sisters, Artur Rubinstein, Carmen Amaya and Her Company, Sophie Tucker, Delta Rhythm Boys, Ted Lewis and His Band, Freddie Slack and His Orchestra, Charles Spivak and His Orchestra, Louis Jordan and His Orchestra (Guest Stars Appearing as Themselves), Maria Montez, Susanna Foster, Louise Allbritton, Robert Paige, Alan Curtis, Lon Chaney, Jr., Gloria Jean, Andy Devine, Turhan Bey, Evelyn Ankers, Noah Beery, Jr., Samuel S. Hinds, Louise Beavers, Clarence Muse, Gale Sondergaard, Peter Coe, Nigel Bruce, Thomas Gomez, Martha O'Driscoll, Maxie Rosenbloom, Lois Collier, Elyse Knox, Randolph Scott, Philo McCullough, Augustin Castellon Sabicas (Stars Glimpsed in Hollywood Victory Committee Sequence).

Credits: Director: A. Edward Sutherland; Producer: Charles K. Feldman; Associate Producer: Albert L. Rockett; Assistant Director: Howard Christie; Original Screenplay: Lou Breslow and Gertrude Purcell; Photography: David Abel; Editor: Fred R. Feitshans, Jr.; Music Director: Leigh Harline; Choreography: George Hale and Joe Schoenfeld; Art Direction: John B. Goodman and Harold H. MacArthur; Sound Recorders: Bernard B. Brown and Robert Pritchard; Costumes: Vera West and Howard Greer; Special Photography:

John P. Fulton. Songs: "Merriment"; "Besama Mucho"; "Sweet Georgia Brown" by Ben Bernie, Kenneth Casey and Maces Pickard, performed by George Raft and Louis Jordan and his Orchestra; "Is You or Ain't You My Baby?" by Billy Austin and Louis Jordan; "Tonight" by Walter Donaldson and Kermit Goell; "I Feel a Song Coming On" by Dorothy Fields, Jimmy McHugh and George Oppenheimer; "The House I Live In" by Earl Robinson and Lewis Allan, sung by Delta Rhythm Boys; "A Better Day Is Comin'" by Jule Styne and Sammy Cahn; "Kittens with Their Mittens Laced" by Inez James; "Some of These Days" by Shelton Brooks, sung by Sophie Tucker; "Liebestraum" by Franz Liszt; "The Bigger the Army and the Navy" by Jack Yellen, sung by Sophie Tucker; "I'll Get By" by Roy Turk and Fred Ahlert, sung by Dinah Shore; "Mad About Him Blues" by Larry Marks and Dick Charles; "I'll Walk Alone" by Jule Styne and Sammy Cahn, sung by Dinah Shore (Oscar Nomination for Best Original Song); "I'll See You in My Dreams" by Gus Kahn and Isham Jones, sung by Jeanette MacDonald; "Beyond the Blue Horizon" by Richard Whiting, W. Franke Harling and Leo Robin, sung by Jeanette MacDonald; "Good Night"; "Shoo Shoo Baby" by Phil Moore, sung by The Andrews Sisters; "Swing Low, Sweet Chariot"; "Bei Mir Bist Du Schoen" by Sammy Cahn, Saul Chaplin, Jacob Jacobs and Sholom Secunda, sung by The Andrews Sisters. Released by Universal on May 5, 1944. Black and white. 110 minutes.

Tagline: "Hollywood's biggest stars come together for a Great Cause."

Synopsis: When the Palace Theatre closes, it means the end of vaudeville. After being fired from their last engagement, the West family (Tony, sister Kitty and father Nick), who were vaudeville headliners as "One Happy

Raft and Vera Zorina in foreground in *Follow the Boys.*

Family," gravitate to Hollywood where Tony lands a job as one of a line of dancers supporting star Gloria Vance. Soon he is able to persuade her to let him become her leading man in a successful series of Hollywood dancing films. Subsequently they fall in love and marry.

When World War II breaks out, Tony tries to enlist, but is rejected as medically unfit. Entertainer Chick Doyle has been drafted and he begs old friends Nick West and Louie Fairweather to put on a show at his local army base. In turn they ask Tony to organize it. This proves to be a big success and this gives him the idea of sending stars to other camp bases, in America and overseas, to entertain the forces. At a meeting of the Hollywood Victory Committee where the Universal stars are gathered, all pledge their support. As Tony expresses it, "They want to see you, talk to you and shake your hand."

When Gloria tries to talk to Tony, he is so immersed in his work that he refuses to listen so they quarrel and separate. When Kitty goes to see Gloria, Gloria admits that she is pregnant. Tony is set for an overseas tour of Australia. On board ship, Kitty breaks her promise to Gloria and tells Tony that the reason Gloria did not see him off was because she is pregnant. He says that he will call her from Australia the following day. Before he can do so, the ship is torpedoed. In searching for Louie, Tony is caught in an explosion and killed. Gloria has a baby boy, but the doctors do not tell her until later about Tony's death. Then Gloria says that she wants to go overseas to entertain as soon as possible. A voice recites the poem "Soldiers in Greasepaint" while the camera flashes to a board which shows the name of stars who have either perished or been badly injured in the line of duty.

Comments: This was the second film which Raft made for director Eddie Sutherland. Some sources give a running time for this film of 122 minutes. The film was premiered at this length, but cut by 12 minutes before its general release. Many of the studios made morale-boosting films with their roster of studio contract players playing themselves and "doing their part." This was Universal's effort. It was not the best of the type, but invaluable from a historic viewpoint as a record of the outstanding contribution made to the war effort by the Hollywood Victory Committee. It was shot on location at the Naval Training Center in San Diego, California. The plot provided an excuse to include generous amounts of actual newsreel footage of several stars performing in front of the armed forces. Oddly, however, many Universal contract players do not feature at all (for example, Abbott and Costello) while other players such as Jeanette MacDonald who were not under contract to the studio feature prominently.

There was one memorable scene for Raft fans. On an earlier tour, Tony West was on board a train when he was approached by a soldier who told him that there was a detachment of soldiers close by and asked if Tony could entertain them. Louis Jordan and his Orchestra and Tony left the train to give an extra performance in the open air for these men. While Tony was dancing to the strains of "Sweet Georgia Brown" on the back of a troop truck, rain started pouring down. Tony shouts, "If you can take it, I can," and completed his dance in the deluge to the delight of the audience. Ironically on the billboard in the film indicating the location of various personalities, Raft himself was shown as being on a USO tour of England, a country he did visit during the war.

Vera Zorina was one of the few leading ladies who did not like Raft. She did not feel his style of dancing combined very well with hers and she would have preferred a younger, slimmer leading man. The moving poem "Soldiers in Greasepaint" by Joe Schoenfeld, which ended the film, was originally published in *Variety*. Patriotism made this film an enormous commercial success with domestic rentals of $2,000,000.

Biography: Vera Zorina was born Eva

Brigitta Hartwig in Berlin, Germany, on January 2, 1917, the daughter of Fritz and Billie Hartwig. Her Norwegian parents were living in Germany at the time. She was educated at the Lyceum for Girls in Berlin. At the age of twelve she was presented to Max Reinhardt who cast her in a couple of his productions. She was seen dancing at London's Gaiety Theatre in 1933 by Leonide Massine who persuaded her to join the Ballet Russe de Monte Carlo for three seasons, both in London and New York. She landed a leading role as Vera in the London version of *On Your Toes* (1937) where Sam Goldwyn saw her, signed her to a contract and brought her to Hollywood. She made her screen debut in his *The Goldwyn Follies* (1938). She was the original choice to play Anna in *For Whom the Bells Tolls* (1943), but two weeks after shooting commenced, Paramount took her off the movie and she was replaced by Ingrid Bergman. Her acting career never recovered. She did however remain in demand for decades as a leading socialite; narrator of records; as a director of serious musical works; and as a director and adviser at Lincoln Center in New York. For years she lived in the East Sixties in Manhattan. She died in Santa Fe, New Mexico, on April 9, 2003, of a cerebral hemorrhage, aged 86. She was married to George Balanchine from 1938 until their divorce in 1946. In 1946 she married Goddard Lieberson, president of Columbia Records, with whom she had two sons.

Nob Hill (1945)

George Raft (Tony Angelo), Joan Bennett (Harriet Carruthers), Vivian Blaine (Sally Templeton), Peggy Ann Garner (Katie Flanagan), Alan Reed (Dapper Jack Harrigan), B.S. Pully (Joe the Bartender), Emil Coleman (Pianist), Edgar Barrier ("Lash" Carruthers), Joe Smith, Charles Dale (Waiters), George Anderson (Rafferty), Carol Andrews (Slummer), Sam Ash (Specialty Singer), Louis Bacigalupi (Bouncer), Merrill Long, Les Clark, Jimmy Cross, Jack Barnett (Members of Specialty Dance Troupe), Joseph E. Bernard (Printer), George Blagoi (Sailor), Olive Blakeney (Carruthers' Housekeeper), Mabel Boehlke (Acrobatic Dancer), Sven Hugo Borg (Sailor), Rory Calhoun (Boxer Sparring with Tony), Doria Caron (Madeleine, French Maid), Chick Chandler (Chinatown Wax Museum Guard), Don Costello (Steve, Fighting Bartender), Ray Dolciame, Marvin Davis (Boys), Tom Dillon (Policeman Chasing Katie), Robert Ferrero (Newsboy), Robert Filmer (Bouncer), Sam Flint (Politician), Benson Fong (Chinese Servant), Dorothy Ford (Tall Girl in Sally's Act), Irving Gump, Gerald Mackey, Hugo Maguire, Eddie Nichols, Danny Shaw, Paul Graeff, Vincent Graeff (Newsboys), Fred Graham (Bouncer), Harrison Greene (Mr. Van Buren), Joseph J. Greene (Headwaiter), Robert Greig (Patton, Carruthers' Butler), William Haade (Big Tim, El Dorado Owner), Eddie Hart, George Lloyd, Ralph Sanford, Arthur Thalasso (Politicians), Freeman High (Specialty Singer), Brooks Hunt (Policeman), William Hunter, John Kelly (Bouncers), Paul Hurst (El Dorado Doorman), John Ince (Doorman), Ben Jade, Virginia Lyndon (Acrobatic Dancers), Bud Jamison (Member of Singing Waiters Quartette), Edna Mae Jones (Dance Hall Girl), Jane Jones (Ruby), Edward Keane (Policeman), Naomi Keene (Acrobatic Dancer), Eddie Lee, Bruce Wong (Chinese Men), George T. Lee (Low, Tony's Chinese Servant), George Leigh (Mr. Van Buren), Arthur Loft (Turner), J. Farrell MacDonald (Cabbie with Katie), William Murphy (Lucky Sailor at Tony's), Forbes Murray (Mayor), Helen O'Hara (Showgirl), Darlene Ottum (Acrobatic Dancer), Nestor Paiva (Luigi, a Bar Owner), Ralph Peters (Policeman), Ronnie Pattirson, David Polonsky, Rudy Wissler (Boys), George Reed (Man at El Dorado), Otto Reichow (Swedish Sailor), Grandon Rhodes (Devereaux), Lillian Salvaneschi, Mario Salvaneschi (Dancers), Syd Saylor (Sailor Tourist at Wax Museum), Susan Scott (Slummer), Barbara Sears (Mrs. Devereaux), Harry Shannon (Policeman in

Left to right: Vivian Blaine, Raft and Joan Bennett in *Nob Hill*.

Chinatown), Will Stanton (Tourist at Wax Museum), Harry Strang (Policeman), The Three Swifts (Specialty Number), Chief Thundercloud (Indian Chief), Teri Toy (Chinese Showgirl), Virginia Walker (Mrs. Van Buren), Priscilla White (Aerial Specialty Act), Larry Williams (Candidate), Bernadene Wolfe (Acrobatic Dancer), Beal Wong (High, Tony's Chinese Servant), Jean Wong (Chinese Showgirl).

Credits: Director: Henry Hathaway; Producer: Andre Daven; Assistant Director: Harry Weinberger; Technicolor Director: Natalie Kalmus; Story: Eleanore Griffin; Screenplay: Wanda Tuchock and Norman Reilly Raine; Photography: Edward Cronjager; Editor: Harmon Jones; Incidental Music Composer: David Buttolph; Musical Direction: Emil Newman and Charles Henderson; Orchestral Arrangements: Gene Rose; Dances Staged by Nick Castle; Art Direction: Lyle Wheeler and Russell Spencer; Sound Recorders: W.D. Flick and Roger Heman, Sr.; Costumes: Rene Hubert; Makeup: Ben Nye; Songs: "I Don't Care Who Knows It": Lyrics by Harold Adamson and Jimmy McHugh, "I Walked Right In with My Eyes Wide Open": Lyrics by Harold Adamson and Jimmy McHugh; "On San Francisco Bay":

Vincent Bryan and Gertrude Hoffman; "What Do You Want to Make Those Eyes At Me For": Written by Howard Johnson, Joseph McCarthy and James Monaco; "San Francisco — The Paris of the USA": Hershel Hendler; "San Francisco": Gus Kahn, Bronislau Kaper and Walter Jurmann; "King Chanticleer" ("Texas Tommy"): Nat D. Ayer; "Chinatown My Chinatown": William Jerome and Jean Schwartz; "Too-Ra-Loo-Ra-Loo-Ra": James Royce Shannon. Released by 20th Century–Fox on June 13, 1945. Technicolor. 95 minutes.

San Francisco at the turn of the century was famed far and wide as the Paris of the USA — a fabulous city of contrasts identified by two extremes — the aristocracy of Nob Hill and the lustiness of the Barbary Coast.

Synopsis: Tony Angelo is the owner of a popular saloon, the Gold Coast, on the Barbary Coast. He has an ill-defined romance with his star showgirl, Sally Templeton. His political opinions carry much weight in the tough part of town. A little Irish lass, Katie Flanagan, comes into his saloon expecting to meet her bartender uncle only to find that he has died. Tony, who was his boss, agrees to take her in for a couple of months until the return boat for Ireland.

Through Katie he meets Harriet Carruthers who lives on Nob Hill. Her brother "Lash" Carruthers is running for office. Brother and sister both realize that an alliance with Angelo could bring in much-needed votes from the slums. With the backing of Angelo and his political machine, Carruthers wins in a landslide. When Sally accidentally overhears a romantic tryst between Tony and Harriet, she packs her wardrobe and defects to sing at a rival club. Carruthers offers Angelo cash for his support, which disgusts Angelo. Tony almost proposes to Harriet who tells him she was only having fun with him. Distraught, Angelo closes his saloon down at the victory gala and seeks solace in drink.

Katie throws a rock through Harriet's window. Attached is a note begging her to sort out the problem. Harriet goes to see Sally, who refuses to listen to her. The two girls have a catfight in which Harriet pins Sally. Harriet tells her that she really fancies Tony and that if Sally really loves him, she had better go to Tony or she will. While Angelo is asleep, his staff return to the saloon and reopen it. When Angelo awakens, he is given a newspaper with a headline which states that "Lash" Carruthers publicly thanks Angelo for his support and will honor all his election pledges. Sally returns to the club and professes her love for Tony. When Tony and Sally go to Katie's room, they find that she has run away and they surmise that she is planning on returning to Ireland because she feels unloved. A major search ensues in which Katie runs through the sinister darkness of the Barbary Coast and Chinatown eluding everyone. Eventually Tony realizes that Katie has gone to a plot of vacant ground on Nob Hill. He and Sally rush there to be tearfully reunited with Katie. Tony promises her that the three of them will always be together.

Comments: This was the third and final film in which Raft was directed by Henry Hathaway. Aside from a couple of times when Raft walked off the set after arguments with Hathaway about the development of his character, it was an easy shoot. The opening montage of San Francisco streets was footage lifted directly from the earlier film *Hello, Frisco, Hello* (1943). The story was a good mixture of sentiment, music, romance, comedy and drama done to a tried-and-true formula. Hathaway was one of the few directors who understood how effective a demoralized George Raft could be and when it occurred in this film, it was his most convincing emoting. It was one of a num-

ber of similar films which 20th Century–Fox made up to the mid-fifties which combined music and nostalgia in a money-spinning formula. While it was not the best of the genre, *Nob Hill* proved to be no exception since it was one of the top-grossing films of the year with domestic rentals of $3,104,000. The most disappointing aspect of this film was that, considering the musical content, Raft did not do any dancing in it. It may be that a dance scene involving him was shot, but ended up on the cutting room floor. The film was notable as being one of only two color films Raft made during his starring days. It was also his most opulent and the photography was beautiful.

Peggy Ann Garner was a gifted child actress whose emoting was natural even when assuming an Irish accent. As the contrasting women in his life, Joan Bennett and Vivian Blaine performed well. Both of these actresses were very fond of Raft in real life. Viewers could easily believe the catfight scene. During the course of shooting this sequence, both Blaine and Bennett tore six identical gowns before achieving the perfect take. All the songs were sung by Blaine. She was given two new ballads to introduce, composed by well-known composers Harold Adamson and Jimmy McHugh. These were "I Don't Care Who Knows It" and "I Walked Right In with My Eyes Wide Open." It was perhaps strange that neither became a standard because they were as good as others in 20th Century–Fox musicals. Blaine also had three production numbers all using standard period songs: "On San Francisco Bay" (1907), "San Francisco — The Paris of the USA" (1912) and "What Do You Want to Make Those Eyes at Me For" (1916).

Biography: Vivian Blaine was born Vivian Stapleton in Newark, New Jersey, on November 21, 1921, the daughter of Lionel Stapleton and Wilhelmina Tepley. She was educated at Newark's Southside High School, and studied at the American Academy of Dramatic Arts. She became a band singer with several bands while in her teens. She was singing in a Manhattan hotel when she was spotted by a 20th Century–Fox talent scout who arranged to have her signed to a contract in 1940. She made her screen debut in *Girl Trouble* (1942). She went on to appear in several musicals for the studio of which *State Fair* (1945) is probably the best remembered. In 1946 her contract with Fox was terminated at her request. She endured a lean time after that until she became the toast of Broadway when she played Miss Adelaide in *Guys and Dolls* in 1950 and of the West End in London in the same role in 1953. She reprised the role in the 1955 film version. She only made a few subsequent films, but went on to star in numerous theatrical musicals and some dramatic plays as well as being a frequent TV guest star. She was married three times. She died in a Manhattan hospital on December 9, 1995, aged 74, of congestive heart failure.

Biography: Peggy Ann Garner was born in Canton, Ohio, on February 3, 1931, the daughter of lawyer William George Huxley Warburton Garner and Virginia Craig. She trained at Marion Venable Dancing School and Alivene Theatre School. She was a model at four and her pushy mother took her to New York. She made her screen debut in *Little Miss Thoroughbred* (1937). She signed a contract with 20th Century–Fox in 1943 and appeared in several films for them until 1947 of which *Nob Hill* was one of the most successful. Her best remembered role was as Francie Nolan in *A Tree Grows in Brooklyn* (1945). In 1945 she received a Special Oscar as "Outstanding Child Actress." From 1950 to 1960 she lived, worked and studied in New York. During this period and into the early sixties, she frequently appeared on television. She moved to an apartment in Brentwood, California. She became a realtor and highly successful fleet motor executive. Her last film was *A Wedding* (1978). She died at the Motion Picture Country Home and Hospital in Woodland Hills, California, on October 16, 1984, aged 53, of cancer. She married and divorced three times to Richard

Hayes (1951–1953), Albert Salmi (1956–1963) and Kenyon Foster Brown (1964). With Salmi she had a daughter named Cassandra, born in 1960. She appeared with Raft again in *Black Widow*.

Johnny Angel (1945)

Cast: George Raft (Johnny Angel), Claire Trevor (Lilah "Lily" Gustafson), Signe Hasso (Paulette Girard), Lowell Gilmore (Sam Jewell), Hoagy Carmichael (Celestial O'Brien), Marvin Miller (George "Gusty" Gustafson), Margaret Wycherly (Miss Drumm), J. Farrell MacDonald (Captain Angel), Mack Gray (Mack, Bartender), Ernie Adams (Steward Leslie), Robert Anderson (Reporter), Virginia Belmont (Cigarette Girl), Don Brodie (Harbormaster's Aide on the *Putnam*), Ann Codee (Charwoman), James Conaty (Harbor Board Member), Aina Constant (Secretary), Marc Cramer (Officer), Kernan Cripps (Official), Wade Crosby (Dock Watchman), Edgar Dearing (Jim, Cop), Marcel De la Brosse (French Civilian), Rusty Farrell (Blonde), James Flavin (Mate of the *Quincy*), John Hamilton (Harbor Master), Eddie Hart (Seedy Sailor), Charles Sullivan, Jimmy O'Gatty, Alf Haugan (Sailors), Leyland Hodgson (Paul Jewell), Burt Holm (Isherwood, Sam's Henchman), John Indrisano (Joe, Bouncer at Cafe LaRue), Carl Kent (Reporter), Rosemary La Planche (Hatcheck Girl), Perc Launders (Official), Eddie Lewis (Boy), George Magrill (Man), Pat McKee (Barfly), Louis Mercier (Cigar Maker), Philip Morris (Joe, Cop), Al Murphy (Ship's Lookout), William J. O'Brien (Bartender), Jack Overman (Biggsy, Sam's Henchman), Theodore Rand (Headwaiter), Joey Ray (Third Mate), Al Rhein (Checker), Jason Robards Sr. (Officer), O.M. Steiger (Frenchman), Bryant Washburn (Reporter), Bill Williams (Big Sailor), Chili Williams (Redhead).

Credits: Director: Edwin L. Marin; Producer: William L. Pereira; Executive Producer: Jack J. Gross; Assistant Director: Sam Ruman;

Based on the Novel *Mr. Angel Comes Aboard* by Charles Gordon Booth; Screenplay: Steve Fisher; Adaptation: Frank Gruber; Photography: Harry J. Wild; Editor: Les Millbrook; Music: Leigh Harline; Musical Director: C. Bakaleinikoff; Art Direction: Albert S. D'Agostino and Jack Okey; Sound Recorder: John Cass; Costumes: Renie; Special Effects: Vernon L. Walker; Montage: Harold Palmer. Song "Memphis in June": Music by Hoagy Carmichael and Lyrics by Paul Francis Webster. Released by RKO on August 2, 1945. Black and white. 79 minutes.

Synopsis: Johnny Angel, a skipper in the Merchant Marines, captains the *Isabel Puttnam*. He comes upon an abandoned ship in the Gulf of Mexico, the *Emmaline Quincy* out of New Orleans, which was captained by his father. The *Quincy* took a cargo of steel rails to Casablanca and was supposed to come back with a cargo of African mahogany. Angel and a couple members of his crew board the ship where they discover signs of violence. They put a salvage crew on board and head for New Orleans. The ships are part of the Gustafson line which is nominally run by George Gustafson and his cheating wife Lilah, but the power behind the throne is Gustafson's former nurse, Miss Drumm, now secretary and treasurer of the company. Lilah and Gustafson are not happily married and he warns her to stay away from the notorious nightclub Jewell Box, run by Sam Jewell and his brother Paul, which is allegedly linked to organized crime.

After reporting to Gustafson, Angel returns to the *Quincy* to explore it. In one of the cabins, he finds a woman's shoe and is told by the dock watchman that he had recently seen a mysterious woman with a suitcase leaving the dock. Angel encounters Celestial O'Brien who takes him on a nightmarish journey of the Latin Quarter in pursuit of the girl, encoun-

Left to right: Raft, Claire Trevor, Marvin Miller and Margaret Wycherly in *Johnny Angel*.

tering one past flame who sneers, "The angel's wearing his halo tonight!" The trail leads to the Cafe LaRue where he finds the girl whose foot fits the shoe perfectly. She tells him that her name is Paulette. She escapes while he is fighting the club bouncer. She has dropped some items on the floor in her haste, one of which is a page torn from the phonebook with the address and phone number of the Jewell Box.

At the Jewell Box Angel goes upstairs to the balcony where he spots Paulette approaching the club. Shots ring out and Paulette dives into a closed shop where she is pursued by the gunman. Angel comes to her rescue, tackling the gunman, but is knocked unconscious. When he is revived, cops are there, but Paulette has vanished. Later he finds out that she has been picked up by Celestial who has taken her to stay with his cousin. Celestial takes Angel to Paulette whom he finds asleep. When she awakens to find Angel there, she is terrified, but he is able to pacify her and win her confidence.

She tells him via flashback the answers to some of his questions. Aboard the *Quincy* there was $5,000,000 in Free French gold entrusted to her father's keeping in Casablanca. The gold was stolen from her father, who was murdered. Paulette found out that the gold was going to be shipped from Casablanca to New Orleans so she decided to follow it and see who received it. Captain Angel, who knew her father previously, agreed to transport her as a passenger. Once underway, they stopped to take on board cargo from a tug which was the gold together with a stowaway who knew Captain Angel. Nothing eventful happened until they reached the Gulf of Mexico when mutiny broke out once the crew were told about the gold by the stowaway. Paulette saw Captain Angel murdered by the stowaway. Attempts were made to murder her, but she managed to fake her own death and hid in a lifeboat on deck. During the night all the murdered men were thrown overboard and the

gold loaded on board the *Dolphin*, Paul Jewell's boat. The seacocks were opened and the *Quincy* was beginning to sink. The few surviving men were shot to death by the stowaway, who then departed on the *Dolphin* without Paulette being able to identify him. She managed to close the seacocks so that the *Quincy* did not sink, but instead drifted until Johnny Angel found the ship.

During a dinner date, Lilah asks Angel whether he would like her and all the gold he can spend. Paulette is subsequently kidnapped and taken by Sam Jewell's henchmen to the Jewell Box where Sam demands to know what happened to his brother and the *Dolphin*. He tries to murder her, but Celestial tells Johnny where she is and he is able to rescue her after a fight. While on board his ship, Lilah visits him and promises to drive him to the gold. The *Dolphin* is moored beneath an isolated house on Teakettle Island with the gold still on board. At the house Angel becomes suspicious and believes Lilah is in league with Sam Jewell. Instead they are confronted by a badly wounded Gustafson, whom Lilah has tried to stab to death. It turns out that he was the mysterious stowaway who killed Angel's father. Miss Drumm arrives in time to shoot and kill Gustafson, but Angel prevents her from shooting Lilah. Drumm and Lilah are turned over to the police. With the mystery solved, Johnny and Paulette can start a proper romance and a new life together.

Comments: This was the first of six Raft films directed by Edwin L. Marin. It was also the first and by far the best of four thrillers which Raft shot for RKO Radio, a studio known for film noir. The plot had echoes of the *Marie Celeste* and the premise had an eerie, haunting quality which resonated throughout the whole film. In *Johnny Angel* the past was almost a character in itself, a ghostly presence from which none of the leading players can escape. *Johnny Angel* was one of the most exciting films Raft ever made and he gave one of the best performances of his career. Raft did some very inspired emoting as he searched the supposedly deserted ship and registered true pain and regret over the death of his beloved father. His no-nonsense quest to find the killer showcased Raft at his most effectual. The film could have done with an extra scene at the end showing Raft discovering the gold in the boat beneath the house.

Variety's reviewer wrote, "Raft is his invariably glowering self as a guy who really handles his mitts." Marin and cameraman Harry J. Wild both deserved praise for photography which oozed mood and atmosphere and was visually arresting. Every shot was framed in a fresh, exciting way. Considering that much of the film was shot in a simulated night or fog or in limited spaces, this made Marin's and Wild's achievement even more remarkable. This was the second of two films in which Raft was cast opposite Claire Trevor, here much more appropriately playing a femme fatale. Signe Hasso, on loan from MGM, registered strongly as the frightened but resilient and resourceful heroine. Hoagy Carmichael was also excellent as the ubiquitous taxi driver who warbles "Memphis in June" even though the film is set in New Orleans. Ironically RKO had very little faith in *Johnny Angel*. Production head Charles Koerner had no enthusiasm for this film calling it, "routine" and "something that won't set the world on fire." Instead *Johnny Angel* turned out to be a box office bonanza which brought profits to the studio of $1,192,000.

Biography: Edwin L. Marin was born in Jersey City, New Jersey, on February 21, 1901, and educated at the University of Pennsylvania. He started in 1919 as a scriptwriter and assistant cameraman. He commenced his directing career in 1933; much of his output was for MGM, RKO and Warner Bros. He directed some of the most profitable films released by RKO during the forties. He was married to actress Ann Morriss from 1940 until his premature death from cancer in Los Angeles on May 2, 1951, aged 50. He was survived by Morriss and three children.

Biography: Signe Hasso was born Signe Eleonora Cecilia Larsson in Stockholm, Sweden, on August 15, 1910, the daughter of Kefas Larsson and Helfrid Lindstrom. Her businessman father died when she was four years old and the family was plunged into poverty. Her expensive private education was paid for by wealthy relatives. She won a scholarship to the Royal Dramatic Academy where she appeared in numerous plays by classical authors. She made her screen debut in *House of Silence* (1933) and won the equivalent of the Swedish Oscar for *Karrier* (*Career*) (1938). In 1941 she emigrated to the United States where she made her stage debut in *Golden Wings*. Her personal notices were excellent and secured her a contract with MGM. She went on to play many roles at different studios of which the best remembered was Elsa Gebhardt/Mr. Christopher, the enigmatic crossdressing spymaster in *The House on 92nd Street* (1945). Her Hollywood film career became moribund around 1950 so she devoted herself to shooting films in Sweden and Germany, appearing on stage and guest shots on television. In 1972 the King of Sweden appointed her Knight First Class of the Royal Order of VASA. Her final film was *One Hell of a Guy* (2000). She was also a songwriter and novelist. She married director-writer-engineer Harry Hasso in 1936, but they divorced in 1942. With him she had a son Henry, born in 1937, who was killed in a car crash in 1957. She married William Langford, but was widowed in 1955. She died in Los Angeles on June 7, 2002, aged 91, of pneumonia following treatment for lung cancer.

Biography: Lowell Gilmore was born in St. Paul, Minnesota, on January 20, 1906. His original ambition was to become a landscape painter, but he turned to commercial art instead. He entered theatrical work as a set designer, subsequently rising to being a Broadway stage manager around 1930. He became a Broadway actor and appeared in plays between 1930 and 1935. After a hiatus he returned to Broadway in 1940, appearing in a few short-lived plays. The momentum was sufficient to propel him to Hollywood where he made his screen debut in *Days of Glory* (1944). He carved a niche for himself as a suave villain in films and television. This activity ceased in 1957. He died in Los Angeles on January 31, 1960, aged 54. His obituary in *Variety* at two lines must be one of the shortest on record for any actor of his eminence.

Biography: Hoagy Carmichael was born Hoagland Howard Carmichael in Bloomington, Indiana, on November 22, 1899. He was the son of Howard Clyde Carmichael. At an early age he learned to play the piano from his mother, but never learned to read music. While attending law school at the University of Indiana, he paid his tuition fees with money he earned from leading a three-piece band. When he failed to become a practicing lawyer, he headed to New York's Tin Pan Alley, where he arranged music. In 1931 he published "Star Dust" which became his biggest hit and one of the most popular songs of the century. He made his screen debut in *Topper* (1937), but only became an active film player in the forties. He and Johnny Mercer shared the Oscar for Best Song for "In the Cool, Cool, Cool of the Evening" from *Here Comes the Groom* (1951). He married three times and had two sons. He died at Rancho Mirage, California, on December 27, 1981, aged 82, from heart problems.

Biography: Marvin Miller was born Marvin Mueller in St. Louis, Missouri, on July 18, 1913. Even as a student at Washington University, he was active in radio. After graduating he became an in-demand radio performer. He made his screen debut in 1945. By far his best remembered role was in the CBS television series *The Millionaire* (1955–1960) in which he played Michael Anthony, personal secretary to the unseen billionaire John Beresford Tipton, who each week instructed his secretary to give an unsuspecting individual a check for $1,000,000. In 1938 Miller married artist Elizabeth Dawson with whom he had a son and a daughter. He died in Santa Monica on February 8, 1985, aged 71, after a heart attack. He also appeared with Raft in *Intrigue*.

Whistle Stop (1946)

Cast: George Raft (Kenny Veech), Ava Gardner (Mary), Victor McLaglen (Gitlo), Tom Conway (Lew Lentz), Jorja Curtright (Fran), Jane Nigh (Josie Veech), Florence Bates (Molly Veech), Charles Drake (Ernie), Charles Judels (Sam Veech), Carmel Myers (Estelle), Jimmy Conlin (Al, the Barber), Jimmy Ames (Barker), Mack Gray (Bartender), Jack George (Joe, Barber Shop Customer), Robert Homans (Sheriff), Jeffrey Sayre (Fran's Dance Partner), Charles Wagenheim (Deputy).

Credits: Director: Leonide Moguy; Producer: Seymour Nebenzal; Based on the Novel by Maritta M. Wolff; Associate Producer and Screenplay: Philip Yordan; Assistant Director: Milton Carter; Dialogue Director: Leon Charles; Photography: Russell Metty; Editor: Gregg Tallas; Original Score and Musical Direction: Dimitri Tiomkin; Choreographer: Jack Crosby; Art Direction: Rudi Feld and George Van Marter; Special Effects: Ray Binger. Song: "Once Again." Released by United Artists on January 25, 1946. Black and white. 85 minutes.

Synopsis: Mary went to Chicago to make money. After a couple of years' absence, she returns to Ashbury, flat broke and jobless, intending to sell the house left to her by her parents. It is currently let to the Veeches. She goes to stay with them temporarily. At one time she was the girlfriend of Kenny Veech, an unemployed gambler who still lives with his family. Although initially they greet each other warmly, they quarrel because Kenny has no prospects and they believe their relationship has no future.

Mary goes to work for unscrupulous Lew Lentz, who runs the Flamingo Club. Fran, a cocktail waitress at Lew's club, is desperately in love with Kenny. Gitlo, a bartender at the club, is Kenny's friend and drinking buddy. He warns Kenny to stay away from the club because Lentz hates him after a brawl in which Kenny knocked him out. Gitlo hates Lentz because years earlier Gitlo committed a crime for which he could go to prison. Lentz helped him escape, but uses this as a form of blackmail to keep him in line. Gitlo tells Kenny that the annual Ashbury fair is taking place in three weeks and persuades Kenny to join him in a scheme to rob and murder Lentz for the $15,000 he will make out of the fair concession. The robbery plan is aborted when Kenny arrives late at the station where they are to murder Lentz, but Lentz is suspicious.

At the fair, Fran is injured in an accident. At the urging of his sister Josie, Kenny goes to visit the dying Fran in the hospital where she declares her love for him. He cannot reciprocate because he loves Mary so he leaves Fran deeply upset. After another fight with Lentz in which Kenny is thrown out of the club,

Mary goes after Kenny and they reconcile. Kenny promises to reform and gets a job on the railroad doing manual labor. For a while he and Mary are very happy.

On Josie's wedding day Kenny and Gitlo are framed for robbery and murder at the club by Lentz. They flee, but in the ensuing chase by police, the gas tank of their car is punctured and Kenny is shot in the arm. Abandoning their car, they hop a freight to Detroit where Gitlo takes Kenny to a roadhouse run by Estelle, whom he has known since Prohibition. Before passing out, Kenny accuses Gitlo and Lentz of framing him, which Gitlo vehemently denies. He returns to the Flamingo Club to clear Kenny's name. On the way he finds Mary and tells her where Kenny is. At the club he is surprised by Lentz who shoots him. Gitlo strangles Lentz, phones the police to tell them that Lentz framed them and then falls to his death. A doctor called to the roadhouse tends Kenny's arm. Mary shows up at the roadhouse where she and Kenny are happily reunited.

Comments: The original novel published in 1941 was a huge, raw tome which was a bestseller of its day. The problem was that it would never have been passed by the censors if it had been filmed as written. This film was a sanitized fragment of the original novel. It was mainly financed by a bank in Palm Springs which had a good return on its investment since the film generally received favorable reviews and did good business. It was also instrumental in launching Ava Gardner to fame. It was worth Raft escaping from the Warner Bros. contract and going freelance for the opportunity of working with her. It had one of the best supporting casts of any later Raft film. Toward the end, Raft disappeared out it for about quarter of an hour, leaving McLaglen to take over the action. Neither Raft nor Gardner were involved in the dramatic climax. Philip

Raft and Ava Gardner in *Whistle Stop*.

Yordan said that both Raft and Gardner were clueless about the characters they were playing and in one scene had to have their dialogue pared to the bone because neither of them could speak the lines as written. Yordan thought that both of them were pathetic acting-wise, but had to admit that in terms of sheer star power they were magic.

Biography: Leonide Moguy was born Leonide Moguilevski in St. Petersburg, Russia, on July 14, 1899. He was educated at the University of Odessa where he studied for a law degree. He worked in the Russian film industry from 1918 and became a director in the newsreel department of the Kiev studio in 1923. In 1928 he was a laboratory chief in Moscow and the following year he emigrated to France where he became a director in the mid-thirties. During World War II he sought refuge in America and directed a few Hollywood films. At the end of the war he returned to Europe where he continued to direct, mainly in France. His final job was as the head of the film department of the International Red Cross. He died in Paris on April 21, 1976, aged 76.

Biography: Ava Lavinia Gardner was born in Grabtown, North Carolina, on December 24, 1922, the daughter of sharecroppers Jonas and Mary Gardner. She was raised in Smithfield, North Carolina, where she graduated from Smithfield High School. She studied to be a secretary at Atlantic Christian College. Her brother-in-law, photographer Larry Tarr, took photographs of her which he showed to MGM executives who signed her to a stock contract in 1940. After playing several bit parts she received her first onscreen credit for *Three Men in White* (1944). She received a Best Actress Oscar nomination for *Mogambo* (1953). Her contract with MGM expired in 1957 and she moved to Spain where she lived and worked for several years before making a final move to London. She was married and divorced three times: to Mickey Rooney (1942–1943), Artie Shaw (1945–1947) and Frank Sinatra (1951–1957). She died at her London home on January 25, 1990, aged 67, of bronchopneumonia following a stroke. Gardner recalled, "I enjoyed *Whistle Stop* mainly because George Raft was such fun.... I think George was always teasing a bit too. We went dancing on a couple of occasions — and George danced like a dream — and although there was always a small wrestling match when he dropped me off, our relationship remained stable. *Whistle Stop* was my first leading role and as such finally did get me noticed."

Biography: Jorja Curtwright was born in Amarillo, Texas, on August 14, 1923. She was the youngest of four sisters and her ambition from childhood was to be an actress. Her father died during the Depression and the family was left very poor. She undertook many odd jobs to pay for her drama tuition. After graduating from high school in 1939 she went to West Texas State College with the intention of becoming a drama teacher. Disliking this profession, she abandoned it and instead undertook a business course which enabled her to obtain a position at a helium plant. At the end of the year she had saved enough money to visit her sisters who were living in Hollywood. A girl friend enabled her to obtain a position as producer Seymour Nebenzal's secretary. When she was given the script of *Whistle Stop* to type, she became determined to play the role of Fran. Eventually she plucked up the courage to ask Nebenzal and Leonide Moguy who agreed to test her, and she was given the part. Her film career continued until 1956. She played several guest shots on television, the last of which was an episode of *The Iron Horse* in 1967. From the fifties onwards she was a highly successful interior designer. She died in Los Angeles on May 11, 1985, of a heart attack, aged 61. She was married to Sidney Sheldon and had one daughter, Mary. Jorja recalled about *Whistle Stop*, "Ava Gardner was my best friend on the picture. We had fun trying to do a little scene-stealing from George Raft and Victor McLaglen. At least we thought we had managed it, but our egos were slightly deflated when we saw the rushes."

Biography: Victor McLaglen was born in Tunbridge Wells, Kent, England, on December 10, 1886. One of eight brothers, he was raised in South Africa where his clergyman father worked. McLaglen lied about his age and enlisted in the Life Guards. After three years he resigned and emigrated to Canada where he worked at several jobs (including professional boxer) before becoming an actor. When World War I broke out in 1914, he enlisted and served as a lieutenant with the Middlesex Regiment. He made his screen debut in *The Call of the Road* (1920) in which he played a boxer and went on to make over a hundred films. He was a particular favorite of director John Ford for whom he appeared as Gypo Nolan in *The Informer* (1935), which won McLaglen a Best Actor Oscar, and as Red Will Danaher in *The Quiet Man* (1952), for which he was nominated as Best Supporting Actor. He was married three times. He died at Newport Beach, California, on November 7, 1959, of a heart attack, aged 72.

Mr. Ace (1946)

Cast: George Raft (Eddie Ace), Sylvia Sidney (Margaret Wyndham Chase), Stanley Ridges (Toomey), Sid Silvers (Pencil), Jerome Cowan (Peter Craig), Sara Haden (Alma Rhodes), Alan Edwards (Pembroke Chase II), Roman Bohnen (Professor Joshua L. Adams), Joyce Bryant (Nightclub Singer), Stanley Andrews (Tomahawk Club Boss), Walter Baldwin (The Bookie), Truman Bradley (Chairman), Lester Dorr (Reporter), Mary Field (Lady with Question), Bess Flowers (Party Guest), Joe Gray (Gentleman Gene Delmont), Mack Gray (Mack), Sam Harris (Dancer), Al Hill (Mack's Henchman), Bert Moorhouse (Election Vote Tallier), Dewey Robinson (Tom), Charles Sullivan (Mack's Henchman).

Credits: Director: Edwin L. Marin; Producer: Benedict Bogeaus; Associate Producer: Arthur M. Landau; Assistant Director: Joseph Depew; Production Assistant: Carley Harriman; Original Story and Screenplay: Fred Finklehoffe; Photography: Karl Struss; Editor: James Smith; Score: Heinz Roemheld; Musical Director: David Chudnow; Sound Recorder: William Lynch; Costumes: Michael Woulfe and Greta; Special Effects: Robert H. Moreland. Song "Now and Then" by Fred Finklehoffe and Sid Silvers, sung by Joyce Bryant and Flennoy Trio. Released by United Artists on August 26, 1946. Black and white. 84 minutes.

Tagline: "The Queen of Politics is holding every card except Mr. Ace." "This story could happen in any city in any state of our union. The story of a challenge to a man and a woman."

Synopsis: During a radio broadcast, Congresswoman Margaret Chase announces she intends to run for governor of the state. She invites political manipulator Eddie Ace to dinner where she seeks his support in her bid for the governorship. At a party he meets Professor Joshua L. Adams who taught her political science at college and who is initially antagonistic towards Ace because he is a racketeer. Ace tells Margaret that he will give her his answer if she will come to his residence the following evening for dinner.

At his home he introduces her to the members of his political machine who call themselves "The Tomahawk Club." Her charm and wit wins them over. Later Ace tells Margaret that he is not going to support her bid for governor because beautiful women do not belong in politics. At Margaret's request Adams hosts a small dinner party where the only guests are Margaret and Ace. After dinner, Margaret manipulates Ace into driving her back seven miles to her country cottage home. Bad weather forces Ace to spend the night on her sofa. In the relaxed atmosphere they fall for each other, but he still refuses to support her candidature. She subsequently enlists the support of Toomey, another powerful and ruthless member of the Tomahawk Club. When Margaret wins the nomination, Ace realizes that Toomey has double-crossed him.

Pembroke Chase II, Margaret's estranged husband, informs her that if she runs for governor, he will file for divorce in the middle of her campaign citing Ace as co-respondent. He has an affidavit from Ace telling of the night of torrid passion they spent together at her country cottage. Margaret decides not to accept the nomination, but instead flies to Reno to divorce Pembroke of her own free will.

Ace goes into reform mode and backs Adams to head an independent party with the aim of having Margaret elected governor. Margaret returns from Reno divorced and bitterly unhappy. Adams tells her that he has established an independent party and wants her to run for governor on a platform against corruption, especially Eddie Ace and the Tomahawk Club. Margaret declares political war on the Tomahawk Club and mounts a hugely successful campaign. Toomey becomes suspicious as the votes pile up in favor of Margaret.

His men bring Adams to the club's political headquarters and hold him prisoner until Ace rescues him. Margaret wins the governorship in a landslide. Afterwards Adams tells Margaret that the idea was masterminded by Ace, which horrifies Margaret because she believes Ace will try to dominate her. When Ace arrives, he tells Margaret that he wants her to be a courageous, honest governor, which will mean a jail sentence for him now and romance later.

Comments: This was the third and final teaming of George Raft and Sylvia Sidney, but previously she had been top-billed whereas this time (nominally at least) he was the star. By this time Sidney had lost the innocent quality which made her so appealing during the Depression years. It was the second and weakest of the six Raft films directed by Edwin L. Marin. It was the first of three Raft films produced by Benedict E. Bogeaus, entrepreneur and self-styled Cecil B. DeMille of the independent movie market. Whereas DeMille was associated with the epic, Bogeaus was frequently synonymous with ennui. Bogeaus did make some enjoyable Westerns and crime

thrillers, but unfortunately they were not the ones which starred George Raft. Bogeaus may have hoped to set the cinema world on fire, but the two forties films he made which starred Raft were not ones audiences flocked to see.

This film was potentially a crime drama, not unlike *The Glass Key* (1935), but conceived in an almost romantic vein so that it lacked both excitement and credibility. The chief villain was the script. The motivation behind Ace's transformation from nefarious political activist to reverential reformer, allegedly because of his love for Margaret Chase, seemed highly unlikely. At one point Roman Bohnen told Raft, "I don't understand you," which just about summed his character up. The script also contained references to women in politics which are antiquated to the point of being untenable in this day and age. A couple of members of the supporting cast, Stanley Ridges and Roman Bohnen, fared better than the two leads. Some viewers have seen a hint of Sapphic passion in the character played by Sara Haden, which was rare at that time. *Mr. Ace* was an outright box office flop, Raft's first such in many years.

Biography: Stanley Ridges was born in Southampton, Hampshire, England, on June 17, 1892, son of a civil engineer. After his discharge from the Royal Flying Corps in 1918, he began his career in musicals on the London stage. His baritone voice brought him to the attention of the Theater Guild which sent him to America for *No, No Nanette* and numerous other productions. Although he made a Vitaphone short, his busy film career really began with *Crime Without Passion* (1934). He returned to New York late in 1950 to concentrate on television and averaged a show a week until the fateful day, April 22, 1951, when he suffered a fatal heart attack in his new home at Westbrook, Connecticut, aged 58. He was married to Dorothea Crawford and had a daughter, but he is understood to have been bisexual. He made appearances in two other Raft films, *Each Dawn I Die* and *I Stole a Million*.

Biography: Roman Bohnen was born in St. Paul, Minnesota, on November 24, 1894. His father Carl was a famous portrait painter. Roman was one of the leading performers at the Group Theater in New York. He first arrived in Hollywood in 1937 (because he needed money to tend his ailing wife Hilda) and made his screen debut in *Vogues of 1938*. He went on to give sterling performances in many films. His name was smeared during the era of attacks on Communism in the film industry and he had difficulties obtaining suitable employment. He was one of the driving forces behind the controversial Actors Lab in whose production of *Distant Isle* he was appearing when he collapsed and died of a heart attack in Los Angeles on February 24, 1949, aged 54.

Nocturne (1946)

Cast: George Raft (Detective Joe Warne), Lynn Bari (Frances Ransom), Virginia Huston (Carol Page), Joseph Pevney (Joe "Fingers" Ford), Myrna Dell (Susan Flanders), Edward Ashley (Keith Vincent), Walter Sande (Detective Lt. Halberson), Mabel Paige (Mrs. Warne), Bernard Hoffman (Erik Torp), Queenie Smith (Queenie, Nora's Roommate), Mack Gray (Gratz), Dorothy Adams (Complaining Neighbor), Robert Anderson (Pat), John Banner (Charles Shawn), Phil Baribault (Dark Room Assistant), Gladys Blake (Movie Theater Cashier), Lillian Bronson (Gotham Cashier), Benny Burt (Bartender), Lucille Casey (Bessie), William Challee (Police Photographer Olsen), Edgar Dearing (Cop with Susan), Virginia Edwards (Mrs. O'Rourke), Antonio Filauri (Nick Pappas), Pat Flaherty (Cop with Susan), Sam Flint (Mr. Barnes), Carol Forman (Receptionist), George Goodman (Manager of Keyboard Club), Greta Granstedt (Clara), Harry Harvey (Police Doctor), Al Hill (Policeman Flynn), Virginia Keiley (Miss Evans, Lotus Model), Donald Kerr (Gaffer), Robert Malcolm (Chief of Detectives Earn), Matt McHugh (Studio Caterer), Bert Moorhouse (Movie Director), Jack Norton (Drunk), Ted O'Shea (Dancer), Lorin Raker (Police Chemist), Al Rhein (Waiter), Rudy Robles (Eujemio, Japanese Houseboy), Janet Shaw (Gracie Andrews, Dance Instructor), Willie Bloom, Roger Creed, James Pierce, Dick Rush (Cops).

Credits: Director: Edwin L. Marin; Producer: Joan Harrison; Executive Producer: Jack J. Gross; Assistant Director: James H. Anderson; Photography: Harry J. Wild; Editor: Elmo Williams; Original Story: Frank Fenton and Rowland Brown; Screenplay: Jonathan Latimer; Music Score: Leigh Harline; Music Director: Constantin Bakaleinikoff; Art Direction: Albert S. D'Agostino; Costumes: Renie; Technical Advisor: Barney Ruditsky; Special Effects: Russell A. Cully; Montage: Harold Palmer. Songs: "Nocturne": Music by Leigh Harline and Lyrics by Mort Greene; "Why Pretend," "A Little Bit Is Better Than None": Music and Lyrics by Eleanor Rudolph. Released by RKO on November 11, 1946. Black and white. 87 minutes.

Synopsis: Keith Vincent, composer and cad, is seated at his piano in his Hollywood home speaking poison in a velvet voice to a woman named Dolores who is sitting in the shadows of the room. He bids her farewell after their affair, placing her as one more conquest among the numerous women whose photos hang on his wall. For each woman he composed a song and plays a medley of them ending with Dolores' song "Nocturne." Before he can finish writing the song down, a gunshot rings out and Vincent falls to the floor dead. His death is then made to look like suicide.

Among the investigating cops is Joe Warne, a cynical homicide detective. The other overworked cops are more than willing to accept Vincent's death as suicide and move on. After an interview with Vincent's wisecracking housekeeper Susan Flanders, Warne has his doubts and decides to pursue it further. Warne discovers that what he considered a lead (the sheet music for "Nocturne" dedicated to Do-

Left to right: Matt McHugh, unidentified player, Raft, Lucille Casey and Lynn Bari in *Nocturne*.

lores) is worthless as Vincent called all his lady friends "Dolores." Taking the photographs off the wall, he begins to track down all the women in the photos. He obtains the photographer's name, Charles Shawn, and his address from the reverse of one of the photos and obtains a list of the girls' real names and addresses from him. One photograph is missing, which intrigues him.

Searching for the missing photo leads him to Frances Ransom, who sometimes works as a movie extra but lives like a princess, indicating that she is a call girl. Through her, Warne meets her sister Carol Page, a nightclub singer; her piano player "Fingers"; and his brutal minder, Erik Torp, who shadows Warne. Although Frances is ostensibly a prime suspect, Warne feels a growing fondness for her.

Warne is suspended from the force for continuing the investigation and for harassment of witnesses. He endures a brutal beating at the hands of Torp. While being treated in a hospital, another victim of a similar beating is there. It turns out to be Susan, who has been attempting blackmail. Through a restaging of the crime by his mother, Warne realizes how the crime was committed. He visits the RKO lot where *Sinbad the Sailor* is being shot. There he spots Frances and explains to her that the first shot to the head killed Vincent. The killer then wiped off his prints, put the gun in Vincent's hand and fired a second round. This time it was a blank cartridge which explains the powder marks on Vincent's head and fingers. The blank cartridge was then removed, making it look like suicide.

Charles Shawn is subsequently murdered. From his studio Warne obtains a photograph and makes good his escape in a taxi, but is spotted by police. He goes to Frances' apartment where he discovers that an attempt has been made to murder her by gas, but again making it appear a suicide. Warne saves her and then returns to the nightclub where a savage fight with Torp ends with Warne throwing coffee in his face which subdues him. Next Warne confronts Carol with the photograph of herself as a brunette and tells her that he thinks she killed Vincent. She admits she was the "Dolores" with Vincent that night. Frances arrives at the club where Warne accuses Carol of trying to murder Frances as well. They are interrupted by "Fingers" playing a near-perfect rendition of "Nocturne" on the piano.

"Fingers" tells Warne that he is the estranged husband of Carol, which Warne already knew. He says that if Vincent had seriously intended to marry Carol, he would have given her a divorce. When he discovered that Vincent was philandering as usual, he turned up at his apartment that evening and shot him dead. He rearranged the murder to look like suicide and then he and Carol left together. Carol told Frances that she had murdered Vincent. Later "Fingers" panicked, killed Shawn and tried to kill Frances. The police arrive to arrest "Fingers," Carol and Torp. Warne produces a letter which he had obtained from a postman on the first day of the investigation showing that at the time of the murder, Frances was on vacation in Mexico so she could not have committed the crime. Warne and Frances are now free to continue their romance.

Comments: *Nocturne* was the third film of Raft's to be directed by Edwin L. Marin. His direction here was very efficient. It was the second Raft film released by RKO. Lynn Bari was borrowed from 20th Century–Fox to play her role. The film was produced by Joan Harrison who was a former scenarist of Alfred Hitchcock and who probably learned the art of suspense from him. This film, the first she produced, was a solid commercial success, generating profits of $568,000. The opening of this film was gripping: The camera moved backwards from downtown Los Angeles into the hills

during the credits, then into a matte painting of a house, coming to rest on a man at the piano playing the title composition. The title song was composed by Leigh Harline and was instantly recognizable, which served the plot well, and it was equally effective as background music. *Nocturne* was a genuine Hollywood-based thriller. It was at its best when it evoked the superficial lives of sunbathing, swimming pools and cocktails of the fast set. It was good when it went behind the scenes of the dream factory and showed Bari on the set of the genuine RKO film *Sinbad the Sailor*. A few scenes such as Raft's search of the photographer's studio were very atmospheric.

The principal weakness of the film was that it did not generate much excitement. It was at its least convincing when trying to explain the convoluted plot towards the end. It was poor in that it withheld information from the audience known to the detective, which was a fault of the script. Another failing was that it was never explained exactly why the composer called each of the women Dolores, although it may have been that he did not differentiate between them because he regarded all of them as nothing more than sexual playmates. Another weakness of the film was that it was difficult to understand the motivation of Raft's character in jeopardizing both his life and career in pursuing a case without any particular reason. With the notable exception of Mabel Paige, who was a delight as Raft's Bingo-playing mother, the supporting cast was competent but did not make much impact. Jane Greer was tested for the role of Frances, but Raft refused to consider her test and insisted on going with a name actress, Lynn Bari, instead.

Biography: Lynn Bari was born Marjorie Schuyler Fisher in Roanoke, Virginia, on December 18, 1913, the daughter of John Manard Fisher and Marjorie Halpen. Her father died in 1920. She was educated at private schools. At the age of 13 the family moved to Los Angeles where her stepfather, the Reverend Robert Bitzer, was appointed head of the Institute of

Religious Science. In 1932 she broke into films as a result of seeing an advertisement in a trade paper (MGM wanted tall girls in bathing suits for their forthcoming film *Dancing Lady*). The film's choreographer, Sammy Lee, liked her so much that he arranged for her to sign a stock contract with Fox. She was best cast as a glamourous, ruthless bitch. She was released by 20th Century–Fox in 1946 after which she freelanced. She was the star of two early television series, *Detective's Wife* and *Boss Lady*. In later years she enjoyed her greatest success on stage in such hits as *Barefoot in the Park* and *The Gingerbread Lady*. She was married and divorced three times and had a son. She died in Goleta Community Hospital, Santa Barbara, California, on November 20, 1989, aged 75, of heart failure.

Christmas Eve (aka *Sinner's Holiday*) (1947)

Cast: George Raft (Mario Torio), George Brent (Michael Brooks), Randolph Scott (Jonathan), Joan Blondell (Ann Nelson), Virginia Field (Claire), Dolores Moran (Jean Bradford), Ann Harding (Aunt Matilda Reed), Reginald Denny (Philip Hastings), Douglass Dumbrille (Dr. Bunyan), Carl Harbord (Dr. Doremus), Dennis Hoey (Williams), Clarence Kolb (Judge Alston), Molly Lamont (Harriet Rhodes), John Litel (FBI Agent Joe Bland), Walter Sande (Mario's Club Manager), Joe Sawyer (Gimlet), Konstantin Shayne (Gustav Reichman), Andrew Tombes (Auctioneer), Claire Whitney (Dr. Bunyan's Wife), Holly Bane (Page Boy at Hotel), Marie Blake (Reporter), James Conaty (Reporter), Edgar Dearing (Police Sergeant), Robert Dudley (Robert, Matilda's Chauffeur), Al Hill (Bartender), Ernest Hilliard (Assistant Bartender), John Indrisano (Gateman), Eddie Parks (Beer Drinker), Charles Sherlock (Reichman Henchman), Brick Sullivan (Policeman).

Credits: Director: Edwin L. Marin; Producer: Benedict Bogeaus; Associate Producer: Arthur M. Landau; Production Assistant: Carley Harriman; Original Story: Laurence Stallings, Arch Oboler and Richard H. Landau; Screenplay: Laurence Stallings and Robert Altman; Photography: Gordon Avil; Editor: James Smith; Music: Heinz Roemheld; Music Supervisor: David Chudnow; Music Arranger: Lowell Mason; Art Direction: Ernst Fegte; Sound Recorder: William H. Lynch; Costumes: Jerry Bos and Greta; Stunt Double for George Raft: John Daheim. Released by United Artists on October 31, 1947. Black and white. 90 minutes.

Synopsis: Wealthy eccentric Aunt Matilda is about to be declared unfit by the courts. Her unscrupulous nephew Philip Hastings seeks to gain control of her estate by being appointed administrator. To prevent this, she seeks to find her three wards whom she adopted when they were boys, but whom she lost touch with when they grew to adulthood.

The first of her boys is Michael, a playboy, who has been passing bad checks and is seeking to marry a wealthy woman. The second is Mario. He has fled to South America to escape the law and become a wealthy club proprietor. He welcomes his girlfriend Claire back from a vacation in the mountains. At the club he is visited by FBI agent Joe Bland who tells him that he is on the trail of Nazi war criminal Gustav Reichman, whom Mario has never heard of. A photo shown to Mario reveals that Claire was Reichman's former mistress.

Mario is kidnapped and taken to a boat by Reichman's goons, who torture him. He discovers that Claire has also been kidnapped. Reichman tells Mario that he originally sent Claire to South America with $10 million in Nazi funds which has disappeared and he wants to know what became of it. Eventually Claire reveals that she really spent the previous weekend making arrangements to return the money to the American Occupied Forces in Berlin. Mario manages to free himself, and in the ensuing gunfight both Claire and Reichman are killed.

The third son is Jonathan who has become a broken-down rodeo rider and near-alcoholic. In the company of Jean Bradford from the Child Welfare Association, he exposes a fake baby adoption racket.

All three of her sons eventually reunite at Aunt Matilda's house on Christmas Eve. Mario reminds Philip that he (Philip) embezzled Aunt Matilda's money in a deal that went sour a decade earlier, and that Mario assumed the blame. Mario forces Philip to leave Aunt Matilda's home forever. Since her three grown-up sons can now look after her estate, the courts decide to take no further action. All of them go to dinner where Aunt Matilda toasts them.

Comments: This was the fourth of six Raft films directed by Edwin L. Marin. It was the second film which Raft made for producer Benedict Bogeaus. Raft appeared after the thirty-minute mark; his segment lasted about twenty minutes and was the most exciting. The George Brent and Randolph Scott episodes were played with humor, but the Raft episode was completely serious. Ann Harding, one of the most popular RKO stars during the thirties, played a character much older than her years. Opinion was sharply divided over how convincing she was in the role and how good her makeup was, but she was undeniably moving in the finale. This film was reworked as a television movie, *Christmas Eve* (1986), which starred Loretta Young in the Harding role.

Virginia Field was paired with Raft, Joan Blondell was paired with Brent and Dolores Moran was paired with Scott. The weakest casting however was Reginald Denny who looked too old to be Aunt Matilda's nephew. Nor did he look intimidating enough to be a ruthless villain although this would not be a barrier to such an individual in real life. The film had a weak denoument which was all talk and no action. It was not really a Christmas film even though the last scene did take place on that day. Benedict Bogeaus liked episodic films, but the public disagreed. Since both films which Raft made in the late forties for him were box office flops, it might be concluded that Raft's career decline was more attributable to Bogeaus than Bogart.

Biography: Virginia Field was born Margaret Cynthia Field in London, England, on November 4, 1917, the daughter of prominent English judge St. John Field and Esmé de la Torre Lee. She was educated in England, Paris and Vienna. She made her screen debut in *The Lady Is Willing* (1934). She was about to make her Broadway bow when she was signed to a contract with 20th Century–Fox

Raft and Virginia Field in *Christmas Eve.*

in 1936. In 1942 she married Paul Douglas with whom she had a daughter, Margaret, but divorced in 1946. She married and divorced Howard Goode within a single year, 1947. She appeared in over forty films, the final one of which was *The Earth Dies Screaming* (1964), opposite her third husband, Willard Parker whom she wed in 1951. Until 1974 when he suffered a serious stroke, he was a successful realtor in Indian Wells near Palm Springs and she owned and managed a boutique. She died in Palm Desert, California, on January 2, 1992, aged 74, of cancer. Field recalled, "I did not want to do *Christmas Eve*, but a $5,000 bonus plus the fact that there was a little house I wanted to purchase convinced me otherwise. This one fell apart during production and George Raft finished the script himself."

Biography: Ann Harding was born Dorothy Walton Gatley in Fort Sam Houston, Texas, on August 7, 1901, the daughter of George Gatley, U.S. Army general, and Elizabeth Crabbe. She was educated at Montclair, New Jersey, and Bryn Mawr College. Her first job after leaving college was as a clerk in an insurance office. She made her Broadway debut in *Like a King* (1921). She broke into films as a script reader for one of the major studios. Her father violently opposed her profession so she changed her surname to that of the then–American president. She was under contract to RKO and her years as a star lasted from 1929 until 1936 after which she became a character actress. She was nominated for a Best Actress Oscar for *Holiday* (1930). In later years she devoted much of her time to stage work and appearing on all the leading anthology television series. She died in Sherman Oaks, California, on September 1, 1981, aged 80, after an illness of several months. She was married and divorced twice and had a daughter.

Intrigue (1947)

Cast: George Raft (Brad Dunham), June Havoc (Mme. Tamara Baranoff), Helena Carter (Linda Parker alias Linda Arnold), Tom Tully (Marc Andrews), Marvin Miller (Ramon Perez), Dan Seymour (Karidian), Jay C. Flippen (Mike), Philip Ahn (Louie Chan), Charles Lane (Hotel Desk Clerk), Marc Krah (Nicco), Nancy Hsueh (Mia, Orphan Girl), Nan Wynn (Dinner Club Singer), Peter Chong (Editor), Michael Ansara (Ramon's Radio Man), Reginald Billado (Air Force Pilot at Bar), Kenneth Chuck (Chinese Boy), Gordon Clark (Hotel Cigar Stand Clerk), Paul Fierro (Warehouse Lead Thug), Bess Flowers (Woman at Table in Bar), Hassan Ezzat, Bob Gilbert, Hassan Khayyam, Alex Montoya, Al Rhein (Karidian's Henchmen), Edna Holland (Miss Carr), Wei F. Hsueh (Hospital Doctor), David Leonard (Headwaiter), Leon Lontoc (Mechanic), Bill Louie, Ronald Louie, Hayward Hoo Soo, Richard Wang (Chinese Boys), Maria San Marco (Ling), Rodd Redwing (Spy in Editor's Office), Philson Ahn (Official), Stan Ross (Warehouse Thug), Phil Taylor (Eddie Lane), Michael Visaroff (Ship's Captain), Ralph E. Waters (Air Force Pilot at Bar), Jean Wong (Hospital Nurse), Victor Sen Yung (Western Union Clerk).

Credits: Director: Edwin L. Marin; Producers: Sam Bischoff, George Raft; Assistant Director: Joseph Depew; Original Story: George Slavin; Screenplay: Barry Trivers, George Slavin and Frances Kavanaugh; Photography: Lucien Andriot; Editor: George Arthur; Musical Director: Louis Forbes; Art Direction: Arthur Lonergan; Sound Recorders: William H. Lynch and Joseph I. Kane; Costumes: Peter Tuesday. Song "Intrigue" by Harry Akst and Samuel Lerner, sung by Nan Wynn. Released by United Artists on December 23, 1947. Black and white. 90 minutes.

Tagline: "I'm a bottle with a label on it. The label says poison ... no antidote."

Synopsis: In Shanghai, Brad Dunham, a former U.S. Army flyer who has been dishonorably discharged, makes a perilous landing with a cargo of contraband. He tells his contact, Ramon Perez, that if he is to continue flying he wants more money and demands to see the mysterious boss of the organization. Dunham finds out what has become of the cargo and hijacks it. He is taken to a stylish apartment above a warehouse where he is amazed to discover the boss is a female named Tamara Baranoff. He informs her that he wants a fifty-fifty split to which she reluctantly agrees.

At the National Hotel where he is a resident, Dunham encounters an old friend, Mark Andrews of the A.T.A. News Service, whom he has not seen in four years. Dunham invites Andrews to share his room, but becomes worried when Andrews tells him that he is writing a series of articles exposing the black market. In the hotel bar Dunham meets and falls for Linda Arnold, a field worker with the International Aid Settlement. In trying to further their relationship, he turns up at the orphanage where she works, but he is spotted by Baranoff who is pretending to be a major supporter of the orphanage. When one of the children collapses from hunger, Linda tells Dunham that there is not enough food for the children because the black marketers are stealing it all. At a later dinner with Dunham and Andrews, she reveals that her real name is Linda Parker and that she is the sister of the late Danny Parker, one of Dunham's crew members who were court-martialed.

At the docks a boat has been attacked and its cargo of rice stolen by a rival gang of river pirates led by the mysterious Karidian. Dunham and a sympathetic Chinese, Louie Chin, ambush a truck carrying the rice and deliver it to the orphanage. Andrews receives a telegram from the U.S. War Department telling him of the involvement of Dunham and other flyers in the black market which led to their court-martial, but there is no proven connection to Baranoff. Andrews goes to see Baranoff to persuade her to exonerate Dunham and the other

Left to right: June Havoc, Raft and Helena Carter in *Intrigue*.

flyers, but she refuses. Subsequently Andrews finds proof of her involvement. Since Andrews has come too close to the truth, she decides to have him eliminated.

When Andrews demands to know from Dunham whether he is involved in the black market, Dunham confesses and they have a fierce argument. When the article which Andrews has written is stolen from the editor's desk by a reporter in league with the black marketeers, Andrews is fatally stabbed by Ramon Perez while delivering another copy. Before he dies, Andrews tells Dunham that in his article Baranoff is named as being responsible for putting the contraband cargo in his plane which led to his court-martial and that Rorke was the only crew member in league with the black marketeers.

Dunham is shattered by Andrews' death and his revelations. After wandering the streets and seeing the poverty, Dunham takes matters into his own hands by opening the warehouse filled with black market goods to the public. In the ensuing fight with the black marketeers, Baranoff is shot dead by Perez but not before she has signed a confession exonerating Dunham. When Linda hears of Dunham's action, she races through the streets and finds him. They embrace and watch as members of the starving crowds take the supplies away.

Comments: This was the first of the two films which Raft made under the banner of his own company, Star Films, in tandem with veteran producer Sam Bischoff. It was the fifth of the six Raft films directed by Edwin L. Marin. This could have been a penetrating study of the postwar black market and the way it operated in Shanghai. Instead, with the introduction of the Chinese orphans, the film declined into sentimentality. There were also budgetary constraints; the river pirates' attack on a cargo vessel cried out to be filmed, but instead was merely described. Marin was shrewd enough to put the emphasis on a few action scenes (with Raft in the thick of them) which were genuinely exciting. Raft was in the right milieu and acquitted himself well as a wronged man with a conscience who became entangled in the black market. Helena Carter as the decent girl and June Havoc as the hypocritical bad girl both provided interesting, contrasting characterizations. Tom Tully as the investigative reporter represented the voice of truth as well as being a fountain of knowledge. Raft's relationship with Tully was well defined.

Raft said of his independent company, "It wasn't a great success for the simple reason that the first picture I made was badly timed. It was called *Intrigue*, all about China. Originally the story was about the smuggling of blood plasma, but then we weren't allowed to use this in the film because the Chinese council said it wouldn't be good for American-Chinese relationships to say we're stealing this. So we had to revert to the old cliché of smuggling whisky and cigarettes which had been done many times before. If we had been able to retain the original idea, it would have been much more exciting."

Biography: Helena Carter was born Helena Ruckert in New York City on August 24, 1923, the daughter of Ruckert and Honorah Sullivan. Her father died when she was seven months old. She was raised in Ireland and New York. She was educated at Hunter College, graduating with a B.A. degree, and went on to become a highly successful Conover model. While on vacation in California, she was tested and signed to a contract by Universal in 1946. *Intrigue* was made on loan-out. Of Raft she recalled, "My mother warned me to be careful of George Raft, but her fears proved groundless. This was my first leading role and naturally I was very nervous. George Raft was a true gentleman and could not have been nicer." After leaving Universal in 1950, she freelanced with some success until 1953 when she married again and decided to retire. In later years she volunteered her services at the Cinema Glamour Shop in Hollywood, which sold off clothes contributed by film stars with the proceeds going to the Motion Picture Country Home and Hospital. She died in Culver City, California, on January 11, 2000, aged 76, of heart problems and diabetes. She was married and divorced from Ralph Bidwell Carter III. She then married Michael Meshekoff, who survived her. She had no children (a son was stillborn in 1959).

Biography: June Havoc was born Ellen Evangeline Hovick in Vancouver, Canada, on November 8, 1912, the daughter of John Olav and Rose Horvick. She was the younger sister of Gypsy Rose Lee. She was the daughter of a Norwegian-American newspaper advertising agent and a stagestruck mother depicted as the indomitable Mama Rose in the musical *Gypsy*. She played roles in short silent films from the age of two and, after her parents divorced, her mother formed a vaudeville act starring "Baby June" with a supporting cast of juveniles including her sister Louise. She eloped with a fellow performer, Bobby Reed, in 1929 to escape her mother's galloping ambition, but the marriage was brief. The two remained partners professionally, however, so when the Depression hit hard they entered the gruelling dance marathons of the era. Her only child, April Kent (1935–1998), was born out of wedlock to June and James Smyth, a marathon promoter. By 1936 she had developed into a statuesque blonde with strong dancing skills and began to appear in Broadway plays and musicals. As an adult she appeared in several films commencing with *Four Jacks and a Jill* (1941). She received a Tony nomination for directing *Marathon 33* (1963), a play based on her memoir about the marathon dance era. In 1982 she took over the role of Miss Hannigan in the original Broadway production of *Annie,* her final Broadway show. Her second husband was Donald Gibbs whom she married in 1935 and divorced in 1942. She wed Los Angeles radio producer William Spier in 1948 and was widowed in 1973. She died in Stamford, Connecticut, on March 28, 2010, aged 97, of age-related causes.

Race Street (1948)

Cast: George Raft (Dan Gannin), William Bendix (Detective Lt. Barney Runson), Marilyn Maxwell (Robbie Lawrence aka Dickson), Frank Faylen (Phil Dickson), Henry Morgan (Hal Towers), Gale Robbins (Elaine Gannin), Cully Richards (Mike Hadley), Mack Gray (Stringy), Russell Hicks (Easy Mason), Richard Powers (Al), William Forrest (Nick Walters), Jim Nolan (Herbie), George Turner (Dixie), Richard Benedict (Sam), Dean White (Big Jack), Freddie Steele (Monty), Eddie Arden, Franklyn Farnum, Mike Lally, George Murray (Men), Reginald Billado, Steven Flagg, Michael St. Angel (Clerks), Barry Brooks (Intern in Hallway), James Bush (Male Nurse on Ward), George Chandler (Herman, Waiter at Billy's Tavern), James Conaty, Larry Steers, Bert Stevens (Nightclub Patrons), Oliver Cross (Turf Club Headwaiter), Robert Dudley (Pop, Stage Door Watchman), George Goodman (Turf Club Waiter), Charmienne Harker, Joan Myles (Cigarette Girls at Turf Club), Cy Kendall (Fatty Parker, Shoeshine Customer), Mary Kent (Central Receiving Nurse-Receptionist), Charles Lane (Switchboard Operator-Clerk), Mickey Martin (Jimmy, Elevator Boy), Frank McClure, William H. O'Brien (Racetrack Spectators), Sam McDaniel (Garage Attendant), Hercules Mendez (Chef), Al Murphy (Drunk), June Pickerell (Woman), Al Rhein (Johnson), Jason Robards Sr. (Apartment Desk Clerk), Edna Ryan (Lucille, Dan's Receptionist), Carl Saxe (Detective), Frank J. Scannell (Burnside, Bar Patron Claiming Deafness), Michael Wallace (Headwaiter at Billy's), Eric Wilton (Bar Patron), Wong Artarne (Lee, Gannin's Houseboy), Jane Worland (Hat Check Girl).

Credits: Director: Edwin L. Marin; Producer: Nat Holt; Executive Producer: Jack J. Gross; Assistant Director: Grayson Rogers; Based on the Story "The Twisted Road" by Maurice Davis; Screenplay: Martin Rackin; Photography: J. Roy Hunt; Editor: Samuel E.

Left to right: Richard Powers, Raft, Mack Gray, William Bendix, Dean White and Richard Benedict in *Race Street*.

Beetley; Musical Score: Roy Webb; Musical Director: C. Bakaleinikoff; Dance Director: Charles O'Curran; Art Direction: Albert D'Agostino and Walter E. Keller; Costumes: Edward Stevenson; Makeup: Gordon Bau; Special Effects: Russell A. Cully. Songs: "I Saw You First": Music by Jimmy McHugh and Lyrics by Harold Adamson, Sung and Danced by Gale Robbins and Cully Richards; "I'm in a Jam with Baby": Music by Ray Heindorf and M.K. Jerome and Lyrics by Ted Koehler, sung by Gale Robbins; "Love That Boy": Music by Gene de Paul and Lyrics by Don Raye, sung by Gale Robbins and Cully Richards. Released by RKO on June 29, 1948. Black and white. 79 minutes.

Taglines: "Raft at his roughest tangles with a dame at her deadliest!" "Racket king Raft and homicide ace Bendix — hunting the same killer — tricked by the same killer."

Synopsis: Former vaudeville singer-dancer turned syndicate head, Paul Dickson, muscles his way into San Francisco's illegal betting dens by shaking down the local bookies for as much as a 25 percent take of their profits going to his protection racket. Crippled bookie Hal Towers, who refuses to accept the syndicate's protection, is taken outside his apartment building and fatally thrown down a flight of steps.

Bookie Dan Gannin, who uses his investment brokerage firm and ownership of the popular night spot The Turf Club as a front for his betting activities, takes it upon himself to track down his friend Hal's killers. The top-billed entertainer at the club is his sister Elaine. Persuading the local bookies not to go to the police, but to let him handle it, alienates Dan's friend, police detective Barney Runson. This attitude results in Gannin being kidnapped, beaten and almost killed by Dickson's thugs. He is later assaulted on the same set of steps as Hal. Runson has a strong desire to capture Dickson, the only quarry who ever eluded him. Runson takes Gannin to an old vaudeville house for coffee and shows him a photo of Dickson and his wife. Gannin is stunned to see that Dickson's wife is Robbie Laurence, Gannin's fiancée. Gannin tells Runson that her husband was killed in the war, but Runson tells him this is not true and that Dickson is very much alive.

Gannin and Runson go to Robbie's apartment where she admits that she is Phil Dickson's wife, but she says that she has not seen him in years. After Runson leaves, Gannin tells her that she is lying and that Dickson had Hal killed. Robbie tells him that she thought Dickson was dead, but he turned up and forced her to help him. To escape Dickson, they decide to leave San Francisco together; Gannin says he will be back in an hour. After he has gone, Robbie phones Dickson and tells him that Gannin knows everything and will be returning shortly. By a ruse, Gannin overhears her conversation, but after Gannin departs, Robbie learns that he eavesdropped.

In Gannin's apartment, Runson tells him that he does not believe Robbie's story and he is placing Gannin in protective custody. Before he has the chance to do this, Al, a bookie who was once a colleague of Gannin's but is now working for Dickson, ambushes them. Dickson emerges from the shadows with the intention of having Gannin and Runson killed. They manage to turn the tables, but Gannin is killed stopping a bullet meant for Runson. He leaves behind a heartbroken Runson who eulogizes, "It's the same town ... a little lonelier."

Comments: This was the third of four Raft films made under his RKO pact. It was the actor's sixth and final film for director Edwin L. Marin. Considerably enhanced by location shooting in San Francisco, it was narrated by William Bendix. It's the only film Raft made between 1945 and 1954 where his character was killed at the end. Interestingly, the protagonist was content at the beginning of the film as he was about to retire from being a bookie, open a club and marry an attractive girl. His life from that point went downhill and ended in tragedy. The majority of the scenes in the film dealt with the relationships between the three leads. Raft was well cast as Gannin, but Gannin was ineffectual in that he tended to be reactive to the threats and violence inflicted on himself and others rather than proactive in hunting down the syndicate leader. One clever touch was having older, benign-looking guys acting as front men for the protection racket. The steps that Harry Morgan was thrown down, and Raft was later beaten up on, were almost an entity in themselves in that they appeared dangerous and gloomy.

In view of the fact that Raft's box office appeal was beginning to falter, this was an attempt by RKO to highlight all three stars rather than to create a Raft vehicle. In Bendix, Raft had an aggressive male co-star to play against which was not the case in his two previous RKO films. The ploy worked to the degree that the film returned a modest profit. One misjudgement on the part of the producers was to advertise the film with taglines which showed that Marilyn Maxwell was playing a crook in league with the gangsters. It was a major twist in the plot which was intended as a surprise, but hardly qualified as one when it was given away in the advance publicity. Maxwell, who was usually better in unsympathetic parts, played the duplicitous female with flair. Another surprise was seeing the blonde bombshell Maxwell appearing in this film as a brunette. Gale Robbins played Raft's sister. Her main function was to perform the songs and dances which were interspersed in the narrative flow of the film. This was one of Raft's films which was dismissed in its day, but has since been revisited and reevaluated by film buffs who have highlighted its merits.

Biography: William Bendix was born in New York on January 14, 1906. His father was Oscar "Max" Bendix, violinist and conductor. William's original ambition was to be a baseball player, but when this proved beyond him he worked in a greengrocer's shop in Orange, New Jersey. When the shop closed during the Depression, he turned to the stage. He was with the New Jersey Federal Theater for two years before trying Broadway where his first six plays flopped. His seventh, *The Time of Your Life*, propelled him into motion pictures; he made his screen debut in *Woman of the Year* (1942). He received a Best Supporting Actor Oscar nomination for *Wake Island* (1942) (but never served in the armed forces in real life because he suffered from chronic asthma). He later starred in two television series, *The Life of Riley* (1953–1958) and *Overland Trail* (1960). He married Teresa Stefanotti in 1928 and had a natural daughter, Lorraine, and an adopted daughter, Stephanie. He died in Los Angeles on December 14, 1964, aged 58, of lobar pneumonia and stomach cancer.

Biography: Marilyn Maxwell was born Marvel Marilyn Maxwell in Clarinda, Iowa, on August 3, 1922. At sixteen she was singing on an amateur radio show in Des Moines. She later sang with the orchestras of Buddy Rogers and Ted Weems. She was a featured radio singer for seven years and appeared regularly on Bing Crosby's radio program. She was at the Pasadena Playhouse in 1941, signed a contract with MGM and made her screen debut in *Stand by for Action* (1942). She toured with Bob Hope during the Korean War and worked in top New York nightclubs. In addition to numerous guest shots on television she was the star of the TV series *Bus Stop* (1961–1962). She was married and divorced three times and had a son. She also had close relationships with Bob Hope and Rock Hudson. She died in Beverly Hills on March 20, 1972, aged 49, of a pulmonary ailment and high blood pressure.

Outpost in Morocco (1949)

Cast: George Raft (Captain Paul Gerard), Marie Windsor (Cara), Akim Tamiroff (Lt. Glysko), John Litel (Colonel D. Pascal), Erno Verebes (Bamboule), Eduard Franz (Emir of Bel-Rashad), Crane Whitley (Caid Osman), Damian O'Flynn (Commandant Louis Fronval), Michael Ansara (Rifle Dispenser), John Doucette (Card-Playing Soldier), James Nolan (Legionnaire Colonel's Aid), Soledad Jiminez (Cara's Companion), Ivan Triesault (Arab Chieftain).

Credits: Director: Robert Florey; Executive Producers: Samuel Bischoff and George Raft; Producer and Original Story: Joseph N. Ermolieff; Screenplay: Paul de Sainte Colombe and Charles Grayson; Script Supervisor: Bobbie Serkes; Assistant Director: Joseph Depew; Photography: Lucien Andriot; Editor: George Arthur; Musical Score: Michel Michelet; Art Direction: Arthur Lonegan; Sound Recorder: Fred Lau; Makeup: Mel Berns. Released by United Artists on May 2, 1949. Black and white. 92 minutes.

We are grateful to the French Government for permission to film this production in the most advanced outpost in South Morocco, with the unreserved assistance of the French Foreign Legion and the Moroccan Spahis Cavalry.

Synopsis: In Teskett, regional headquarters of the French Colonial Army in Morocco, French Foreign Legion Captain Paul Gerard has gained a reputation for his military exploits and his sexual prowess. Colonel Pascal sends Gerard's orderly, Bamboule, in search of Gerard to escort Cara, the daughter of the emir of Bel-Rashad, back to her father's province. Since she is returning early and Bel-Rashad is a forbidden place for Frenchmen, Pascal suspects that a plot is being hatched to overthrow the French. Bamboule searches all the nightspots and eventually finds Gerard dancing the tango with a mysterious and beautiful woman who erroneously believes that he is a professional dancer.

En route, Cara is stunned to discover that her dancing partner is none other than Gerard who is in charge of the convoy. The two fall in love, exacerbating a dangerous situation. Gerard is invited to meet the emir inside Bel-Rashad. After Gerard has gone, the emir tells his daughter that he intends to destroy the French. At the fort, one of the sentries is shot with a bullet from a brand new rifle. Gerard disguises himself as a native and goes undercover to obtain one of the new guns. He succeeds in his attempt, but is chased by the rebels. While in the palace, he encounters Cara, who believes he has come to visit her, and they have a passionate reunion. With her help, he makes good his escape. When she discovers his deception, she is upset. After he returns to the fort, he is ordered to start for Teskett with Lt. Glysko and bring reinforcements.

Upon their return with a fresh garrison, they find that the Legionnaires have all been massacred and the wall of the fort breached. The emir uses the massacre as a strong argument to convince the other tribal chieftains to join him. Gerard intends to lead a raiding party to blow up the Bel-Rashad ammunition dump, but Glysko insists on doing it himself. When Glysko arrives, the emir has disappeared and the arsenal is empty so he takes Cara prisoner instead.

The rebels manage to cut off the water supply to the fort and the cavalrymen are forced to turn their horses loose in the desert. Gerard professes his love for Cara and tells her that the garrison is going to make a break for it before releasing her. There is a downpour of rain which makes the repaired wall very vulnerable. Instead of fleeing, Gerard and his men lay a minefield outside the fort. When the emir and his forces attack at dawn, the Legionnaires are prepared for them. Cara rides after her father in a doomed effort to prevent further blood-

Left to right: Raft, Marie Windsor and Soledad Jiminez in *Outpost in Morocco*.

shed. At a signal from Gerard, the mines are detonated, killing both the emir and Cara. After the battle the other tribes emerge, surrender their weapons and renew their loyalty to the French. With Cara's death, Gerard is left desolate, but with the knowledge that his actions have strengthened French sovereignty in that part of North Africa.

Comments: A sturdy action picture, this was one of Raft's best postwar films and he gave an excellent performance. This was the first and only time Raft was directed by Robert Florey. Although he was not an "A"-list director, Florey handled many minor films with flair and efficiency. In this film there were some very exciting scenes, notably where the horses were turned loose in the desert and the final charge towards the fort. *Outpost in Morocco* was Florey's personal favorite of his own films. This was the second film Raft co-produced with Sam Bischoff.

One outstanding aspect of the film was Lucien Andriot's desert photography. The film had some good dialogue as when Glysko says, "All women are unfair," to which Gerard replied, "If they weren't, there would be no Foreign Legion." While the film was not one of Raft's biggest box office hits, it is understood to have turned a reasonable profit in the action market. Raft went to French Morocco to shoot exterior scenes for this film in 1947. He recalled, "You really had to be tough to play in that picture. While we were working it was 150 degrees in the sun and not more than a degree cooler in the shade. It was so hot that the horses had to be rested every third day, but the actors, including French Legionnaires, worked every day."

Sultry Marie Windsor, a name well known to film buffs, could ignite the screen with her presence. The nightclub scene in which Raft danced the tango with her was performed with tremendous grace and was very romantic. In some respects this was a standard heroine assignment and yet she still managed to bring to it a smoldering sexuality. She had another memorable scene where she appeared to be swimming naked. The role was somewhat more complex in that it remained uncertain throughout much of the film whether she will side with her father or her lover Gerard. She also rode a horse extremely well, a prime requirement for this film. Arguably she was Raft's best postwar leading lady. In the supporting cast, Akim Tamiroff gave a sterling performance as Raft's second-in-command. In view of the recent conflicts between insurgents and peace-keeping forces in North Africa and other countries, *Outpost in Morocco* is a film which still has some contemporary relevance.

Biography: Robert Florey was born in Paris on September 14, 1900. Fascinated by films from childhood, he started work as a journalist (initially as a sportswriter) but later as a critic. In 1919 he entered the film industry in Switzerland as actor, writer and assistant director of a series of shorts. He went to Hollywood in 1921 and received his first directorial credit with Tiffany-Stahl as the director of a series of two-reelers. In America he was very active on the social scene in the twenties and worked mainly as a publicist. His first feature as a director was *One Hour of Love* (1926). He returned to Europe, directing movies in France, Germany and England. Between 1929 and 1950 he directed in excess of sixty films, some of which are highly regarded by film buffs. Afterwards he became a prolific television director. He died in Santa Monica on May 16, 1979, aged 78, of cancer. In 1939 he married Virginia Dabney, who survived him.

Biography: Marie Windsor was born Emily Marie Bertelson in Maryvale, Utah, December 11, 1919, the daughter of Lane Bertelson and Etta Long. She attended Brigham Young University for two years and was elected "Miss Utah," a phantom beauty title. In 1940 she went to Hollywood where she studied with Maria Ouspenskaya. She lived at the Hollywood Studio Club where, at the suggestion of one of the residents, she changed her star surname to Windsor. She was working as a cigarette girl at the Mocambo Club when she was spotted by producer Arthur Hornblow, Jr., which led to her screen debut in *All American Co-ed* (1941). She moved to New York where a role in a Broadway revue, *Follow the Girls*, led to a short term contract with MGM. From there she went on to play leads in Westerns at Republic such as *Hellfire* (1949) and such thrillers as *The Narrow Margin* (1952) and *The Killing* (1956). She did a lot of stage work in Los Angeles during the 1980s and obtained a licence to practice as a realtor. During the 1990s she was beset with numerous health problems and eventually died a day short of her 81st birthday of cardiopulmonary arrest in Beverly Hills on December 10, 2000. Her first marriage to Ted Steele in 1946 was annulled in 1947. She married realtor Jack Hupp in 1954 and with him had a son named Richard (born in 1963) and a stepson named Chris. Although she seldom headed the cast of a film, her name was usually worth more to film buffs than many a toplined star. She recalled, "George Raft was a great gentleman and a very sweet, kind man. I loved working with him. He certainly wasn't a great actor, but he exuded 'star' quality. He just had that air about him. He was courteous and friendly to everyone. One day a delivery man came by the set with a TV which someone had sent him. He turned right around and asked me if I would like to have it. I was thrilled."

Biography: Akim Tamiroff was born in Baku, Russia, on October 29, 1899. In 1918 he was one of four selected from 500 applicants for admission to the Moscow Art Theater School, from which he graduated in 1921. In 1923 he came with a group to America to present several Russian plays and decided to stay. After several New York Theater Guild productions and work in a Chicago nightclub, he decided to try films so he and his actress wife Tamara Shayne drove to Hollywood. In 1934 he signed with Paramount and went on to appear in numerous films as a top-of-the-line character actor. Cecil B. DeMille once called him "the finest workman as an actor I've ever seen." He was twice nominated as Best Supporting Actor, for *The General Died at Dawn* and *For Whom the Bell Tolls*. He died in Palm Springs, California, on September 17, 1972, aged 72. He also appeared with George Raft in *Rumba* and *Spawn of the North* and they both made appearances in *Ocean's 11*, but did not share any scenes together.

Johnny Allegro (aka *Hounded*) (1949)

Cast: George Raft (Johnny Allegro), Nina Foch (Glenda Chapman), George Macready (Morgan Vallin), Will Geer (Schultzy), Gloria Henry (Addie), Ivan Triesault (Pelham Vetch), Harry Antrim (Pudgy), William "Bill" Phillips (Roy), Thomas Browne Henry (Frank, T-Man), Walter Rode (Grote), Eddie Acuff (Maintenance Man), Mary Bear (Nurse), Paul E. Burns (Gray), Matilda Caldwell (Servant), Frank Dae (Dr. Jaynes), Sol Gorss (Jeffrey), Chuck Hamilton (Guard), George Offerman, Jr. (Elevator Boy), Joe Palma (Guard), Steve Pendleton (Young Man), Cosmo Sardo (Waiter), Fred F. Sears (Desk Clerk), Brick Sullivan (Guard), Larry Thompson (Operator), Harlan Warde (Coast Guard Officer).

Credits: Director: Ted Tetzlaff; Producer: Irving Starr; Assistant Director: Earl Bellamy; Original Story: James Edward Grant; Screenplay: Karen De Wolf and Guy Endore; Script Supervisor: Pearl Leiter; Photography: Joseph Biroc; Editor: Jerome Thoms; Assistant Editor: Andy Anderson; Music Score: George Duning; Music Director: Morris Stoloff; Art Direction: Perry Smith; Sound Recorder: Jack Goodrich; Costumes: Jean Louis; Makeup: Irving Berns. Released by Columbia on May 26, 1949. Black and white. 81 minutes.

Synopsis: U.S. Treasury agents are shadowing Glenda Chapman. She manages to outwit them by embracing Johnny Allegro, the florist in the hotel where she is staying, and pretending that he is her husband. In his shop Allegro is visited by T-man Schultzy, who reminds him of his previous history as Joe Rock, a gangster escapee from Sing Sing and later as a World War II hero in the O.S.S. Schultzy wants his cooperation in shadowing Glenda. When Allegro goes to her room, Glenda tells him that she is leaving and needs his help to escape. In the process he pretends to shoot a T-man with an automatic. Since he is now ostensibly a wanted man, he insists on accompanying her. Allegro drives her to a private airfield where a waiting plane takes off with Allegro and Glenda on board. They touch down in Florida where they board a small boat steered by a vicious thug named Roy who takes them to a small island off the Florida coast. There Glenda introduces Allegro to her husband, a madman named Morgan Vallin who is a crack shot with bow and arrow. The following day Allegro sees a boat arrive at the dock and two mysterious men, Vetch and Groat, disembark.

Vallin takes Allegro and Glenda to the Florida races where Allegro is given a package which he delivers to an office. At a restaurant Allegro feigns a malaria attack and is taken to a Veterans' Hospital where Schultzy is waiting. Schultzy tells him that Vallin is a criminal mastermind in league with ex–Nazis who are providing him with counterfeit money printed by the Japanese during World War II. The intention is to flood America with counterfeit money, thereby disrupting the national economy. He instructs Allegro to find out where the island is located and to notify the Coast Guard by radio.

Back on the island Vallin falls out with ex–Nazis Vetch and Groat and murders them both. Vallin tells Allegro and Roy that they are quitting the island and to load the boat. Allegro uses the boat radio to alert the Coast Guard. Vallin discovers that the automatic Allegro used to "kill" the T-man is loaded with blanks and realizes that Allegro is working with the authorities. Glenda begs Allegro to flee the island in the boat, but Allegro refuses to go without the counterfeit money. Reluctantly Glenda shows him where the money is hidden in a cave. There Allegro discovers Roy apparently trying to take the counterfeit money to the boat. A fight ensues in which Allegro manages to overcome Roy and trap him in the cave. Vallin stalks Allegro and Glenda with his bow and arrows. He corners Allegro close to the boat, intending to finish him off, but Glenda manages to deflect his aim which gives Allegro time to reach Vallin and, in the ensuing fistfight, knock him off a cliff. Glenda declares her love for Allegro, and Allegro reveals to her the deal to reduce his jail sentence if he tracked Vallin down. Schultzy arrives with the Coast Guard and congratulates Allegro on a job well done.

Comments: *Johnny Allegro* was one of only

Nina Foch and Raft in *Johnny Allegro*.

a couple of films which Raft made for Columbia, a major studio. It was the first and superior of the two Raft films directed by Ted Tetzlaff. Years earlier Raft had walked off the set of *The Princess Comes Across* because he alleged that the cameraman was favoring his co-star Carole Lombard. The name of the cameraman was Ted Tetzlaff. The latter half of *Johnny Allegro* had plot elements which seem to be derived from *The Most Dangerous Game*.

Of the batch of Raft postwar thrillers, *Johnny Allegro* was one of the most exciting and the most commercially successful. It was well shot in black and white with a good cast. Raft, who was always convincing in crime films, gave his usual reliable performance. The musical score was very effective and the set decorations were elaborate, particularly of Vallin's house. An intriguing noir element was the sense of the remoteness of the island and of the hero and heroine almost being beyond help. Overall this was an interesting, well-plotted and fast-paced film which was worth watching for its mystery, the placing of characters in a desperate situation and the underlying theme of loyalty. The film tied the various strands together extremely well. The interplay between hero Allegro and the villain Vallin, with respect and mutual distrust being displayed on both sides, anticipated some of the dialogue and plotting of the James Bond films in future decades.

Biography: Ted Tetzlaff was born Dale H. Tetzlaff on June 3, 1903. He entered the film industry in 1923 as a camera assistant before working his way up to being director of photography by 1926. During the thirties he was active at Columbia and Paramount, where he photographed some prestigious films. In 1941 he turned director, helming 14 films before he retired in 1959. He died at Fort Baker, California, on January 7, 1995, aged 91.

Biography: Nina Foch was born Nina Consuelo Maud Fock in Leyden, Holland, on April 20, 1924, the daughter of orchestra conductor Dirk Fock and actress Consuelo Flowerton. Her parents divorced when she was a child and she was raised in New York City where she was educated at Lincoln School, Art Students League and Parsons Art School. She became interested in acting at an early age and trained at the American Academy of Dramatic Arts. She appeared on stage in regional theaters before signing a contract with Columbia in 1943. She received a Best Supporting Actress Oscar nomination for *Executive Suite* (1954). During the latter stages of her career, in addition to television and theater acting she became an acclaimed drama coach and college lecturer. She married and divorced three times and had a son. She died in Los Angeles on December 5, 2008, aged 84, of myelodysplasia, a blood disorder.

Biography: George Macready was born George Peabody in Providence, Rhode Island, on August 29, 1899, the son of George Peabody and Grace Clark. He was educated at Brown University where he studied Greek and mathematics. His first job was as a reporter in New York. He appeared on stage in Detroit and studied at the Boleslawski Theater in New York. He was on vacation in Paris when he read that Gordon Craig, famed scenic designer, was going to stage *Macbeth* on Broadway. He returned to New York and landed a small part. Then he progressed to leading roles opposite Katharine Cornell and Helen Hayes on Broadway before going to Hollywood where he made his screen debut in *Commandos Strike at Dawn* (1942). He went on to play a number of important roles in films, frequently cast as a suave villain. He was under contract to Columbia for many years. On television he played the role of Martin Peyton in *Peyton Place* (1964–1968). The scar on his right cheek was the result of a car accident. He was an expert on art and a close friend of Vincent Price, with whom he ran a Los Angeles art gallery. He married actress Elizabeth Dana, whom he divorced in 1942. They had a son and two daughters. He died in Los Angeles on June 2, 1973, aged 73, of emphysema. He had roles in two other Raft films, *Follow the Boys* and *Jet Over the Atlantic*.

Red Light (1949)

Cast: George Raft (John Torno), Virginia Mayo (Carla North), Gene Lockhart (Warni Hazard), Raymond Burr (Nick Cherney), Harry Morgan (Rocky), Barton MacLane (Detective Lt. Strecker), Arthur Franz (Jess Torno), Ken Murray (Himself), Stanley Clements (Bellhop at Carlson Hotel), William Frawley (Hotel Clerk), Arthur Shields (Father Redmond), Frank Orth (William "Wally" Stoner), Philip Pine (Pablo Cabrillo), William "Bill" Phillips (Detective Jim Ryan), Movita Castenada (Trina), Paul Frees (First Bellhop), Claire Carleton (Waitress), Soledad Jiminez (Pablo's Mother), Robert Espinoza (Miguel), Mack Gray, Leonard Bremen (Gamblers), Chuck Hamilton (Detective Arresting Cherney), Al Hill (Bert), Bob Jellison (Man in Hotel Room), Phyllis Kennedy (Chambermaid), Joe Kirk (Reporter in Newsreel), Knox Manning (Newsreel Commentator), Edwin Max (Max Appleby aka Burt Adams), Jack Overman (Hotel Clerk), Brick Sullivan (Red, Truck Driver), Bob Perry (Red's Helper), Victor Sen Yung (Vincent, Houseboy).

Credits: Director-Producer: Roy Del Ruth; Associate Producer: Joseph Kaufman; Based on the Story "This Guy Gideon" by Donald Barry; Screenplay: George Callahan; Additional Dialogue: Charles Grayson; Photography: Bert Glennon; Editor: Richard Heermance; Music: Dimitri Tiomkin; Art Direction: F. Paul Sylos; Sound Recorder: Frank Webster; Costumes: Jack Masters; Special Effects: Robert H. Moreland. Second Unit Director: D. Ross Lederman; Assistant Director: Robert Aldrich; Sound Recorder: Frank McWhorter; Photographer: James Van Trees. Production Dates: January to March 1949 Filming Locations: Carmel Mission, Carmel, California, San Francisco and El Capitan Theater, Vine Street, Los Angeles. Released by United Artists on September 30, 1949. Black and white. 83 minutes.

Taglines: "Raft is on the prowl for big game with luscious Virginia Mayo as his 'killer bait!'"

"It takes everything Mayo has to stop a guy like Raft."

"I'm giving you a job to do baby. Don't ask questions and you won't get hurt."

"You're going too far this time, Torno. The law is breathing down your neck."

This is the story of one of the most unusual cases in the criminal records of San Francisco. The criminal, a cruel, sadistic killer was never apprehended, judged or convicted by the law — yet on the books the case is marked "closed" to which someone has added the words, "Man Proposes and God Disposes."

Synopsis: Johnny Torno, owner of San Francisco's Torno Freight Lines Company, welcomes his brother Jess, an army medical chaplain, back after five years of war in the South Pacific. This is captured on a newsreel which is seen by San Quentin inmates, including Nick Cherney and Rocky. Cherney, a former employee of Torno's, was sent to prison for embezzlement. The newsreel gives him the idea of revenging himself on Johnny by murdering Jess. One evening Johnny visits his brother's room at the Carlson Hotel and finds him dying of bullet wounds. When Johnny asks him who did it, Jess answers, "Written in the Bible," before dying. Warni Hazard, Torno's accountant, reveals that Nick Cherney has been released from San Quentin. Torno goes to a bowling alley where he threatens Cherney in the men's room. Cherney tells him that he was in San Quentin at the time of the killing.

Johnny realizes that his brother was referring to the hotel room's Gideon Bible, which is now mysteriously missing. From the bellhop he obtains a list of the five guests who have occupied the room since Jess. At the top of the list is showgirl Carla North, who gives her address as "Ken Murray's Blackouts" in Hollywood. Johnny traces Carla to the Samson Hotel where, in her absence, he searches her room and finds a photo of Jess and other soldiers. Upon her return he challenges her, but

Left to right: Philip Pine, Movita Castenada and Raft in *Red Light*.

ing. Unknown to Torno, Cherney is hiding in the room, but he and Rocky make good their escape. On a train, Rocky tries to blackmail Cherney which leads Cherney to hurl him off the train, intending to murder him. When Cherney discovers that Warni has found out that Cherney was in Reno, he murders Warni. Back in Los Angeles, Carla demands to know what she is involved in. When Johnny tells her, they argue and she leaves him. The police arrive at Johnny's business. Detective Lt. Strecker tells him that they are keeping him under surveillance, but he eludes them.

Torno goes to Monterey where he finds Pablo Cabrillo and his family. Cabrillo is blind, but admits to taking the Bible. Torno demands it back, but is told that Carla has arrived ahead of him and taken it. Cherney arrives at Torno's

she replies that her brother, who was in the photo, was killed shortly after the photo was taken and that his personal effects were returned to her by Jess. Johnny hires her to trace the rest of the people on the list. Cherney turns up at Torno's office, ostensibly searching for a job, but in reality snooping. He overhears Torno telling Warni that he and Carla are tracking the people on the list and that Jess has told him he wrote the murderer's name in the Gideon Bible.

The trail takes Torno and Carla from Max Appleby, a bookie in San Francisco, to Wally Stoner, a short order cook in Reno. Stoner turns out to be a dead end, but Rocky goes to Reno where he is spotted by Torno, who relieves him of his gun and forces him to take him to the Globe Hotel where Rocky is stay-

business where Torno hires him to phone all the hotels in town and find where Carla is staying. Carla arrives followed shortly afterwards by the police. When Johnny examines the Bible, he finds no name in it, only a message from Jess reading, "Johnny, thou shalt not kill." Lt. Strecker tells him they have searched his office and found the gun he grabbed from Rocky; tests have proved it was the one which killed Jess. Johnny realizes Rocky is the murderer.

As Cherney is leaving, a badly injured Rocky suddenly appears, threatening him, but Cherney shoots him. The shots are heard by Johnny, Carla and Strecker. When they rush to the dying Rocky, he points to Cherney and tells them he was paid to murder Jess. Cherney flees to the roof of the building where Torno intends to kill him, but remembers Jess' message and has a change of heart. In a twist of fate, Cherney is electrocuted by one electric sign, while another sign nearby flashes "24 Hour Service."

Comments: This was the fourth and last Raft film directed by Roy Del Ruth. Raft was reportedly paid a $65,000 salary for this film. *Red Light* was a blend of film noir and religion. Johnny Torno was one of Raft's more complex characterizations to which he brought considerable depth and credibility. His customary cool facade was allowed to crack at times and he expressed a myriad of emotions ranging from deep regret at the brutal murder of his brother to cold rage as he resolutely pursued the killer on a multi-state journey. Leading businessmen are frequently ruthless and Raft conveyed this single-mindedness very effectively. The ruthlessness which enabled him to establish a successful business, he applied to avenging the death of his brother. After a while his brother's murder became secondary as the quest became an end in itself. In the process he alienated virtually everyone around him. His sudden violent eruption inside the church, where the sympathetic priest pleaded with him to forgo vengeance, was one of the most memorable scenes in the film. There were frequent visits from the police telling him to let them handle it, which he ignored. Barton MacLane had the final line in the film: "It looks like someone else was on the job" as the neon sign flashes "24 Hour Service." Both of these are references to God.

Raft's quest was accompanied by multiple cinematic devices which made the film noir cycle so worthwhile: grotesquely lit close-ups; rainwashed streets; brutal fights; and chases in the dark. The gloom was so deep and disturbing that it is almost possible to wallow in it. Dimitri Tiomkin's score seemed a little heavy-handed as it moved from one religious theme to another. The title of the film is rather a mystery. It could be a warning to stop the mounting violence or more likely a reference

to the electrocuting signage that ended the movie.

Virginia Mayo first appeared about half an hour into the film. Raft usually established a good rapport with his leading ladies, but there was a total lack of chemistry between Raft and Mayo. Coincidentally, she was one of the few leading ladies who intensely disliked him. This was one of the few films from this period where Raft did not do any dancing. Nor was there any hint of romance between Raft and Mayo. Raft tried to incorporate a unique mannerism in his characterization, one borrowed from "Bugsy" Siegel: Siegel had a hair-combing habit and Raft suggested to Roy Del Ruth that he would like to use it in his performance. Del Ruth refused to let him do this on the grounds that an audience would find this highly unlikely.

The supporting cast was excellent. In particular Raymond Burr and Harry Morgan were as brutal a pair of villains as ever appeared in a film noir. Morgan was making his second appearance in a Raft film, but his role here could not have been more different from the Raft buddy whom he played in *Race Street*. The film was at its weakest where coincidence played too large a part in the proceedings. Burr frequently appeared at exactly the right moment to overhear some important piece of information. Although this moved the plot along, the number of such coincidences strained credulity.

Gene Lockhart did a fine job as Warni. He had some good dialogue as when he says, "My old man always said liquor doesn't drown your troubles — just teaches 'em to swim." One memorable noir scene occurred late at night when a badly frightened Warni goes down to the truck garage and finds that his car has been sabotaged. He has a panic attack and takes refuge under a truck trailer. Only the legs of his pursuer are seen as he approaches Warni's hiding place and kicks the bricks away which prop up the trailer, causing its full weight to crush Warni. The camera pans upwards to reveal a smug Cherney.

Biography: Virginia Mayo was born Virginia Clare Jones in St. Louis, Missouri, on November 30, 1920. She studied dance at the Wientge School of Dramatic Expression. Following graduation from high school in 1937, she spent a season as a member of the ballet of St. Louis Municipal Opera. Then she joined a well-known vaudeville act called "Pansy the Horse" as ringmistress. She went into the New York revue Billy Rose's Diamond Horseshoe, where she was seen and tested by a talent scout. The test was eventually seen by producer Samuel Goldwyn who signed her to a contract. She initially appeared in the chorus of *Up in Arms* (1944). Then she was leading lady to Danny Kaye and Bob Hope. After leaving Goldwyn she was signed to a longtime contract at Warner Bros. In 1947 she married actor Michael O'Shea with whom she had a daughter, Mary Catherine, born in 1953. She was widowed in 1974. She died in a nursing home in Thousand Oaks, California, on January 17, 2005, aged 84, of pneumonia and heart failure. She appeared with Raft in two films, *Red Light* and *Jet Over the Atlantic*.

Biography: Raymond Burr was born in New Westminster, British Columbia, Canada, on May 21, 1917. He was the son of William Johnston Burr Sr., a hardware salesman, and his wife Minerva Smith, a music teacher. He was educated at San Rafael Military Academy and Willard Junior High School. He was appearing in a Broadway play, *The Duke in Darkness* (1944), when he was seen by a Hollywood agent who got him a film contract at RKO Radio. For the next decade he played mainly hulking villains. He hit the television jackpot when he played the title characters in *Perry Mason* (1957–1966) and *Ironside* (1967–1975). In 1946 he married Isabella Ward, but his only marriage ended in divorce in 1949. Burr, who was a homosexual, died in Geyserville, Sonoma County, California, on September 12, 1993, aged 76, of metastatic cancer of the liver.

A Dangerous Profession
(aka *The Bail Bond Story*) (1949)

Cast: George Raft (Vince Kane), Ella Raines (Lucy Brackett), Pat O'Brien (Joe Farley), Bill Williams (Claude Brackett), Jim Backus (Detective Lt. Nick Ferrone), Roland Winters (Jerry McKay), Betty Underwood (Elaine Storm), Robert Gist (Roy Collins/Max Gibney), David Wolfe (Matthew Dawson), Harry Brown (Room Clerk), Dick Dickinson (Thin Man), Don Dillaway (Young Drunk), Jim Drum (Wally), Gloria Gabriel (Kane's Secretary), Mack Gray (Fred, Taxi Driver), Jonathan Hale (Roger Lennert), Charmienne Harker (Cigarette Girl), Phyllis Kennedy (Maid in Kane's Apartment), Mike Lally (Policeman), Paul Maxey (Judge Thompson), Frances Morris (Mrs. Frances Farley), William J. O'Brien (Clerk), Allan Ray (Hotel Dorsey Clerk), Lynn Roberts (Miss Wilson), Yvonne Rob (Vi), Dick Ryan (Gus, Policeman), Frank Shannon (Barman), Michael St. Angel (Roberts, Law Firm Receptionist), Bork Symon (Herman), Nancy Valentine (Dawson's Secretary), Alan Wood (Bellhop).

Credits: Director: Ted Tetzlaff; Producer: Robert Sparks; Executive Producer: Sid Rogell; Assistant Director: James Casey; Screenplay: Martin Rackin and Warren Duff; Photography: Robert de Grasse; Editor: Frederic Knudtson; Score: Frederick Hollander and Roy Webb; Musical Director: C. Bakaleinikoff; Art Direction: Albert D'Agostino and Al Herman; Sound Recorders: Earl Mounce and Clem Portman; Costumes: Michael Woulfe. Released by RKO on November 26, 1949. Black and white. 79 minutes.

Synopsis: In Los Angeles, Vince Kane, a former police officer, and Joe Farley are partners in a bail bond business, posting bonds for accused persons which allows them freedom providing that they guarantee to appear in court at the appointed time. Kane and Detective Lt. Nick Ferrone, a friend and former colleague, go to a nightclub brawl where Ferrone spots and arrests Claude Brackett, a gang fugitive. Two years earlier Brackett cashed $150,000 for two other men which turned out to be stolen and Brackett fled. Brackett is residing at the Dorsey Hotel. Kane and Ferrone go to his hotel room where Kane leaves his card. The following day he is surprised to find Lucy Brackett, a woman with whom he once had a brief but passionate romance, and Roger Lennert, her lawyer, in his office. Bail has been set at $25,000, but Brackett only has assets of $4,000. Against the advice of Farley, Kane agrees to put up a bond.

Unscrupulous attorney Matthew Dawson arrives at Kane's office also claiming to represent Mrs. Brackett and asking for a bond. He hands Kane an envelope containing $12,000 cash. Lennert arrives almost simultaneously with $4,000. Although Kane introduces them, neither attorney has ever met the other. Shortly afterwards Kane posts the bond and Brackett is released. Neither of the Bracketts claim to know Dawson. Brackett absconds leaving a note. Ferrone takes Kane to the morgue to view the body of the murdered Brackett. Farley warns Kane not to investigate Brackett's murder, but nevertheless Kane goes to see Dawson, who tells him that a man named Max Gibney, whom he had never heard of, gave him the money for the bond.

Kane manages to trail Gibney to a boarding house where he discovers that Gibney's real name is Roy Collins, together with a link to another sinister underworld figure named Jerry McKay who runs a nightclub. He goes to see McKay, accusing him and Collins of masterminding the original robbery and of murdering Brackett. Kane pretends to turn crooked and agrees to keep quiet if McKay pays him $50,000. Farley arrives and McKay accuses Kane of a shakedown. Farley explodes and dissolves the partnership for which he will pay Kane $25,000 for his end of the business. Kane tells both men to meet him at the following morning at this apartment.

The following day, Lucy, who is being watched by the police, goes to Kane's apartment and hides. McKay and Farley arrive at Kane's apartment where they pay him the money. Kane tells McKay that he is not satisfied and wants Collins arrested for the murders of Brackett and a police officer named Benny Kafka at the original robbery. Kane, who becomes aware of Lucy's presence, is able to slip her a note telling her to contact Ferrone. Kane, Farley and McKay pile into a car, pick up Collins and drive to the Hollywood Hills pursued by the police. Kane provokes an argument which turns nasty between McKay and Collins. In the ensuing gunfight, Collins shoots Farley in the arm before Kane knocks Collins out. Kane and Lucy are reunited and plan a new life together while Ferrone and Farley argue over whether Kane should rejoin the police force or continue in the bail bond business.

Comments: This was the fourth and final Raft film for RKO. Director Ted Tetzlaff had earlier helmed Raft in the more exciting *Johnny Allegro*. This was the second of three films in which Raft co-starred with Pat O'Brien. Co-starring Raft, O'Brien and Ella Raines was really an attempt to make this an all-star cast rather than a George Raft vehicle although Raft had the lion's share of the screen time. As a sign of postwar economy, two key sequences (namely the one where Raft originally encountered Raines and the one where Bill Williams was murdered, both of which needed to be shown) were merely described. Another weakness of the film was that the character of Elaine Storm, Kane's girlfriend, went nowhere. The major merit of the film was that the Hollywood Hills climax was genuinely exciting.

Pat O'Brien recalled of this film, "A real dog. 'Everyone,' my agent said, 'connected with it should have been locked up without benefit of bail before it ever went into production.' No one knows where it ever played, probably the shelf in the cutting room." In actuality the film was nowhere near as bad as both film historian Leonard Maltin and O'Brien say it is. The real problem was that the bail bond business was not a particularly interesting one as the subject of a motion picture. Nevertheless the film turned a modest profit, which meant that none of the four films Raft made for RKO lost money. That studio made the kind of movies to which Raft was well suited and he might have continued there had it not been for Howard Hughes acquiring the studio at that point and within a short time virtually destroying it. It has to be said that Raft's career in the forties, in contrast to James Cagney who revived his career with *White Heat,* ended with a whimper rather than a bang.

Jim Backus recalled, "I made a film with George Raft called *A Dangerous Profession.* We had a scene in a car, backscreen projection, me at the wheel. Rehearsal went fine, but Raft goofed take after take. Finally, the director Ted Tetzlaff took me aside and told me that Raft had to look an actor straight in the eyes while doing a scene, or he'd lose concentration. I protested that since I was supposed to be driving a car, I had to keep my eyes on the road. Tetzlaff said to look Raft in the eyes or we'd be there all night. I did my best, looking Raft straight in the eyes with quick side glances ahead to preserve the illusion of driving as much as possible. The take went fine."

Biography: Ella Raines was born Ella Wallace Raubes in Snoqualmie Falls, Washington, on August 6, 1921, the daughter of a lumber company engineer. She was educated at the University of Washington where she studied drama. With some little theater experience, in 1942 she set out for New York intending a stage career. She made a screen test which eventually secured her a contract with Howard Hawks and Charles Boyer who formed BH Productions with her as its sole asset. She made her screen debut in *Corvette K-225* (1943) before her contract was sold to Universal. When her contract expired in 1947 she successfully freelanced at other studios. She later appeared on Broadway in *The Wisteria Trees* (1955) and was the star of the successful syndicated series *Janet Dean, Registered Nurse* (1954–1955) for which she scripted a few episodes. She married and divorced twice, to Captain Kenneth Trout (1942–1945) and Major Robin Olds (1947–1978). With the latter she had two daughters, Christina (born in 1951) and Susan (born in 1953). She died in Sherman Oaks, California, on May 30, 1988, aged 66, of throat cancer.

We Will All Go to Paris
(aka *Nous Irons à Paris*) (1950)

Cast: Philippe Lemaire (Jacques Lambert), Francoise Arnoul (Micheline Grosbois), Henri Genes (Julien), Christian Duvaleix (Paul), Pasquali (Monsieur Grosbois), Max Elloy (Honorin), Maryse Martin (Maman Terrine), George Lannes (Director of French Radio), Ray Ventura and His Orchestra. Guest Stars: George Raft, Martine Carol, Peters Sisters, Henri Salvador.

Credits: Director: Jean Boyer; Producer: Jean Darvey; Assistant Director: Jean Bastia; Script: Franz Tanzler; Adaptation: Jean Boyer; Dialogue: Serge Veber; Photography: Charles Suin; Editor: Fanchette Mazin; Music Score: Paul Misraki; Art Direction: Raymond Negre; Sound Recorder: Antoine Petitjean. Released by Les Films Corona/Hoche Productions on February 8, 1950. Black and white. 93 minutes.

Synopsis: Micheline Grosbois is in love with impoverished radio singer Jacques Lambert, who is disapproved of by her overbearing father, the manufacturer of the Lotus corset. Jacques and his friends Julien and Paul, frustrated by their lack of prospects, are fired from the official French radio station. They make their way to the South of France where they live on the farm of Maman Terrine and establish a trendy, peripatetic pirate radio station which becomes a big success. They are joined on the air by Micheline and later by Ray Ventura and His Orchestra. The station goes from strength to strength. The girl's father, erroneously believing his daughter to have been kidnapped, sets the police on their trail. Eventually the station broadcasts from a boat. Micheline goes back to Paris where she pleads their cause. The group are apprehended by the police, but instead of being arrested, they are taken to the Concord Square in Paris where they broadcast before a huge crowd and are awarded a radio contract to broadcast legally every day.

Comments: When the three friends are on the air, they devise a gag where they later dress as Western bandits, stop a car on the highway and force the driver to perform. The car they stop is driven by none other than George Raft. They introduce him to their listeners as "the famous Hollywood gangster, George Raft." When they explain their trick, Raft laughs and then excuses himself as he has a rendezvous with a beautiful moll! Raft's cameo was done during a French vacation which he took in 1949. This lightweight film, which was shot in France, was a box office hit in Europe but never released in the United States. It was a far-sighted film because pirate radio stations became a very popular form of entertainment in Europe during the 1960s.

Biography: Jean Boyer was born in Paris on June 26, 1901. He was the son of noted singer-songwriter Lucien Boyer and the brother of chanteuse Lucienne Boyer. He began writing songs for musical films in 1930. He commenced writing screenplays in 1931 and directed his first film in 1932. He went on to helm over seventy light but entertaining films which caught the mood of the time and were catnip to French audiences, but not shown much outside their country of origin. He died in Paris on March 10, 1965, aged 63.

Lucky Nick Cain (aka I'll Get You for This) (1951)

Cast: George Raft ("Lucky" Nick Cain), Coleen Gray (Kay Wonderly), Enzo Staiola (Toni), Charles Goldner (Massine), Walter Rilla (Eric Mueller), Martin Benson (Frankie Sperazza), Peter Illing (Armando Ceralde), Hugh French (Miles Travers), Peter Bull (Hans), Elwyn Brook-Jones (The Fence), Donald Stewart (Kennedy), Constance Smith (Nina), Greta Gynt (Claudette Ambling), Margot Grahame (Mrs. Langley), Norman Shelley (Mr. Langley), Martin Miller (Photographer), Hannah Watt (Prison Matron), Anthony Dawson (Treasury Agent), Valerie de Cadenet (Blonde), Jack La Roc (Orchestra Leader).

Credits: Director: Joseph M. Newman; Producer: Joseph Kaufman; Assistant Director: Philip Shipway; Based on the 1947 Novel *High Stakes* by James Hadley Chase; Screenplay: George Callahan and William Rose; Photography: Otto Heller; Editor: Russell Lloyd; Music Score: Walter Goehr; Art Direction: Ralph W. Brinton; Sound: John W. Mitchell; Costumes: Elizabeth Hennings. Songs: "Leni" by Ray Ventura and Bruno Coquatrix, "La Cumparsita" by Gerardo Matos Rodriguez. Released by 20th Century–Fox on March 3, 1951. Black and white. 87 minutes.

Synopsis: "Lucky" Nick Cain, a professional gambler, arrives in San Paolo on the Italian Riviera. He is befriended at the railway station by Toni, a shoeshine boy. Initially he is welcomed by Frankie Sperazza the casino manager, Miles Travers the hotel manager and Armando Ceralde the police chief. He is puzzled as to the reason. At the casino he is joined by Kay Wonderly, a budding artist who loses heavily at the gambling tables. When she confesses she is broke to Sperazza, he tells her he will forget the debt if she will make herself pleasant to Cain and become his girlfriend. As Cain is leaving the casino, an American named Kennedy stops him and says that he needs to speak to him urgently. Cain tells him that he will meet him tomorrow.

At Cain's hotel, he and Kay have a nightcap which is drugged and they both collapse. When they are revived hours later by the police, they find that they have been framed for the murder of Kennedy, a United States treasury agent whose body is lying in their room. Cain and Kay manage to escape and try to steal a car, but are held at gunpoint by Massine who is masquerading as a flower seller, but in reality is an Italian treasury agent. Massine believes their story and helps Cain and Kay hide in a ruined village. Kay tells Cain that she had seen Kennedy at the casino in the company of a woman named Claudette Ambling.

Cain breaks into Ambling's villa where he overhears a conversation between Ambling and a German named Mueller. He steals a photo of Mueller and escapes, pursued by police, but is rescued by Messine who does not recognize Mueller. They go to see the photographer who snapped the photograph and he identifies Mueller. Resting in the ruins, Kay has nightmares, but Cain returns to comfort her. He tells her that Sperazza and Ceralde both work for Mueller and that Messine is trying to find his address. Cain leaves Kay again and the trail leads him to a sinister encounter with underworld figures at a bar. En route he spots Toni, whom he tells to find Kay and stay with her until he returns. Toni finds Kay, but foolishly she becomes impatient and leaves the ruins to find Messine. En route she is recognized and arrested by police. She is imprisoned and tortured by a sadistic prison matron who wants to know where Cain is.

At Messine's house, Cain finds counterfeit money. Messine returns and says that he has been trailing the gang, but lost them. He tells Cain that treasury agents have been pursuing Mueller for years because he has the Hitler plates which enable him to manufacture counterfeit money and flood Europe with it. Messine takes Cain to a rocky point on the seashore where he lost the gang. Toni finds them and tells them that Kay has been arrested. They find a secret entrance on the hillside which leads them directly into the prison. Cain, Messine and treasury agents enter the prison. In the ensuing fight, the counterfeit notes and plates are recovered; Kay is rescued; Ceralde

is arrested; and Sperazza and Travers are killed. Mueller is trying to escape to Tunis with Messine in pursuit. Cain and Kay are reunited with Toni, and Cain promises to take them both back with him to America.

Comments: The only time that Raft was directed by Joseph M. Newman was in this independent film released by 20th Century–Fox. It was an early example of a U.S.–British co-production. The producer, director and stars were all American while the supporting cast was comprised of thespians whose careers were mainly spent in British films. One of its main virtues was the lineup of villains who were played by some of the best talent available for such roles in British films of the fifties. The location was breathtaking, but the film would have been improved if it had been shot in color. Several key scenes took place either at night or in darkness which made the film a little confusing at times.

Coleen Gray recalls, "We worked in San Remo, Italy, a beautiful town on the Italian Riviera. Scenes were shot in the casino and on the streets. A good deal of the film was shot in San Remo Vecchia, a deserted village which had been ruined by an earthquake." There was a delightful sequence in this film in which Raft and Gray danced the tango. She recalls, "How lucky can a girl get? To be taught the tango by the master of the tango is a gift from Heaven. George was an incredibly graceful dancer and, of course, the tango is the most beautiful, romantic dance. Sometimes I wish those lessons could have gone on forever."

One misconception about films is that they are always inferior to the literary sources from which they originate. *Lucky Nick Cain* did not fall into this category. The original novel *High Stakes* by James Hadley Chase was a badly written piece of pulp fiction, and the screenplay represented a dramatic improvement. One rather strange aspect of the film concerned the climax. The leading villain Mueller was not caught on screen, but was last seen escaping to Tunis with the leading Italian treasury

Coleen Gray (laughing) and Raft on the set of *Lucky Nick Cain*.

agent, Massine, chasing him. Neither character was shown at the climax and it was left to another treasury agent, who had not appeared before, to explain this to Cain, Kay and the audience. It was almost as though one or both of the actors had been called away for other assignments before the film had wrapped.

Raft was a tough guy with a sentimental streak. In this film there was a scene where Enzo Staiola had to tell Raft that his girlfriend Gray had been arrested. Raft was so moved at the child's acting that tears came to his eyes. As he expressed it, "I've got a soft side in spite of all my tough roles. I can easily be moved to tears." Other members of the film unit who witnessed this incident confirmed that it was true.

Raft was usually close to his best whenever he found himself in the crime genre and *Lucky Nick Cain* was an example of this. The *New York Times* critic noted, "George Raft is working in a tailor-made role. He is laconic, a smooth tango dancer, tough on dastards and easy on the eyes of several ladies." Coleen Gray adds, "George Raft was a lovely gentleman, quiet and shy. He told me he was in awe of me because I had a college degree and he had not gone to college. We got over that. I admired him for his many fine qualities. He knew his lines and was motivated to do his best at all times. He had a good sense of humor. He was kind, thoughtful and generous. He offered me the use of his car, a Bentley, on days when I was not working. I remember driving to Genoa, having lunch in a restaurant and then driving back to San Remo. The steering was on the right side of the auto which made it difficult for an American girl. I marvel that George had so much confidence in me."

Biography: Joseph M. Newman was born in Logan, Utah, on August 7, 1909. He commenced his career in the film industry at MGM as an office boy, later becoming a script clerk, assistant director and director of shorts. During World War II he joined the Signal Corps, rose to the rank of major and directed several shorts. After being discharged he resumed his film career and began to direct mainly action-orientated feature films. He later became a television director of some merit. He died in Simi Valley, California, on January 23, 2006, aged 96. He also directed *The George Raft Story* (1961). Of him, Coleen Gray recalls, "Joe Newman was a sensible director, 100 percent American 'meat and potatoes.' He had patience with the father of Enzo Staiola and a good sense of humor."

Biography: Coleen Gray was born Doris Bernice Jensen in Staplehurst, Nebraska, on October 23, 1922. She was raised on a farm near Hutchinson, Minnesota, by Danish parents. She obtained a Bachelor of Arts degree from Hamline University in 1943 and then followed her fiancé to Southern California. When they split up, she moved to Los Angeles where she worked numerous jobs to survive. She joined a little theater and drama school where she appeared in plays; as a result, an agent offered to represent her. Shortly afterwards she signed a contract with 20th Century–Fox. She made her screen debut in a bit role in *State Fair* (1945). Two of her most successful films were *Kiss of Death* (1947) and *Red River* (1948), appearing in the latter only briefly. The studio released her from contract in 1950 and she freelanced successfully thereafter. She made her Broadway debut in *Leaf and Bough* (1949) and had running parts in the television soap operas *Days of Our Lives* and *Bright Promise*. In 1945 she married Rod Amateau, a writer-director with whom she had a daughter Susan before divorcing in 1949. She then married Lockheed executive Bill Bidlack in 1953 and had a son, Bruce Robin Bidlack, before being widowed in 1978. Since 1979 she has been married to Fritz Zeiser. Among other activities since 1990 she has been a part of Cantori Domino, a fifty-member choral group that has toured worldwide.

Biography: Charles Goldner was born in Vienna, Austria, on December 7, 1900. He was the son of Marc Goldner and Rose Pollack. He studied for the stage at the Academy of Dramatic Art in Vienna and made his first stage appearance at that city's Lustspiel Theater in 1919. He had a flourishing career as an actor and producer in Germany and Austria until 1938. The following year he fled to England where he enjoyed success both as a stage and film actor. Notable West End stage successes were *The Doctor's Dilemma* (1942) and *Watch on the Rhine* (1943). His first British film was *Room for Two* (1940) and he went on to appear in nearly thirty more before he died in London on April 15, 1955, aged 54. His estate amounted to £6,846. He was married to Maureen Leslie. He was allegedly fluent in nine languages.

Biography: Walter Rilla was born Walter Wilhelm Karl Ernst Rilla in Neunkirchen, Saar, Germany, on August 22, 1894. He was the son of railway engineer Friedrich Wilhelm Rilla and his wife, Caroline Grunder. He was educated at the University of Koenigsberg in Breslau and Berlin. He initially worked as a journalist for *The Latest Breslau News* and founded the literary journal *Erde*. He made his stage debut at Berlin's Die Tribune Theater in 1921 and enjoyed considerable success in Berlin as an actor. His first film in Britain was *The Scarlet Pimpernel* (1934). After this he returned to Berlin, but fell under Nazi suspicion. His first wife was Jewish and he refused to leave her behind. They managed to escape to England in 1936 and in 1940 he became a British citizen. In 1939 he joined the BBC European Service and was later appointed a producer, working there until 1945. He contributed memorable performances in both British and international films for the next thirty years, frequently playing distinguished politicians, scientists and, ironically, Nazis. He was also a successful West End actor and wrote novels. He returned to Germany in 1957 and continued to act and direct until the late seventies. His first wife was actress Therese Roland Klausner, who died in

1948. With her he had a son, director Wolf Rilla (1920–2005). His next wife was writer Alix Degrelle-Hirth du Frenes, whom he married in 1959. He died at Rosenheim, Germany, on November 21, 1980, aged 86.

Loan Shark (1952)

Cast: George Raft (Joe Gargen), Dorothy Hart (Ann Nelson), Paul Stewart (Lou Donelli), John Hoyt (Vince Phillips), Helen Westcott (Martha Gargen Haines), Henry Slate (Paul Nelson), Russell Johnson (Charlie Thompson), Margie Dean (Ivy), Benny Baker (Tubby), Lawrence Dobkin (Walter Kerr), Mike Ragan (Maxie), Robert Bice (Steve Casmer), Claire Carleton (Nagging Wife), Virginia Carroll (Netta Casmer), Jack Daley (Borrower), George Eldredge (Mr. Howell), Ross Elliott (Norm), Robert Karnes (Police Lieutenant), Charles Meredith (F.L. Rennick), Spring Mitchell (Nancy), William H. O'Brien (Waiter), Frank O'Connor (Bartender), William "Bill" Phillips (Baski), William Phipps (Ed Haines), Keith Richards (Buckley), Brick Sullivan (Card Player), William Tannen (Rourke), Harlan Warde (Detective Lt. White), Robert B. Williams (Scully), Barbara Woodell (Mrs. Hilton).

Credits: Director: Seymour Friedman; Producer: Bernard Luber; Original Story: Martin Rackin; Screenplay: Martin Rackin and Eugene Ling; Photography: Joseph F. Biroc; Editor: Al Joseph; Music Composer and Director: Heinz Roemheld; Song Supervisor: David Chudnow; Art Direction: Feild M. Gray; Sound Recorder: Frank Webster. Song "Peru" by Victor Young and Edward Heyman. Released by Lippert on May 23, 1952. Black and white. 79 minutes.

Synopsis: A vicious loan shark organization is terrorizing workers at the Delta Tire Factory. An ex-convict on parole, Joe Gargen, returns from prison to stay with his sister Martha in her apartment. Martha's husband Ed Haines works in the factory. Martha introduces Joe to Ann Nelson, who lives in the same building and is secretary to F.L. Rennick, the general manager of the factory. An interview is arranged between Rennick and Gargen in which Rennick asks him to go undercover to expose the heads of the loan shark racket, but Gargen indignantly refuses. He is given an ordinary job instead. When Ed Haines is viciously murdered, Gargen changes his mind. Gargen borrows $50 from the loan shark racket. When he falls behind with his payments, he is attacked, but Gargen overpowers the thug instead.

Impressed with Gargen, Donelli and Phillips, two of the bosses of the loan shark organization, hire him as a collections agent. Gargen tells Rennick, accepts the job and resigns from the plant. Gargen is taken to the gang's headquarters in a rough part of town where he is introduced to bookkeeper Walter Kerr. Joe's involvement with the loan sharks alienates both Ann and Martha. Gargen suggests to Phillips that they set up a laundry service to ensnare housewives into the loan shark racket by lending them money at extortionate interest rates. Since Phillips does not promptly agree, Gargen suspects he is not the head man. The idea is later accepted and the loan sharks buy a laundry business and install Gargen as its head. Gargen is given 10 percent of the business, which flourishes.

Phillips and Donelli tell Gargen that Ann's brother Paul is causing trouble and want Gargen to teach him a lesson. Gargen gives him a beating, witnessed by Ann and Martha. Martha later tells him that she and Ann are going to the police and that he will be returned to prison as a parole violator. Gargen tells Rennick that he will try to pressure Phillips into taking him to see the head man, but Donelli overhears him. At gunpoint Gargen is taken to the deserted boiler room of the laundry where he manages to gain the upper hand against Donelli and throws his body in a boiler.

Gargen tells Phillips that, as a parole violator, he needs to leave town in a hurry. He de-

Raft and Dorothy Hart in *Loan Shark*.

mands $50,000 for his 10 percent of the laundry business. Since Phillips professes not to have sufficient cash, he takes Gargen to a deserted theater where the boss lives in an upstairs apartment. The mysterious leader of the organization turns out to be Walter Kerr. Instead of giving him the money, Kerr tries to shoot Gargen. In the ensuing gunfight, Gargen shoots both Phillips and Kerr. Gargen manages to smash the loan shark racket much to the satisfaction of the police and the tire plant management and he is reunited with Ann.

Comments: This was the first and best of three low-budget thrillers Raft made for producer Bernard Luber (1906–1981). This was the first of the two films in which Raft was directed by Seymour Friedman. The budget for this film was $250,000. Raft's salary was $25,000 plus 25 percent of the profits. While it is very hard to believe that the film did not return a profit, creative accounting meant that

Raft did not receive any extra money beyond his salary. The original leading lady was intended to be Gail Russell, but she had to withdraw because of personal problems. Dorothy Hart was a very acceptable substitute.

This was a very well-paced thriller in which Raft's motivation for behaving and reacting the way he does was much better defined than in a few of his other films. It is still topical today since loan sharks exist in most countries. There was an excellent pre-credits sequence which showed a victim of the racket, trying to leave town, being chased by thugs through dark streets until they caught and beat him. Another highlight was the vicious fight between Gargen and Donelli in the boiler room of the laundry against a shadowy background. There was also an exciting climax involving a shootout in a theater where the leading villain resided. The villains were very well characterized and played by capable actors. Raft performed well against them and, if the viewer were not aware of where his loyalties lay, he might be convinced that Raft had gone to the bad.

Biography: Seymour Friedman was born in Detroit, Michigan, on August 17, 1917. He was educated at Cambridge University, England, and St. Mary's Hospital Medical School in London. He entered films in 1937 as an assistant editor and then became an assistant director. After World War II service, he returned to films as a director of low-budget films, mainly at Columbia. His later career was spent as a television production executive. He died in Los Angeles in April 2003, aged 85, of a heart attack.

Biography: Dorothy Hart was born in Cleveland, Ohio, on April 3, 1922. She was educated at Dennison University and started acting while at college, but began her career as a model. In 1944 she won the National Cinderella Cover Girl contest sponsored by Columbia Pictures to publicize their film *Cover Girl* (1944). She continued to model until she made her screen debut in *Down to Earth* (1947). At different times she was under contract to Universal and Warner Bros. *Loan Shark* was her final film; she had grown disenchanted with the industry. Despite winning the Photoplay Gold Key Award that year, she made no further films but continued to appear on television in episodes of anthology series and panel game shows. By the mid-fifties she had become involved in charity work, often acting as guest speaker for the United Nations. She also helped to raise the profile of the Motion Picture Fund and a number of animal charities. After a second divorce in 1966 she moved to North Carolina to be near her parents. She died in Arden, North Carolina, on July 11, 2004, aged 82, of complications of Alzheimer's Disease. She was survived by a son.

Biography: Paul Stewart was born Paul Steinberg in New York on March 13, 1908, the son of Maurice D. Sternberg and Nathalie

Nathanson. He was educated at Columbia University and Brooklyn Law School. He made his Broadway debut in *Two Seconds*. He moved into radio and in total made nearly 5,000 broadcasts. Between 1935 and 1939 he was part of Orson Welles' Mercury Theater Group working on the *March of Time* radio series. He also acted as co-producer of *Mercury Theater of the Air* including the notorious *War of the Worlds* broadcast in 1938 which panicked America. Welles took him to Hollywood where he made his screen debut in *Citizen Kane* (1941) in the role of Raymond, Kane's valet. After the war he worked in a creative capacity for both David O. Selznick and Dore Schary. In the late forties he resumed his acting career and notched up several fine characterizations mainly, as gangsters, but also as agents and business managers. He died in Los Angeles on February 17, 1986, aged 77, following a heart attack. In 1939 he wed vocalist Peg LaCentra who survived him.

Biography: John Hoyt was born John McArthur Hoysradt in Bronxville, New York, on October 5, 1904, son of a Wall Street broker. He attended Yale University and was briefly a history teacher. When he realized that he wanted a different career, he joined the Summer Theater at South Hampton, Long Island. He then appeared in Stuart Walker's repertory company in Cincinnati. He was a frequent Broadway performer between 1930 and 1940. In 1935 he turned to musical shows and performed in *The Ziegfeld Follies*. Between 1936 and 1946 he put together a cabaret act billed as "The Master of Satire," doing impressions of celebrities. In 1945 he did a U.S.O. tour of the South Pacific with Gertrude Lawrence, which led to a starring role in *Blithe Spirit*. One night a member of the audience was the chairman of the board of Paramount Studios, who encouraged him to come to Hollywood. Hoyt made his screen debut in *O.S.S.* (1946) and went on to appear in numerous films, frequently cast as a suave villain. On television he played Stanley Kanisky in the situation comedy *Gimme a Break* (1982–1987). He was also famous for playing Mr. Creety in the Midas Muffler commercials. He died in Santa Cruz, California, on September 15, 1991, of lung cancer at age 85. He was twice married and had a son.

Escape Route (aka *I'll Get You; Traitor's Gate; Traitor's Highway*) (1952)

Cast: George Raft (Steve Rossi), Sally Gray (Joan Miller), Clifford Evans (Michael Grand), Reginald Tate (Colonel Wilkes), Patricia Laffan (Irma Brooks), Frederick Piper (Detective Insp. Reid), Roddy Hughes (Porter), June Ashley (Ann), John Warwick (Security Chief Brice), Grace Arnold (Neighbor), Howard Douglas (Taxi Driver), Norman Pierce (Detective Inspector Hobbs), Arthur Lovegrove (Detective Phillips), Cyril Chamberlain (Bailey), Anthony Pendrell (Rees), Harry Towb (Immigration Officer).

Credits: Directors: Seymour Friedman and Peter Graham Scott; Executive Producer: Bernard Luber; Producer: Ronald Kinnoch; Screenplay: John V. Baines; Additional Dialogue: Nicholas Phipps; Photography: Eric Cross; Editor: Tom Simpson; Additional Photography: Freddy Ford; Music Score: Hans May; Art Direction: George Paterson; Sound Recorders: Leslie Hodgson and Charles Tasto; Makeup: Jill Carpenter. Second Unit Assistant Directors: Pat Kelly, Eric Pavitt, Billy Russell. Scenes from the Tate Gallery through the cooperation of the Trustees and Director Thereof. Released by Lippert on January 16, 1953. Black and white. 78 minutes.

Tagline: "It's loaded with Searing, Screaming, Suspense!"

Synopsis: Several atomic scientists in various countries have suddenly and swiftly disappeared, the latest being Dr. Halas from America. He is the boss of Steve Rossi, production manager of Alliance Aircraft Corporation. Rossi is told that it is likely the scientists are being taken behind the Iron Curtain and the name of the man thought to be behind the kidnappings is Michael Grand. Grand had once offered Rossi a job and is understood to be in London.

Rossi flies to England where he dodges immigration at the airport and hitches a ride to London. A contact gives him British currency, a new wardrobe and Michael Grand's last known address. Upon going to this address, he encounters Joan Miller who claims to be Grand's secretary. Unexpectedly she pulls a gun and insists that Rossi accompany her to see her real boss who turns out to be a military intelligence chief named Colonel Wilkes. Wilkes tells him about the way scientists are being shipped out of the country and that they believe Grand is behind it all, but he has disappeared. They need Rossi's help because he is the only one who knows what Grand looks like.

Rossi and Miller discover that Grand's apartment is being rented on his behalf by Irena Brooks, who runs a secretarial school. She gives Rossi the address of Grand's London office which turns out to be a derelict apartment block, badly damaged during the blitz. Upon entering the building he encounters Grand, who makes two attempts to kill him and then escapes. Rossi and Miller return to the secretarial school where Irena Brooks suffers a panic attack when she discovers Rossi is still alive. She later goes to a hairdresser's shop followed by Rossi and Miller. While investigating this, they are arrested by the police and taken in for questioning. Before long Colonel Wilkes arrives and confirms that Joan Miller is an M.I.5 agent and Rossi is an undercover FBI agent. Wilkes whisks them off to the morgue where he asks Rossi to identify two bodies found in a burned car. Rossi is able to identify Miss Brooks, but doubts that the other body is that of Grand.

They return to the hairdresser's shop where they discover a hidden cellar in which Grand is burning documents. Grand tries to shoot

Raft in *Escape Route.*

Rossi, but escapes again. Surviving fragments of burned documents indicate that Grand is planning on leaving the country almost immediately. Police inform Rossi that a Communist embassy staff member has been making nocturnal visits to the Crown and Anchor, a sleazy hotel located near the docks and mainly frequented by seamen. Changing into a seaman's uniform, Rossi goes to the docks and spots Grand. Rossi pursues Grand, leaving chalk marks on the streets to enable Miller and the police to follow him. On top of a warehouse near London Bridge, Grand ambushes him. A terrific fistfight ensues in the descending goods elevator until Rossi overpowers Grand. On the ground again, Rossi is reunited with Miller, Wilkes and Detective Inspector Reid. When Reid asks about the whereabouts of Dr. Halas, Rossi points to a ship anchored nearby in the Thames and tells him that it is where Grand was headed and that Halas is un-

doubtedly on board. Once this is confirmed, Rossi and Miller stroll away together to start a romance.

Comments: This was the second and weakest of the three films which Raft made for producer Bernard Luber. This was the second time that Raft was directed by Seymour Friedman, although here he shared directorial credit with Peter Graham Scott. Even the least discriminating of filmgoers would realize that there were a number of plot loopholes which were not resolved. These included what happened to the scientists once the Communists had them and whether any of them, apart from Halas, were ever rescued. A montage at the beginning of the film showed these scientists being kidnapped with relative ease. If the scientists were really important to political security, the protection level afforded to them would probably have been higher. What the filmmakers did was to try to substitute a chain of exciting incidents in place of a coherent plot, although important and wealthy people have disappeared in bizarre circumstances in real life.

This film has been criticized for being more of a travelogue than a fictional movie, but the location photography was excellent, incorporating famous London landmarks such as the Tate Gallery and London Bridge; World War II bombed-out buildings; and the River Thames. At the time Sally Gray said, "Locations are being shot all around London. George Raft is delighted with his role. I went out on location with him one day and exciting shots were made all around the blitzed areas of St. Paul's." Some film buffs categorize this as a film noir, but it was a spy mystery thriller. Raft and Gray made an attractive team although their romance proceeded at such a rapid pace that it was unconvincing. This was the only Raft film shot entirely on location in London.

Biography: Peter Graham Scott was born East Sheen, Surrey, England, on October 27, 1923. He entered films in 1940 as an assistant director. He worked with the Ministry of Information's film division during the early years of World War II, making propaganda documentaries with London's Colonial Film Unit. He served in H.M. Armed Forces between 1942 and 1944. On being invalided out he joined Greenpark as chief editor. After the war he worked for Rank for their series of short films under the *This Modern Age* umbrella. Scott was a pioneer in producing television dramas. He worked for the BBC as a trainee in the late 1940s and joined ITV in 1955. He went on to direct numerous television episodes and created two of the BBC's most popular series, *The Troubleshooters* and *The Onedin Line.* He married actress Eve Martell in 1950 and had four children. He died on August 5, 2007, aged 83.

Biography: Sally Gray was born Constance Vera Stevens in London, England, on February 14, 1915, one of five children of a widowed bal-lerina named Green. Trained for the stage at the Fay Compton School of Dramatic Art, she "trod the boards" from childhood and made her screen debut in *School for Scandal* (1930) billed under her real name. She appeared in cabaret and in 1936 made her West End debut in *Over She Goes.* In 1935 she shot her second film, *Cheer Up*, and went on to appear in more films over the next several years, of which the most popular was *Dangerous Moonlight* (1941). In 1942 after the death of her mentor and frequent co-star, Stanley Lupino, she suffered a nervous breakdown and did not film again until 1946. Between 1946 and 1949 she starred in a further six films including the classic *Green for Danger* (1946). After an absence she shot *Escape Route*, her final film. She became the third wife of Lord Oranmore and Browne in December 1951 and subsequently retired from the screen. They settled in Castle McGarret in County Mayo, Ireland, where she developed a passion for gardening. When the estate fell into financial difficulties, they ended up raising pigs in the drawing room. Eventually they sold the estate and moved into an apartment in Belgravia London in the early 1960s. Her husband died at the age of 100 in 2002. She died in London on September 24, 2006, aged 91.

Biography: Clifford Evans was born in Cardiff, South Wales, on February 17, 1912, the son of David Hugh Evans and his wife, Dinah Daniel. He was educated at Llanelly Grammar School. For the first eight years of his life, he spoke no English. At the Royal Academy of Dramatic Art where he studied for the stage, he was a prize winner. He made his screen debut in *The River House Mystery* (1935). He joined H.M. Forces as a private in the army in 1943 and was demobilized in 1946. As with many actors who were in a similar position, he had to start again from scratch. During the fifties his film roles were mainly second features in which he played either police inspectors or wealthy but treacherous men. During the sixties his most high-profile acting job was as

Caswell Bligh in the successful British television series *The Power Game*. He died in Shrewsbury, Shropshire, England, on June 9, 1985, aged 73. He was married to actress Hermione Hannen.

The Man from Cairo (aka *Cairo Incident*; *Adventure in Algeria*; *Secrets of the Casbah*; *Dramma nella Kasbah*) (1953)

Cast: George Raft (Mike Canelli), Gianna Maria Canale (Lorraine Beloyan), Massimo Serato (Basil Constantine), Guido Selano (Emile Touchard), Irene Papas (Yvonne Lebeau), Alfredo Varelli (General Dumont alias Professor Crespi), Leonardo Scavino/Leon Lenoir (Police Capt. Akhim Bey), Mino Doro (Jules Moreau alias Major C. Blanc), Angelo Dessy (Pock Mark Thug), Richard McNamara (Agent Charles Stark), Franco Silva (Armeno), Rossana Galli (Princess Zoraide).

Credits: Director: Ray Enright; Producer: Bernard Luber; Assistant Directors: Edoardo Anton and Ugo Velona; Original Story: Ladislas Fodor; Screenplay: Eugene Ling, Philip Stevenson and Janet Stevenson; Photographer: Mario Albertelli; Editor: Mario Serandrei; Music Score: Renzo Rossellini; Musical Direction: Franco Ferrara; Art Direction: Giulio Bongini; Costumes: Marilu Carteny. Released by Lippert on November 27, 1953. Black and white. 81 minutes.

Synopsis: In 1940 all the gold reserves of the Free French were transported to Algeria and stored in different locations. One of the convoys was ambushed with all the soldiers being massacred except Emile Touchard. The head of operations, General Dumont, was arrested, but before he could be tried for treason, he escaped. The gold, amounting to $100 million, is hidden somewhere in the Sahara desert. Since then the thieves have murdered five intelligence agents and have outwitted both the French Secret Service and the police. Police Captain Bey sends for an American agent,

Charles Stark, to discover who the thieves are. Stark's cover is that he is a geologist who is to spend a couple of weeks in Saudi Arabia before flying on to Algiers.

At the Cairo airport during a short stopover, he runs into an old acquaintance, Mike Canelli, an entrepreneur en route to Algiers. Arriving in Algiers, Canelli is met by the police who take him to see Captain Bey. He is also spotted by the racketeers who mistake him for the American agent. While being pursued by racketeers, Touchard ducks into a shop which specializes in voice recordings. He cuts a record in which he tells of his involvement in the gold theft. He sends it to his girlfriend Yvonne, a nightclub dancer. He arranges to meet Canelli at his hotel. En route he is stabbed to death. Canelli goes to the hotel where he encounters Yvonne in the tub in Touchard's room. He is drugged and passes out. When he comes to, he finds Yvonne has been strangled and the record stolen.

In quick succession he meets Professor Crespi, a stamp collector and gold seeker who is actually General Dumont in disguise; Lorraine Beloyan, a friend of Yvonne's and a chanteuse at the Algeria Club owned by Basil Constantine, who is later murdered; and Major Blanc, who purports to be working for French Intelligence. Canelli is kidnapped and tortured by the racketeers, but is released alive. He remembers the face of one of his captors and traces him to the French Africa Transport Company, a scrap metal firm owned by the mysterious Jules Moreau. Later Canelli receives a telephone call from Blanc who has been searching Lorraine's house for the record. The conversation is cut short by a gunshot. Canelli and Lorraine rush to the house, but find no trace of Blanc.

Canelli, who has fallen in love with Lorraine, finds the record, which reveals that General Dumont was innocent and that the theft was masterminded and executed by Jules Moreau. The house is attacked and Lorraine is kidnapped. Canelli pursues the kidnappers to the trucking company base where Lorraine has been taken on board a freight train. Canelli rescues her, but they find themselves being held at gunpoint by Moreau, alias Colonel Blanc, who shows them the train fittings which conceal gold coins. This is the method used to transport the gold from the desert. When Bey and his men stop the train, Canelli attacks Moreau and overpowers him. The gang members are arrested. Lorraine retrieves a few gold coins which she keeps as souvenirs, while she and Canelli decide to go to America together. At the airport Canelli runs into a bemused Stark who has just arrived to solve the case. Canelli shoves a newspaper into his hands with the headline "General Dumont and American tourist solve lost gold mystery."

Comments: With interiors shot in Italy and exteriors in North Africa, this was the third and last Raft film produced by Bernard Luber. It was the only time Raft was directed by Ray Enright. The last released film in which Raft had top billing, it received poor reviews. But while it was one of Raft's lesser vehicles, it was far from being unwatchable. It was professionally assembled with a competent American director, Enright, at the helm. There were quite a number of U.S.–foreign co-productions shot on foreign soil during the sixties and seventies which were inferior to *The Man from Cairo*. The complicated plot was a peg on which to hang a few exciting action sequences, particularly the climax on board the train. This film recycled some elements from previous Raft films, one example being the missing Free French gold (a key plot point of *Johnny Angel*). Leading lady Gianna Maria Canale had the distinction of the largest age gap between Raft and one of his leading ladies. Some sources such as the IMDb give *Crime Squad* as an alternative title to this film, but this is incorrect.

Biography: Ray Enright was born in Anderson, Indiana, on March 25, 1896. For a short time he worked at the *L.A. Times*. He served with the American Expeditionary Force in France. He entered films in 1914 as a cutter and editor and for seven years was with Mack Sennett. He made his debut as a director in 1927. He was one of the founders of the Masquers Club. *The Man from Cairo* was his final film. He died in Hollywood on April 3, 1965, aged 69, after a heart attack.

Biography: Gianna Maria Canale was born in Reggio di Calabria, Italy, on September 12, 1927. She was of Greek descent and a former typist. In 1947 she entered the Miss Italy contest and came in second. In 1948 she met director Riccardo Freda and the two began a torrid love affair culminating in marriage in 1948. They shot two films in Brazil before returning to Italy because she preferred the climate. She resided in Rome throughout most of her career, which continued until 1964. She retired when she was still somewhere close to the peak of her fame, allegedly because of the breakdown of

Gianna Maria Canale and Raft in *The Man from Cairo*.

her marriage. After this she lived very privately, declining all requests for interviews. She died in Florence, Italy, on February 13, 2009, aged 81.

Rogue Cop (1954)

Cast: Robert Taylor (Detective Sgt. Chris Kelvaney), Janet Leigh (Karen Stephanson), George Raft (Dan Beaumonte), Steve Forrest (Eddie Kelvaney), Anne Francis (Nancy Corlane), Robert Ellenstein (Detective Sidney Y. Myers), Robert F. Simon (Ackerman), Anthony Ross (Father Ahearn), Alan Hale, Jr. (Johnny Stark), Peter Brocco (George "Wrinkles" Fallon), Vince Edwards (Joey Langley), Olive Carey (Selma), Roy Barcroft (Detective Lt. Vince D. Bardeman), Dale Van Sickel (Manny), Ray Teal (Patrolman Mullins), Jimmy Ames (News Dealer), Nicky Blair (Marsh), Nesdon Booth (Detective Garrett), Dallas Boyd (Patrolman Higgins), Paul Brinegar (Arcade Clerk), Paul Bryar (Marx, Patrolman at Morgue), Benny Burt (Apartment Proprietor), Robert Burton (Inspector Adrian Cassidy), Budd Buster (Parker), Lillian Buyett (Gertrude), Phil Chambers (Detective Dirksen), Gene Coogan (Truck Driver), Richard Deacon (Stacey), Herb Ellis (Bartender), Michael Fox (Rudy), Paul Hoffman (Clerk), Russell Johnson (Patrolman Carland), Mitchell Kowall (Guard), Connie Marshall (Frances), Harold Miller (Turf Club Patron), Gilda Oliva (Italian Mother), Milton Parsons (Tucker), Guy Prescott (Detective Ferrari), Dick Ryan (Elevator Man), George Selk (Parker), Dick Simmons (Detective Ralston), George Taylor (Dr. Leonard, Coroner), Jack Victor (Morgue Orderly), Joseph Waring (Rivers), Carleton Young (District Attorney Powell).

Credits: Director: Roy Rowland; Producer: Nicholas Nayfack; Assistant Director: Ridgeway Callow; Based on the 1952 Novel *Rogue Cop* by William P. McGivern; Screenplay: Sydney Boehm; Photography: John F. Seitz; Editor: James E. Newcom; Music: Jeff Alexander; Art Direction: Cedric Gibbons and Hans Peters; Costumes: Helen Rose; Hair Stylist: Sydney Guilaroff; Makeup: William Tuttle; Special Effects: A. Arnold Gillespie. Released by MGM on September 17, 1954. Black and white. 92 minutes.

Synopsis: A drug pusher is stabbed to death in a penny arcade by George "Wrinkles" Fallon. Fallon is seen and later identified by police patrolman Eddie Kilvaney. His brother, Detective Sgt. Chris Kelvaney, is given Fallon's whereabouts by his informant, news vendor Selma. They arrest Fallon in a pool room. The story appears in the papers together with Eddie's name. Chris, who is in the pay of the syndicate, is summoned to the racetrack where he meets crime czar Dan Beaumonte and his alcoholic mistress, Nancy Corlane. Beaumonte tells Chris that Fallon would embarrass him and fellow mobster Ackerman; that Eddie had better not identify him at the trial; and to offer Eddie a bribe of $10,000.

Chris goes to the Fanfare Club where chanteuse Karen Stephanson is Eddie's girlfriend. Chris informs Eddie of Beaumonte's proposition, but Eddie indignantly refuses. They are joined by Karen, whom Chris recognizes as the former mistress of a mobster. He uses her background as damaged goods to try to persuade Eddie to accept the bribe, but to no avail. Nevertheless, Chris tells Beaumonte and Ackerman that his brother will cooperate and they tell him to bring Eddie to see them the following night. Neither Beaumonte nor Ackerman believe him and decide to hire an outside hitman to kill Eddie. At the appointed time Chris goes to Beaumonte's apartment where he finds a drunken Nancy. Beaumonte, Ackerman and their bodyguard, Johnny Stark, arrive. Chris tries to stall them, but the gangsters tell him that he is lying. A fight breaks out in which Chris overpowers both Beaumonte and Stark. Nancy makes the mistake of mocking Beaumonte after Chris has gone. Beaumonte beats her up and forces Stark to take her to the sadistic Fonzo's joint.

Left to right: Alan Hale, Jr., Robert Taylor, Robert F. Simon, Raft and Anne Francis in *Rogue Cop*.

Chris goes to the Fanfare Club where he finds Karen and tells her that Eddie is in danger. Beaumonte reaches Chris at the club pretending to make a truce for forty-eight hours, but in actuality his purpose is to lower Chris's guard so that the hitman can kill Eddie. Chris returns to sleep at his apartment, but is woken in the dead of night by a badly battered Nancy who tells him that Beaumonte has thrown her out and that Eddie has been shot dead in the street outside of Karen's apartment after dropping her off. After identifying the body of his brother, Chris goes to the police station where he is summoned to see Detective Lt. Bardeman, who gives him a grand jury subpoena and informs him that he has been suspended from duty. Bardeman agrees to delay the suspension if Chris will work on the inside while the other police investigate from the outside.

Chris is informed that the syndicate want Nancy dead so he takes her to stay with Karen. Nancy tells him that Mullins, a street photographer turned policeman, had taken an incriminating photograph years earlier of Beaumonte and Ackerman committing a heinous crime and has been blackmailing them ever since. Karen is lured away, leaving Nancy alone. When Chris returns to Karen's apartment, he finds the body of Nancy, drowned in the bath. His informant, Selma, tells him that Joey Langley is the killer and gives him Langley's address. Chris tells her to send word to Beaumonte that he is going to arrest Langley. In the street he spots Detective Myers, who has been detailed to follow him. Together they go to Langley's apartment where Chris bluffs his way in, overpowering and arresting Langley. Outside Beaumonte and Ackerman are waiting for them and open fire. In the ensuing gun battle, Chris shoots and kills Ackerman; Beaumonte shoots Chris in the back; and Beaumonte is killed by the wounded Myers.

Comments: *Rogue Cop* was one of the fastest films from script to screen in the history of MGM since only four months elapsed between buying the story and the final preview. The whole film was shot at MGM and it was a box office winner. This was the only time that Raft was directed by Roy Rowland. Raft obtained this part as a result of an emotional plea for work at a Friar's Club roast in his honor. Dore Schary, the head of MGM, was there and offered Raft the part. Ironically, Raft was going to reject this role and only agreed to play the part after the star of the film, Robert Taylor, went to him and pleaded with Raft to accept it. "It was the script that made me change my mind. I hope I can do justice to it," was Raft's comment at the time.

Raft gave one of the best performances of his career as crime kingpin Dan Beaumonte. He was in exactly the right cinematic environment and his performance was genuinely frightening whether as a manipulator of people for criminal gain or, on a more personal level, in his sadistic treatment of his mistress, Nancy. He was remorseless and he never forgave or forgot if he was crossed. He did not recognize any authority except his own and that of the criminal empire in which he was involved. As such he was beyond redemption and the fight against him was a fight to the death.

One of a cycle of "dirty cop" films shot during the early fifties, it faithfully derived from a solidly written thriller by William P. McGivern. The character actors, notably Robert Ellenstein as Myers, were as important to the development of the story as the leads. The film did not end as one might have supposed with a clichéd clinch between hero and heroine, but with Robert Taylor and Ellenstein on their way to the hospital. It was uncertain whether Taylor ultimately lived or died. The final shootout between the cops and gangsters was one of the most realistic and exciting of any film. The film focused on the high end of or-

ganized crime in which sharp-suited mobsters live in spacious apartments and discuss the murder of incorruptible cops over dry martinis. The comparison between the affluence of the criminals and the austerity of the more honest characters was effectively depicted.

Cinematographer John F. Seitz received an Oscar nomination for Best Black and White Cinematography for his work on this film. In its drive for realism, the film has virtually no background music. In the course of their long careers, Raft and Humphrey Bogart only made one film apiece released by MGM. Raft's *Rogue Cop* looked like a masterpiece of cinematic art in comparison to Bogart's *Battle Circus* (1953). This was one time Raft definitely came out ahead.

Biography: Roy Rowland was born in New York City on December 30, 1902. After he studied law at the University of Southern California, he began his career as a script clerk, then became an assistant director and director of shorts including entries in *Crime Does Not Pay* series. He signed a contract with MGM where he directed feature films from 1942 onwards. He became one of their leading in-house directors and did most of his best work for them. His wife's name was Ruth and one of their children, Steve, became an actor. Rowland died in Orange, California, on June 29, 1995, aged 92.

Biography: Robert Taylor was born Spangler Arlington Brugh in Filley, Nebraska, on August 5, 1911. The son of a country doctor, he enrolled at Donne College, Nebraska, where he studied music and then followed his cello teacher to Pomona College in California from which he graduated. His performance in a college production led to a screen test and a long-term contract with MGM, to whom he remained under contract for over 20 years, initially as a handsome hero, but later in more complex roles in films of many different genres. During World War II he served as a flight instructor with the Navy's Air Transport. After his stature as a film star declined, he starred in two successful television series, *The Detectives* and *Death Valley Days*. He married actress Barbara Stanwyck in 1939, but they divorced in 1952. In 1954 he married Ursula Thiess, adopted her two children and had a son and a daughter. He died in Santa Monica, California, on June 8, 1969, aged 57, of lung cancer.

Biography: Anne Francis was born in Ossining, New York, on September 16, 1930, the daughter of Philip Francis and Edith Abbertson. She moved to Manhattan at the age of seven and became a child model and a frequent radio performer. She made her Broadway debut in *Lady in the Dark* (1942). In the late forties she was under contract to MGM where she made her screen debut in *Summer Holiday* (1948). Between 1950 and 1954 she was under contract to 20th Century–Fox and between 1954 and 1957 she was under contract to MGM. Her best remembered film at MGM was *Forbidden Planet* (1956) as Altaira. After that she successfully freelanced. In 1965 and '66 she played a female private investigator in the television series *Honey West*, receiving an Emmy Award nomination. Over the succeeding decades she became one of the most frequent and highest paid guest stars on American television. Her last appearance was an episode of *Without a Trace* in 2004. She was twice married and divorced and had a daughter. She also adopted a girl, Margaret West Francis, in 1971. A memoir, *Voices from Home: An Inner Journey*, was published in 1982. She died at a retirement home in Santa Barbara on January 2, 2011, aged 80, of pancreatic cancer after being diagnosed with lung cancer in 2007. Of her experience in *Rogue Cop*, Anne Francis recalled, "I made this film because I was under contract to MGM. George Raft was charming and fun to work with."

Black Widow (1954)

Cast: Ginger Rogers (Lottie Marin/Carlotta Mullen), Van Heflin (Peter Denver), Gene Tierney (Iris Denver), George Raft (Detective Lt. C.A. Bruce), Peggy Ann Garner (Nancy "Nanny" Ordway), Reginald Gardiner (Brian Mullen), Virginia Leith (Claire Amberly), Otto Kruger (Gordon Ling), Cathleen Nesbitt (Miss Lucia Colletti), Skip Homeier (John Amberly), Hilda Simms (Anne), Harry Carter (Police Sgt. Welch), Geraldine Wall (Miss Gwen Mills), Richard Cutting (Police Sgt. Owens), Mabel Albertson (Sylvia), Aaron Spelling (Mr. Oliver), Wilson Wood (Costume Designer), Tony De Mario (Tony), Virginia Maples (Model), Frances Driver (Maid), James Stone (Fritz, Stage Doorman), Michael Vallon (Coal Dealer), Ralph Brooks, Bert Stevens, Franklyn Farnum (Party Guests), Forbes Murray (Man in Hallway).

Credits: Director, Producer and Screenplay: Nunnally Johnson; Based on a Novel by Patrick Quentin; Assistant Director: A.F. Erickson; Photography: Charles G. Clarke (CinemaScope); Editor: Dorothy Spencer; Music Score: Leigh Harline; Musical Conductor: Lionel Newman; Orchestrator: Edward B. Powell; Art Direction: Lyle Wheeler and Maurice Ransford; Sound Recorders: Eugene Grossman and Roger Heman; Costumes: Travilla; Makeup: Ben Nye. Released by 20th Century–Fox on October 28, 1954. Color. 95 minutes.

Taglines: "An electrifying drama about a predatory female!," "All the Suspense Your System Can Take!," "One of them will kill her tonight and your guess is as good as ours!," "The first crime of passion story filmed in CinemaScope."

Synopsis: Peter Denver, a Broadway producer, puts his wife Iris on the plane for New Orleans where her mother is ill and then goes to a cocktail party at the apartment of Lottie Marin, star of his current Broadway hit, and her husband Brian Mullen. At the party he meets Nancy Ordway, a lonely, ambitious young writer from Savannah, Georgia, who has crashed the party. That night on the long distance phone, Peter tells Iris that he took

Nancy to dinner, just for companionship, but never again because "the kid ate too much."

There is then a flashback to the day Nancy arrived in New York. She contacts her uncle Gordon Ling, an actor, and through him meets Claire Amberly, a painter, and her brother John. Nancy begins her climb up the social ladder by moving into Claire's apartment when she learns Claire is a wealthy Bostonian. She also meets Brian Mullen who falls for her. Nancy continues to pursue Peter and eventually moves into his apartment. When Iris returns from New Orleans, there is evidence of Nancy's presence all over the apartment. Peter protests that he was only trying to befriend Nancy. When Iris discovers Nancy's body hanging in the bathroom, all evidence points to Peter. In trying to clear himself, Peter learns that Nancy has had many men and was strictly a hustler.

Detective Lt. Bruce's search for evidence takes him to Lottie's apartment and suspicion points away from Peter to Brian and Lottie. It develops that Lottie had gone to Denver's apartment to quiet Nancy about her relationship with Brian but, after a quarrel, she choked Nancy to death. Bruce delivers the final piece of evidence when he shows Lottie a crumpled piece of paper with doodles on it that he found in her apartment, written by the same ballpoint pen supposed to have been used by Nancy. Lottie makes a break for the window, but is restrained by Bruce. Later, in Denver's apartment, Bruce, Iris and Peter speculate on what the outcome of Lottie's trial will be.

Comments: This was the first and only time that Raft appeared with Ginger Rogers. They were two of the screen's finest dancers, but in this film neither of them did any dancing. It was the only time that Raft was directed by Nunnally Johnson. The one leading member of the cast with whom Raft had previously appeared was Peggy Ann Garner. They had co-starred in *Nob Hill* (1945) when she was a child. In *Black Widow* they did not share any scenes since she had been murdered before he

appeared. This was the fourth and final Raft film released through 20th Century–Fox. This film featured an all-star cast and was one of several attempts by Fox during the fifties to halt the decline of the cinema and combat the onslaught of television. The film was notable as Fox's first murder mystery in CinemaScope and it was Raft's second film in color. Despite the excellent cast and good production values, the film was not a big commercial success. The title and the brief introduction before the credits gave a very strong indication of who the murderer was so the viewer was robbed of the element of suspense. The major demerit of the film was that it was an interesting rather than exciting film.

Publicity at the time laid a great deal of emphasis on Raft continuing his onscreen reformation: After a succession of gangster roles, he had "gone straight" in recent years. After playing a cop in his television series *I'm the Law*, he was now playing one in a major film. ("Being on the right side of the law is a good feeling," he said.) When producer Nunnally Johnson offered Raft the detective part in *Black Widow*, he eagerly cut short his vacation in London and Rome to fly to Hollywood to begin work. This film is another bête-noire of film historian Leonard Maltin, who made derogatory remarks about the performances of Raft and Ginger Rogers. In actuality they were both very competent and professional. While Raft's part was definitely a subordinate one, his character appeared after half an hour, featured prominently and had the penultimate line.

Biography: Nunnally Johnson was born in Columbus, Georgia, on December 5, 1897. He began his career as a newspaper reporter for various papers. He became a writer of short stories, some of which were published as a book in 1930. He went to Hollywood in 1932 and the following year he commenced a career as a screenwriter of polished, literate scripts. In 1935 he became a producer and in 1943 he formed International Pictures, which was later taken over by Universal. Johnson then joined 20th Century–Fox where he became a triple threat director, producer and writer. He was married and divorced twice, then from 1939 onwards to actress Dorris Bowdon. He died in Hollywood on March 25, 1977, aged 79, of pneumonia, survived by Bowdon and five children.

Biography: Ginger Rogers was born Virginia Katherine McMath in Independence, Missouri, on July 16, 1911, the daughter of William Eddins McMath and Lela Haworth (aka Lela Owens and Lela Rogers). She was nicknamed "Ginger" by a cousin. In 1916 her mother went to Hollywood to become a screenwriter, leaving Ginger with her (Ginger's) grandparents. In 1919 her mother married John Rogers, who adopted Ginger. She was educated at Forth Worth, Texas. In 1925 she won a Charleston competition which led to her dropping out of school and entering dance competitions. Eventually she became a dancer at the Paramount Theatre in New York. She made her screen debut in *Young Man of Manhattan* (1930). She shot five films at Paramount's Long Island studio while appearing on stage. Then she went to Hollywood where she played small parts until she created a sensation when she partnered with Fred Astaire in *Flying Down to Rio* (1933). They appeared in ten films together in total. She became established as a dramatic actress in *Stage Door* (1937) and won a Best Actress Oscar for *Kitty Foyle* (1940). By 1943 she was the highest paid actress in Hollywood. Her final film was *Harlow* (1965) as Mama Jean. In the 1990s she suffered two strokes and was confined to a wheelchair. Nevertheless she received a couple of Lifetime Achievement Awards in person. She died at Rancho Mirage, California, on April 25, 1995, aged 83, of acute myocardial infarction and arteriosclerosis. She married and divorced five times, to Jack Culpepper (from 1928 to 1931), Lew Ayres (1934 to 1941), Jack Briggs (1943 to 1949), Jacques Bergerac (1953 to 1957) and William Marshall (1961 to 1972).

A Bullet for Joey (1955)

Cast: Edward G. Robinson (Insp. Raoul Leduc), George Raft (Joe Victor), Audrey Totter (Joyce Geary), George Dolenz (Dr. Carl Macklin), Peter Van Eyck (Eric Hartman), Toni Gerry (Yvonne Tremblay), William Bryant (Jack Allen), John Cliff (Morrie), Steven Geray (Raphael Garcia), Joseph Vitale (Nick Johonus), Sally Blane (Marie Tremblay), Peter Hansen (Fred), Kaaren Verne (Mrs. Viveca Hartman), Henri Letondal (Dubois), Stan Malotte (Paul), Ralph Smiley (Paola), Mal Alberts (Adams), John Alvin (Constable Dan Percy), Tina Carver (Counter Girl), Roy Engel (Detective, Truck Driver), John Frederick (Cason), Carmelita Gibbs (Cuban Girl), John Goddard (Driver, Police Car), Frank Hagney (Nightclub Bartender), William Henry (Michael, Artist), Fred Libby (Booking Officer), Rory Mallinson (Rent-a-car Clerk), Peter Mamakos (Ship's Captain), Paul Marion (Detective Posing as Gardener), John Merrick (Policeman in Car), Carlyle Mitchell (Benson), Bill Neff (Sergeant), Barry Regan (Crocker), Frank Richards (Ship's Officer), Carlos Rivero (Portuguese Waiter), Sandy Sanders (Telephone Man), Joel Smith (René), Sandra Stone (Rosie), Paul Toffel (Ten-Year-Old Boy), Alan Wells (Armand).

Credits: Director: Lewis Allen; Producers: Sam Bischoff and David Diamond; Assistant Director: Bert Glazer; Original Story: James Benson Nablo; Screenplay: Daniel Mainwaring (Geoffrey Holmes) and A.I. Bezzerides; Photography: Harry Neumann; Editor: Leon Barsha; Music Score: Harry Sukman; Orchestrations: Henry Vars; Art Direction: Jack Okey; Sound Recorder: John C. Grubb; Wardrobe: Chuck Keehne; Makeup: Mel Berns. Released by United Artists on April 15, 1955. Black and white. 85 minutes.

Synopsis: In Montreal, a Red spy masquerading as an organ grinder snaps a photograph of atomic scientist Dr. Carl Macklin. In the process, policeman Dan Percy is murdered.

The organ grinder takes the photo to Eric Hartman, a Red spymaster masquerading as a rare book dealer, and his wife Viveca. Hartman is pleased with the photo, but incensed when he learns of the death of the policeman.

In Lisbon, deported American gangster Joe Victor is offered $100,000 if he will kidnap Macklin. Victor is given the false identity of Ernest Steiner together with a passport and a passage by ship to Canada. Upon arrival in Canada, Victor is met by Dubois and taken to Maple Leaf Farm where he meets Hartman. Victor arranges for his old gang to fly to Montreal. He suggests to Hartman that Macklin should be introduced to femme fatale Joyce Geary, a former flame of Victor's. She is reluctant, but contrives to meet Macklin at a golf club where he gives her some instruction in golf and later chess and she becomes genuinely fond of him. Another member of Victor's gang, Jack Allen, becomes involved with Yvonne Temblay, Macklin's secretary, who resides with her repressive and suspicious older sister Marie. Allen obtains information from Yvonne, but when she becomes suspicious and tries to run away from him, he panics and murders her. Allen passes the information on to Victor and is paid off without telling him that Yvonne is dead.

The police find Yvonne's body and Insp. Raoul Leduc deduces that the common link between all three murders is Macklin. Fingerprints on a rental car match those of Allen. A photograph of him is identified by Marie Temblay. The FBI knows that Allen is a member of Victor's gang and Leduc asks them to trace the whereabouts of Victor and the other gang members, but he is not aware of Joyce. Leduc tracks Macklin to the golf club where he is introduced to Joyce, informs them of the murder of Yvonne and tells him that he may be the target. Hartman arrives at the farm and shows Victor the newspaper story which deals with the slaying of Yvonne. Victor arranges for a hit man to liquidate Jack Allen while gambling in L.A. Leduc is able to trace the call setting up the hit to Morrie in a Montreal bar. Morrie is followed to Maple Leaf Farm, but Dubois spots a police officer up a telegraph pole and the gangsters make a swift escape.

Victor goes to the Hartmans' place where he finds Joyce writing a confession for Leduc. Victor persuades Joyce to phone Macklin and tell him she is leaving that afternoon. Macklin offers to drive her to the airport, but when he turns up at the Hartmans' house, he is kidnapped. Victor pretends to pay Joyce off, but when she tries to leave, he insists she turn over the confession to him and prevents her going. The Hartmans take Macklin and Joyce to a freighter which is soon going to sail. On the highway, Leduc and another officer are flagged down, kidnapped and taken to the same ship. On board Victor finds Hartman and demands his money which Hartman reluctantly gives him. After the freighter sets sail, Victor goes to the captain, pulls a gun and demands that he and his men be allowed to disembark. The captain and his men overpower Victor and he is taken to the saloon where Leduc tells him that Macklin is a scientist who has been kidnapped by Communists for their own ends. Victor and his gang attack the freighter's crew and a gunfight ensues. In the confusion, Leduc manages to fire a distress flare which alerts the river patrol. Victor has an attack of conscience and he and Hartman shoot and kill one another. Joyce and Macklin are saved. Before he dies, Victor gives Joyce's letter to Leduc and begs him to scatter his ashes in the U.S.

Comments: This was the only time that George Raft was directed by Lewis Allen. It was the third time that Raft appeared in a film produced by Samuel Bischoff, his former business partner. This was the second occasion in which Raft co-starred with Edward G. Robinson, but this time there was no reported friction on the set. *A Bullet for Joey* was a modestly budgeted production with a slow pace, but the supporting players were all well cast and there was no shortage of extras. It was a topical thriller designed to cash in on the Red menace which was then frightening people in many free countries of the world. In spite of this, the film was a box office flop. There was a speech in this film delivered by Robinson to Raft which was reckoned to be a highwater mark in terms of anti–Red hysteria: "Joe, you've pulled all kinds of deals during your lifetime ... gambling, the numbers racket, smuggling, the occasional rub-out. All of these are petty crimes compared to the one you committed when you handed Macklin over to this mob."

Victor's change of heart towards the end of the film came across as rather unconvincing. Indeed the character of Joe Victor was so disreputable that it might be wondered why Raft accepted it. The reasons were because of the dearth of other offers together with the fact that Raft wanted to use his salary to buy shares in a gambling casino. A.I. Bezzerides was also responsible for writing the original novel on which *They Drive by Night* was based. Of *A Bullet for Joey* he recalled, "Robinson wanted me to polish his dialogue. He gave me $5,000 to do it. Just his dialogue. The hell with George Raft. And I went through the script and polished his dialogue. But what it did to the other guy's dialogue they couldn't believe. And Raft got wind of it and he said, 'Hey, how about me?' So I shrugged and said, 'More money.' Raft said, 'I'll pay.' So I did his."

Biography: Lewis Allen was born in Oakengates, Telford, Shropshire, England, on December 25, 1905. He commenced his career on stage as an actor in England. He worked with impresario Gilbert Miller supervising stage productions in the West End of London and on Broadway. He began working at Paramount in the early 1940s and made his directorial debut with the classic *The Uninvited* (1944). The critical and commercial failure of *Valentino* (1951) largely wrecked his film career and hastened his transition to television where he directed numerous episodes. He died in Santa Monica on May 3, 2000, aged 94. He

was married to Dorothy Skinner and later to Trudy Colmar, who survived him.

Biography: Audrey Totter was born in Joliet, Illinois, on December 20, 1917, of an Austrian father and Swedish mother. She was educated at Joliet High School. Upon graduating she went to Chicago where she became extremely active in Chicago's flourishing radio soap operas and later in New York where she developed a reputation for being able to affect any accent. She made her screen debut in *Main Street After Dark* (1944) and was under contract to MGM for seven years and then successfully freelanced. After marriage to Dr. Leo Fred in 1952 and giving birth to a daughter in 1954, she downscaled her career. She did however have regular roles in three television series, of which the longest was *Medical Center* (1972–1976) as Nurse Wilcox. She was widowed in 1995. At last report she was a resident of the Motion Picture Country Home and Hospital in Woodland Hills, California.

Around the World in 80 Days (1956)

Cast: David Niven (Phileas Fogg), Cantinflas (Passepartout), Shirley MacLaine (Princess Aouda), Robert Newton (Inspector Fix), Charles Boyer (M. Gasse, Clerk, Thomas Cook, Paris), Joe E. Brown (Station Master, Fort Kearney), Martine Carol (Girl in Railroad Station, Paris), John Carradine (Colonel Proctor, San Francisco Politico), Charles Coburn (Clerk, Hong Kong Steamship Office), Ronald Colman (Official of Great Indian Peninsular Railway), Melville Cooper (Mr. Tulley, Steward, R.M.S. *Mongolia*), Noël Coward (Roland Hesketh-Baggott, London Employment Agency Manager), Finlay Currie (Member of the Reform Club, London), Reginald Denny (Inspector, Bombay Police), Andy Devine (First Mate, S.S. *Henrietta*), Marlene Dietrich (Owner, Barbary Coast Saloon), Luis Miguel Dominguin (Bullfighter, Spain), Fernandel (Coachman, Paris), Sir John Gielgud (Foster, Fogg's

Ex-Valet), Hermoine Gingold (Tart, London), José Greco (Flamenco Dancer, Cave of the Seven Winds), Sir Cedric Hardwicke (Sir Francis Cromarty, Bombay-Calcutta Train), Trevor Howard (Denis Fallenstin, Reform Club Member), Glynis Johns (Tart, London), Buster Keaton (Train Conductor, San Francisco to Fort Kearney), Evelyn Keyes (Tart, Paris), Beatrice Lillie (Leader of Revivalist Group, London), Peter Lorre (Japanese Steward, S.S. *Carnatic*), Edmund Lowe (Chief Engineer, S.S. *Henrietta*), A.E. Matthews (Billiard Player, Reform Club), Mike Mazurki (Drunk, Hong Kong Dive), Tim McCoy (Commander of U.S. Cavalry, Fort Kearney), Victor McLaglen (Helmsman, S.S. *Henrietta*), John Mills (London Cabbie), Robert Morley (Ralph, a Governor of the Bank of England), Alan Mowbray (British Consul, Suez), Edward R. Murrow (Commentator in Prologue), Jack Oakie (Captain, S.S. *Henrietta*), George Raft (Bouncer, Barbary Coast Saloon), Gilbert Roland (Achmed Abdullah), Cesar Romero (Henchman of Achmed Abdullah), Frank Sinatra (Piano Player, Barbary Coast Saloon), Red Skelton (Drunk, Barbary Coast Saloon), Ronald Squire, Basil Sydney (Members of Reform Club, London), Harcourt Williams (Hinshaw, Aged Steward, Reform Club).

Credits: Director: Michael Anderson; Producer: Mike Todd; Associate Producers: William Cameron Menzies, Kevin McClory; Based on the Novel by Jules Verne; Screenplay: James Poe, John Farrow, S.J. Perelman; Photography: Lionel Lindon; Editors: Howard Epstein, Gene Ruggiero, Paul Weatherwax; Music Score: Victor Young; Choreographer: Paul Godkin; Art Direction: James Sullivan; Sound Recorder: Joseph Kane; Costumes: Miles White; Special Effects: Lee Zavitz. Released by United Artists on October 17, 1956. Color. 175 minutes.

Synopsis: At the Reform Club in London during the days of Queen Victoria, Phileas Fogg makes a wager of £20,000 that he can circle the globe in 80 days accompanied by his

Man Friday, Passepartout. A bold bank robbery from the Bank of England of £55,000 complicates matters. Fogg, suspected of the crime, is pursued by the dogged Inspector Fix.

One adventure takes them to the Barbary Coast of San Francisco which is in the midst of a turbulent political campaign. Passepartout drifts into a saloon where a drunk is in process of stuffing his pockets with food from the free lunch counter until the bouncer collars him and heaves him into the gutter. Fogg enters the same saloon searching for Passepartout, but is waylaid by the attractive female saloon owner. She invites him to linger at her table, but their conversation is interrupted by the angry bouncer. Fogg and Passepartout leave. Meanwhile the saloon pianist in a bowler hat and sleeve garters never misses a beat.

Comments: This film received Oscars for Best Color Cinematography, Best Scoring of a Dramatic or Comedy Picture, Best Film and Best Adapted Screenplay, plus nominations for Best Direction and Best Color Costume Design. This was notable as the film George Raft appeared in which won an Oscar as Best Picture. The budget was $6,000,000. It was also the most commercially successful film Raft ever appeared in with domestic rentals of $23,120,000. He did not want to accept such a small role, but agreed to do it when he was told that three of his friends (Frank Sinatra, Marlene Dietrich, Red Skelton) would be in the sequence with him.

Biography: Michael Anderson was born in London on January 30, 1920. The son of stage actor Laurence Anderson, he entered the film industry in 1935 as an office boy at Elstree Studios, later graduating to assistant director and unit manager. After war service he became a director both in England and Hollywood commencing with *Private Angelo* (1949). He married and divorced Betty Jordan and Vera Carlisle and since 1977 he has been married to Adrienne Ellis. He has six children, one of whom, Michael Anderson, Jr., is a well-known actor.

Some Like It Hot (1959)

Cast: Marilyn Monroe (Sugar Kane Kowalczyk), Tony Curtis (Joe-Josephine), Jack Lemmon (Jerry-Daphne), George Raft (Spats Columbo), Pat O'Brien (Detective Mulligan), Joe E. Brown (Osgood Fielding III), Nehemiah Persoff (Little Bonaparte), Joan Shawlee (Sweet Sue), Billy Gray (Sig Poliakoff), George E. Stone (Toothpick Charlie), Dave Barry (Beinstock), Mike Mazurki, Harry Wilson, Pat Comiskay (Spats' Henchmen), Beverly Wills (Dolores), Barbara Drew (Nellie), Edward G. Robinson, Jr. (Johnny Paradise), Al Breneman (Bellhop), Marian Collier (Olga), Grace Lee Whitney, Penny McGuiggan, Joan Fields, Mary Foley (Band Members), Paul Frees (Funeral Director), Joe Gray (Mobster at Banquet), Ted Hook, Harold Hart (Officials), John Indrisano (Waiter), Tom Kennedy (Bouncer), Jack McClure (Spats' Driver), Laurie Mitchell (Mary Lou, Trumpet Player), Helen Perry (Rosella), Fred Sherman (Drunk), Tito Vuolo (Mozzarilla), Sandra Warner (Emily).

Credits: Director and Producer: Billy Wilder; Associate Producers: I.A.L. Diamond and Doane Harrison; Assistant Director: Sam Nelson; Original Story: R. Thoeren and M. Logan; Screenplay: Billy Wilder and I.A.L. Diamond; Photography: Charles Lang, Jr. (Oscar nomination); Editor: Arthur P. Schmidt; Score: Adolph Deutsch; Musical Supervision: Matty Melneck; Music Editor: Eve Newman; Set Decorator: Edward G. Boyle (Oscar nomination); Art Direction: Ted Haworth (Oscar nomination); Sound Recorder: Fred Lau; Costumes: Orry-Kelly (Oscar winner); Wardrobe: Bert Henrikson; Hair Stylists: Alice Monte and Agnes Flanegan; Special Effects: Milt Rice and Daniel Hays; Stunts: Polly Burson and Joe Gray. Released by United Artists on March 29, 1959. Black and white. 120 minutes.

Synopsis: Detective Mulligan gains access to a speakeasy behind a funeral parlor with the aid of stool pigeon Toothpick Charlie. There he tangles with gangster Spats Columbo shortly before a police raid. Columbo surmises that Toothpick Charlie betrayed them. As an act of revenge, he arranges for Toothpick Charlie to be gunned down in a garage as part of the infamous St. Valentine's Day Massacre. Joe and Jerry, two itinerant musicians playing at the speakeasy, accidentally witness the massacre and flee. To escape Columbo's wrath, Joe and Jerry disguise themselves as females, Josephine and Daphne, and join an all-girl band led by Sweet Sue. On the train to Florida they meet Sugar Kane, another band member. When they arrive in Florida, Daphne is pursued by multi-married millionaire Osgood Fielding III. Josephine reverts to being Joe for a date and, using Osgood's facilities, pretends to be a millionaire so Sugar Kane falls in love with him.

Spats Columbo arrives in Florida with Mulligan in pursuit. Columbo and his henchmen are attending the tenth anniversary of the Italian Opera Association — in reality, a front for the Mafia headed by Little Bonaparte, whose pal was Toothpick Charlie. The gangsters spot Josephine and Daphne and realize they are not women. A madcap chase ensues until Josephine and Daphne hide under a table at the gangsters' meeting. At the meeting a cake is wheeled in, celebrating the birthday of Spats Columbo — except it is not his birthday. At the end of the celebratory song, Johnny Paradise leaps from the cake armed with a machine-gun and sprays Columbo and his henchmen with bullets. Josephine and Daphne race from the hotel while Mulligan arrests the remaining gangsters. Josephine and Daphne leap into a boat with Osgood at the wheel. Sugar Kane realizes that Josephine is really Joe and at the last minute joins them in the boat. Joe and Sugar Kane profess their love for each other. Jerry reveals to Osgood that he cannot marry him because he is not a woman, but Osgood shrugs and tells him, "Nobody's perfect!"

Comments: This was the first and only time that George Raft was directed by Billy Wilder. This was the third and last time that

Raft appeared with Pat O'Brien. It was the only comedy which Raft appeared in that was an unqualified success. Raft played it straight as the sinister gangster, Spats Columbo, so-called because he always wore spats, and as such he is much more effective. It was one of the most commercially successful films that Raft ever appeared in with domestic rentals of $8,127,835. Jack Lemmon received an Oscar nomination for his performance. Wilder and I.A.L. Diamond received a Best Screenplay Based on Material from Another Medium nomination, and Wilder received a Best Director nomination.

Raft was originally hired for a week's work, but because Marilyn Monroe frequently failed to arrive on the set, Wilder shot extra scenes with him to fill up the time. He even taught Jack Lemmon and Joe E. Brown how to tango. Raft actually worked on the film for four months. Raft said that Marilyn Monroe suggested that she and Raft should tango into the sunset at the end of the film, but this was obviously impossible given that Raft had been killed earlier in the film. Raft's only display of temperament was when he blew up on the last day. When Wilder gently asked him what the problem was, Raft admitted that he so enjoyed shooting the film that he did not want to see it end. Of all the films Raft made, this is the one for which he is best remembered. There was one particularly memorable scene where Columbo sees Johnny Paradise flipping a coin and asks, "Where did you pick up that cheap trick?"— a reference to Raft's trademark. The role of Little Bonaparte was originally offered to Edward G. Robinson, but he declined not because of antipathy to Raft, but because he was appearing in a play and the schedules conflicted.

Biography: Billy Wilder was born Samuel Wilder in Sucha Galicia, Austria-Hungary (now Poland), on June 22, 1906. The son of a Jewish hotelier, he began his career as a newspaper reporter, initially in Vienna and later in Berlin where he later became a scriptwriter. In 1933 when Hitler came to power, Wilder was forced to flee to Paris and in 1934 to America via Mexico. In 1938 he started a highly successful collaboration with Charles Brackett, initially as a writing team, and later as a production team with Wilder directing and Brackett producing. Wilder won Best Director Oscars for *The Lost Weekend* (1945) and *The Apartment* (1960). After the split, Wilder's penchant for cynicism and vulgarity became more prominent. He served mainly as his own producer, but collaborated on many scripts with I.A.L. Diamond. Wilder died in Los Angeles on March 27, 2002, aged 95, of pneumonia. He was married and divorced from Judith Coppicus and was married to Audrey Young from 1949 onwards.

Biography: Tony Curtis was born Bernard Schwartz in New York on June 3, 1925, the son of a Hungarian immigrant tailor. He grew up in the tough environment of the Bronx. After serving in the Navy during World War II, he studied drama at New York's Dramatic Workshop. He commenced his professional career with a stock company that toured the Catskills. He appeared briefly off–Broadway and then in 1949 he signed a contract with Universal-International who built him into a star in a wide range of films. The fifties, his most successful decade, culminated in a Best Actor Oscar nomination for *The Defiant Ones* (1958). His later acting career declined in stature, but he developed a successful secondary career as an artist. He died in Henderson, Clark County, Nevada, on September 29, 2010, aged 85, of cardiac arrest. He was married five times and divorced on four occasions. From 1998 onwards he was married to Jill Vandenberg, who survived him along with five of his six children. Curtis recalled, "I enjoyed working with George Raft. He was a wonderful man."

Biography: Jack Lemmon was born John Uhler Lemmon III in Boston, Massachusetts, on February 8, 1925. The son of the president of a doughnut company, he was educated at

Harvard. He served in the Navy as an ensign, then embarked upon an acting career. After appearing on Broadway, he was signed to a contract by Columbia and made his screen debut in *It Should Happen to You* (1954). He won a Best Supporting Actor Oscar for *Mister Roberts* (1955) and a Best Actor Oscar for *Save the Tiger* (1973). He played a wide diversity of roles, frequently in parts in which he was an individual caught in a bureaucratic web. He made a number of comedies in which he co-starred with Walter Matthau. Lemmon died in Los Angeles on June 27, 2001, aged 76, of colon cancer and metastatic cancer of the bladder. In 1950 he married Cynthia Stone, with whom he had a son before divorcing in 1956. In 1962 he wed Felicia Farr with whom he had a daughter; both of them survived him.

Biography: Marilyn Monroe was born Norma Jean Mortenson or Norma Jean Baker in Los Angeles on June 1, 1926. Her father was a baker, Edward Mortenson, while her mother was Gladys Pearl Monroe, a Mexican film cutter. She was brought up in a succession of foster homes. She was working in the Radio Plane factory in Van Nuys, California, where she was discovered by photographer David Conover, who had been sent to take photographs of women helping the war effort. On the strength of the photographs taken, she signed on at a model agency where she was known as Jean Norman. She signed with 20th Century–Fox in 1946 and made her screen debut in *Dangerous Years* (1947). She was dropped from her original contract, but then Fox signed her again in 1951. *Niagara* (1953), in which she played unfaithful wife Rose Loomis, made her a star. When she formed her own production company, Marilyn Monroe Productions, in 1955, this caused great conflict with the studio, but eventually a new contract was negotiated in 1956. She went on to star in other successful films notably *Some Like It Hot.* Her final released film was *The Misfits* (1961). The last film she worked on, the appropriately titled *Somethings Gotta to Give,* was left incomplete at the

time of her death. She died in Los Angeles on August 5, 1962, aged 36, of acute barbiturate poisoning; her death certificate states "probable suicide." Her death has been the subject of endless speculation and conspiracy theories over the years, but in view of the state of her mental health at the time, it hardly seemed necessary to murder her.

Jet Over the Atlantic (1959)

Cast: Guy Madison (Brett Matoon/Murphy), Virginia Mayo (Jean Gurney), George Raft (Charles Stafford), Ilona Massey (Mme. Galli-Gazetti), George Macready (Lord Robert Leverett), Anna Lee (Lady Ursula Leverett), Margaret Lindsay (Mrs. Lanyard), Venetia Stevenson (June Elliott), Mary Anderson (Maria), Brett Halsey (Dr. Vanderbird), Argentina Brunetti (Miss Hooten), Frederic Worlock (Dean Halltree), Tudor Owen (Mr. Priestwood), Cindy Lee (Laura Lanyard), Hilda Moreno (Mrs. Priestwood), Tito Junco (General Ramirez), Rebeca Iturbide (Stewardess), Carlos Muzquiz (Purser), Cesar Ugarte (Co-pilot), Armando Saenz (Captain Reyes), John Kelly (Garbatz), José Epinosa (Carson), Rafael Alcaide, Breck Martin, Selene Walters (Passengers), Gene Roth (Policeman at Airport).

Credits: Director: Byron Haskin; Producer: Benedict Bogeaus; Assistant Director: Jamie Contreras; Screenplay: Irving H. Cooper; Photography: George Stahl; Editors: James Leicester and Thomas Pratt; Music Score: Lou Forbes; Art Direction: John Mansbridge and Ramon Rodriguez Granada; Sound Recorders: Bert Schoenfeld and José Carles; Costumes: Gwen Wakeling. Song "What Would I Do Without You?": Music by Lou Forbes, Lyrics by Jack Hoffman, Sung by The King Sisters. Released by Inter Continent Films Incorporated on November 4, 1959. Black and white. 95 minutes.

Tagline: "They knew it was now or never ... when they were thrust into the jet-heat of this Desperate Affair! Jet-Hot Action! Jet-Hot

Suspense! Jet-Hot Thrills! Panic in the Skies Jet Screaming to New Heights of Excitement!"

Synopsis: In Madrid, two Americans, Brett Matoon and Jean Gurney, a singer-dancer at the Club Lido, meet and fall in love. On what would have been their wedding day Jean is telephoned by Matoon and told that their wedding plans are indefinitely postponed because he has been arrested by Stafford, an FBI agent, for extradition to the United States as an escaped convicted murderer. Matoon is handcuffed and taken aboard a jet airliner, Flight 400, bound for New York. Jean buys a ticket and also boards the plane. There is a flashback sequence to Chicago where Matoon has stopped by a neighborhood bar when two men enter and try to force the owner into paying for "protection." When Matoon tries to intervene, they knock him unconscious, kill two barmen and frame Matoon by placing the gun in his hand. He is found guilty of the double murder and sentenced to the electric chair.

Lord Leverett, whose wife is aboard the plane to visit her family in the States and whose daughter Laura has recently died, also boards the flight. The tragedy has unhinged his mind and turned him into a psychopathic murderer. He contrives to place on board the plane a bomb triggered to burn and release deadly fumes. Other passengers include Mme. Galli-Gazetti, a fading opera star en route to appear at Carnagie Hall, paid for by Charles Harrington, her lover; Miss Hooten, a rich, kind old spinster; Dean Halltree, a famous English clergyman; Vanderberg, an affluent doctor en route to New Guinea to establish a hospital for the natives; and Jane Elliott, who is going to see her father in New York for the first time in fifteen years. In the course of the flight Vanderberg and Elliott become close.

When Matoon discovers Jean on board after takeoff, Stafford allows him to join her in the lounge. Busybody Miss Hooten overhears Matoon tell Jean that he was framed for two murders. The lovers, with a marriage license and no time left to be united in matrimony, are too much for the sentimental Hooten, who contrives to have Stafford suggest to the couple that they be married on the plane and convince Dean Halltree to perform the ceremony.

Fumes from Leverett's device in the forward luggage compartment seep into air ducts, killing the flight crew. Matoon, a former Air Force pilot, investigates with Stafford the cause of the tragedy and is forced to kill Leverett when the madman threatens them with a gun. He maneuvers the plane to New York's Idlewild Airport. After a belly landing, he attempts to make a break, but is winged in the leg by Stafford, who has saved him from being mowed down by police and FBI agents surrounding the area. The criminal responsible for Matoon's murder conviction is brought to the airport where he confesses to having framed Matoon. Stafford assists the wounded Matoon into an ambulance along with Jean and the ambulance takes them to the hospital.

Comments: This was the only time that George Raft was directed by Byron Haskin. This was the third and last of the Raft films produced by Benedict Bogeaus. The "jet" referenced in the title was actually a propeller aircraft (in the film it's called a turboprop). The movie was a precursor of the disaster genre. Although he was not top-billed, Raft appeared in both the first and last scenes and had the final line. It was the last time that he had a prominent role in a Hollywood film. Of this experience he said at the time, "It's a real test for an actor. I had to keep fighting all along to portray the FBI man like he should be played. I could feel the old gangster character creep up and show itself in the way I talked, the way I walked, and even in the way I stood when I held a gun." What Raft strove for was to reveal his character as tough, but more of a rugged toughness than the bestial toughness of the bad guy. To a large extent he succeeded.

Brett Halsey recalled, "We shot that picture in Mexico City. George Raft was a wonderful character. He was a very macho man, but very ill at the time. He had to have oxygen since

Mexico City is located at a very high altitude. Once at dinner he got into an argument with the producer, Ben Bogeaus. He just turned and grabbed him and growled, 'I'll kill you, you son of a bitch!' I don't remember the issue, but the producer quickly agreed to whatever Raft wanted. Everyone relaxed and the meal continued in a calm, pleasant manner. I found it interesting to learn that Raft never drank. Many people were surprised to see him drinking milk with his meals. George Raft was really one-of-a-kind. He always insisted on a Rolls-Royce to take him back from work. We weren't really good friends, but he was a major star in my youth, so I was respectful."

Biography: Byron Haskin was born in Portland, Oregon, on April 22, 1899. He moved with his family to San Francisco as a child. He attended the University of California at Berkeley for three years before enlisting as a naval aviation cadet during World War I. On demobilization he worked briefly as a newspaper cartoonist and advertising man, then entered films as a newsreel cameraman in 1918. In 1919 he gravitated to Hollywood where he became an assistant cameraman, assistant director and director of photography. Between 1927 and 1928 he directed four films, then resumed his career as a cinematographer. Between 1929 and 1932 he was a production executive in England. Between 1937 and 1945 he was head of the special effects department at Warner Bros. In 1945 he resumed directing with a particular bias towards science fiction films. He died in Montecito, California, on April 16, 1984, aged 84.

Biography: Guy Madison was born Robert Ozelle Mosely in Bakersfield, California, on January 19, 1922. The son of Benjamin J. Mosely, he attended Bakersfield Junior College and was working as a telephone lineman when he was drafted during World War II. He was serving at a U.S. naval base in San Diego when he attended a radio broadcast. Sitting in the audience, he was noticed by agent Henry Willson. Willson brought him to the attention

of Selznick International Pictures who signed him to a contract. When he made his screen debut in *Since You Went Away* (1944), the studio was deluged with fan letters. He graduated to playing the hero of a number of action films and starred in a highly successful television series, *The Adventures of Wild Bill Hickok* (1951–1958). Later he worked extensively in Europe. He married actress Gail Russell in 1949, but they divorced in 1954. In 1955 he wed Sheila Connolly, with whom he had four children, but they divorced in 1963. He died in Palm Springs, California, on February 6, 1996, aged 74, of emphysema.

Ocean's 11 (1960)

Cast: Frank Sinatra (Danny Ocean), Dean Martin (Sam Harmon), Sammy Davis, Jr. (Josh Howard), Peter Lawford (Jimmy Foster), Angie Dickinson (Beatrice Ocean), Richard Conte (Anthony Raymond "Tony" Bergdorf), Cesar Romero (Duke Santos), Patrice Wymore (Adele Ekstrom), Joey Bishop ("Mushy" O'Connors), Akim Tamiroff (Syros Acebos), Henry Silva (Roger Corneal), Ilka Chase (Mrs. Restes), Buddy Lester (Vince Massler), Richard Benedict ("Curly" Steffens), Jean Willes (Gracie Bergdof), Norman Fell (Peter Rheimar), Clem Harvey (Louis Jackson), Hank Henry (Mr. Kelly, Mortician), Lew Gallo (Jealous Young Man), Robert Foulk (Sheriff Wimmer), Murray Alper (Deputy), Don "Red" Barry (McCoy), Marjorie Bennett (Mrs. Allenby), Rummy Bishop (Castleman), Nicky Blair (Gangster), Richard Boone (Voice of Minister), Norman Brooks (Himself), Paul Bryar (Cop), David Carlile (Attendant), Laura Connell (Honeyface, Massler's Wife), John Craven (Cashier), Ronnie Dupo (Timmy Bergdorf), George Fenneman (Voice on Phone), West Gale (Red Cap), Gregory Gaye (Freeman), John George (Midget), Leonard George (Police Operator), Jay Gerard (Cab Driver), Hoot Gibson (Roadblock Deputy), Bob Gilbreath (Helicopter Pilot), Joe Gray (Pit Boss), John Holland (Man),

Dick Hudkins (Drunk), John Indrisano (Texan), Jessica James (Go Go Dancer), Barbara Sterling, Helen Jay (Girls), William Justine (Parelli), Sparky Kaye (Riviera Manager), Mike Lally (American Legionnaire at Funeral Service), David Landfield (Flamingo M.C.), Forrest Lederer (Sands Manager), Pinky Lee (Himself), Nelson Leigh (Doctor), David Leonard (Rabbi), Shirley MacLaine (Tipsy Girl), Charles Meredith (Mr. Cohen, Mortician), Tom Middleton (Dan Murphy, TV Newscaster), Red Norvo (Vibraphonist), Ted Otis (Cashier), Steve Pendleton (Major Taylor), Carmen Phillips (Hungry Girl), Louis Quinn (DeWolfe), Myrna Ross (Passenger), Jack Santoro, Buddy Shaw (Cashiers), Shiva (Snake Dancer), Al Silvani (Burlesque Club Manager), Richard Sinatra (Attendant), John Slosser (Squad Leader), Joan Staley (Helen), George E. Stone (Proprietor), H.T. Tsiang (Houseboy), Jerry Velasco (Harmonica-Playing Garbageman), James Waters (Disposal Attendant), Dave White (Burlesque Club Stagehand), Harry Wilson (Man), Norma Yost (Airline Hostess). Guest Stars: George Raft (Jack Strager), Red Skelton (Gambler).

Credits: Director and Producer: Lewis Milestone; Associate Producer: Henry W. Sanicola; Assistant Directors: Ray Gosnell, Jr., and Richard Lang; Original Story: George Clayton Johnson and Jack Golden Russell; Screenplay: Harry Brown and Charles Lederer; Photography: William H. Daniels; Editor: Philip W. Anderson; Music: Nelson Riddle; Art Direction: Nicolai Remisoff; Sound Recorder: M.A. Merrick; Costumes: Howard Shoup; Makeup: Gordon Bau; Special Effects: Franklyn Soldo; Title Design: Saul Bass. Released by Warner Bros. on August 10, 1960. Color. 127 minutes.

Synopsis: Eleven friends who know each other from World War II service plan to rob five of the biggest casinos in Las Vegas in one night. They develop and execute a master plan, but afterwards the scheme goes awry with an ironic outcome. After the casinos have been robbed, Jack Strager convenes a meeting of the other casino owners. At this meeting he tells the group that he has partners who are none too happy about the robberies. He introduces Duke Santos to the company. Santos offers to retrieve the money for a finders fee of 30 percent which the others reluctantly agree to. Santos asks Jack Strager to call the sheriff's office to obtain cooperation. The next scene takes place in the sheriff's office where the voice of Jack Strager is heard on the phone asking the sheriff to go and see Duke Santos. That was all of George Raft's contribution to this film.

Comments: This was the only time that George Raft was directed by Lewis Milestone. *Ocean's 11* was made because Frank Sinatra and the Rat Pack were appearing in Las Vegas and wanted a project to do during the daytime when they were not appearing in the clubs. Raft was pitifully underused in this film. Conversely the latter stages of the film were dominated by Cesar Romero, which must have been something of a disappointment for fans who thought they were going to see more of the Rat Pack. Another demerit was that some of the characters (including Angie Dickinson and Patrice Wymore) were not properly developed and disappeared abruptly out of the film. The film ran to excessive length and never became really exciting. Nevertheless it was a box office hit with $5,650,000 in domestic rentals. *Ocean's 11* (2001), which starred George Clooney, borrowed the title and the basic theme, but was otherwise a different story.

Biography: Lewis Milestone was born Lev Milstein in Chisinau, Moldova, on September 30, 1895. The son of a prosperous Jewish clothing manufacturer, he quit university on an impulse and on his own went to the United States where he spent five years working at various menial jobs. In 1917 when he enlisted in the U.S. Army for World War I service, he was assigned to the Signal Corps where he learned much about filmmaking. Following his discharge in 1919 he changed his name to Lewis Milestone and headed for Hollywood and entered the industry as an assistant film cutter. He then became an assistant director, editor and script collaborator before becoming a film director in 1925. He won Best Director Oscars for *Two Arabian Knights* (1927) and *All Quiet on the Western Front* (1930) and received an Oscar nomination for *The Front Page* (1931). His retirement came in 1963 following a series of strokes. He was married to actress Kendall Lee from 1935 until she died in 1978. Milestone died in Los Angeles on September 25, 1980, aged 84.

The Ladies Man (1961)

Cast: Jerry Lewis (Herbert H. Heebert), Helen Traubel (Miss Helen Wellenmellon), Kathleen Freeman (Katie), Madlyn Rhue (Miss Intellect), Hope Holiday (Miss Anxious), Pat Stanley (Fay), Lynn Ross (Miss Vitality), Lillian Briggs (Lillian), Mary La Roche (Miss Society), Alex Gerry (Mr. Zoussman), Jack Kruschen (Graduation M.C. Professor), Vicki Benet (Frenchie), Dee Arlen (Miss Liar), Gloria Jean (Gloria), Sylvia Lewis (Sylvia), Ann McCrea (Miss Sexy Pot), Caroline Richter (Miss Southern Accent), Sheila Rogers (Miss Reed), Doodles Weaver (Soundman), Beverly Wills (Miss Hypochrondriac), Westbrook Van Voorhis (TV Personality), Roscoe Ates (Pet Shop Owner), Don Brodie (Makeup Man), Fritz Feld (Mrs. Wellenmellen's Hairdresser), John Indrisano (TV Technician), Kerner G. Kemp (Graduation Attendee), Kenneth MacDonald (Papa Heebert), Michael Ross (The Grocer), William Wellman, Jr. (Soda Jerk/Rod Reason), Dave Willock (Assistant TV Program Director), Roger Bacon (TV Cableman), Dick Bernie (Second Floor Man), Charles Cirillo (TV Repairman), Ira Cook, Abe Lax, Peter Potter, Michael Tomack, Mickey Finn, Jack Fisher (Men on Date), Jerry Gordet (Speedy Armature), Bob Hopkins (Announcer), Gretchen Houser, Francesca Bellini, Bonnie Evans (Dancers), Gloria Tracy (Gloria Glands), Patricia Blair, Karyn Kupcinet, Kay Tapscott, Patty Thomas, Faye Michael Nuell, Dolores Erickson, Marianne Gaba, June Kenney, Paula Lane, Patricia Olson, Kathy Potter, Cecile Rogers, Darlene Tompkins, Meri Welles (Working Girls); Jack LaLanne (Himself), Guest Stars: George Raft, Harry James, Marty Ingels (Themselves), Buddy Lester (Willard G. Gainsborough).

Credits: Director and Producer: Jerry Lewis; Assistant Directors: C.C. Coleman, Jr., and Ralph Axness; Associate Producer: Ernest D. Glucksman; Assistant Producer: Arthur P. Schmidt; Screenplay: Jerry Lewis and Bill Richmond; Photography: W. Wallace Kelley; Editor: Stanley Johnson; Art Direction: Hal Pereira and Ross Bellah; Music: Walter Scharf; Choreographer: Bobby Van; Orchestrators: Leo Shuken and Jack Hayes; Music Coordinator: Phil Boutelje; New Songs: Harry Warren and Jack Brooks; Costumes: Edith Head; Jerry Lewis' Wardrobe: Sy Devore and Nat Wise; Makeup: Wally Westmore; Special Photographic Effects: John P. Fulton. Released by Paramount on June 28, 1961. Color. 95 minutes.

Synopsis: Jilted by his fiancée, Herbert Heebert decides to have nothing further to do with the opposite sex. Then he finds himself working as a maintenance man in an upmarket boarding house for aspiring actresses. Two thirds of the way into the film Heebert enters a room to find George Raft sitting there waiting for one of the girls. Raft eventually introduces himself, but Heebert disputes that he is George Raft. Raft tosses a coin to prove his identity, but misses. He then dances a tango with Lewis before leaving with his date.

Comments: Jerry Lewis recalls, "George Raft did a cameo. He was wonderful." His cameo appearance lasted about four minutes. According to Raft, Lewis said that he could do a cameo in any of his pictures. This was the first of his two appearances in Lewis films. The other was *The Patsy* (1964).

Biography: Jerry Lewis was born Joseph Levitch in Newark, New Jersey, on March 16, 1926. His parents were in show business and he became a performer at an early age. In 1946 he met another struggling performer, Dean Martin, and since neither had been successful as a solo, they decided to form a partnership which became highly successful in clubs, radio, the stage and television. Producer Hal B. Wallis signed them for films in 1949 and their success continued. The team split in 1956 after which Lewis signed a production deal with Paramount to direct and star in his own comedies, which continued until the end of the sixties. He was married to vocalist Patty Palmer from 1944 until they divorced in 1982. Since 1983 he has been married to SanDee Pitnick.

For Those Who
Think Young (1964)

Cast: James Darren (Gardner "Ding" Pruitt III), Pamela Tiffin (Sandy Palmer), Paul Lynde (Uncle Sid Hoyt), Tina Louise (Topaz McQueen), Bob Denver (Kelp), Robert Middleton (Burfold Sanfold "Nifty" Cronin), Nancy Sinatra (Karen Cross), Claudia Martin (Sue Lewis), Ellen McRae [Ellen Burstyn] (Dr. Pauline Swenson), Woody Woodbury (Himself), Louis Quinn (Gus Kestler), Sammee Tong (Clyde), Addison Richards (Dean Watkins), Paul "Mousie" Garner (Mousie), Benny Baker (Lou), Anna Lee (Laura Pruitt), Sheila Bromley (Mrs. Harkness), Jack LaRue, Allen Jenkins, Robert Armstrong (Cronin's Business Associates), John Christopher, Mickey Dara, Byron Garner, Ian March, Michael Nader, Don Voyne, Gordon Westcourt, Larry Weston (College Boys), Edie Baskin, Laurie Burton, Pam Colbert, Lada Edmund, Marie Edmund, Linda Feldman, Lara Hale, Susan Hart, Jan March, Maureen O'Hanlan, Leslie Perkins, Donna Russell, Maria White (College Girls), Harry Antrim (45th Anniversary Husband), Eleanor Audley (45th Anniversary Wife), Byron Kane (Reporter), Alberto Morin (Marion, the Butler), George Raft (Detective), Roger Smith (Smitty, the Detective).

Credits: Director: Leslie H. Martinson; Producer: Hugh Benson; Executive Producer: Howard W. Koch; Assistant Director: Arthur Jacobson; Assistant Producer: Red Doff; Dialogue Coach: Alberto Morin; Original Story: Dan Beaumont; Screenplay: James and George O'Hanlon; Script Supervisor: Dolores Rubin; Photography: Harold E. Stine; Editor: Frank P. Keller; Score: Jerry Fielding; Choreographer: Robert Tucker; Art Direction: Arthur Lonergan, Hal Pereira; Sound Editor: Howard Beals; Sound Recorders: Hugo Grenzbach, John Wilkinson; Costumes: Grace Harris; Makeup: Wally Westmore. Released by United Artists in June 1964. Color. 93 minutes.

Synopsis: College students Ding Pruitt and Sandy Palmer fall in love. Along with their fellow students they live for sun, sand and surf. When not at the beach, they spend their time at a comedy and musical club, Surfs Up, run by Sandy's uncles, Sid and Woody. Ding is the grandson of a major sponsor of the college, B.S. Cronin, who does not consider Sandy worthy of Ding. College faculty member Pauline Swanson goes into the club to make a report to shut it down, but her report is unsatisfactory and indeed she falls for Woody. Incensed, Cronin plots to plant evidence of underage drinking and gambling in the club and arranges for a police raid. Sid and Woody are arrested. An old newsreel shows that Cronin himself was a bootlegger during Prohibition. The tables are turned, the lovers are reunited and the club remains open. Towards the end of the film, when the police raid the Surfs Up club, their leader turns out to be a detective played by George Raft. He enters the place and has a short, sharp exchange with another detective played by Roger Smith. Raft's one scene lasts only a couple of minutes.

Comments: This was the only time that Raft was directed by Leslie H. Martinson. This film was a curio from a bygone era, contrived and derivative. Any similarity to real life in the pre-flower power, pre–Vietnam era was purely coincidental. The college kids depicted as being so "with it" in this film were in actuality very conservative by contemporary standards. It had quite a lot of veteran talent on board. Raft and Roger Smith were uncredited in the film probably because the credits were prepared before they signed contracts to appear. This film basically functioned as a long commercial for Pepsi Cola. Even the title of the film was a direct quote from a catchphrase used in Pepsi radio and television commercials of the early 1960s. There were blatant product placements throughout the film, notably a huge Pepsi dispensing machine placed directly in the center of several shots in the nightclub bar.

Biography: Leslie H. Martinson was born in Boston, Massachusetts, on January 16, 1915. He was educated at Boston University and Boston Conservatory of Music. He worked in the advertising department of a newspaper before going to Hollywood in 1936 and working as a script clerk at MGM for fifteen years. He left MGM in 1952 to direct for television and subsequently directed numerous episodes of popular series. He also directed some lightweight feature films. He is married to Connie Frye Martinson, a well-known television host.

The Patsy (1964)

Cast: Jerry Lewis (Stanley Belt), Ina Balin (Ellen Betz), Everett Sloane (Caryl Ferguson), Phil Harris (Chic Wymore), Keenan Wynn (Harry Silver), Peter Lorre (Morgan Heywood), John Carradine (Bruce Alden), Hans Conried (Professor Mulerr), Richard Deacon (Sy Devore), "Scatman" Crothers (Shoeshine Boy), Del Moore (Policeman), Neil Hamilton (The Barber), Buddy Lester (Copa Cafe M.C.), Nancy Kulp (Helen), Lloyd Thaxton (Himself), Norman Alden (Bully at the Gym), Jack Albertson (Theatergoer with Helen), Henry

Slate (Paul), Gavin Gordon (Executive on Golf Course), Phil Foster (Mayo Sloan), Clyde Adler (Bald Man), Phil Arnold (Bartender), Richard Bakalyan (Boy at Spring Hop), Ned Wynn, Bob Denver, Billy Beck (Band Members), Billy Bletcher (Table Captain #3 at Italian Café), Murray Alper, Don Brodie (Bowlers), Robert Carson (Table Captain #2 at Italian Café), Chick Chandler (Hedda Hopper's Escort), Harry Cheshire (Police Sergeant), Robert Christian (Barbershop Porter), Isabelle Dwan, Adele Claire (Elderly Ladies), Jerome Cowan (Business Executive), Lorraine Crawford (Manicurist), Fay De Witt (Woman at Party), Jerry Dexter (Man), John Dexter (Radio Newscaster), Jerry Dunphy (TV Newscaster), William Enge (Barbershop Porter), Herbie Faye (Tailor), Fritz Feld (Maitre D'), Joel Finnegan (Reporter at Party), Marlene Maddox, Joanne C. Quakenbush, Nancy Patricia Fisher, Marianne Gaba (Waitresses), Kathleen Freeman (Katie), John Gallaudet (Barney), Richard Gehman (Reporter at Party), Bob Harvey (Waiter), Jerry Hausner (Floorman), Robert Ivers (Boy at Spring Hop), Bobby Jordan, Joey Johnson (Barbershop Porters), Byron Kane (Table Captain #1 at Italian Café), Norman Leavitt (Newsboy), William Leyden (TV Announcer), David Lipp (Frozen Store Man), Darlene Lucht (Checkroom Girl), John Macchia (Student), Michael Mahney (Copa Café Heckler), John Marlowe (Waiter), Dee Jay Mattis (The Broad), Bob May (Fireworks Boy), Peggy Mondo, Barbara Pepper (Bowlers), Mantan Moreland (Barbershop Porter), Hollis Morrison (Juke Box), Terry Naylor (Barbershop Customer), Quinn O'Hara (Cigarette Girl), Sherwood Price (Bellboy), Sheila Rogers (Woman at Party), Michael Ross (Truck Driver), Benny Rubin (Waiter #1 at Italian Café), Eddie Ryder (Man at Party), Ernest Schworck (Man), Vernon Scott (Himself), June Smaney (Pedicurist), Mabel Smaney (Woman in Phone Booth), Walter Smith (Barbershop Porter), Harry Spear (Salesman), Anthony Spinelli (Man on the Phone), Joe Stabil (Lead Musician), Ed Sullivan (Himself), Joan Swift (Girl), William Wellman, Jr. (Band Member), Edward C. Widdis (Man), Dave Willock (Alec). Guest Stars: Rhonda Fleming, Hedda Hopper, George Raft, The Step Brothers, Mel Tormé, Ed Wynn (Themselves).

Credits: Director: Jerry Lewis; Producer: Ernest D. Glucksman; Assistant Director: Ralph Axness; Associate Producer: Arthur P. Schmidt; Screenplay: Jerry Lewis and Bill Richmond; Photography: W. Wallace Kelley; Editor: John Woodcock; Music: David Raksin; Music in Silent Movie Sequence: Victor Young; Art Direction: Hal Pereira and Cary Odell; Sound Recorders: Hugo and Charles Grenzbach; Costumes: Edith Head; Makeup: Wally Westmore; Special Effects: Paul K. Lerpae. Song "I Lost My Heart in a Drive-In Movie": Lyrics by Jack Brooks, Music by David Raksin. Released by Paramount on August 12, 1964. Color. 97 minutes.

Synopsis: When comedian Wally Brantford is killed in a plane crash, his creative management team decide that if they want to retain their standard of living, they need a replacement fast. They accidentally encounter bellboy Stanley Belt whom they try to groom for stardom, leading to all kinds of mayhem. About fifteen minutes into the movie, George Raft does a silent bit: Lewis is in a men's store trying on some new clothes to go with his image. When asked which male movie star he most admires, he replies, "George Raft!" Stanley is fitted with a jacket, glances in a mirror and sees his idol. Raft performs a bit of a pantomime with Stanley and then walks past him, leaving Stanley amazed.

Comments: This was the second time that Raft appeared in a film starring and directed by Jerry Lewis.

Casino Royale (1967)

Cast: Peter Sellers (James Bond 007/Evelyn Tremble), Ursula Andress (Vesper Lynd), David Niven (Sir James Bond), Orson Welles (Le Chiffre), Joanna Pettet (Mata Bond), Daliah Lavi (The Detainer), Woody Allen (Jimmy Bond/Dr. Noah), Deborah Kerr (Agent Mimi/Lady Fiona McTarry), William Holden (Ransome), Charles Boyer (Le Grand), John Huston (M/McTarry), Kurt Kasznar (Smernov), George Raft (Himself), Jean-Paul Belmondo (French Legionnaire), Terence Cooper (Cooper), Barbara Bouchet (Moneypenny), Angela Scoular (Buttercup), Gabriella Licudi (Eliza), Tracey Crisp (Heather), Elaine Taylor (Peg), Jacky Bisset (Miss Goodthighs), Alexandra Bastedo (Meg), Anna Quayle (Frau Hoffner), Derek Nimmo (Hadley), Ronnie Corbett (Polo), Colin Gordon (Casino Director), Bernard Cribbins (Taxi Driver), Tracy Reed (Fong Leader), John Bluthal (Casino Doorman/M.I.5 Man), Geoffrey Bayldon (Q), John Wells (Q's Assistant), Duncan Macrae (Inspector Mathis), Graham Stark (Casino Cashier), Chic Murray (Chic), Jonathan Routh (John), Richard Wattis (British Army Officer), Vladek Sheybal (Le Chiffre's Representative), Percy Herbert (First Piper), Penny Riley (Control Girl), Jeane Roland (Captain of the Guards), Jennifer and Susan Baker (Le Chiffre's Assistants), R.S.M. Brittain (Sergeant Major), Erik Chitty (Sir James Bond's Butler), Frances Cosslett (Michele), Alexander Doré (Extra), Valentine Dyall (Vesper Lynd's Assistant/Dr. Noah's Voice), Veronica Gardnier (Bond Girl), Bob Godfrey (Scottish Strongman), John Hollis (Monk), Anjelica Huston (Agent Mimi's Hands), Burt Kwouk (Chinese General), John Le Mesurier (M's Driver), Yvonne Marsh (Bond Girl), David Lodge, Barrie Melrose (Men), Stirling Moss (Driver), Caroline Munro (Control Room Girl), Peter O'Toole (Piper), David Prowse (Frankenstein's Creature), Milton Reid (Temple Guard), Robert Rowland (M.I.5 Agent).

Credits: Directors: John Huston, Ken Hughes, Val Guest, Robert Parrish, Joseph McGrath; Producers: Charles K. Feldman, Jerry Bresler; Associate Producer: John Dark; Assistant Directors: Roy Baird, John Stoneman, Carl Mannin; Second Unit Directors: Anthony Squire and Richard Talmadge; Based on the Novel by Ian Fleming; Screenplay: Wolf Mankowitz, John Law and Michael Sayers; Photography: Jack Hildyard; Editor: Bill Lenny; Music: Burt Bacharach; Choreographer: Tutte Lemkow; Art Direction: John Howell, Ivor Beddoes, Lionel Couch; Sound Editor: Chris Greenham; Costumes: Julie Harris; Makeup: Neville Smallwood; Titles and Montage Effects: Richard Williams; Main Title Theme: Herb Alpert and the Tijuana Brass; Song "The Look of Love": Music: Burt Bacharach, Lyrics: Hal David, Singer: Dusty Springfield. Released by Columbia on April 28, 1967. Color. 131 minutes.

Synopsis: The original Sir James Bond is called back from retirement to stop SMERSH and Le Chiffre, whose gambling winnings support the villainous organization. Bond thinks up the ultimate plan namely that every agent will be called James Bond to confound the enemy. One of the Bonds, whose real name is Evelyn Tremble, is dispatched to take on Le Chiffre in a game of baccarat, but all the Bonds become involved in the action, especially when the head villain, Dr. Noah, turns out to be Bond's nephew, Jimmy Bond. Towards the end of the film Raft is shown flipping a coin. During a massive fight sequence which occupies the entire last part of the film, Raft is shown with a gun in his hand at the bar when a shot rings out. He gasps, "I've been framed. This gun shoots backwards. I've just shot myself!" before collapsing.

Comments: When this film was originally shown, many cinemagoers emerged from theaters warning those outside not to bother to see it. Since then it has been included on many lists of the worst films ever made. It was one of a number of surreal films which tried to capture the essence of the swinging sixties in London. Raft's scene was shot in a single day. He was lectured for a morning by a young director on how to play his part. When the scene was shot in the afternoon, he totally ignored

the advice, but played it with his customary professionalism. Ironically he was one of the few people to emerge from this farrago with any credit. Raft's only comment on this film was that he did not understand it. The film was very loosely reworked as *Casino Royale* (2006) with Daniel Craig borrowing the title and the story outline, but little else.

Rififi in Panama (aka *Du Rififi a Paname; Rififi in Paris; The Upper Hand*) (1967)

Cast: Jean Gabin (Paul Berger aka Paulo the Gems), George Raft (Charles Binnaggio), Gert Frobe (Walter), Nadja Tiller (Irene), Claudio Brook (Mike Coppolano), Mireille Darc (Lili Princesse), Claude Brasseur (Giulio), Daniel Ceccaldi (Commissioner Noel), Marcel Bozzuffi (Marque Mal), Jean-Claude Bercq (Jo le Pale), Dany Dauberson (Lea), Claude Cerval (René), Carlo Nell (Sergio), Christa Lang (Mario's daughter).

Credits: Screenplay and Director: Denys de La Patelliere; Producer: Maurice Jacquin; Executive Producer: Raymond Danon; Based on the Novel by Auguste Le Breton; Dialogue: Alphonse Boudard; Italian Dialogue: Franco Dal Cer; Photography: Walter Wottitz; Editor: Claude Durand; Music: George Garvarentz; Costumes: Jacques Fonteray. A co-production of Les Films Copernic, Paris; Gloria Film, Munich; and Fida Cinematografica, Rome. Released in France by Comacico on March 2, 1966 and in the U.S. by Paramount on July 26, 1967. Color. 93 minutes.

Synopsis: Two veteran Paris-based gangsters, Paul Berger and Walter, run an international gold smuggling ring. The situation is slightly complicated by the fact that Irene, Walter's wife, is a former mistress of Paul Berger. The success of their operation is based on using a number of different couriers in different countries. They recruit an unemployed journalist, Mike Coppolano, who pretends to need the money to fund a relationship with

Lili Princesse. In reality he is a C.I.A. agent whose mission is to find the link between the Parisian gangsters and the American Mafia headed by Charles Binnaggio. There is no existing link, but members of the American syndicate want to create one and begin to murder the French syndicate's couriers. Eventually they kill Walter. The American syndicate forces a meeting between the two sides at a Parisian hotel. At the second meeting the wily old smuggler Berger makes an excuse to exit the room, leaving behind a bomb which explodes, killing the Americans. He is apprehended and arrested by the police. When Coppolano congratulates Berger on the success of his operation, Berger knocks him cold.

Comments: This was the only time that Raft was directed by Denys de La Patelliere. On the French DVD release the dialogue is all spoken in French except when Raft appeared. He had such a distinctive voice that the dialogue in his scenes was all spoken in English with French subtitles. Raft made a late appearance: He was shown arriving at the airport and then later entering into some negotiations with Gabin. He was ignorant of the killings of the couriers and Walter which were masterminded by his underlings. When the bomb exploded, he was killed. The film did very well commercially. Raft and Gabin enjoyed working together so much that they intended to make other films, but nothing ever materialized and this was their only collaboration.

Biography: Denys de La Patelliere was born in Nantes, France, on March 8, 1921, and directed numerous films between 1955 and 1995.

Five Golden Dragons (1967)

Cast: Bob Cummings (Bob Mitchell), Margaret Lee (Magda), Rupert Davies (Commissioner Sanders), Klaus Kinski (Gert), Maria Rohm (Ingrid), Sieghardt Rupp (Peterson), Roy Chiao (Inspector Chiao), Dan Duryea, Brian Donlevy, George Raft, Christopher Lee (Dragons), Maria Perschy (Margret), Yukuri Ito (Guest Singer).

Credits: Director: Jeremy Summers; Producer: Harry Alan Towers; Executive Producer: Norman Williams; Assistant Director: Anthony Waye; Based on the Novel by Edgar Wallace; Screenplay: Peter Welbeck [Harry Alan Towers]; Photography: John von Kotze; Editor: Donald J. Cohen; Score: Malcolm Lockyer; Art Direction: Scott MacGregor; Sound Editor: Roy Piper. Songs "Five Golden Dragons" and "Time of Our Lives" by Malcolm Lockyer, Hal Shaper and Sid Colin, sung by Margaret Lee with the Voice of Domino. Production Company: Blansfilm. Released by Commonwealth United on August 4, 1967. Color. 104 minutes.

Synopsis: After American playboy Bob Mitchell receives a mysterious note with only the words "Five Golden Dragons" written on it, he is drawn into the intricate underground world of Hong Kong and becomes the prime suspect in the murder of Margret. He escapes from the police only to be entangled further in the web of secrecy surrounding "Five Golden Dragons" whose identities are unknown even to each other. They control the illicit trafficking of the world's gold. In order to organize a final sale to the Mafia, they must meet for the first time and Hong Kong is chosen as the rendezvous point.

The Dragons are shown arriving in Hong Kong by different routes and transport methods. Raft arrives by helicopter. His next scene involves the meeting of four of the Dragons, but wearing dragon masks and undergoing a test before they unmask. In the next scene in which they appear, a fifth Dragon has joined them; he fails the test and is killed. The police move in to rescue Mitchell and arrest the remaining Dragons.

Comments: This was the only time that Raft was directed by Jeremy Summers. The film was produced by Harry Alan Towers who made some colorful thrillers during this period, often set against an exotic backdrop and filled with beautiful girls. Bob Cummings was a liability in this film because he played it as a comedy despite the threats to his life. This lethargic film worked better as a travelogue for Hong Kong than it did as a thriller. The film had little action and several sequences were unnecessarily protracted. One twist in the plot near the end came as a genuine surprise. Although Raft's role was small, he was integral to the plot. He had less dialogue than some of the other Dragons, but was present in the last few scenes of the film.

Biography: Jeremy Summers, the son of director Walter Summers, was born in St. Albans, Hertfordshire, England, in 1931. He shot a number of international films and was active between 1960 and 1999.

Skidoo (1968)

Cast: Jackie Gleason (Tony Banks), Carol Channing (Flo Banks), Frankie Avalon (Angie), Fred Clark (Tower Guard), Michael Constantine (Leech), Frank Gorshin (The Man), John Phillip Law (Stash), Peter Lawford (The Senator), Groucho Marx (God), Burgess Meredith (The Warden), George Raft (Captain Garbaldo), Cesar Romero (Hecky), Mickey Rooney (George "Blue Chips" Packard), Arnold Stang (Harry), Doro Merande (The Mayor), Phil Arnold (Mayor's Husband), Slim Pickens, Robert Donner (Switchboard Operators), Richard Kiel (Beany), Tom Law (Geronimo), Jaik Rosenstein ("Eggs" Benedict), Stacy King (The Amazon), Renny Roker, Roman Gabriel (Prison Guards), Harry Nilsson (Tower Guard), Austin Pendleton (Fred, the Professor), Alexandra Hay (Darlene Banks), Donyale Luna (God's Mistress).

Credits: Director and Producer: Otto Preminger; Casting: Erik Kirkland [Erik Lee Preminger]; Screenplay: Doran William Cannon; Photography: Leon Shamroy; Editor: George R. Rohrs; Music: Harry Nilsson; Musical Director: George Aliceson Tipton; Art Direction: Robert Emmet Smith; Costumes: Rudi Gern-

reich; Makeup: Web Overlander; Special Effects: Charles Spurgeon; Titles: Sandy Dvore. Released by Paramount on December 19, 1968. Color and Black and white. 97 minutes.

Tagline: "It takes two to Skidoo!"

Synopsis: Tony Banks is a retired gangster turned businessman who lives with his wife Flo and daughter Darlene, but has an acrimonious relationship with both. He particularly objects to his daughter's infatuation with hippie Stash. Tony is visited by fellow gangster Hecky, who insists on Tony accepting an order from lead gangster, God, to eliminate "Blue Chips" Packard, who is in a maximum security prison preparing to turn state's evidence. Tony is reluctant to do this, but when his wife and daughter are threatened, he capitulates. He allows himself to be taken to the same prison without telling his wife and daughter where he is. Darlene and Stash go to visit God to persuade him to cancel Tony's mission. Instead they are kidnapped aboard God's luxury yacht. Tony finds that he cannot go through with the hit and escapes from the prison hospital via hot air balloon. Eventually the balloon is shot down and lands on God's yacht. The yacht is invaded by hippies. Tony is reconciled with his wife and daughter. God escapes and is last seen embracing the hippie culture. In a few scenes as the captain of God's yacht, Raft exchanged some dialogue with Groucho Marx, was seen ordering his men to fire at the balloon and the hippies, and performed a marriage ceremony. At this wedding service, his manual was clearly seen as "The Death of God."

Comments: *Skidoo* was the first and only time that Raft was directed by Otto Preminger. It was a truly embarrassing comedy which was very reflective of its era. It showed how mainstream Hollywood could not come to terms with the hippie culture. It is frequently included by film buffs on lists of the worst films ever made. Its natural running time was artificially extended by two pointless LSD sequences involving drugs, hippies and free love.

Biography: Otto Preminger was born in

Wiznitz, Bukovina, Austria-Hungary (now Ukraine), on December 5, 1905. The son of a successful lawyer, he graduated with a law degree from the University of Vienna. He was more interested in the theater and he became assistant to Max Reinhardt. Later he went to Zurich as an actor and stage director. He returned to Vienna and founded a small theater there before becoming involved with films. After directing several Austrian talkies, he was summoned by Joseph Schenck to direct in Hollywood in 1936. He directed two Hollywood films, spent two years directing and producing stage plays and for a time was attached to the Drama School of Yale University. In 1942 he was brought back to Hollywood by 20th Century–Fox to play Nazis. He was allowed to direct Fox's *Laura* (1944), a huge commercial and critical success which garnered him a Best Director Oscar nomination. Between 1943 and 1952 he directed a number of films for Fox. In 1953 he turned independent producer and directed a number of prestigious, but increasingly elephantine movies, some of which were successes while others were total turkeys. He was also received a Best Director Oscar nomination for *The Cardinal* (1963). His bombast and cruelty led to him being detested by many of the players whom he directed. He died in his New York City apartment on April 23, 1986, aged 80, of cancer.

Deadhead Miles (1972)

Cast: Alan Arkin (Cooper), Donna Anderson (Waitress), Madison Arnold (Hostler), Paul Benedict (Tramp), Bruce Bennett (Johnny Mesquitero), Oliver Clark (Durazno), Patrick Dennis-Leigh (Loader), William Duell (Auto Parts Salesman), Charles Durning (Red Ball Rider), Hector Elizondo (Bad Character), Allen Garfield (Juicy Brucey), Barnard Hughes (Old Man), Philip Kenneally (State Trooper), Richard Kiel (Big Dick), Bill Littleton (Chicken Farmer), Bill McCutcheon (Used Car Dealer), John Milius (Second State Trooper), Sue Carol Perry

(Woman Tramp), John Quade (Spud Holder), Dan Resin (Foreman), Avery Schreiber (The Boss), Diane Shalet (Donna James), John Steadman (Old Sam), Loretta Swit (Woman with Glass Eye), Tom Waters (Truck Driver), Larry Wolf (Pineapple), Ida Lupino (Wife at Gas Station), George Raft (Husband at Gas Station).

Credits: Director: Vernon Zimmerman; Producers: Tony Bill and Vernon Zimmerman; Associate Producer: John Prizer; Screenplay: Terrence Malick; Photography: Ralph Woolsey; Editors: Danford B. Greene, George Hively, Eva Newman and Bud S. Smith; Music: Dave Dudley and Tom T. Hall; Art Direction: Spencer Quinn; Sound Recorder: Charles T. Knight; Costumes: Richard Bruno. Released by Paramount. Color. 84 minutes.

Synopsis: Cooper is party to the hijacking of a Peterbilt eighteen-wheeler which he then proceeds to steal from the thieves. Along the way he picks up a hitchhiker named Tramp who later unsuccessfully tries to rob him. They have various minor adventures including eluding the cops and encountering a ghostly trucker clad in black. Eventually Cooper leaves the rig behind and takes a hitchhike to nowhere. In the early scene at a gas station where Cooper steals the rig after locking his confederate in a toilet, the confederate escapes and gives chase in a stolen car. The car in question belongs to an apparently affluent older couple played by George Raft and Ida Lupino billed as special appearances. They utter some abuse at the disappearing thief.

Comments: This was the only time Raft was directed by Vernon Zimmerman. Raft and Lupino did cameos in this film because *They Drive by Night* (1940), in which they previously appeared together, was one of producer Tony Bill's favorite films. Shelved by the studio, this was an aimless film. Alan Arkin was recently asked why this film was not generally released, to which he replied, "Because it wasn't any good. It was a weird road movie with completely insane characters." Arkin was impressive, but there is only so much a good actor can do when faced with a script as poor as this one. Oddly, the film did have elements which might have made a decent film such as Johnny Mesquitero, apparently a ghostly trucker in black played by Bruce Bennett, whose role should have been expanded. "Deadhead Miles" is a trucker's expression for driving a semi with no load in the trailer. Ironically, Arkin's character did carry a load in the trailer in this film.

Biography: Vernon Zimmerman was a writer and director of some offbeat films. He currently lives in Los Angeles, works as a script analyst and teaches screenwriting courses at UCLA.

Hammersmith Is Out (1972)

Cast: Elizabeth Taylor (Jimmie Jean Jackson), Richard Burton (Hammersmith), Peter Ustinov (Doctor), Beau Bridges (Billy Breedlove), Leon Ames (General Sam Pembroke), Leon Askin (Dr. Krodt), George Raft (Guido Scartucci), John Schuck (Henry Joe), Marjorie Eaton (Princess), Lisa Jak (Kiddo), Linda Gaye Scott (Miss Quinn), Mel Berger (Fat Man), Anthony Holland (Oldham), Brook Williams (Pete Rutter), Carl Donn (Cleopatra), José Espinoza (Duke), Stan Ross (Patient).

Credits: Director: Peter Ustinov; Producer: Alex Lucas; Executive Producer: Frank Beetson; Assistant Director: Newton Arnold; Production Assistant: Brook Williams; Screenplay: Stanford Whitmore; Photography: Richard H. Kline; Editor: David Blewitt; Music: Dominic Frontiere; Production Designer: Robert Benton; Costumes: Edith Head; Makeup: Ron Berkeley. Production Company: J. Cornelius Crean Inc. Released by Cinerama Releasing Corporation on May 12, 1972. Color. 100 minutes.

Synopsis: With the aid of a dim-witted psychiatric nurse Billy Breedlove, psychopathic murderer Hammersmith escapes from an asylum. They link up with waitress Jimmie Jean Jackson. By successively murdering people they acquire a topless bar, a pharmaceutical factory and an oil empire. Later they support a puppet politician who is elected president of the United States. When Billy falls out with Jimmie Jean, he insists Hammersmith murder her. Instead Hammersmith gets her pregnant and causes an accident which paralyzes Billy, subsequently leading him to shoot himself. When the leading doctor from the asylum arrives at a castle, the headquarters of Hammersmith's empire, Hammersmith willingly goes back to the asylum with him.

Early in the film, Raft as Guido Scartucci turns up as master of ceremonies and part owner of a topless bar which Hammersmith aspires to own. Hammersmith insists on meeting him the following day at the top of a building where he claims to be a resident. He tells Scartucci to come alone and bring along the deed to the bar. When Scartucci appears at the rendezvous, he is quickly thrown out of the top storey window and lands dead in his own car.

Comments: This was the only time that Raft was directed by Peter Ustinov. This appallingly bad film defied all genres and was in thoroughly bad taste. This was Richard Burton and Elizabeth Taylor's last of nine films together. Raft's appearance was brief. It was incredible that a character as streetwise as Raft would arrive without bodyguards at such a dangerous rendezvous.

Biography: Peter Ustinov was born Peter Alexander Freiherr von Ustinov in London on April 16, 1921, the son of a journalist father of Russian descent and an artist mother of French descent. He trained for the stage at the London Theatre Studio and made his stage acting debut in 1938. He made his screen bow in 1940 and went on to become an outstanding star character actor, writer and director. He won Best Supporting Actor Oscars for *Spartacus* (1960) and *Topkapi* (1964). He was married to Isolde Denham, Suzanne Cloutier and (from 1972 onwards) Helene du Lau d'Allemans. He died on March 28, 2004, aged 82, of heart failure at a clinic near his home by Lake Geneva, Switzerland.

Sextette (1979)

Cast: Mae West (Marlo Manners aka. Lady Barrington), Timothy Dalton (Sir Michael Barrington), Dom De Luise (Dan Turner), Tony Curtis (Alexei Karansky), Ringo Starr (Laslo Karolny), George Hamilton (Vance Norton), Keith Moon (Dress Designer), Rona Barrett, Regis Philbin (Themselves), Walter Pidgeon (Mr. Chambers, the Chairman), George Raft, Gil Stratton (Themselves), Ed Beheler (President Jimmy Carter), Van McCoy (Delegate), Harry Weiss (The Don).

Credits: Director: Ken Hughes; Producers: Daniel Briggs and Robert Sullivan; Executive Producers: Warren G. Toub and Don Henderson; Dialogue Director: Irving Rapper; Associate Producer: Harry Weiss; Based on a Play by Mae West; Screenplay: Herbert Baker; Photography: James Crabe; Editor: Argyle Nelson; Music: Artie Butler; Additional Music: Van McCoy; Choreographer: Marc Breaux; Art Direction: James Clayton; Costumes: Edith Head. Released by Crown International in July 1979. Color. 91 minutes.

Synopsis: Marlo Manners, actress and covert worker for the State Department, marries her sixth husband, Sir Michael Barrington, in London. In the same hotel, an international trade conference is taking place. The Russian delegate, Alexei Karansky, is threatening to vote against the agreement unless he can have one more liaison with Marlo. Marlo has also made a tape of her projected memoirs containing intimate details of her various marriages and affairs which both her manager and her fifth husband, gangster Vance Norton, are seeking to locate and destroy. Raft, playing himself, encounters old flame Marlo in an elevator in the hotel. They exchange some banter and then part company. His cameo appearance lasts only a minute.

Comments: This was the only time that

Raft was directed by Ken Hughes. This incredibly poor film was allegedly privately financed by one of Mae West's fans. West and Raft had previously appeared together in *Night After Night* (1932) when both were close to the peak of their game.

Biography: Ken Hughes was born in Liverpool, England, on January 19, 1922. He started in the film industry as a cinema projectionist and later worked as a BBC sound engineer. During army service he was assigned to a unit making training films and learned the craft of filmmaking. Upon being demobbed he began directing documentaries and shorts. He started directing feature films in 1952, initially B movies with American leads. His direction of *The Trials of Oscar Wilde* (1960) led to him enjoying a decade of more prestigious assignments, but his career nosedived during the seventies and by the eighties he was virtually out of films altogether. He died in Panorama City, California, on April 28, 2001, aged 79, of complications from Alzheimer's disease.

The Man with Bogart's Face (aka *Sam Marlow, Private Eye*) (1980)

Cast: Robert Sacchi (Sam Marlow), Franco Nero (Hakim), Michelle Phillips (Gena), Olivia Hussey (Elsa Borscht), Misty Rowe (Duchess, Marlow's Secretary), Victor Buono (Commadore Alexander Anastas), Herbert Lom (Mr. Zebra), Sybil Danning (Cynthia Ashley/Lena Z.), Dick Bakalyan (Detective Lt. Bumbera), Gregg Palmer (Detective Sgt. Hacksaw), Jay Robinson (Wolf Zinderneuf), Joe Theismann (Jock), Aleshia Brevard (Mother), Buck Kartalian (Nicky), Peter Mamakos (Spoony Singh), Martin Kosleck (Horst Borsht), Philip Baker Hall (Dr. Inman), Mike Masters (Hulio), Larry Pennell (George), Kathleen Bracken (Mona), Ed McCready (Garbage Man), Alan Foster (Driver), Rozelle Gayle (Mastodon), Bill Catching (Nero's Uncle), Everett Creach

(Buster), Wally Rose, Ralph Carpenter (Gunmen), James Bacon, Frank Barron, Marilyn Beck, Robert Osborne, Will Tusher, Dick Whittington (Reporters). Special Appearances: George Raft (Petey Cane), Yvonne De Carlo (Theresa Anastas), Mike Mazurki (Driver), Henry Wilcoxon (Chevalier, Bookseller), Victor Sen Yung (Mr. Wing).

Credits: Director: Robert Day; Producer, Screenplay and Original Novel: Andrew J. Fenady; Executive Producer: Melvin Simon; Production Manager and Associate Producer: Eddie Saeta; Assistant Directors: David McGiffert and Rafael Elortegui; Photography: Richard C. Glouner; Editor: Houseley Stevenson, Jr., Music: George Duning; Production Designer: Robert Kinoshita. Songs "The Man With Bogart's Face" and "Looking at You": Music by George Duning and Lyrics by Andrew J. Fenady. Released by 20th Century–Fox on October 3, 1980. Color. 106 minutes.

Synopsis: Sam Marlow has his face altered by plastic surgery to resemble Humphrey Bogart. He opens a private detective agency in Hollywood and is hired to find a pair of enormous sapphires called "The Eyes of Alexander." Along the way he encounters various people in pursuit of the same jewels. This leads to a climax off Catalina Island. Fairly early on, Marlow is hired by Gena to accompany her to a nightclub where blackmailer Petey Cane (Raft) is holding compromising photos of her. Marlow is told to wait outside, but muscles his way in. There he encounters Cane and exchanges some tough talk before knocking him unconscious and retrieving the photographs.

Comments: This was the only time that Raft was directed by Robert Day. The budget was $3,500,000 and the shooting schedule was forty days. It was a hardboiled thriller with a complex plot and multiple characters. It remains a highly watchable film with a uniformly excellent cast. Andrew Fenady recalled, "Everything was going along beautifully. Mel Simon

Productions bankrolled the picture and I brought it in under budget. Then 20th Century–Fox said they would distribute it.... A new regime came in over there ... and the picture was torpedoed ... they completely mishandled it.... The whole thing just went in the crapper. Despite that, it was a rewarding picture to do."

Sybil Danning recalled, "This was a fun film. George Raft was a legend in his own lifetime and he lived up to the legend. He took us all out for a day at Santa Anita Racetrack where we all had a fabulous time." Fenady further recalled, "I went and had lunch with Raft. He lived in Beverly Hills and we went to the Brown Derby in Beverly Hills. He had read the script and he just loved it, so he said, 'Sure, sure I'll do it.' It was one day, one scene ... I rented space at MGM. All of a sudden there were more people on that set and on that stage. It was all the executives, secretaries, producers and directors who were on the lot who came down and wanted to see George Raft." This was Raft's final film and a good one to go out on.

Biography: Robert Day was born in Sheen, England, on September 11, 1922. He entered British films in 1938 as a camera assistant and became a director of photography during the forties. He directed his first feature film in 1955 and went on to helm some lightweight films and dozens of television episodes, many of them in Hollywood. From 1969 until her death in 2010 he was married to actress Dorothy Provine. At last report he was living in Bainbridge Island, Washington State.

George Raft also appeared in the following shorts:

1933: *Hollywood on Parade*
1934: *The Fashion Side of Hollywood*
1937: *Screen Snapshots* series 16 and 17
1938: *Screen Snapshots* series 18
1941: *Meet the Stars: Stars at Play*
1949: *Screen Snapshots: Vacation at Del Mar*

OTHER FILM APPEARANCES

Gold Diggers of Broadway (1929)

This is a lost musical film, a few fragments of which still exist. Directed by Roy Del Ruth for Warner Bros., the story concerns three showgirls searching for rich husbands. Raft may have appeared as a dancer in it.

Love Is a Racket (1932)

This film was directed by William Wellman for Warner Bros. Raft was cast in the small role of a crook named Sneaky, but his scenes were deleted before the film was released.

Two Guys Abroad (1962)

Synopsis: Two nightclub owners are constantly in trouble.

Comments: Director Don Sharp recalls, "*Two Guys Abroad* was made in March 1962 at Shepperton Studios, England, for producer Ian Warren's Summit Films. At that time there was a fashion for these 'products.' They were made for a double purpose: as a pilot episode for a possible TV series; if that failed, for release as a B movie supporting the main feature. Very few of them even made the grade.

"I got on very well with George — the complete Hollywood pro. He was amiable, always ribbing Maxie [Rosenbloom, his co-star]; constantly doing his coin-flipping act; and likely at any moment to break into a few dance steps — for no particular reason. There is a photo of me and my camera operator on the camera dolly with George doing the grip's job of pushing it because, he said, he always wanted to do a real job." Diana Decker and Diane Todd also appeared in the film.

Biography: Don Sharp was born in Hobart, Tasmania, on April 19, 1922. From 1945 to 1948 he was an actor in Australia. From 1948 to 1949 he was an actor in England. He spent 1950 to 1951 in hospital. In 1952 he entered the film industry initially as a scriptwriter and then as a director, which he remained for decades, most productively for Hammer Films. He also directed many television episodes. He was married to actress Mary Steele. Sharp lived for many years in Cornwall where he died on December 18, 2011, aged 89.

Silent Treatment (1968)

In this curious film produced and directed by Ralph Andrews using the silent film technique, Raft allegedly had a cameo, but since the film was never released this has been impossible to verify.

The Great Sex War (aka *Make Love Not War*) (1969)

In this oddity directed by Norman Foster in Mexico, Raft allegedly had a cameo. Since the film has never been released, this has been impossible to verify.

MISCELLANEA

Paramount Years (1932–1939)

No Man of Her Own (1932)

Raft was considered for the role of Babe Stewart, which was ultimately played by Clark Gable.

The Story of Temple Drake (1933)

Raft rejected the role of Trigger partly because the character was a heartless villain who raped the heroine and partly because he did not want to work with Miriam Hopkins again. He was replaced by Jack LaRue. The film was panned by critics and did not do well at the box office so this was one of the few occasions when Raft's judgment was reckoned to be sound.

Belle of the Nineties (1934)

Raft rejected the role of Tiger Kid opposite Mae West in this film (originally titled *It Ain't No Sin*) because he claimed the script favored her rather than himself. Roger Pryor replaced Raft.

It's a Pleasure to Lose (1934)

This was a projected film about Nick the Greek, a famous bookie, in which Raft was set to play the lead. It was never made.

R.U.R. (1934)

This was a projected film derived from writer Karel Capek's play about robots, but it was abandoned. Raft was slated to star.

Hold 'Em Yale (1935)

Raft was cast in this footballing story, but was replaced by Cesar Romero.

The Princess Comes Across (1936)

Raft was cast in the role of King Mantell opposite Carole Lombard. He left the production after he claimed that cameraman Ted Tetzlaff was favoring her, and he was replaced by Fred MacMurray. When Tetzlaff became a director, he helmed two Raft movies. *Johnny Allegro* (1949) and *A Dangerous Profession* (1949).

Dead End (1937)

Sam Goldwyn wanted to borrow Raft from Paramount for the role of "Baby Face" Martin in this prestigious film. Raft rejected the role, which was then played by Humphrey Bogart.

Caviar for His Excellency (1937)

Raft was offered this after *Souls at Sea*, but rejected it.

Stolen Heaven (1938)

Raft rejected the lead in this minor film, originally titled *Dream of Love* and *Strange Fascination*, opposite his *Souls at Sea* co-star Olympe Bradna, but was replaced by Gene Raymond. This film made very little impact.

Argentina Love (1939)

Raft was offered the leading role opposite Dorothy Lamour or Carole Lombard in this dance film. He declined the part. The film was never made.

The Magnificent Fraud (1939)

Raft rejected a secondary role in this minor film partly because he disliked the gangster he was assigned to play and partly because it was not a prestige film. He was replaced by Lloyd Nolan.

Beau Geste (1939)

Raft was under serious consideration for an unspecified role in this adventure classic. Some sources state that he rejected it, but this seems unlikely. In the released version of the film, none of the roles seemed remotely suitable for him.

St. Louis Blues (1939)

Raft rejected the role of Dave Guerney opposite Dorothy Lamour. The part was subsequently played by Lloyd Nolan.

Warner Bros. Years (1939–1943)

The Dealer's Name Was George

Whenever a rival studio wanted to borrow Raft for a film throughout his Warners years and Jack Warner did not feel like lending him, the reason given was because the studio wanted him to appear in a film with this title. In fact, this was a phantom film. The script was not written and the film was never made.

Dillinger (1939)

Warner Bros. announced that Raft would play the lead in a biopic of the famed criminal, but then never made such a film.

A Free Soul (1940)

At the time when Raft was going out with Norma Shearer, MGM announced plans to co-star them in a remake of their 1931 film. Nothing came of it.

The World We Make (1940)

Again during the Raft–Norma Shearer romance, MGM announced that they would star in this film, which again was never made.

'Til We Meet Again (1940)

Warner Bros. announced a remake of *One Way Passage* to star Raft and Norma Shearer. When the film was made, it co-starred George Brent and Merle Oberon.

The Patent Leather Kid (1940)

The original film made in 1927 starring Richard Barthelmess was one of Raft's favorites and he tried to interest Warners in a remake. According to some sources this was set to be made, but by this time Raft was too fat to fit into boxing trunks and the production was abandoned.

Two Sons (1940)

After the huge success of *Each Dawn I Die*, Raft was offered this film which would have given him the opportunity to work with James Cagney again. After reading the script, Raft declined the part because it was so subordinate to that of Cagney.

South of Suez (1940)

Raft rejected the role of John Gamble and was replaced by George Brent. Watching the released film, it is very hard to imagine Raft in the part.

City for Conquest (1940)

When Raoul Walsh was set to direct this boxing melodrama, Raft was offered the role of Murray Burns. When Walsh was instead assigned to *High Sierra*, director Anatole Litvak was substituted. Raft rejected the role and was replaced by Anthony Quinn.

Blues in the Night (1941)

Raft rejected the role of Jigger Pine which was subsequently played by Richard Whorf.

The Sea Wolf (1941)

Edward G. Robinson was assigned the role of Captain Wolf Larsen. Raft rejected the role of George Leach. According to a telegram dated October 23, 1940, from Raft to Hal B. Wallis, "You told me in your office that it would be a fifty fifty part. I am sorry to say it is just the opposite.... [T]his is just a little better than a bit." Wallis replied by telegram (October 23, 1940), "It is the kind of part you have been wanting to play namely the romantic lead in a good, gutty picture. You are not a heavy and you get the girl." The role of Leach was subsequently played by John Garfield.

High Sierra (1941)

Raft rejected the role of Roy "Mad Dog" Earle because the character was a vicious gangster who died at the end. The part was subsequently played by Humphrey Bogart in the film directed by Raoul Walsh, which was a box office hit. According to scriptwriter W.R. Burnett, Bogart talked Raft out of appearing in it because he argued the part of Earle did not suit Raft.

The Maltese Falcon (1941)

Raft rejected the role of private investigator Sam Spade on the advice of his agent Myron Selznick. The film was budgeted as a B picture; the story had been filmed twice before and had twice flopped; and Raft felt that he could not entrust his talent to a first-time director like John Huston. Sam Spade was then played by Humphrey Bogart and the film became a clas-

sic. In a letter dated June 6, 1941, to Jack Warner, Raft wrote, "I strongly feel that *The Maltese Falcon* which you want me to do, is not an important picture." Raft had obviously forgotten that *The Glass Key* (derived from a novel by the same author, Dashiell Hammett) had been one of his most successful films of the thirties. If Raft had accepted *The Maltese Falcon*, it is highly unlikely it would have become a classic because Huston tended to judge actors on their capacity for drink. He and Bogart had a rapport because they were drinking buddies. Raft practiced total abstinence.

I Wake Up Screaming (aka Hot Spot) (1941)

Twentieth Century–Fox entered into negotiations to borrow Raft for the role of Frankie Christopher. It is uncertain whether Raft rejected the role or if negotiations broke down, but Victor Mature ended up playing the part in this film noir which is more highly regarded now than at the time.

All Through the Night (1942)

Raft rejected the role of Gloves Donahue which was subsequently played by Humphrey Bogart. This is reckoned to be the last time Raft turned down a role and Bogart stepped in.

Juke Girl (1942)

Raft was assigned the role of Steve Talbot, but he so disliked the part that he did not even show up on the set for work and was replaced by Ronald Reagan.

The Mayor of 44th Street (1942)

RKO entered into negotiations to borrow Raft for this odd amalgam of crime and music, but he rejected the role of Joe Jonathan which was subsequently played by George Murphy.

Casablanca (1943)

Contrary to popular belief, Raft did not reject the role of Rick Blaine in *Casablanca*. He was nixed from the project in an exchange of memoranda dated April 1942. On April 2, Jack Warner sent a memo to Hal B. Wallis which stated, "What do you think of using Raft in *Casablanca*? He knows we are going to make this and is starting a campaign for it." On April 13, Wallis replied, "I have thought over very carefully the matter of George Raft in *Casablanca* and I have discussed this with Mike Curtiz, and we both feel that he should not be in the picture. Bogart is ideal for it and it is being written for him and I think we should forget Raft for this property." In later years Raft liked to say that he had rejected *Casablanca*, presumably because it gave him a feeling of power.

Independent Years (1943–1980)

Double Indemnity (1944)

Raft was offered the role of Walter Neff, which he rejected. Allegedly 28 actors in total rejected the part before Fred MacMurray reluctantly accepted it. As director Billy Wilder later said, "It was when George Raft turned it down, we knew we had a good movie."

Unnamed Paramount Project (1944)

There was some discussion of Raft returning to Paramount to do a film in which he played a Roman Catholic priest who befriends a delinquent boy. The film was never made, allegedly because the theme was too similar to *Going My Way* (1944) with Bing Crosby.

Hoodlum Empire (1951)

Republic offered Raft $150,000 to play racketeer Frank Costello in a biopic, but Raft rejected the role because he knew Costello personally. The script was subsequently completely rewritten.

The Big Heat (1953)

Columbia offered Raft $150,000 to play racketeer Mike Lagana in this classic crime drama. He rejected the role and was replaced by Alexander Scourby.

The Miami Story (1954)

Columbia offered Raft the role of gangster Tony Brill in this B film. He initially accepted it but then backed out, allegedly because the Mob disapproved. He was replaced by Luther Adler.

Morning Call (aka *The Strange Case of Dr. Manning*) (1957)

Raft rejected the role of Nick Logan in this obscure British thriller and was replaced by Ron Randell. He was offered and accepted another script, *Women of the Night*, but he was refused a work permit to shoot this film in England. It was never made.

Earl of Chicago (1963)

Raft announced plans to direct an English remake of a 1940 MGM film which starred Robert Montgomery. Nothing came of it.

Robbery (1967)

Raft was offered a small role in this thriller about the British Great Train Robbery, which was to be shot entirely in England. But Raft was banned from the country before he could shoot his scenes.

Madigan's Millions (1967)

Raft was offered the title role as a dying gangster in this Italian film produced by

Sidney Pink, but failed to show up on the set and was replaced by Cesar Romero. Some sources still erroneously credit him with an appearance in it. It is understood that legal problems and conflicting schedules caused by the Colony Club debacle prevented him from appearing.

Don't Make Waves (1967)

Raft was offered a cameo in this poor film which starred Tony Curtis, but it is understood that the legal problems stemming from the Colony Club involvement prevented him from appearing.

TELEVISION APPEARANCES

In one respect, Raft's television career was unique. Aside from the television series *I'm the Law*, he did virtually no other acting on television. He made frequent appearances on television, but these were usually of the chat or game show variety. There were many other contemporaries of Raft whose film careers had hit the skids, but they sustained their careers by guesting on many of the most prestigious drama shows of the period. Raft did not. He would have been an asset to the guest lineup of many of the leading crime shows of the period, but he was conspicuously absent from all of them.

I'm the Law

It was at a low point in his film career that Raft turned to television with a syndicated series called *I'm the Law*. This consisted of 26 half-hour black and white episodes in which Raft played Detective Lt. George Kirby of the NYPD. It was a Cosman production bankrolled by Lou Costello, the comedian. His brother Pat was the executive producer. The series was used at least once to advertise an Abbott and Costello movie. In one of the better episodes (domestic violence camouflaged a plot to kill a woman's husband for the insurance), there was a scene set in a cinema. The audience is shown roaring with laughter at the antics of Abbott and Costello's latest feature *Jack and the Beanstalk* (1952).

Raft started work at eight in the morning and quit at six in the evening and found the pace gruelling. In common with many stars from the golden era of movies, he was not used to the frenetic pace of television. His agents, Charles Feldman and Jules Levy, wanted to buy three of the half-hour episodes, edit them into a feature film and pay Raft $125,000 for the privilege, but he refused. They went ahead and did it anyway. The feature *Crime Squad* played briefly in Europe and overseas. Raft was supposed to receive a salary of $90,000 for the series, but after expenses he wound up with virtually nothing. The series sat on the shelf for a while and was eventually shown in 1953, when it was a modest success. Two years later it was reissued under the title *The George Raft Casebook,* but again Raft was cut out of the profits. Of this experience Raft said, "I thought it was a lousy series."

The talent involved was professional enough on both sides of the camera. The scripts, however, contained great gaps in logic, and key action scenes took place off-screen. Some of the stories incorporated clever ideas, but made insufficient use of them. One particularly unconvincing aspect of the series was the frequency with which Raft deliberately went alone into situations he knew were potentially fatal instead of requesting back-up. One of the better elements of the series was the location shots of New York which were shown over the closing credits. *Variety*'s review stated, "Raft's a natural in the role of a cop, a role he's done often enough. He commands attention throughout without overplaying."

One organization that was not a fan of the series was the FBI whose Los Angeles Office reported that the series did not always picture law enforcement in a favorable light. Raft used many slang expressions which had long since become obsolete in law enforcement.

Episode Title	*Original Air Date*
The Fight Fix Story	February 13, 1953

189

Episode Title	*Original Air Date*
The Cowboy and the Blind Man Story	February 20, 1953
The Model Agency Story	February 27, 1953
The Powder Box Smuggling Story	March 6, 1953
The McClury Brothers Story	March 13, 1953
The Firebug Story	March 20, 1953
South American Money	March 27, 1953
Who Killed Evelyn?	April 3, 1953
The Stool Pigeon Story	April 10, 1953
The Juvenile Murder Story	April 17, 1953
The Mad Cartoonist Story	April 24, 1953
The Wish and the Shoplifter	May 1, 1953
The Moon Man	May 8, 1953
O Sole Mio	May 15, 1953
The Trucking Story	May 22, 1953
The Impossible Death	May 29, 1953
The Suspect	June 5, 1953
The Countess Bobo Story	June 12, 1953
Husband and Wife Murder Story	June 19, 1953
The Bust of Plato	June 26, 1953
The Killer	July 3, 1953
Sleep with Terror	July 10, 1953
Sob Sister	July 17, 1953
Falling Star	July 24, 1953
The Button Story	July 31, 1953
The Train to Auburn	August 7, 1953

Additional Television Appearances

1951: *The Colgate Comedy Hour*
1952: *The Colgate Comedy Hour*

1953: *I've Got a Secret, What's My Line, The Name's the Same, The Colgate Comedy Hour, The Milton Berle Show*

1954: *The Milton Berle Show*

1955: *The Name's the Same, The Colgate Comedy Hour* (two), *The Jimmy Durante Show*

1956: *The Jimmy Durante Show* (two), *The Tonight Show with Jack Paar*

1957: *Toast of the Town, The Gisele Mackenzie Show*

1958: *It Could Be You*

1959: *The Arthur Murray Dance Party, Masquerade Party, The Jack Paar Show*

1960: *About Faces, Red Skelton Timex Special*

1961: *Here's Hollywood, Truth or Consequences*

1962: *Your First Impression*

1964: *Toast of the Town*

1965: *The New London Palladium Show*

1966: *The Eamonn Andrews Show, Hippodrome*

1967: *The Joey Bishop Show, Batman* (episode: "Black Widow Strikes Again")

1968: *The Joey Bishop Show*

1969: *The Merv Griffin Show, The David Frost Show, The Tonight Show*

1970: *The Movie Game, The Tonight Show*

1971: *Laugh-In* (two), *The Tonight Show, The Chicago Teddy Bears* (episode: "The Rivalry")

1972: *Tribute to Humphrey Bogart*

1974: *The American Film Institute Salute to James Cagney*

1979: *The Hollywood Greats*

RADIO BROADCASTS

The Cases of Eddie Ace

This was a well-written syndicated half-hour radio show from Paragon Productions broadcast between June 4 and September 3, 1947, in which Raft starred as Eddie Ace, the sole owner of the Ace Detective Agency located on 6th Avenue in New York City. Ace talked tough and had an eye for the ladies. He was also very loquacious because each week he sat down and recounted one of his cases to Dr. Karen Gayle, who was compiling a book about criminal behavior and wanted the viewpoint of a tough, cynical private investigator. This radio series was created by Jason James (Jo Eisinger) and morphed into the television series *The Cases of Eddie Drake* with Don Haggerty. Raft also starred in a film called *Mr. Ace* (1946), but the character was not the same.

Rocky Jordan

This was broadcast on CBS between June 27 and August 22, 1951. Raft played the title character, proprietor of the Café Tambourine located not far from the Mosque Sultan Hassan. As an American (born in St. Louis) restaurateur in a North African country, Jordan is similar to Rick Blaine in *Casablanca* though the Café Tambourine is apparently a much more downmarket establishment than Rick's Café. The announcer described it as being "crowded with forgotten men and alive with the babble of many languages." Each episode sees Jordan confronted with a crime, a mystery or a beautiful woman or a combination of two or all three. Precisely why Jordan is in Egypt is deliberately left vague though he has enemies in St. Louis so he cannot return to America.

The show was originally broadcast on CBS from 1948 to 1950 with Jack Moyles, but Raft took over for the 1951 run. Radio was a medium Raft liked because he did not have to learn any lines.

Lux Radio Theatre

This was a long-running, classic radio anthology series broadcast on the NBC Blue Network, CBS and NBC at various times. The series adapted Broadway plays during its first two seasons before it began adapting films. These hour-long radio programs were performed live before studio audiences. It became the most popular dramatic anthology series on radio, broadcast for more than twenty years, and morphed into television as *Lux Video Theatre* throughout the fifties. Raft was heard on the following broadcasts:

1936: *Cheating Cheaters*
1938: *Spawn of the North*
1941: *They Drive by Night*
1942: *Manpower, Broadway*
1943: *Each Dawn I Die, Air Force*
1944: *Action in the North Atlantic*
1948: *Intrigue*

Miscellaneous Radio Broadcasts

1936: *Kraft Cheese Program*
1937: *Kraft Cheese Program, Standard Brands Hour*
1939: *Screen Guild Theatre: A Mug, A Moll and A Mountaineer, Proctor and Gamble's Knickerbocker Playhouse: Bulldog Drummond*
1941: *Campbell Soup Play House: A Free Soul,*

America Calling, Kraft Music Hall (two), *Bristol Meyer's Time to Smile, Bendix Corporation's Treasury Hour*

1942: *The Chase and Sandborn Program, Screen Guild Theatre: Torrid Zone, Philip Morris Playhouse: Brother Orchid, Kraft Music Hall*

1943: *Colgate's Sports Newsreel, The Abbott and Costello Show, Bristol Meyer's Time to Smile, Philip Morris Playhouse: The Glass Key, Radio Readers Digest*

1944: *Ed Sullivan Entertains, Report to the Nation, Texaco Star Theatre, Sealtest Village Store, The Abbott and Costello Show, The Silver Theatre: The Sun Field*

1945: *The Bill Stern Sports Show, Tonight in Hollywood, Which Is Which Quiz Show, Sealtest Village Store*

1946: *Bill Stern Sports Newsreel of the Air* (two), *Campbell Soup's Request Performance, The Silver Theatre: The Private Eye, Duffy's Tavern*

1947: *This Is Hollywood: Mr. Ace, Broadway and Vine*

1948: *Colgate Sports Newsreel*

1949: *Chesterfield Supper Club, Proctor and Gamble's Welcome Travellers, Colgate Sports Newsreel*

1950: *Colgate Sports Newsreel* (two)

1951: *Martin and Lewis Show, Bob Hope Show*

1953: *Martin and Lewis Show*

1954: *Bob Hope Show*

APPENDIX A:
THE FILMS, BY STUDIO

Paramount

25 titles (*Dancers in the Dark, Madame Racketeer, Night After Night, If I Had a Million, Under-Cover Man, Pick-Up, Midnight Club, All of Me, Bolero, The Trumpet Blows, Limehouse Blues, Rumba, Stolen Harmony, The Glass Key, Every Night at Eight, Yours for the Asking, Souls at Sea, You and Me, Spawn of the North, The Lady's from Kentucky, The Ladies Man, The Patsy, Rififi in Panama, Skidoo, Deadhead Miles*)

United Artists

15 titles (*Palmy Days, Scarface, The Bowery, The House Across the Bay, Stage Door Canteen, Whistle Stop, Mr. Ace, Christmas Eve, Intrigue, Outpost in Morocco, Red Light, A Bullet for Joey, Around the World in 80 Days, Some Like It Hot, For Those Who Think Young*)

Warner Bros.

9 titles (*Queen of the Nightclubs, Taxi!, Winner Take All, Each Dawn I Die, Invisible Stripes, They Drive by Night, Manpower, Background to Danger, Ocean's 11*)

RKO

5 titles (*Side Street, Johnny Angel, Nocturne, Race Street, A Dangerous Profession*)

20th Century–Fox

5 titles (*It Had to Happen, Nob Hill, Lucky Nick Cain, Black Widow, The Man with Bogart's Face*)

Universal

4 titles (*Night World, I Stole a Million, Broadway, Follow the Boys*)

Columbia

3 titles (*She Couldn't Take It, Johnny Allegro, Casino Royale*)

Lippert

3 titles (*Loan Shark, Escape Route, The Man from Cairo*)

Fox

3 titles (*Quick Millions, Goldie, Hush Money*)

Les Films Corona

1 title (*We Will All Go to Paris*)

MGM

1 title (*Rogue Cop*)

Inter Continent

1 title (*Jet Over the Atlantic*)

Summit

1 title (*Two Guys Abroad*)

Commonwealth United

1 title (*Five Golden Dragons*)

Cinerama Releasing

1 title (*Hammersmith Is Out*)

Crown International

1 title (*Sextette*)

APPENDIX B:
THE FILMS, BY DIRECTOR

Edwin L. Marin
  6 titles (*Johnny Angel, Nocturne, Mr. Ace, Christmas Eve, Intrigue, Race Street*)

Raoul Walsh
  5 titles (*The Bowery, Every Night at Eight, They Drive by Night, Manpower, Background to Danger*)

Alexander Hall
  5 titles (*Madame Racketeer, Midnight Club, Limehouse Blues, Yours for the Asking, The Lady's from Kentucky*)

Roy Del Ruth
  4 titles (*Taxi!, Winner Take All, It Had to Happen, Red Light*)

Henry Hathaway
  3 titles (*Souls at Sea, Spawn of the North, Nob Hill*)

Eddie Sutherland
  2 titles (*Palmy Days, Follow the Boys*)

Archie Mayo
  2 titles (*Night After Night, The House Across the Bay*)

James Flood
  2 titles (*Under-Cover Man, All of Me*)

Marion Gering
  2 titles (*Pick-Up, Rumba*)

Frank Tuttle
  2 titles (*The Glass Key, I Stole a Million*)

Ted Tezlaff
  2 titles (*Johnny Allegro, A Dangerous Profession*)

Seymour Friedman
  2 titles (*Loan Shark, Escape Route*)

Jerry Lewis
  2 titles (*The Ladies Man, The Patsy*)

Bryan Foy
  1 title (*Queen of the Nightclubs*)

Mal St. Clair
  1 title (*Side Street*)

Rowland Brown
  1 title (*Quick Millions*)

Benjamin Stoloff
  1 title (*Goldie*)

Sidney Lanfield
  1 title (*Hush Money*)

David Burton
  1 title (*Dancers in the Dark*)

Howard Hawks
  1 title (*Scarface*)

Hobart Henley
  1 title (*Night World*)

Harry Wagstaff Gribble
  1 title (*Madame Racketeer*)

H. Bruce Humberstone
  1 title (*If I Had a Million*)

George Somnes
  1 title (*Midnight Club*)

Wesley Ruggles
  1 title (*Bolero*)

Stephen Roberts
  1 title (*The Trumpet Blows*)

Alfred L. Werker
  1 title (*Stolen Harmony*)

Tay Garnett
  1 title (*She Couldn't Take It*)

Fritz Lang
  1 title (*You and Me*)

William Keighley
  1 title (*Each Dawn I Die*)

Lloyd Bacon
  1 title (*Invisible Stripes*)

William A. Seiter
  1 title (*Broadway*)

Frank Borzage
1 title (*Stagedoor Canteen*)

Leonide Moguy
1 title (*Whistle Stop*)

Robert Florey
1 title (*Outpost in Morocco*)

Jean Boyer
1 title (*We Will All Go to Paris*)

Joseph M. Newman
1 title (*Lucky Nick Cain*)

Peter Graham Scott
1 title (*Escape Route*)

Ray Enright
1 title (*The Man from Cairo*)

Roy Rowland
1 title (*Rogue Cop*)

Nunnally Johnson
1 title (*Black Widow*)

Lewis Allen
1 title (*A Bullet for Joey*)

Michael Anderson
1 title (*Around the World in 80 Days*)

Billy Wilder
1 title (*Some Like It Hot*)

Byron Haskin
1 title (*Jet Over the Atlantic*)

Lewis Milestone
1 title (*Ocean's 11*)

Don Sharp
1 title (*Two Guys Abroad*)

Leslie H. Martinson
1 title (*For Those Who Think Young*)

Joseph McGrath
1 title (*Casino Royale*)

Denys de La Patelliere
1 title (*Rififi in Panama*)

Jeremy Summers
1 title (*Five Golden Dragons*)

Otto Preminger
1 title (*Skidoo*)

Vernon Zimmerman
1 title (*Deadhead Miles*)

Peter Ustinov
1 title (*Hammersmith Is Out*)

Ken Hughes
1 title (*Sextette*)

Robert Day
1 title (*The Man with Bogart's Face*)

BIBLIOGRAPHY

Books

Beck, H. *Inside Hollywood: Intimate Story of United Artists*, Parts 2 and 3. Glasgow: McKenzie, 1947.

Behlmer, Rudy. *Inside Warner Bros. (1935–1951)*. New York: Simon & Schuster, 1985.

Bergan, Ronald. *The United Artists Story*. London: Octopus, 1986.

Cohn, Art. *Around the World in 80 Days*. New York: Random House, 1956.

Crane Wilson, Ivy *Hollywood Album No. 1*. London: Samson Low, Marston, 1947.

Deschner, Donald. *The Films of Spencer Tracy*. Secaucus, N.J.: Citadel, 1968.

Dickens, Homer. *The Complete Films of Gary Cooper*. Secaucus, N.J.: Citadel, 1970.

Dickens, Homer, and Jerry Vermilye. *The Complete Films of Marlene Dietrich*. Secaucus, N.J.: Citadel, 1992.

Dietrich, Marlene. *My Life*. London: Weidenfeld & Nicolson, 1989.

Donnelley, Paul. *Fade to Black*. London: Omnibus, 2000.

Eames, John Douglas. *The MGM Story*. London: Octopus, 1977.

_____. *The Paramount Story*. London: Octopus, 1985.

Everson, William K. *The Detective in Film*. Secaucus, N.J.: Citadel, 1972.

_____. *Hollywood Bedlam*. Secaucus, N.J.: Citadel, 1994.

Finch, Christopher, and Linda Rosenkrantz. *Gone Hollywood*. London: Weidenfeld & Nicolson, 1980.

Fitzgerald, Michael. *Universal Pictures*. New Rochelle, N.Y.: Arlington House, 1977.

Freedland, Michael. *The Warner Brothers*. London: Harrap, 1983.

Gardner, Ava. *Ava: My Story*. New York: Bantam, 1992.

Hardy, Phil. *The BFI Companion to Crime*. London: Cassell/BFI, 1997.

_____. *Gangsters*. London: Aurum, 1998.

Hirschhorn, Clive. *The Columbia Story*. London: Pyramid, 1989.

_____. *The Hollywood Musical*. London: Octopus, 1981.

_____. *The Universal Story*. London: Octopus, 1983.

_____. *The Warner Brothers Story*. London: Octopus, 1979.

Jarvis, Everett. *Final Curtain: Deaths of Noted Movie and Television Personalities*. Secaucus, N.J.: Citadel, 1996.

Jewell, Richard B., and Vernon Harbin. *The RKO Radio Story*. London: Octopus, 1982.

Jones, Ken, and Arthur McClure. *Hollywood at War*. New York: A.S. Barnes, 1973.

Lahue, Kalton C. *Winners of the West*. New York: A.S. Barnes, 1970.

Lamparski, Richard. *Whatever Became Of?* 3rd and 8th series. New York: Crown, 1970, 1982.

Maltin, Leonard. *The Real Stars 2*. New York: Curtis Books, 1973.

McCarty, Clifford. *The Complete Films of Humphrey Bogart*. Secaucus, N.J.: Citadel, 1965.

McClelland, Doug. *Forties Film Talk*. Jefferson, N.C.: McFarland, 1992.

McGilligan, Pat. *Backstory*. Los Angeles: University of California Press, 1986.

Mell, Eila. *Casting Might-Have-Beens*. Jefferson, N.C.: McFarland, 2005.

O'Brien, Pat. *The Wind at My Back*. New York: Doubleday, 1964.

Parish, James Robert, and Alvin H. Marill. *The Cinema of Edward G. Robinson*. New York: A.S. Barnes, 1972.

Parish, James Robert, and Steven Whitney. *The George Raft File*. New York: Drake, 1973.

Picture Show Annual. London: Amalgamated, 1934, 1936, 1938, 1941, 1949, 1952 and 1954.

Picturegoer's Who's Who of the Screen Today. London: Odhams, 1933.

Pink, Sidney. *So You Want to Make Movies*. Sarasota: Pineapple Press, 1989.

Quinlan, David. *British Sound Films: The Studio Years, 1928–1959*. London: Batsford, 1984.

Quirk, Lawrence. *The Films of Fredric March*. Secaucus, N.J.: Citadel, 1972.

_____. *The Films of Robert Taylor*. Secaucus, N.J.: Citadel, 1975.

Server, Lee. *Screenwriter Words Become Pictures*. Pittstown, N.J.: Main Street Press, 1987.

Silver, Alain, and Elizabeth Ward. *Film Noir*. London: Secker and Warburg, 1980.

Springer, John. *All Talking! All Singing! All Dancing!* Secaucus, N.J.: Citadel, 1971.

Steen, M.F. *Celebrity Death Certificates 2*. Jefferson, N.C.: McFarland, 2005.

Thomas, Tony. *The Complete Films of Henry Fonda*. Secaucus, N.J.: Citadel, 1983.

_____, and Aubrey Soloman. *The Films of 20th Century–Fox*. Secaucus, N.J.: Citadel, 1979.

Truitt, Evelyn Mack. *Who Was Who on Screen*. New York: Bowker, 1984.

Turner, Roland. *The Annual Obituary*. New York: St. Martin's, 1980.

Vermilye, Jerry. *More Films of the Thirties*. Secaucus, N.J.: Citadel. 1989.

Wallace, Stone. *George Raft: The Man Who Would Be Bogart*. Albany, GA: Bear Manor Media, 2008.

Willis, John. *Screen World*, Volume 32. London: Muller, 1981.

Winchester, Clarence. *Screen Encyclopedia*. London: Winchester, 1948.

Yablonsky, Lewis. *George Raft*. London: W.H. Allen, 1975.

Articles

Blumenfeld, Simon. "Gang Show." *The Stage*, August 5, 1999.

Briggs, Colin. "Helena Carter — The Colleen from New York" *Films of the Golden Age* 30, Fall 2002.

Brodie, Ian. Obituary. *Daily Telegraph*, November 25, 1980.

Bury, Lee. "Mr. Unlucky." *Daily Express*, September 7, 1978.

"Escape Route." *Picture Show*, February 14, 1953.

"George Raft Banned Again." *The Guardian*, 1974.

"George Raft Banned from Britain." *Daily Express*, February 24, 1967.

"George Raft Feels Like Communist or Spy." *Sunday Express*, February 25, 1967.

Hamill, Pete. "The Last Caper." *New York Post*, March 4, 1967.

Kohler, Renate. "Raft Adrift ... and No Help in Sight." *Radio Times*, October 24, 1974.

"Life Story." *Picture Show*, October 7, 1939.

Mepean, Edith. "Around the British Studios." *Picture Show*, August 23, 1952.

Miller, Mark A. "Marie Windsor." *Filmfax* 30, January 1992.

Mooring, W.H. "Tough Guy Raft." *Picturegoer*, July 23, 1949.

Obituary. *Daily Express*, November 25, 1980.

Obituary. *Liverpool Daily Post*, November 25, 1980.

Obituary. *Liverpool Echo*, November 25, 1980.

Obituary. *Variety*, November 26, 1980.

Plume, Kenneth. "Interview with Screenwriter A.J. Fenady." July 5, 2000.

Rabin, Nathan. "Interview with Alan Arkin." *The A.V. Club*, August 2, 2006.

Richards, Brad. "Old Black Snake: The Coiled Menace of George Raft." *Films of the Golden Age* 38, Fall 2004.

Russell, Frederick. "Hollywood's Dancing Gangster." *Film Pictorial*, May 19, 1934.

Sklair, Astor. "Constance Cummings." *Movie Memories* 27, Spring 1997.

"The Cost of Being Good." *Picturegoer*, July 3, 1954.

Wall, Michael. "An Early Decision about Mr. Raft." *The Guardian*, February 23, 1967.

_____. "Mr. Raft Not Allowed to Land in Britain." *The Guardian*, February 24, 1967.

Williams, Michael. "A Movie Tough Guy." *Radio Times*, 1967.

Williams, Tony. "Brett Halsey." *Psychotronic* 40, 2004.

Woman Biography 1960s.

"You've Got to Be Tough with Hollywood." *Films and Filming*, 1962.

Miscellaneous Documents

Black Widow Pressbook.

Death certificate.

George Raft Declassified FBI Files.

Anne Francis letter to the author, 2005.

Coleen Gray letter to the author, 2007.

Will Hutchins letter to the author, 1989.

Jet Over the Atlantic Pressbook.

1910 census.

Nous Irons à Paris Pressbook.

Don Sharp letter to the author, 2011.

Marie Windsor letter to the author, 1998.

Interviews

Tony Curtis, 2008.

Sybil Danning, 2006.

Websites

www.imdb.com

INDEX

Page numbers in *bold italics* indicate illustrations

199